Advanced Highway Driving

Tactics for Safety and Optimization

Paul Maravelias

Copyright © 2014, 2015 Paul Maravelias

Printed by CreateSpace
Charleston, SC, United States of America

"Advanced Highway Driving Tactics for Safety and Optimization"
First Edition

First printed January 7th, 2015

ISBN-13: 978-0692340851

ISBN-10: 0692340858

BISAC: Transportation / General

All rights reserved. No part of this publication may be reproduced or transmitted in any form or by any means, electronic or mechanical, including photocopying, recording, or any other information storage or retrieval system, without the prior written permission of the author.

The information contained herein is provided on an "as-is" basis with no implication of warranty or fitness. The author shall have neither liability nor responsibility to any person or entity with respect to any loss or damages arising from the information contained in this book.

Send all inquiries to:

Paul Maravelias
34 Mockingbird Hill Rd
Windham, NH 03087
contact@highwaydriving.org

Written in Massachusetts and New Hampshire, USA

Illustrations Copyright © 2014, 2015 by Paul Maravelias. Some figures partially derived from public domain materials.

Cover design Copyright © 2014, 2015 by Paul Maravelias

6" x 9" (15.24 x 22.86 cm)
12.5pt Garamond

HighwayDriving.org

Printed in the United States

Advanced Highway Driving

Tactics for Safety and Optimization

Paul Maravelias

Windham, New Hampshire, USA

Copyright © 2014, 2015

For Chrysoula, my driver

Acknowledgements

We gratefully acknowledge Kathy L. and her employer Granite State Driving School for the conceptual inspiration of this work.

Additionally, we thank the Dartmouth College Library, in particular the DartDoc research service, for affording reliable access to the academic literature referenced throughout the present text.

We would be remiss to omit thankful posthumous acknowledgement of the late President Dwight D. Eisenhower for his fervent support of the Federal Aid Highway Act of 1956, which carried America's world-leading Interstate Highway System from theory to reality.

Advanced Highway Driving Tactics for Safety and Optimization

Paul Maravelias

Table of Contents

Part I Introduction 19

    CHAPTER 1 PURPOSE OF WORK 20

Part II High-level Strategic Model for Highway Driving 29

    CHAPTER 2 HIGHWAY DRIVING STRATEGY 30

Part III Tactical Model for Highway Spatial Maneuvering .. 39

    CHAPTER 3 SPATIAL AWARENESS 40

    CHAPTER 4 HIGHWAY ENTRANCE MERGING PROCEDURES . 76

    CHAPTER 5 LANE OPTIMIZATION 121

    CHAPTER 6 SPEED OPTIMIZATION 177

    CHAPTER 7 FUEL-EFFICIENCY OPTIMIZATION 216

    CHAPTER 8 INTERVEHICULAR DYNAMICS 238

    CHAPTER 9 OTHER DEFENSIVE TACTICS 277

Part IV   Vehicular Control and Interface Tactics 289

CHAPTER 10 VEHICLE CONTROL 290

Part V   Additional Considerations 319

CHAPTER 11 DRIVING ENVIRONMENT 320

CHAPTER 12 CANONICAL FREEWAY ACCIDENT SITUATIONS AND AVOIDANCE METHODS 334

Part VI   Conclusion 363

Part VII   Appendices 367

Detailed Table of Contents

Part I Introduction 19

  CHAPTER 1 PURPOSE OF WORK 20

    "Safety and Optimization" defined 22

    Appreciating the nuances of freeway driving 23

Part II High-level Strategic Model for Highway Driving 29

  CHAPTER 2 HIGHWAY DRIVING STRATEGY 30

    Balancing safety with other optimizations 30

    Navigational strategy 33

    "Control loop" mental processing model 35

Part III   Tactical Model for Highway Spatial Maneuvering .. 39

  CHAPTER 3 SPATIAL AWARENESS 40

    Path-of-travel and line-of-sight 40

    Primary spatial awareness regions 41

    Non-visual spatial awareness sensory stimuli 44

    Visual information source #1: Primary frontal view through the front windshield 46

    Visual information source #2: Center (rear-view) and "side" or "wing" mirrors 49

Visual information source #3: Usage of the rear-lateral windows of the vehicle 53

    Head-check procedure *54*
    Peripheral vision *58*
    Pillar structure *59*
    Differences in wing-mirror construction *61*
    Traditional vs. wide mirror alignment *64*

Vehicular status awareness 71

Intravehicular spatial awareness and human factors 72

CHAPTER 4   HIGHWAY ENTRANCE MERGING PROCEDURES . 76

Allovehicular terminology and spatial zones 76

Highway entrance merging psychology 77

Highway entrance merging phases 78

Preparatory factors 81

Entrance ramp procedure 87

Acceleration zone and merging lane procedure 96

    Speed-adjustment feedback loop *96*
    Risk analysis *97*
    Spatial awareness model *99*
    General acceleration-incentivizing factors *101*
    Behavior-predictive observational analysis *102*
        Frontal merging vehicles *103*
        Lateral traffic-lane vehicles *105*
    Action and assertiveness signaling *109*
    Merge execution tactics *114*

Weave lanes 118

Multi-lane ramps 120

CHAPTER 5   LANE OPTIMIZATION 121

General factors 121

Lane-switch maneuver dynamics 123
   Lateral speed *123*
   Lateral acceleration profile *125*
   Directional signal usage *126*
   Lane switch abortion *127*

Geometric economy: the curve-distance interlane disparity effect 128

Longitudinal-axis safety margin and following distance optimization 137

Predictive deceleration and collision zone avoidance 152

Lane closure and obstructive object avoidance 158

Lane designation compliance 164

Visibility optimization 167

Lateral safety clearance optimization 168

Highway egress anticipation 171

Special Cases 173
   High Occupancy Vehicle (HOV) lanes *173*
   Breakdown lane *174*

Lane Optimization Conclusion 175

CHAPTER 6 SPEED OPTIMIZATION 177

Determination of the freeway-vacant ideal travel speed 178
   General time-urgency and safety balancing theory *180*
   Fuel-efficiency factors *181*
   Marginal analysis of speed increases: risks vs. benefits *193*
   Situational factors of enforcement risk *200*
   Basic speed rule *203*
   Assured Clear Distance Ahead (ACDA) *204*

Sectional prioritization and discretized risk analysis 207

Additional safety factors 213

Speed Optimization Conclusion 215

CHAPTER 7 FUEL-EFFICIENCY OPTIMIZATION 216

Acceleration profile effects 216

Initial acceleration to freeway speed 217
Optimal engine power vs. brake-avoidance 218
Maintenance of even throttle, load, and speed 219
"Pulse-and-glide" tactic 220

Gravitational potential energy related methods 222

Drag reduction 224

Dynamical changes to the drag coefficient 224
Drafting 228
Critique of drafting 230

Non-drafting intervehicular effects 235

CHAPTER 8 INTERVEHICULAR DYNAMICS 238

Intervehicular aerodynamics 239

Topographic factors 242

Following distance effects 242
Visibility obstruction 244

Road Curvature 246

Entrance and exit ramp hazards 246
Intrafreeway curvature 247

General Passing 252

Incentives and procedures 252
Passing on the right 253
Speed responses to being passed 257
Large allovehicle aerodynamic optimization and safety passing 260

Passing lane situations 261

Passing lane situation #1: slower adjacent-lane travel 262

    Immediate speed response options 263
    Allovehicular-driver psychological optimization of passing-lane-entrance directional signal activation 264
    Passing lane situation #2: faster adjacent-lane travel 266
    Passing lane situation #3: faster passing-lane travel 267
    Passing lane situation #4: slower passing-lane travel 269

  Two-lane freeway considerations 271

  High urgency situations 272

  High-congestion traffic conditions 274

CHAPTER 9 OTHER DEFENSIVE TACTICS 277

  Vehicular proximity response 277

    Longitudinal proximity 277
    Lateral proximity 279
    Collision response procedure 280

  Driver impairment and road rage 280

  Stationary object anticipation and avoidance 283

  Interlane position in high traffic density 286

Part IV   Vehicular Control and Interface Tactics 289

CHAPTER 10 VEHICLE CONTROL 290

  Speed control 290

    Cruise control vs. manual speed control 290
    Tactical model for cruise control usage 292

  Braking 298

    Braking distance 298
    Downforce 300
    Tire slip 301
    Brake fade 302
    Cadence braking and ABS 303

    Foot position and left-foot braking.. *304*

  Steering control 306

    Handling and dynamics.. *306*
    Steering hazards.. *308*
    Grip and hand position.. *311*

  Control loop effects of operating devices 313

  Driver communication 314

    High-beams.. *314*
    Brake lights.. *316*

Part V Additional Considerations 319

CHAPTER 11 DRIVING ENVIRONMENT 320

  Low-lighting and night conditions 320

  Atmospheric and solar effects... 321

    Hydrometeors *321*
        Identifying warm-wet and frozen-wet road surfaces.......................*322*
        Visibility limitation...*323*
        Hard ice accretion..*324*
    Hydroplaning *325*
    Wind... *327*
    Extreme heat and cold.. *328*
    Glare and albedo.. *329*

  Pre-drive automobile optimizations.. 330

  Physiological considerations... 331

  Psychological considerations 332

CHAPTER 12 CANONICAL FREEWAY ACCIDENT SITUATIONS AND AVOIDANCE METHODS... 334

  1. Frontal collision due to rapid, unnoticed deceleration of frontal vehicle 335

2. Posterolateral collision due to tight passing attempt and accelerating posterolateral vehicle 337

3. Anterolateral collision due to tight passing attempt and decelerating anterolateral vehicle 340

4. Lateral collision with vehicle in blind spot during lane switch 342

5. Lateral collision from another vehicle switching lanes 344

6. Rearwards or lateral collision by lane-switching out of stalled high-traffic lane into high-speed neighboring lane 347

7. Rear-end collision due to overactive deceleration 350

8. Lateral collision due to drifting interlane position 352

9. Posterolateral collision in tight merging maneuver 354

10. Frontal collision during merging maneuver due to extended blind spot spatial awareness check and resulting ignorance of frontal vehicle deceleration 357

11. Collision due to lack of road friction for corrective deceleration and/or steering 360

Part VI Conclusion 363

Conclusion 364

Part VII Appendices 367

US Listing of Location-Specific Considerations by State
.... 368

Eisenhower Interstate System Signage and Conventions
.... 389

Stopping Distance at Various Speeds 390

Table of Figures 391

GLOSSARY	393
BIBLIOGRAPHY	404

Part I

Introduction

CHAPTER 1

Purpose of work

Considering the concurrent necessity, routineness, and potential lethality of driving on the highway, being so for most adult citizens of developed countries, we find that a shocking lack of attention is devoted to the subject both in published driver's education literature and by social attitudes prevailing among informal circles. We hold that neither devote sufficient attention to the particular concern of vehicular *highway* travel as is justly merited by the comparative attention which other topics in the driver's education field are given.

This opinion derives from a general advocacy for more comprehensive driving education which may be honorably extended to all contexts of operating a motor vehicle, including any non-freeway context, as most constructed roads by length do not constitute that which is the specialization of this book: *multi-lane controlled-access highways*. However, a well-established field of resourceful literature is freely available in the way of general driver's safety education – a statement which does not hold true under the narrow lens of our current, specialized focus.

This book therefore takes the opportunity to luxuriate in the details of a certain part of the broader driving experience and accordingly provides an exhaustive, technical discussion on the particular topic of highway driving.

The terms "highway", "freeway", "expressway", "motorway", and "interstate" are defined, on the whole, in highly variable manners specific to country and even region, and with some degree of mutual exchangeability – therefore we will operate with only a general understanding of key terminology for consistent usage throughout this book. Technically speaking, the term "highway" properly commands the broad definition of any public land road, with different contexts and common usages of the term spanning across British and North American usage. In the latter usage, the term "highway" is colloquially limited to that of the proper *freeway*; this book assumes the focus of *controlled-access* highways, also synonymously called "freeways", "motorways", or (in Europe) "autoroutes", which are canonically typified by the absence of traffic lights, high speed limits, the prohibition of pedestrians (and usually cyclists), and the usage of a bi-directional, separated dual carriageway (or "divided highway" in North American terminology) layout. Therefore we will use the terms "highway" and "freeway" synonymously throughout this book in reference to the same controlled-access, high-speed road structures. While maintaining an international relevance, we will primarily refer to America's Dwight D. Eisenhower National System of Interstate and Defense Highways – the second greatest interstate system in the world by total road length (second to China's) and, in our opinion, the best and most representative of the quintessential freeway driving experience which defines this book's topic. The contents of this book will also apply to limited-access highways (i.e. "expressways", by which they are sometimes distinguished) in the respects through which they are similar to the freeway, our primary focus.

It is difficult to exaggerate the prevalence of highway driving in industrialized societies, warranting therefore the focused and exhaustive discussion this book will devote to the particular subject. In 2011, United States drivers spent around 25% of all driven miles, both rural and urban, on the US's Eisenhower Interstate Highway

System (Office of Highway Policy Information, 2011)[1], notwithstanding the comparative 1.1% relative length which these interstate roads constitute to that of all other public roads in the US. Safety on such roads is a critical subject especially for the many drivers who use them on a quotidian basis, such as urban workers who live in and commute from suburbs. For them especially this book may prove a worthwhile study endeavor, since the consequences of even non-lethal controlled-access highway accidents will challenge their economic as well as physical vitality. This book has been written with the highest expectation of practicality in mind, in order to be a wise investment for such patrons of the highway system. We will include, however, many extended theoretical discussions necessary for full driver appreciation of safety and optimization principles and assume an already moderate-to-professional level of driving experience in the reader.

"Safety and Optimization" defined

This book was titled with both the terms *safety* and *optimization* to underscore their mutual and dynamic role in professional highway driving: by enacting the strategies and tactics about to be discussed, the driver may elect to "spend" their collective optimization benefit on either safety (as is normally recommended), on another optimization enterprise (such as fast arrival to destination, fuel-efficiency, to the avoidance of speeding tickets, etc.), or on some combination of these. As this book will expound upon in great detail, interstate driving is a game of balancing many different multivariate factors (and typically far more than only a few, as it was simplified above) that themselves may not be of constant or equal value. We define "optimization" as any driving method or technique which leads to greater efficiency in a particular area, holding all other factors constant. From a probabilistic point of view, safety

---

[1] Office of Highway Policy Information, 2011. Table VM-1. *Highway Statistics Series.*

techniques always count as optimization techniques, since the decreased risk of damage to human and physical property satisfies the economic requirements of the more generally defined "optimization" benefit. All optimizations are not always necessarily safety techniques however (and in fact are often quite at odds with safety), and therefore we will assume a healthy focus on the latter, though we will also describe the dynamic interplay between the two such that drivers will be able to judge their own individual balance based on their varying motivations for driving. As this book will demonstrate, highway driving is a quite technical balancing act of many inversely proportional, competing factors. In outlining the theoretically ideal and safety-optimum spatial maneuvering tactics on the freeway, we will refer to "the professional driver", or simply, "the driver", to indicate the instructional perspective of the reader – the ideal freeway-driving expert who is distinguished from the other drivers on the freeway in the perspective from which our technical discussions are written. We have attempted to write with great clarity and consistency in our nomenclature describing such (at times, very complicated) intervehicular dynamical situations, so that the reader may learn from both the presented perspective of the professional driver and also from that of the other drivers (or "allovehicular" drivers) which surround the professional driver on the freeway.

Appreciating the nuances of freeway driving

Though many drivers may regard a motor vehicle's operation on the freeway as a mostly passive and relaxed activity in comparison to that of other driving contexts, the professional driver will perform highly active, nuanced, and precise vehicular operation on the freeway, reaping the perhaps-astounding optimizations such techniques are able to create. Highway driving takes on a set of variables and considerations potentially more confined and predictable than that of driving on urban or rural secondary/tertiary roads, and therefore the skill can be mastered in much shorter time than the latter by repeated habituation to applying the practices about to be discussed.

Before we begin, let us consider the potential efficacy any such nuanced highway driving strategies may hold for the driver. Though the exact proportion may be debated, a certain and large part of the driving populace holds a simplistic model for highway driving which typically is not compellingly more detailed nor advanced than the following four-step simplified tactical model:

1. Enter the freeway through the entrance ramp and merge into traffic consulting the left mirror.

2. Graduate the vehicle's lane position to the left or middle lane if the destination exit is more than a mile or two away.

3. Maintain a "comfortable" speed with the accelerator and check for sudden slow and/or merging other vehicles ahead in the vehicle's path-of-travel.

4. An exit or two before the destination exit, merge back over to right lane and finally decelerate into the exit ramp.

Even if this simplistic highway driving model were sufficiently thorough to the ends of personal safety, it still entirely ignores the hundreds of optimization strategies at the driver's fingertips which can be used to increase personal safety, increase fuel-efficiency, decrease risk to other drivers, or arrive at the destination more quickly – and often, moreover, which can be applied to a combination of more than one of these benefits. It is apparent that these driving goals extend secondary benefits which maximize overall social utility for not only the driver but for everyone else, such as the lowered time-expenditure cost associated with faster arrival, the human social benefit of safer transportation methods, the lowered environmental impact of optimized vehicular energy expenditure, the financial attractiveness of increased fuel-efficiency, the avoided burden to the insurance industry of covering avoidable accidents, and the avoided pre-occupation of law enforcement resources from traffic stops that never occur – to name only a few. The economic nature of highway driving choices is evident from this simple cost-benefit analysis, and we believe that optimization potential for vastly positive economic improvements exists in an overwhelming majority of freeway drivers' freeway driving.

What if vehicles could always follow the inner curve (i.e. shortest distance) of a heading-variable highway? What if drivers were able to identify and pre-emptively avoid dangerous road rage situations before coming into fruition by analyzing key signs of aggressive drivers? Which lane switches are theoretically optimal, and which are only risky and expensive? What if the 70mph-average-speed travelling driver subject to a traffic-enforcement stop for momentarily (and accidentally) going 77 mph at the wrong time were to *increase* his or her average speed to 73 mph but with proper consistency that both the ticket be avoided and the destination be reached more quickly? What if this speed regulation process were however too mentally demanding any may cause risk for an accident from inattention to a merging vehicle? What if the merging vehicle were a large truck travelling at 75mph and therefore creating a large wind shadow in front of the passenger vehicle, altering fuel-efficiency and lateral maneuverability due to decreased air resistance? What if the truck however needed to decelerate quickly and therefore collide with the first driver, since he or she was following him too closely for the sake of the aforementioned optimization benefit? What if a traffic accumulation of unknown cause creates large pressure to merge into a clear passing lane, only for the aforementioned pattern to reverse itself half a mile later? What if a crosswind blows the visibility-obstructing precipitation spray cloud behind a semi-truck into an adjacent-lane vehicle who is unable to pass due to longitudinal constrictions? What if the flow of traffic greatly exceeds the speed limit, however the driver wishes neither to risk collision nor a traffic enforcement stop? What if it is dangerous to obstruct the faster (and speeding) flow of traffic in a precariously tight down-hill curve yet simultaneously preferable to decelerate due to enforcement risk and wet-road traction limitations enhanced by lane position and geometric road curvature? How can a slower vehicle pass a faster vehicle around a curve without increasing speeding risks? How does the professional driver identify and respond to impaired allovehicular drivers? What if a left-lane vehicle enters a new state in which the lane is unknowingly reserved for passing only? Is it appropriate to pass on the right? Who has right of way in simultaneous highway exit and entrance ramp lanes? Which lanes are more likely to include hydroplaning or frozen-ice-patch hazards?

The exercise of asking rhetorical questions which illuminate the multivariate nature of highway driving considerations could be continued at length, but only a small amount of them is necessary to demonstrate that the simplified, common, and mainstream highway driving model listed above is at best suboptimal, realistically a waste of energy, time, and resources, and at worst, a recipe for potentially lethal human tragedy. This book will outfit highway drivers with a thorough understanding of all the subtle factors and variables alluded to above (and many more), which will enable them both to respond optimally in critical situations and to apply sound optimization strategies on an everyday basis. We sincerely hope and confidently expect that the information contained herein, properly and consistently applied, will pay over for this book's cost countless times and to a potentially remarkable degree.

Part II

High-level Strategic Model for Highway Driving

CHAPTER 2

Highway Driving Strategy

It is impossible to have a meaningful discussion of specific highway driving *tactics* without first identifying the higher level driver *strategies* which will inform his or her specific maneuvers and decisions on the freeway.

Balancing safety with other optimizations

The different highway driving strategies we will discuss stem from different goals and purposes inherent to the driver's cause for using the freeway. For example, someone using an interstate in the morning for a work-related commute (and therefore, a perhaps economically sensitive temporal arrival deadline) will likely choose a strategy which places higher relative focus on speed than a weekend beach-goer, who is far wiser to lend safety a greater relative role in his or her strategy (since there is little to no time-sensitivity to their arrival time) – given an even time constraint (which is, of course, easily avoided by extra-freeway strategic considerations, such as earlier departure time). This is not to suggest that safety is at times an ignorable factor in formulating driving strategy, but rather that there are times in which there is no reason not to increase by even more the already (and hopefully) paramount estimation to which safety has already been elevated, and that safety is naturally a lesser priority in times that are not so, relatively speaking. Absolutely speaking, safety is prioritized in all situations, just by even more in some situations versus that of others. Consider the sanctioned existence of travel-permitted breakdown lanes that are time-regulated to correspond with periods of higher anticipated traffic (such as stretches of I-93 Northbound in Massachusetts, USA on which Boston commuters may use the additional lane from 3pm to 7pm on weekdays): this is an example of affording a slight, calculated reduction in safety for a greater marginal economic benefit of decreased congestion (and not to mention the systemic increase of safety in highway usage as a whole, since vehicles arrive to their destination more quickly and therefore spend less time in which there is a chance for an accident). This elucidates the concept that different high-level freeway driver strategies may balance their constituent factors (including safety) without being guilty of marginalizing safety as it may seem. If this is morally flawed, then we wish to avoid an *argumentum ab auctoritate* fallacy in mentioning the state-sanctioned existence of breakdown lane travel at certain times; this useful example only insulates us from criticism which could not also concurrently remonstrate reputable Departments of Transportation (MassDOT, in our particular example) in their adoption of a similarly utilitarian philosophy on highway driving safety. We will now proceed under the assumption that we are safe from any misunderstanding criticism that this text is advocating the acceptability of occasional risky behavior (i.e. excessive preoccupation with speed and/or efficiency optimization) at the unsafe expense of increasing risk cost – we are simply advocating the economic reality (as is accepted by many public Departments of Transportation, per the example above) that there are appropriate balances of safety vs. other optimizations in which the optimal point gives safety considerations a higher value in some strategic cases than in others. We will accordingly assign a highly utilitarian, economic model to the risks, benefits, and optimizations of highway driving in the development our tactical model for highway driving.

By employing optimization techniques, it is possible to improve any performance metric of driver strategy – however to incur these optimization benefits in the field of safety is the consistent recommendation of this book. This will not limit us from considering the place of alternative driver utility-maximizing strategies, in which the driver's subjective assessment of an improved speed or efficiency benefit outweighs the risk-cost of sacrificing a bit of safety. Freeway drivers must make their own subjective strategy for using the freeway and apply the following tactics in accordance thereto, since strategic differences will lead to vast differences in tactical choices on the road (e.g. in response to questions such as: "should I switch lanes?" or "should I increase or decrease following distance?", etc.)

Formulating these subjective utility assessments, however, must be done with wisdom and full consideration. Research indicates that speeding behavior which is intended to optimize arrival time in fact does not often accomplish this to the full degree of expected effectiveness (Tranter, 2010)[1], in which case a more conservative and careful driving strategy would be appropriate for the mislead, hurried driver. The increased risk of traffic enforcement stops also, quite obviously, stands as an additional obstruction to fast-arrival solely from the lens of the speed optimization metric – wholly discounting the potential financial, legal, and psychological effects of such stops. The purpose of this paragraph is not to insinuate that some situations will not appropriately call for freeway driving strategies that lend proportionally greater emphases to speed, but rather to reaffirm that care and wise judgment must be used to make such speed-emphases in formulating a driving strategy, since their potential costs are often mistaken to be lower than they actually are by means of the factors explained above. The entire system of roads taken as a whole, the underlying assumption of increased speed's inherent danger derives from simple physical processes of increased potential collision force (Yowell, 2005)[2], even though (fortunately) higher speeds are far safer in the freeway context.

Fuel-efficiency is another strategic end which usually runs at odds against safety. Any usage of vehicle brakes wastes energy in the form of heat generated by friction between the brake pads and tire rotor discs (in the case of the most-common disc brakes) – and even alternate, more efficient braking technologies which conserve

---

[1] Tranter, P. J., 2010. Speed Kills: The Complex Links Between Transport, Lack of Time and Urban Health. *Journal of Urban Health,* March, 82(2), pp. 155-166.

[2] Yowell, R. O., 2005. The evolution and devolution of speed limit law and the effect on fatality rates. *Review of Policy Research,* 22(4), pp. 501-518.

some of the lost energy as electricity still involve a certain amount of thermal loss, which is thermodynamically unavoidable. Therefore decreased usage of braking stands as a broad category of optimizations aimed at fuel-efficiency – however this also betokens decreased maneuverability, which in many situations further constitutes a safety cost. A holistic view of driver strategy will appropriately balance these factors as well and appreciate their careful interactions.

Navigational strategy

A freeway driver's high-level strategy will also be influenced greatly by his or her navigational intentions. Common sense dictates that longer trips will demand a higher relative safety requirement due to the increased time spent on the road and, therefore, the increased probabilistic chance of being involved in a motor vehicle accident. Driving in unfamiliar areas must also increase driver attention to safety per the increased risk of unknown structural disruptions such as closed lanes, road work, disabled vehicles, etc. Though not as important for simple trips involving the usage of only one stretch of one certain freeway, longer trips will frequently demand the traversal of new and changing freeway routes; in these situations, the navigational optimization of full cognition and basic working memory of freeway travel directions pre-drive will constitute additionally a safety benefit due to its likely tendency to decrease moments of confusion and indecision. Such moments are not infrequently caused by over-trusting electronic, voice-dictating navigational instruments, which may contain static and perhaps obsolete road information, potentially conflicting with newly posted signs or other *in situ* visual road navigation aids and thereby creating an indecisive moment of conflict to the driver's navigational understanding about how to proceed with vehicular maneuvering. Many of the highway accidents which we will review occur in a state of indecision and tension – moments which are best avoided in the first place just as much by sound navigational strategy as by professional, precise vehicular control tactics in moments of danger that could have been avoided in the first place.

Increased navigational awareness pre-drive may also inform safety and efficiency factors in the way of deciding whether or not it is even optimal to use the highway in the first place. Though per-mile accident rates are consistently lower on freeways than on secondary urban and suburban roads (Zeeger & Williams, 1994)[3], many of these controlled-access highway accidents occur during both entrance and exit merging phases inherent to freeway travel of even the smallest duration; it is accordingly possible to conceive of a situation in which travel on a low-traffic secondary road to a certain proximate destination is in fact safer than a freeway option of comparable length, even though an electronic navigation service may have suggested otherwise by simplistically eschewing such precise considerations to each route and weighing only the predicted distance or time each route will take. An example of the opposite nature is also conceivable (and exceedingly more likely): potentially unaware of mitigating traffic or road-surface condition factors, an electronic navigation instrument may elect to recommend a slightly shorter route on a secondary road while in fact a marginally longer freeway route may extend a greater safety benefit than time cost due to the factors about which the device is ignorant. Deliberate and high-awareness navigational strategy is therefore a large component of overall highway-usage strategy which has the potential to afford speed and/or safety optimizations even before a driver enters the freeway.

---

[3] Zeeger, C. V. & Williams, C., 1994. Calculation of Accident Rates by Roadway Class for HSIS States. *University of North Carolina Highway Safety Research Center.*

"Control loop" mental processing model

On the freeway, drivers must concomitantly multi-task a balancing act of visually scanning manifold factors, many of them quickly changing, and decide within split seconds how their strategy will combine with their observations to perform a certain tactic (i.e. interfacing with the controls of the vehicle) – a cycle which is repeated throughout the course of driving on the highway. However, this theoretical and even algorithmic requirement seems to contradict a growing psychological body of evidence which suggests that the human mind cannot effectively multitask, at all times, information processing of every visual and auditory stimulus with perfect, immediate motor response, as the freeway driving task truly requires[4]. Instead, the human brain approximates multitasking by rapidly "task-switching" between tasks in an efficient and interlinked manner. This brings us to our "Control Loop" model of driver cognition, observation, and response.

The professional freeway driver will continuously execute a cyclical "Control Loop" while operating a vehicle on the highway, which allows him or her to manifest the chosen high-level freeway strategy into specific vehicular control tactics, and which may be very approximately outlined by the three following, general, high-order, categorical steps:

1. Sensory observation (i.e. spatial and situational awareness primarily by means of visual and auditory stimuli)

2. Conscious processing of sensory observations (i.e. identifying potential risks and optimization benefits from spatial awareness)

---

[4] Further reading on "task-switching" in psychology literature may fascinatingly illuminate this topic's inherent relevance to the mental task of driving a vehicle in any context, especially that of the freeway.

3. Tactical response by means of vehicle control (e.g. physical vehicle maneuvering, adjusting vehicle user inputs, etc.)

For example, maintaining proper lane position is probably the most basic and continuous manifestation of this cycle. Through only mere moments (a second or two) of missed sensory observation (#1 above) as a result of, for instance, an extended glance at an electronic instrument or an adjustment of the passenger radio apparatus – processes #2 and #3 above are delayed by great enough a lag interval such that one's vehicle has by now strayed out of proper position and perhaps into dangerous proximity to allovehicular paths of travel such that the distracted driver issues a quick, correctional jerk to the steering wheel in a brief moment of elevated tension in order to restore the vehicle's path-of-travel to the proper geometric constraints. However, varying situations will indeed call for the appropriation of sensory input (and rightly so) that may be distracting to a concurrent yet necessary task as well, such as glancing into the rear mirror before applying immediate pressure to the brakes in the hope of sparing a rear-end collision while concurrently having a safety obligation to visually monitor the stopping (or already stopped) vehicle in front of the driver such that the driver him or herself does not rear-end-collide into the car in front. We could extend this constrained hypothetical to more elaborate cases in which even more external observations would be beneficial to the driver's consideration, but cannot be performed all at the same time due to the limits of human physiology (i.e., drivers do not have two sets of eyes for looking ahead and into mirrors simultaneously). Therefore the thrust of our control loop model is not to suggest that human drivers should or even could behave as procedurally and deterministically as computers, but rather to suggest that holistic driving judgments need to be made from often-incomplete understandings of spatial awareness, and that a proper balance of observational activities (depending on situation) must be made in procuring such situational awareness.

The aforesaid "spatial awareness" is the professional freeway driver's all-important lifeline for making defensive safety maneuvers, pre-emptive safety optimizations, and even efficiency-augmenting Pareto improvements to his or her freeway driving. The real substance of this book, the following tactical model for highway driving, will therefore start with a thorough discussion of this critical first step to being an advanced, safe, and professionally competent freeway driver.

Part III

Tactical Model for Highway Spatial Maneuvering

CHAPTER 3

Spatial Awareness

If the reader were to select only one narrow part of this entire book for thorough mastering, our present discussion on spatial awareness would likely be the sole most important section and the most auspicious to improving driver safety and success on the highway. Virtually all of the safety and optimization techniques we will discuss stem from an understanding of the vehicle's spatial position relative to the geometries of the road, of other vehicles, and of any other objects in proximity to the path-of-travel.

Path-of-travel and line-of-sight

The terms *path-of-travel* and *line-of-sight* will be important to define for this section. We refer to the vehicle's path-of-travel most basically to indicate the geometric areas which are bound to be occupied by a vehicle given the driver's intention to follow a certain road and (hopefully) a certain lane position within that road. In this sense, it is to be hoped that the vehicle's path-of-travel remains always an area defined and bound by a road – if, for instance, a sharp turn is made on an icy surface, and directional control of the vehicle is lost, then unfortunately the vehicle's path-of-travel may veer away from a road and into a ditch – perhaps even in a vector direction that is not parallel to the front/back orientation of the vehicle or the direction of the tires. The term *line-of-sight* therefore is not synonymous with the vehicle's path-of-travel, since the direct line of frontward vision extending from the driver's view may not always align with the projected motion of the vehicle (for instance, if the driver is executing a turn around a bend in which his or her line-of-sight represents the instantaneous direction of the vehicle, but also in which his or her vehicle's path-of-travel represents a curved area which bends away from the line-of-sight). It will be important also to think of a vehicle's path-of-travel as a two-dimensional area or even as a three-dimensional volume of air which the vehicle will occupy – as opposed to the one-dimensional *line* of sight of the vehicle's vision.

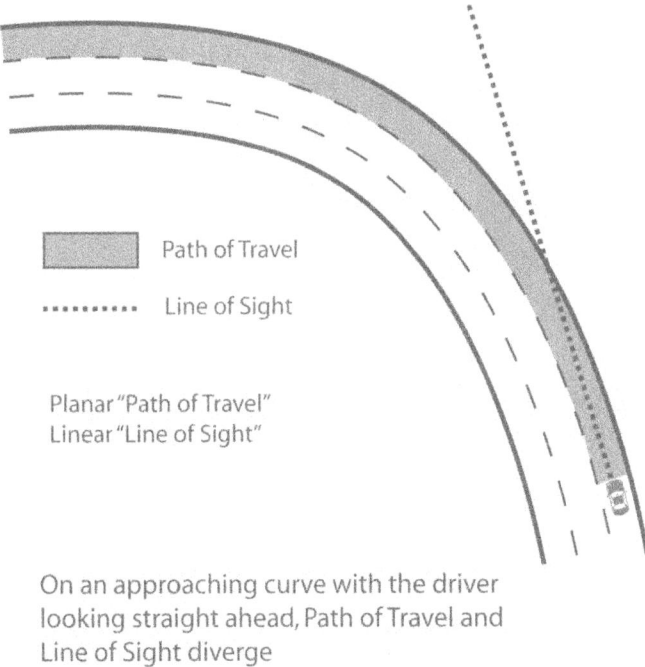

Figure 1 – *Formal differences between the path-of-travel and the line-of-sight, illustrated by their divergence at a curve. Furthermore, the former covers a surface area whereas the latter is entirely one-dimensional. Note that our present formal definition of the line-of-sight may vary slightly from some other definitions which may simply name it the "visible" section of the path-of-travel.*

Primary spatial awareness regions

Freeway driving, firstly and foremostly, demands constant visual attention to the frontal path-of-travel in order to identify any of the following factors (and perhaps more) which will call for appropriate driver response when necessary:

- Other vehicles merging into the path-of-travel of the driver's vehicle

- Lane/road curvature demanding steering adjustments

- Changes in road elevation and traffic patterns which demand an according adjustment to speed

- Obstructive physical objects errantly lying (or walking, blowing, rolling, etc.) through or in the vehicle's path-of-travel

- Allovehicular collisions and/or identifying the likelihood of impending allovehicular collisions which pose a risk to infringe the vehicle's path-of-travel with debris, fire, and perhaps even the disabled vehicles themselves

- Traffic enforcement officers, who may be signaling the necessity of a lane switch for upcoming road work or for any such related closure (of an exit, etc.), or who may be watching for speeders

- An overall reduction in the speed of vehicular traffic flow, necessitating braking or other decelerative measures

It is apparent from the above (inexhaustive) list of potential hazards that maintaining constant attention to the objects in front of the vehicle constitutes a critical safety priority. But this attention alone is insufficient for the professional driver's obligation to maintain a holistic, three-dimensional, 360-degree spatial awareness including areas to the side (lateral) and rear of the vehicle. There is a natural tendency in freeway driving for these areas (and especially the latter) to be of less importance than the aforementioned frontal areas given the relative velocity of the vehicle, however they are still critically important for spatial understanding lest the driver undertake the following risks:

- Lateral collisions with undetected passing vehicles as a result of an ill-informed lane switch

- Rear-end collisions in situations of high speed variation (e.g. traffic congestion)

- Rear-end collisions due to rapid deceleration prompted instinctively by any sizeable and immediate perception of danger from a frontal-zone risk identification

- Rear-end collisions due to only minimal deceleration yet excessive proximity to another (rear-zone) vehicle having just merged into the vehicle's lane, unbeknown to the ignorant driver

- Risks associated with emergency vehicles travelling faster than the flow of traffic

- Risks associated with aggressive, enraged, and/or inebriated drivers approaching from behind travelling both faster than the safe flow of traffic and with untrustworthy acuity with regards to avoiding lateral collisions (due to compulsive and risky lane switches, etc.)

- Failing to identify being stopped by a traffic enforcement officer for a long enough period as to create the perception that the driver is attempting to evade the stop, leading to the necessity of increased aggression in the enforcement officer's driving which may pose an additional safety risk to both vehicles

The necessity for the professional freeway driver of a holistic, 360-degree spatial awareness technique is therefore established. Our method will employ a dynamic interplay of three visual informational sources:

1. Primary frontal view through the front windshield

2. Usage of the one center and two side mirrors

3. Usage of the view through other lateral windows of the vehicle (typically at least two and sometimes four) and the rear window

Our visual spatial awareness technique will omit only the direct use of the rear window, since performing a head-check of such extreme angularity represents an unwise safety cost in comparison to merely using the central mirror for which it is purposed (we will discuss the controversy surrounding head-checking vs. aligned mirror usage in a following section). Likewise, there is rarely if ever an informational value to any small area covered by any side windows which extend not directly behind the driver's seat but along a tertiary row of rear seats (if the vehicle even has them by being an SUV or minivan, for instance), and which normally would produce view of an area already visible in the side mirror, if properly aligned.

Non-visual spatial awareness sensory stimuli

Before elaborating on the specific execution tactics of our spatial awareness method, it is important also to identify non-visual sources of spatial awareness information. Sound is virtually the only other conceivable sensory channel through which useful spatial awareness information can be obtained (if tactile feedback from a collision is detected, clearly the driver has already failed to maintain proper spatial awareness and is now concerned with proper accident response strategies, and likewise the olfactory sense's ability to detect smoke would also likely betoken only a formerly completed accident). We except the tactile sense's limited role in steering wheel operation tactics, to be described in a different section not pertaining to spatial awareness. The gustatory sense is therefore the one sensory channel which is *completely* ignorable to the professional highway driver, though everything other than auditory and visual stimuli is *virtually* ignorable in all standard circumstances.

Auditory perception may be relevant to the advanced freeway driver in any of the following situations:

1. A passing driver signals their horn to dissuade a mistaken driver from executing a declared lane switch

2. A passing driver exhibits signs of road rage for the driver's noticing by means of signaling his or her horn and/or verbally exclaiming confrontational language through the window

3. A traffic enforcement officer activates his or her siren to inform the driver that he or she is being pulled over

4. A driver seeking to merge into a slow-moving, traffic-congested lane uses verbal confirmation in the event of sufficiently proximate and open windows to signal his or her merging intention, or being the recipient of such rare exchanges

5. The horn of another vehicle within the path-of-travel is activated due to some invisible frontal obstruction noticed by the driver of this other vehicle, and which thereby indicates a heightened likelihood of rapid deceleration, and which furthermore may occur before the likely visual indications of braking and noticed deceleration

Therefore it is necessary to balance these considerations with the potential benefits which may be elicited through the use of alternate, competing sound sources, such as the vehicle's radio. Radio usage is capable of holding a tactical value for navigational purposes (e.g.

live traffic information) and, depending from driver to driver, psychological purposes (e.g. loud music to stay awake during states of fatigue), the latter of which will be discussed in a later section. It is relevant to the present topic of spatial awareness merely to notice that internal sources of sound compete with the potential benefits of external auditory perception enumerated above, and should therefore be balanced in volume accordingly. The professional driver understands the utter unacceptability of wearing head-mounted, silencing audio apparatus during freeway driving which may severely limit or entirely obstruct external auditory perception, including but not limited to earphones, headphones, earbuds, noise-cancelling devices, or any other related instruments. The usage of such devices on the road, furthermore, is outlawed in many jurisdictions. In the discouraged, curious, and potentially illegal event of wearing such a device on only one ear, to leave the other open for external auditory perception, it is recommended that the free ear is chosen according to lane position and the side on which there exists the highest probability of "action". This is variable throughout the course of driving and would necessitate adding an additional expenditure of control loop resources to switch ears during travel as lane position accords, one of the many reasons that could be stated for why wearing such devices even only on one ear is strongly discouraged.

Let us now turn attention back to the visual sense and its supreme role in maintaining comprehensive spatial awareness.

Visual information source #1: Primary frontal view through the front windshield

The eyes of the advanced highway driver will spend a majority of the time scanning and looking ahead at the road in front, gaining a constantly updating geometric understanding of the vehicle's path-of-travel and its contents. This information leads directly to the conscious identification of physical objects which either do exist in the vehicle's path-of-travel or are predicted to do so.

The nuanced factor with regards to frontal view visual scanning is that different *regions* of the driver's view are more or less likely to contain, or be about to contain, physical objects in need of driver identification depending on situation. Potential hazards occupying the left shoulder, for instance, are far less relevant to a driver in the center lane than one occupying the left-most lane. However the center lane driver should assign a higher visual emphasis to the immediate frontal lane area due to the comparatively higher probability that another driver may merge into that center lane in front of him or her. (That is, the left-most lane is only bordered by one other lane whereas interior lanes are surrounded by two lanes, increasing the statistical likelihood that another driver's lane switch will involve an area lying within the vehicle's path-of-travel.) By this example, it is a concern even to the center-lane driver to scan for any such obstructive projections on the left shoulder, due to their likelihood of prompting a left-lane driver to execute the aforementioned lane switch into the center lane. This demonstrates the necessity of analyzing the proper priority emphases which certain areas should merit for the driver's visual scanning, since such obstructions on the left shoulder, which may pose a hazard to a passing left-lane driver, would only rightly attract such a large increase in a center-lane driver's visual attention if a driver to his or her left were present; if the center lane driver were travelling alone on the freeway at 3am in the morning, the relative priority to which he or she should assign these lateral areas, removed from his or her vehicle's immediate path-of-travel, should be comparatively less – since there are no drivers to merge into his or her lane upon encountering the hypothetical road obstruction (insofar, of course, as any obstructions on the left are not egregious enough to infringe closely on his or her own path-of-travel itself). This is not to say that absolutes can be drawn with regards to visual scanning prioritization (i.e., as it would be to say falsely that, at 3am, a driver may safely ignore all areas other than his or her frontal path-of-travel), since other reasons for scanning our example left-shoulder region still do exist (e.g., identification of a moving obstruction such as a moose or of important sign notifications such as a new speed limit or a lane closure). The aforementioned limited example, however, is merely to demonstrate that every variable in a driving situation should and will influence the professional driver's areas of visual priority while scanning his or her surroundings in the most efficient manner possible to effect the most wholesome spatial awareness relevant to a particular situation.

Constant attention to all primary frontal visual areas, however, is a crucial requirement for the professional highway driver; we only seek to optimize the relative and changing proportion to which some areas are visually examined than others. Stretches of road curvature demand a marginally greater temporary emphasis on the immediate frontal lane area so that the driver may steer accordingly, which occupies eye scanning resources such that less visual emphasis may be given to other areas; however the same factor of road curvature may concurrently increase the importance of scanning in other areas. Is there a sudden, abrupt region of slower or stopped traffic immediately after the curve (caused, for instance, by an accident or by road-work-related lane closures)? The utter necessity also of long-range anticipation scanning is therefore established, as indeed an extremely common freeway accident situation is rear-end collision (Davis & Swenson, 2006)[1] – which can occur not only in slow traffic, but also at high-speed during continued failure to identify an abrupt frontal traffic halting as described above. We have now arrived at a seemingly paradoxical conclusion that there is need to prioritize two mutually exclusive (i.e., spatially distant) visual areas while following a curve on the freeway: the immediate frontal position for lane maintenance, and the long-range path-of-travel distance scanning for anticipation of slowed traffic, which itself may be made more abrupt from not having been visible before the curve. Our "control loop" model illustrates the appropriate, adaptive response: the professional driver must rapidly scan different visual sources according to optimized

---

[1] Davis, G. A. & Swenson, J., 2006. Identification and Simulation of a Common Freeway Accident Mechanism: Collective Responsibility in Freeway Rear-end Collisions.

prioritization and never stare in the same place for too long, compromising other critical areas of spatial attention.

It may seem obvious that keeping eyes fixed in one visual perspective for too long, without consulting other visual areas, is a safety hazard – however this behavior is not at all uncommonly carried out to a suboptimal degree, and is related to anything from general lack of attention to conditions described as "highway hypnosis" such as may occur under fatigue. Maintaining decided and controlled eye motion in accordance with our visual scanning techniques will ensure the greatest understanding of spatial awareness that human physiology is capable of achieving, since drivers have only two eyes, and two eyes which are physically constrained to view in unison at the same object or place with each other without independence.

Visual information source #2: Center (rear-view) and "side" or "wing" mirrors

Not only must the professional driver scan every region of the full field of vision, regions which are prioritized according to particular circumstance as noted above, but he or she must also make informed switches between this field of vision and that of the vision provided in his or her mirrors – adding an additional layer of complexity to the ideal spatial awareness method. Since mirrors are so much closer to the driver's vision than are the outdoor and perhaps distant sceneries around him or her, a small delay for optical refocusing on the new, closer focus point constitutes a time cost of switching between windshield view and mirror view, even though such refocusing delay is likely negligible (Charissis & Naef, 2007)[2]. However, total ignorance of mirror information is clearly more disadvantageous than is any minimal refocusing time cost (in addition to the obvious cost of not looking at the road for an

---

[2] Charissis, V. & Naef, M., 2007. Evaluation of prototype automotive head-up display interface: testing driver's focusing ability through a VR simulation. *Intelligent Vehicles Symposium, 2007 IEEE*.

increasingly dangerous time), and so mirror usage must be optimized and balanced according to situation.

Under stable driving circumstances, it should be part of the expert freeway driver's spatial awareness check to refer to side and rear-view mirrors every 4-10 seconds under moderate traffic conditions, yielding awareness to potentially passing drivers on either side of the vehicle. Under conditions in which the highway is nearly deserted, whether for its physical remoteness, time of night, or by whatever cause, it is optimific to increase priority of visual-scanning focus on the road ahead in detection of potential hazards – not only due to the decreased likelihood of encountering other vehicles, but also due to these circumstances' propensity (lateness of night, remoteness, etc.) to increase hazard risk to begin with, such as the risk of large mammalian wildlife crossings. Indeed, the frontal area of visual scanning always occupies foremost priority for the professional driver, as side mirrors themselves were non-standard and considered luxury options on automobiles up until as recently as the 1960s.

In the case of higher traffic congestion levels, frequent mirror consultation becomes a much higher relative priority due to the likelihood of rapid deceleration and rear-end collisions. The absolute guilt of a driver who rear-ends another, regardless of the other's deceleration, is frequently touted in drivers' education courses as a persuasive argument for maintaining focus on solely the frontal area of the vehicle, and ensuring compliance with the basic speed rule without worrying about other drivers' behavior (since such worrying about the driver behind may reduce forward attention such that the worried driver his or herself rear ends the next vehicle – in effect, becoming the executor of the very action he or she was fearing from the driver behind, and only due to such fear). While this instructional technique is perhaps an efficient method for addressing novice and typically adolescent drivers, who are just beginning to internalize the subtleties of vehicular dynamics, and who have perhaps little experience in driving over stretches of highway with high, traffic-related speed differentials, it is however insufficient for the professional driver who, by our definition, finds the very optimum response given the *entire* body of spatial knowledge attainable. Therefore rear-view mirror presence in the visual scanning control loop is not inappropriate especially in high-congestion circumstances, and may just as well prevent an accident from occurring (by, for instance, suddenly allowing a few extra feet of forward distance for a rapidly, nervously decelerating rear vehicle spotted in the rear-view mirror). In this hypothetical, the expert driver identified the momentary spike in the importance of rear-zone spatial awareness due to his or her own rapid deceleration. This section itself is quickly pointing towards two key facts to highway driving safety and optimization which we will examine later in more extensive detail: firstly, that vehicular deceleration always prompts a heightened need for rear-zone spatial awareness, and secondly and even more importantly, that generous following distances are critical for highway driving safety. However, let us return to the present discussion of mirrors' role in proper spatial awareness technique.

The relative distances to each mirror from the driver's present eye direction also bear merit; it is of course the aim of the professional driver to minimize the split-second delay in which his or her eyes are moving from the left mirror and well across the field of view into the right mirror. During this entire five-step interval (focusing on left mirror, identifying mirror contents, switching to the right, and repeating the first two steps for this side), the eyes have absolutely no visual input from the direct road in front of the vehicle. While this delay still constitutes only a fraction of the time some other distracting operations may take, such as operating the vehicle's radio or climate control system, it still promises a field in which Pareto improvements could be made to visual scanning tactics. Assuming there is no imminent time-sensitivity to rearwards spatial awareness, a middle glance at the vehicle's path-of-travel between the visual switch of mirror sides could provide a useful bit of information which prompts the driver to take an appropriate evasive action he or she would not otherwise have taken. This, of course, comes at the expense of a refocusing delay between the near side mirror and the likely distant (by comparison) road surface. The professional driver will meticulously care to his or her visual scanning practice as to make geometric and temporal optimizations both in eyeball movement and focusing, allowing the greatest and most relevant amount of information to be processed by the driver.

Mirrors sometimes produce distortion artifacts which may dangerously lend an inaccurate sense of three-dimensional space to the side of and behind the vehicle, especially to less experienced drivers who have not developed a complete internalization of correlating mirror images to spatial positions, or to drivers who operate an unfamiliar vehicle with potentially deviant mirror constructions. This effect can be particularly pronounced for North American drivers switching to a non-North American vehicle and vice-versa, due to varying regulations between jurisdictions. Canadian and American standardizations require the driver's side mirror to be an entirely undistorted, flat mirror[3]. Meanwhile, other (European and elsewhere – those party to the United Nations Economic Commission for Europe's World Forum for Harmonization of Vehicle Regulations) specifications allow for convex or even aspheric lens shapes, which afford a greater field of vision but which also cause objects to appear smaller and more distant than they actually are, hence the famously common printed warning typically seen on passenger side mirrors. Passenger side (right) mirrors are near-universally distorted with some form of non-flat lens, due to the increased necessity of a widened field of view brought about by the greater distance from the driver's eye. For all these reasons, mirrors are ideally to be used as a supplement to direct eye line-of-sight checking methods, especially when the driver is preparing to execute a potentially collisional maneuver, such as a lane switch.

The former statement has attracted much controversy among driver's education instructors and certainly deserves a separate

---

[3] United States Federal Motor Vehicle Safety Standards and Regulations, Standard 111. U.S. Department of Transportation.

discussion, as it pertains to whether or not physical "head-checks" or "shoulder-checks" should be taught as part of proper lane switching procedure. We will now discuss this intriguing point as part of the third visual information source for spatial awareness.

Visual information source #3: Usage of the rear-lateral windows of the vehicle

Primarily pertaining to lane switches and any multi-lane lateral motion of the vehicle's path-of-travel, the rear-lateral windows of the vehicle afford the driver a direct, undistorted view of areas which must be cleared before the driver executes such a maneuver. The interplay between mirror usage and direct visual scanning through these windows centers mostly on the well-known occurrence of "the blind spot" – a region invisible to the driver scanning solely his or her mirrors (or, perhaps, lateral windows as well) in which vehicles of high collisional risk can escape the spatial awareness of the driver. There may in fact be multiple blind spots depending on vehicle dimensions and the particulars of its mirror configuration, and smaller vehicles (such as motorcycles and even bicycles) can exacerbate the spatial awareness challenges inherent to the phenomenon of the blind spot.

Since the driver's seat faces forward and is situated in front of the aforementioned rear windows, all or some of the vision which they provide extends back beyond the peripheral vision of the forward-facing driver. A physical, left-or-right turning motion of the head is therefore required to make any appreciable use of this visual information source, which necessitates removing the driver's eyes from the vehicle's forward path-of-travel and larger frontal field of view for a split second while the "head-check" or "shoulder-check" maneuver is executed (with the latter term deriving from the fact that the driver looks over his or her shoulders, "checking" for vehicles in and around the blind spot). This typically accompanies an investigation on the possibility of a lane switch, however the importance of spatial awareness of the lateral surroundings of the vehicle is not limited to this most common circumstance to the professional driver.

Head-check procedure

Proper head-checking procedure requires the professional driver to execute a quick head rotation in the direction of spatial investigation with absolutely no other related movements below the neck. The speed of the extending and returning rotation should be as fast as comfortably possible, and the glance should be maintained for as short a period as possible to obtain a quick line-of-sight visual image through the focused visual portion of the rear mirrors. Eyeballs are to be slanted in the direction of spatial interest, which requires a marginally smaller angle of head rotation than if the eyes were held straight, which in turn minimizes the time cost of the maneuver. Due to the double integral relation of steering wheel angle and lateral road position (which we explain in a later section), a firm, stationary, regulatory grip should always be applied to the steering wheel during the approximately half-second to full-second (depending on driver expertise) head check maneuver. Rotating only the head is a critical execution point, as inexperienced drivers are known also to twist their shoulder and upper torso in conjunction with the head twist, which has a deleterious safety effect by its tendency to affect steering angle in an unintended manner, the danger of which is exacerbated by the driver's temporary inattention to the small yet accumulating heading error he or she would introduce by twisting the upper body, and by the tendency of this heading to direct the vehicle towards the blind spot itself being investigated by the head-check maneuver.

Criticism of the aforementioned (and widely unknown) steering-error effect pales in comparison to that of the general lack of frontal visibility, however momentary, from the critics of head-checking within driver's education and expert circles. This argument against head-checking insists that the side mirrors can be configured to eliminate blind spots (a dubious statement, as we shall see) and that complete visual ignorance of the frontal area of the vehicle increases the risk of frontal collisions and otherwise decreases the driver's allotted response time for approaching hazards within the path-of-travel. They purport a fear that removing eye focus from the road in front poses a safety hazard of greater effect than merits the safety benefit of increased lateral spatial awareness afforded by head-checking. We strongly disagree with this sentiment and insist that the professional driver will at all times balance differing regions of spatial priority – the accurate appropriation of which will frequently lend to head-checking, especially in the freeway setting. Adherence to the basic speed rule assures against frontal collisions (we will detail speed optimization in a future section), and situations of high anticipated or observed traffic speed differential institute an accordingly higher visual scanning priority on frontal regions of the driver's vision. A corpus of traffic safety research supports this position; safe head-checking has been considered as "an underlying assumption" to research on the effects and benefits of automated blind spot detection systems (Kiefer & Hankey, 2008)[4] and is formally instructed to novice drivers. Accordingly, in a study focusing on senile driver ability, Marottoli et al. (1998) discovered that decreased capacity for head rotation can nearly double crash risk[5].

The criticism which some driving instructors opine concerning head-checking should only serve as a semi-obvious reminder that a comprehensive frontal analysis of the road in front of the vehicle should be conducted before the head-check in preparation for a momentary loss of visual feedback of the vehicle's path-of-travel. This preparatory analysis includes not only a visual scan of the path-of-travel, but also a predictive consideration of vehicles and/or other obstructions which may enter the seemingly clear path-of-travel while the head-check is being executed. The minimal time cost of a head-check, lasting in any appropriate or rehearsed form

---

[4] Kiefer, R. J. & Hankey, J. M., 2008. Lane change behavior with a side blind zone alert system. *Accident Analysis & Prevention,* 40(2), pp. 683-690.
[5] Marottoli, R. A. & Richardson, E. D., 1998. Confidence in, and Self-rating of, Driving Ability among Older Drivers. *Accident Analysis and Prevention,* 30(3), pp. 331-336.

for no longer than three quarters of a second to a full second, should also be noted – a time cost which may be trivial compared to any other common operations requiring visual abandonment of the path-of-travel, such as operating a climate control or radio setting on the vehicle's interface panel – operations which do not provide critical collision-preventative lateral spatial awareness information, as does head-checking.

Our discussion on the appropriateness of rotational head-checking for lateral spatial awareness is an apt occasion to introduce a useful concept which can be applied to this context and many others throughout this book. In the majority of cases, if experimental research indicates the tendency of a certain cautionary driver behavior to increase with some sort of decreasing safety feature, or is better yet correlated with greater driver experience, then it is usually safe to assume that the behavior is at least aimed towards some well-intentioned and beneficial end – and often that it is a sound behavior altogether. This seems naturally correct as driving a vehicle is a learned process of intelligence, with mistakes and errors usually being momentary deviations from said learned driver-intelligence due to some sort of distraction, human imperfection, or competing circumstance. In other words, the common and regular intelligent driver behaviors (which account for successful operation of a vehicle) are typically sound and valid, with accidents occurring usually at only rare departures from this learned norm. In this manner a further advocacy for sensible head-checking (especially as a precursor behavior to lane switches and any lateral movement of the vehicle) can be made by analyzing the behavior's widespread usage among drivers. Tijerina et al. (2005) analyzed the incidence rate of passenger vehicle driver failure to execute an over-the-shoulder head-check during lane switching in the direction of the lane switch, finding an 87% failure rate for rightwards maneuvers and 71% for leftwards lane switching maneuvers[6]. In other words, drivers were far more cautious and certain to visually head-check the left blind zone during left lane switches than that of the right blind zone during right lane switches. Interestingly, a 1994 NHTSA report documents a slightly higher crash rate for LCM (Lane Change/Merge) crashes on the left side for passenger vehicles – likely explaining the extra caution naturally imbued into drivers' sense of leftwards head-checking priority as reflected in Tijerina's data (Wang & Knipling, 1994)[7]. An expectable objection to this interpretation is that perhaps the heightened tendency to perform an over-the-shoulder head check during left lane switches is in fact that cause of the slightly higher left-side crash rate, instead of a programmed response to counter whatever other tendencies which may cause it to be so. But in fact the crash report data in this part analyzes only sideswipe, lane-switching collisions, not the type of forward crashes that critics of head-checking are eager to warn about. Furthermore, researchers have commented on a wide variation in driver habits which accords with our statistical interpretation that the two aforementioned groups (the ones who perform frequent head checks and the ones who get into lateral collisions) are distinct groups, occupying different ends of the wide driver-behavior spectrum.

As it pertains to this third visual information source (the rear windows requiring a rotational, over-the-shoulder head check), the professional driver must be aware of various factors that will assign an accordingly greater or lesser need to performing head-checks for the appropriation of spatial information for lateral regions in which

---

[6] Tijerina, L., Garrott, W. R., Stoltzfus, D. & Parmer, E., 2005. Eye glance behavior of van and passenger car drivers during lane change decision phase. *Transportation Research Record: Journal of the Transportation Research Board*, 1937(1), pp. 37-43.

[7] Wang, J.-S. & Knipling, R. R., 1994. Lane change/merge crashes: problem size assessment and statistical description. *US Department of Transportation, National Highway Traffic Safety Administration,* January.Volume DOT HS 808-075.

the vehicle may travel. Since head-checking necessarily involves some transitory moment of time during which the frontal vision field is outside the driver's peripheral vision, it should be minimized when less necessary and prioritized when more needed. Factors contributing to this delicate balance include width of the peripheral vision field, car structure/pillar arrangement, and the peculiarities of the vehicle's side mirrors. The professional driver is aware of all of these factors in establishing his or her critical, dynamic balance of frontal vs. lateral visual scanning, and therefore we will examine each of these three in detail.

Peripheral vision

It is commonly assumed that the human eye is able to see a full 180-degree field of view including the very periphery of vision, which is false. Burg (1968) found that the maximum angle of peripheral vision is a function of age, reaching a maximum of 176-degrees at age 20 and decreasing to 150-degrees by age 70[8]. Furthermore, total visual field is slightly greater in females (Burg, 1968)[9]. Therefore the professional driver of an older age and of less capable peripheral vision should prioritize safely conducting a rotational head check before executing lateral movements of the vehicle, and should also practice head stretching/rotation exercises as a warm up to his or her driving (so that the maneuver may be made more quickly and comfortably). Transportation authorities typically require a satisfactory field of vision as part their licensing process, usually varying from 120 to 140 degrees as a minimum passable threshold. The eyes of the ideal, professional driver will see among the widest of visual fields, and those who are less physiologically gifted will compensate by enacting more deliberate and aware lateral awareness methods. The common senile inaccessibility for head rotation is cited as a common benefit for the blind-spot-free mirror configuration (which we will explain in a future part), since the need

---

[8] Burg, A., 1968. Vision test scores and driving record: Additional findings.

[9] Burg, A., 1968. Lateral visual field as related to age and sex. *Journal of Applied Psychology*, 52(1), pp. 10-15.

for head-checking is purportedly eliminated – however we must first return to the mastery of proper head-checking procedure before any dubious and oversimplified optimizations can be made to mirror configuration and scanning strategy.

Pillar structure

An increased prioritization and suitability for head-check-based lateral awareness ought to be appropriated while driving a vehicle whose physical structure is less conducive, or perhaps even obstructive, to comprehensive spatial awareness of the sides and blind spots of the vehicle. Varying widths and pluralities of the vehicle's rear pillars (the structural support elements of the vehicle which connect the lower body to the roof), in addition to variations in window size, contribute to potentially vast differences in size and location of blind spot(s) compared to that of another vehicle the driver may be more accustomed to operating. The professional driver will therefore identify such constraints on lateral and rear visibility according to vehicle design, and compensate accordingly by means of adjusting the emphasis on head-checking in his or her visual scanning routine. Research has been conducted on the effect of letter-identified (according to the pictured diagram) pillar positioning and thickness on lateral crash rates; the University of Michigan Transportation Research Institute found that four-door models of the same vehicle type were 17% more likely to be involved in lateral lane-switch collisions than their two-door counterparts due to more forward B-pillar placement (Sivak, et al., 2006)[10]. Furthermore, Sivak et al. 2007 established a correlation between higher lateral crash rates and two factors concerning the A-pillar: its width (unsurprisingly), and angularity away from the

---

[10] Sivak, M., Schoettle, B. & Reed, M. P., 2006. Influence of visibility out of the vehicle cabin on lane-change crashes. *Accident Analysis & Prevention,* 38(5), pp. 969-972.

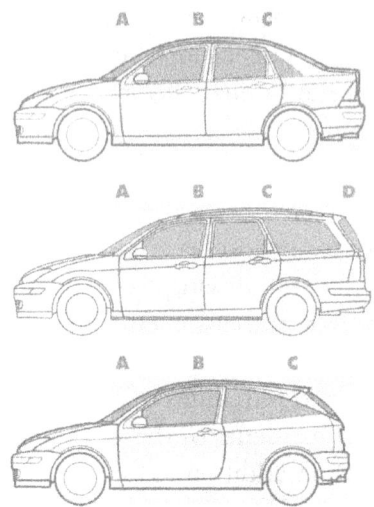

Figure 2 - Common vehicle body styles and corresponding pillar identifiers. Reproduced from public domain materials.

driver's straight ahead view[11]. The professional driver should therefore be aware of his or her present vehicle's pillar positioning as it pertains to his or her past experience with pillar arrangements of different qualities, which may be more or less conducive to lateral awareness given the scientific findings cited above. Given these considerations, if a driver determines his or her vehicle's visual pillar configuration to accord with a higher lateral crash probability, he or she should take more caution in performing lane switches or any other lateral motion of the vehicle, especially in high traffic conditions, due to the heightened statistical likelihood of collision.

The reader may ask, "why not spend a copious amount of visual scanning resources to cautiously scan the lateral regions before a lane switch in all conditions and vehicle types, favorable or unfavorable, whatsoever?" The answer, we should recapitulate, is that a proper prioritizing balance must be made due to the scarcity of visual scanning resources; visual investigation of the lateral areas of the vehicle – whether by mirror checking or, more expensively, head-checking – necessarily constitutes a decreased attention to the straight forward view of the vehicle's path-of-travel, which is generally the most important area for spatial awareness scanning (especially at highway speeds, whereupon unforeseeable

---

[11] Sivak, M., Schoettle, B., Reed, M. P. & Flannagan, M. J., 2007. Body-pillar vision obstructions and lane-change crashes. *Journal of safety research*, 38(5), pp. 557-561.

obstructions may enter the vehicle's path-of-travel). Merging into adjacent lane on the highway is a task that must call for an appropriate balance (and wise timing) of lateral versus frontward spatial attention due the necessity of understanding both – as other vehicles may enter a driver's path-of-travel as he or she is inattentive to that area and busy scanning the lateral region to which he or she intends to merge. (As we shall see in a common collision setup, the sudden decrease in speed of a driver in front of a merging driver causes a rear-end collision due to the merging driver's spatial ignorance of the rapidly slowing car in front of him or her, due to that vehicle's own lane-switching initiative robbing the driver's eyes of frontal scanning attention[12].) The competition for limited sensory scanning resources is the reason that the professional driver must analyze the factors which contribute to the higher or lower emphasis on lateral scanning; we have discussed two of these factors (variations in peripheral vision ability and vehicular pillar construction), and will now examine a third.

Differences in wing-mirror construction

The construction peculiarities of a vehicle's side mirrors (the driver's side mirror, in particular, in the case of left-side spatial interest) may contribute extensively to an accurate estimation of the vehicle's propensity to require more or less lateral scanning attention for safe lane switches and for reason motivating the acquisition of lateral spatial awareness. The professional driver should be aware of the planarity of the left-side mirror; while the right-side mirror is almost always spherically distorted in some fashion to afford a greater field of visibility, United States and Canadian traffic regulations require flat, planar mirrors of "unit magnification" on the driver's side. This instills a vastly greater lateral awareness burden (that is, head-checking necessity) for the American driver compared to the European or Japanese driver, who may likely enjoy the effects of a multiradius or convex driver's side mirror – which may completely eliminate any problematic blind

---

[12] See Chapter 12, accident situation #10

spot(s) in some cases. (It should be noted that this statement holds true under standard mirror configurations; we will discuss alternate mirror configuration methods for American drivers in a proceeding section.) Another factor which should be known to the North American driver is that planar mirrors have been found to reflect more glare into the driver's eyes than aspheric and convex mirrors – depending on the intensity of the glare and the driver's sensitivity to light, this may be considered an advantage or disadvantage to spatial awareness; on one hand, more visible light could potentially save visual scanning resources in the control loop execution by affording the opportunity to respond to the light-stimulus as an initiation (or prioritization) of subsequent lateral scanning (due to the knowledge of a nearby vehicle) as opposed to consistently checking the area, expending frontal scanning resources, when a vehicle may not even be present (this statement is naturally more applicable dark, low-traffic situations). On the other hand, glare of too great an intensity may challenge the vision of the driver as it pertains to the other areas of spatial awareness.

The most persuasive argument for the North American regulation requiring flat driver-side mirrors concerns the minifying image distortion presumably associated with aspheric ("multiradius") or convex mirrors. The NHTSA's 2008 report on driver performance with aspheric mirrors indicates that "underestimation of distance decreases as mirror radius of curvature increases" – that is, planar mirrors are safer due to their tendency to cause the driver to underestimate the distance to image, which accordingly represents an increase in safety clearance amount (since the imaged vehicle would in reality be farther away than it is perceived to be)[13]. This effect was not however shown to be significant, and, on the whole, drivers are largely able to compensate for mirror minification effects (as stated in the report, "drivers do not appear to judge distance on

---

[13] National Highway Traffic Safety Administration, 2008. Study of diver performance/acceptance using aspheric mirrors in light. *US Department of Transportation, National Highway Traffic Safety Administration,* Volume DOT HS 810-959, 33.

the basis of image size.") We generally hold the increased field of vision associated with non-planar mirrors to be a greater safety advantage than is the associated risk of distance-to-object overestimation. This means that American highway drivers must prioritize alternate blind-spot scanning methods (in essence, the head-check maneuver), while European drivers must take care to avoid overestimating the distance to mirror-minified vehicles while making left lane switches – to remember that objects in mirror, truly, "are closer than they appear". Of course, for rightwards lateral movement, this must be remembered for the invariably non-planar right wing mirror design regardless of locale.

Some wing-mirrors are equipped with a SBZA (Side Blind Zone Alert) system which automatically detects and visually warns passing traffic on either side of the vehicle – aiding in the process of blind spot checking. Kiefer & Hankey (2008) found that a well-implemented SBZA system can reduce leftwards lane change attempts by 31% and rightwards attempts by 23% - before the driver looks into the mirror or, even more expensively, performs a head-check[14]. That is to say, notification from an SBZA system of a passing vehicle is beneficial to the professional driver since it entirely rules out the possibility of executing a lane switch, whereas mirror glancing and/or head checking control-loop resources would otherwise need to be expended to arrive at the same conclusion. An SBZA system alert must therefore be used as a prohibitory mechanism but not the inverse – that is, lack of an SBZA warning is insufficient clearance for a lane switch due to the possibility of failure on the system's part.

Prior to driving on the freeway, there are various optimizations the professional driver can make to his or her mirror system which may prove beneficial to spatial awareness on the highway. A relatively well known method of overcoming the restrictions imposed by the American ban on non-planar driver side mirrors is to install "stick

---

[14] Kiefer, R. J. & Hankey, J. M., 2008. Lane change behavior with a side blind zone alert system. *Accident Analysis & Prevention,* 40(2), pp. 683-690.

on" convex mirrors over the side or edge of the left mirror. Studies have discovered the existence of such mirrors on 6.6% of 620 sampled vehicles, suggesting some sort of (at least perceived) safety augmenting value (Olson & Winkler, 1985)[15]. While such mirrors may technically eliminate the blind spot, they carry at least two less-appealing downfalls: firstly, their visible surface area is small, and only the edge portions of the mirror do provide any new, useful visual information that isn't already present in the default mirror (which is why their usage requires, at least, high visual acuity); secondly, they reduce the effective width of the primary planar mirror which can significantly reduce its field of view. George Platzer (1995) proposed an intelligent method of overcoming these downfalls by advocating the design of a mirror whose bottom strip is "canted" as to provide a wider field of view solely in that area, which does not affect the field of view of the planar section – however this design is not implemented in mainstream vehicles and is likely out of reach for most professional drivers[16].

Traditional vs. wide mirror alignment

Platzer, working with the Society of Automotive Engineers (SAE), therefore proposed an alternative arrangement of unmodified side mirrors which attempts to eliminate the blind spot – now a decently well-known technique which the reader may have already heard of or even presently use (the "SAE Method", as it is sometimes named, or the "BGE/blind-glare-elimination mirror setting", or "setting the mirrors wide").

---

[15] Olson, P. L. & Winkler, C. B., 1985. Measurement of crash avoidance characteristics of vehicles in use. Final report.. October.
[16] Platzer, G., 1995. The geometry of automotive rearview mirrors-why blind zones exist and strategies to overcome them.. *SAE Technical Paper Series*, 1 February. Volume 950601.

Essentially, the SAE technique involves shifting the side mirror's field of visibility such that two blind spots on either side are created, but of half the angular size as the original blind spot such that the resulting two half-size blind spots are insufficient to fully hide a vehicle. The method is purported as an alternative to the traditional

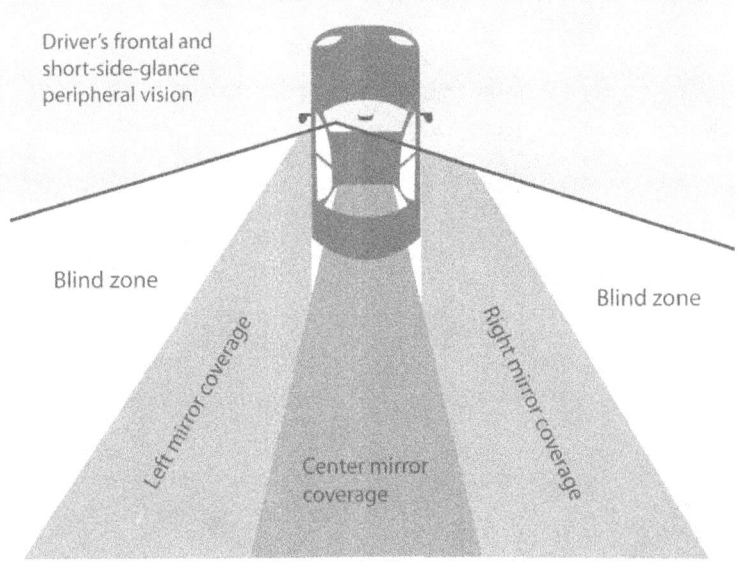

Figure 3 - Mirror visibility zones and blind spot coverages of the traditional alignment method

mirror configuration requiring head-checking, and is said therefore to be more suitable for "older and physically restricted" drivers as Platzer pointed out. Furthermore, the eliminated necessity of interrupting frontward vision is touted as a large benefit of the method. These seeming advantages explain why the technique is even currently taught in many introductory driver's education courses. In general, we discourage usage of this modern mirror configuration and advocate the traditional setting which maintains rear-wards view along the side edge of the vehicle, and which necessitates head-check maneuvers; this however is not a steadfast absolute for the ideal spatial awareness method of the professional driver. We will analyze this increasingly common method and review in detail its benefits and deficiencies as it concerns the optimal freeway driving mirror configuration; this detail will be necessary to defend our position on wide mirror settings from predictable criticism, as this is a controversial topic among driving educators.

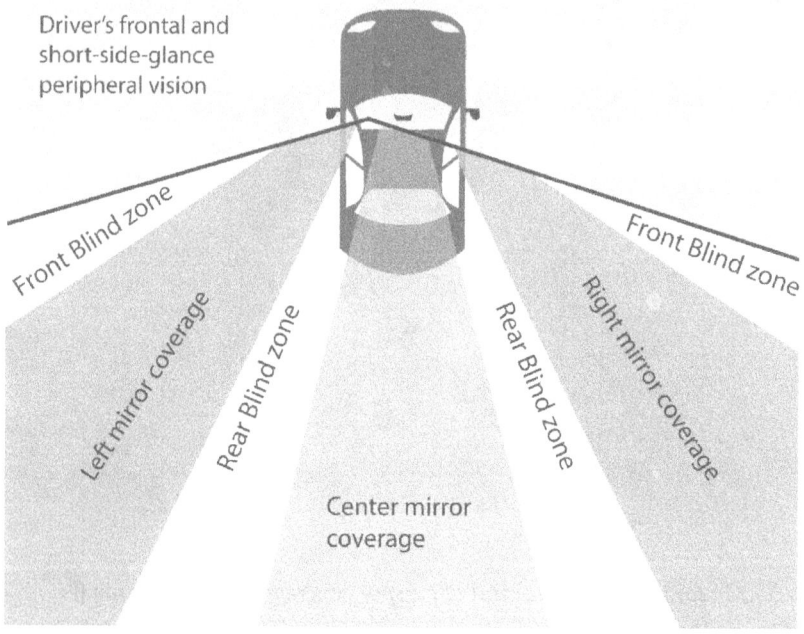

Figure 4 - Modern "Wide" or "SAE" mirror configuration method, showing the creation of two additional (yet smaller) blind spots

The illustrations above, drawn intentionally out of scale for simple conceptual illustration, demonstrate the effect of the SAE method's "widening" the outer mirrors and the consequent creation of two extra (though narrower) blind spots on each side. This wide mirror configuration method can be implemented through the following steps:

1. Center the rear-view mirror such that its reflecting vision directly centers over the lane behind the vehicle.

2. With eyes laterally aligned just to the side of or at the left/driver window of the vehicle (i.e., the adjuster's head is spatially translocated over towards the window), adjust the left wing mirror so that the right-most part of the image therein aligns just along the edge of the vehicle.

3. Place eyes in the center of the vehicle, lining up directly with the center mirror, and adjust the right wing mirror as to cause the left-most edge of its vision to barely reach the right side of the vehicle.

At least in the freeway environment, we contend that the SAE mirror alignment method, and resulting lateral spatial awareness strategy, is suboptimal and inferior to the traditional method of mirror alignment combined with well-executed head-checks, in most circumstances, for a variety of reasons. Firstly, the traditional method provides a degree of overlap between the left-most image of the rear-view mirror, and the right-most of the left-side mirror (and vice versa for the center and right mirror). This overlap (i.e., two places in which to see the same theoretical image) is crucial for comprehensive spatial awareness, since many varied human and/or environmental factors may serve to disrupt the center mirror's view of the regions no longer covered by the side mirrors in the SAE method (namely, the rear-side posterolateral areas of the vehicle necessary for viewing posterolateral vehicles – which is crucial in a plethora of highway driving circumstances). Head restraints in the rear of the vehicle, passengers, and even the C and/or D pillars of the car's structure themselves will combine to create various small angular blind spots in the rear-view mirror on each rear-side area – blind areas which are visualized in the side mirrors under the traditional method, since vision extends in each mirror along the edge of the vehicle and back behind it on this longitudinal axis. Additionally, the rear windows are often tinted, further limiting center mirror visibility, whereas the driver and passenger windows (through which the driver examines the side mirror images) are untinted by federal regulation. This means that even if center-mirror blind spots were nonexistent, the image of these side-rear areas is still more visible to the driver in the side mirrors – which are angled to omit this area in the SAE method.

The main thrust of the SAE mirror alignment method is that the two blind spots found on either side of the vehicle, made essentially from cutting the first blind spot in half by shifting the mirror field of view, are of insufficient angular width as to fully hide a vehicle, which is not true for the size of the one larger blind spot created by the traditional alignment method. The fact is that this assumption is not sufficient to the professional driver and his or her safety purposes, since motorcycles and potentially other hazards smaller than a full passenger vehicle may still hide in these blind zones – a likelihood which is exacerbated by any factors limiting peripheral vision, such as senility. The method itself is largely a design in response to the "annoyance" of performing head-checks, and so its usage is frequently associated the abandonment of the necessity of performing such shoulder glances altogether. For reasons already established, and foremostly the possibility of motorcycles to hide in the reduced-width blind spots, neglecting direct line-of-sight lateral spatial awareness is not acceptable to the professional driver. The stubborn proponent of the SAE method may persist that the mirror alignment can therefore be safely practiced along with the continued usage of head-rotational shoulder checks, and that the mirror configuration may simply provide a device which more frequently causes the abandonment of impossible lane changes before expending the time and frontal-road-inattention of doing a head-check to achieve the same conclusion – which certainly would be an advantage (such is the advantage of electronic SBZA systems, as we already stated). We consider this an insufficient retort in defense of the SAE method for two reasons; firstly, potentially dangerous vehicles unknown to driver in need of lateral spatial attention will tend to have approached the vehicle from behind in their lane, rather than having decelerated in their lane from in front of the vehicle, for the obvious reason that drivers face forward relative to the direction of the vehicle, and that any such decelerating vehicle entering a driver's side zone would likely have already been seen by the driver. Therefore, since unnoticed, side-blind-zone-occupying vehicles will almost always have come from behind instead of from ahead, and since the traditional mirror configuration points backwards along their approaching trajectory, the SAE method is probabilistically no better or faster of a lane-switch-abandonment-causing device than is the traditional mirror alignment – and is in fact slower due to the longer time which advancing vehicles must spend accelerating into the longitudinally farther-forward rearmost edge of the side mirror's field of vision under the SAE mirror alignment method.

Our second objection to the aforementioned defense of the SAE method concerns the efficiency of combined rotational head-eye movements; the largest time expenditure during the head-check constitutes the ocular readjusting/refocusing to the new viewing region and then the processing of this visual data – whereas the initial physical twisting of the head and turning of the eyes happens very quickly by comparison. Therefore, head-checking both blind spots under the SAE method not only requires becoming very familiar with their exact positioning, but also requires two separate iterations of the turn/refocus/visual-processing time demand, which lengthens the head-check maneuver at the expense of safety, due to the concurrently unchecked (and rapidly advancing) path-of-travel of the vehicle, which is largely or completely out of peripheral vision during a head check. The cumbersomeness of executing a head-check over both blind spots in the SAE method lies in contrast with the masterable, neuromuscularly-programmable, fast, practiced, cohesive, and familiar head-check to the one simple and well-known blind spot created by the traditional mirror alignment method.

The SAE mirror configuration will also have the effect of reducing glare/light reflectivity from the imaged vehicles, which may be desirable or undesirable depending on circumstance and driver physiology, as we discussed while comparing planar and non-planar mirrors. Either way, we have shown the problems inherent to relying solely on information from SAE method-aligned mirrors, and have also shown the suboptimalities inherent to "covering" these deficiencies with using head-checking in conjunction with the SAE method. This leaves us to declare that the professional driver will use the traditional mirror configuration (assuming standard mirror equipment and vehicle design) in conjunction with expertly executed and wisely prioritized head-checks. Senile drivers, for whom the SAE method's purportedly safe elimination of head-checking is stated to largely benefit, may simply lean their head forward temporarily, to increase side-mirror field of vision, before a head-check in order to reduce the amount of neck-rotation necessary to procure the same field of vision from a head-check as would the upright head-checking driver (as is ideal, if physiologically possible). Bhise et al. (1981) conducted a study which parameterized various head movements of drivers and found that such movements are capable of changing the field of vision within the mirror to a potentially consequential degree[17]. We would therefore recommend to the persisting dissenter to our general disapproval of the SAE method to make such lateral head movements while consulting the wide-adjusted side mirrors in order to enlarge their effective visual field and narrow (or possibly eliminate) the two blind spots which they create (however, like SAE method head-checking, this still constitutes an unwanted time and attention expenditure).

Advances in mirror design and electronic side blind-zone notification systems do hold promise for aiding the speed by which the professional driver obtains lateral spatial awareness; one interesting mirror design is formed from a standard planar surface mirror, which bends into a curvature on and only on the outer-side, affording vision of the blind zone without sacrificing the crucially important rear-side view along the edge of the vehicle which the SAE method removes from mirror vision, and without shrinking

---

[17] Bhise, V. D. et al., 1981. Driver head movements in left outside mirror viewing. *SAE Technical Paper Series,* Volume 810761.

the effective width of the mirror such as occurs with self-adhesive convex mirrors. However, such non-standard mirrors may extend beyond the bounds of present regulatory possibility and/or the reality of the vehicular hardware which the professional driver must operate. We therefore confirm our general disapproval of the SAE mirror-alignment method, and the associated head-check-eschewing scanning strategy, and do incorporate the traditional side mirror alignment configuration and incumbent head-checking procedure, as we have extensively detailed above, as the primary mechanical method of ingesting visual information about lateral spatial awareness into the mental processing control loop in this discussion regarding our third enumerated source of visual information: usage of the direct, line-of-sight vision afforded by the rear-lateral windows of the vehicle.

Vehicular status awareness

We have hereunto defined a tactical model for the ideal appropriation of spatial information concerning space and objects external to the vehicle, however this is still insufficient to the professional driver who will maintain a constant awareness of his or her vehicle itself – as such measures of awareness thereabout (fuel levels, service lights, navigation instructions, etc.) constitute physical mechanisms in some form (however micro-scale), and therefore they fall under the umbrella of spatial awareness. Such knowledge of the vehicle's operating status itself can be critical to both safety and optimization depending on circumstance. For instance, for cars with built-in tire pressure sensors accessible to the driver by some sort of wheel-button-operated electronic display interface, the driver could anticipate circumstances in which a flat tire would be more likely (such as exiting the freeway onto an unpaved, rocky road in subzero temperatures – not at all an unlikely prospect for more remote areas which may have such extreme climatic temperature conditions), and make a predictive adjustment to his or her route based on low-tire-pressure information which may not otherwise be made, since only more traditional factors of route planning (distance, speed limit, etc.) would be considered. Monitoring gas levels is largely a routine and self-explanatory process, and as it occurs, coming to a halt mid-lane on a freeway due to expired gasoline reserves is an incredibly rare phenomenon (as even untrained highway drivers have the common sense to merge into the breakdown lane if they find themselves in a futile gas-station-arrival situation – which is itself decreasingly likely due to the increased prevalence of auditory and/or visual electronic, low-gas warning systems built into any newer vehicle). The point as it pertains to the professional driver's spatial awareness method is to judge sage prioritizations and timings when glancing or interfacing with the vehicle in order to procure operational information, since it is the external spatial awareness which, on the whole, has the most constant and pressing need for continued attention.

Intravehicular spatial awareness and human factors

In addition to the status of the vehicle itself, the professional driver's encompassing concept of spatial awareness extends also to that of the interior cabin area of the vehicle (which may not be an entirely enclosed space, depending on vehicle style and construction). Useful spatial awareness of the interior of the vehicle pertains almost exclusively to human and/or environmental factors which could come to constitute, by predictive analysis, an obstruction to the professional driver's physical interfacing with the vehicle or his or her psychological attentiveness and information processing to the road by repeating the master "control loop" of tactical decision making. Loose physical objects, such as comestibles once contained by a designated holding device, or objects which are otherwise subject to free motion on the floor, must be attended such that they do not fall or travel into the region under the vehicle's pedal interfaces (accelerator, brake, and sometimes clutch), which would constitute a large safety hazard. Human factors are of equal or even greater importance, due to adversarial passengers' ability to completely overpower the driver, who is defenseless in his or her visual subjugation to the road and vehicular maneuvering, with hands, feet, and eyes all concomitantly dedicated to that same purpose. Even the unarmed passenger could easily exert full submissive control over the driver by means of gradations of violence up to yet inferior to armed threatening. Although physical defense tactics for professional drivers who must also attend to their highway-speed-travelling vehicle do exist, they are beyond the scope of this book and so we will therefore emphasize the importance of preventative measures, insofar that the professional driver will attempt to minimize or eliminate travelling with passengers of violent and/or suicidal inclinations, excessive noisiness as to challenge auditory stimuli contributing to spatial awareness, excessive proclivity towards motion which may contribute to the obstruction of visual line-of-sight information gathering, or quite simply of such height which would create a blind zone through the rear window as viewed from the center mirror. The tallest passenger should be seated in the passenger seat, as his or her height is least obstructive in this place. Accordingly, passengers in the rear left side of the vehicle should be shorter than those on the rear right, since (as mentioned before), lateral spatial awareness is slightly more challenging on the left side of the vehicle, and such leftwards lane-change-related crashes are slightly higher than that of the right side (and, additionally, right wing mirrors are always non-planar, offering a potentially wider field of vision than the left side mirror in North American legislative areas (which typically ban non-planar driver side mirrors) which may supplement the blind spots created by the taller passengers while executing a rightwards head-check). Passengers also reduce fuel-efficiency and maximum speed of the vehicle by their added weight. If heavy passengers unevenly disturb an equal weight distribution relative to the axles of the vehicle, this may constitute a safety and well as efficiency sub-optimality (since the physics of the maneuverability of the vehicle will be altered, and since uneven amounts of friction-causing downforce will be placed on certain tires – this is known as weight transfer and is explained in our later discussion on vehicle control). Macuga et al. (2006) confirmed the "importance of inertial information" while executing lane switches[18], confirming that drivers are trained to rely on subtle, somatosensory inertial cues from the vehicle's angular tilt (and, presumably, the tactile, resistive steering-wheel feedback) during lane changes – which could be altered appreciably by an uneven (and unfamiliar) distribution of overweight passengers. The aforementioned height-related passenger arrangement optimization (as it pertained to line-of-sight spatial awareness) must therefore be balanced with evenly distributing the weight of passengers, with (in all but extreme cases) an emphasis on the former.

HOV (high-occupancy vehicle) lanes are an interesting exception to the general rule that reducing or eliminating passengers constitutes an optimization. It is certainly possible to illegally drive into an HOV lane while being the only occupant of the vehicle, and depending on area, the chances of being caught may be very low. However the validating existence of extra passengers eliminates whatever risk there may be to the aforesaid behavior, and verifies this special case as an exception to the passenger-unfriendly optimization rule stated above. This point extends back to the first part of this book, when we examined highway driving strategy and the role of navigational preplanning and route familiarity. For what distance on the intended route is there an HOV lane option? What are the lane's effectual times of day? What is the probability that slower traffic will be avoided, and what is the comparative safety of riding in one versus riding in the traffic? These additional questions cast a more complicated light onto the question of passengers and of HOV lanes' implication that having more is generally suboptimal for safety and optimization; we will analyze HOV lanes in detail in a following section. Regardless of pre-drive optimizations to passenger identity and count, active spatial awareness on the human factors interior to the vehicle is a crucial responsibility to the professional driver who must ensure an environment conducive to

---

[18] Macuga, K. L. et al., 2006. Changing lanes: inertial cues and explicit path information facilitate steering performance when visual feedback is removed. *Experimental brain research,* 178(2), pp. 141-150.

carrying out his or her other, most important, and psychologically demanding attention to operating the vehicle as a product of the control loop and the processing of spatial information therewith.

We have dissected the multifaceted components to the professional driver's expert spatial awareness technique and have hopefully demonstrated the importance of its overlooked peculiarities as it concerns safety and, as we shall see later, analyzing the potential for optimization. This information, if practiced and consistently applied, already sets the practitioner at a vastly higher level of freeway driving expertise compared to the average driver who omits head-checks, scans frontal regions with un-optimized regional prioritization, and who ventures overextended visual abandonments of the vehicle's path-of-travel in order to execute small (and often avoidable) tasks. The professional driver's mastery of continually maintaining the highest possible degree of spatial awareness serves as the basis by which the following discussions concerning spatial maneuvering tactics are applied.

CHAPTER 4

Highway Entrance Merging Procedures

In this section, we will discuss the freeway driver's first experience of any highway trip: getting onto the highway by means of an entrance ramp and successfully into the flow of traffic.

Merging into different lanes, as part of a lane switch, will be discussed in the next section, as for now we are concerning primarily with the assumption that an initially slow-moving vehicle will need to accelerate to highway speeds and merge into traffic travelling faster than what may always be feasible by means of on-ramp acceleration (especially in circumstances in which the on ramp is held to a stand-still due a frontal vehicle's ongoing inability to merge into the right lane of the freeway). This differs from merging into lanes while on the highway, which involves vehicles typically of similar speed, and so those cases are reserved for the following chapter.

Allovehicular terminology and spatial zones

We will need to establish a consistent terminology for referencing the other vehicles surrounding the professional driver (referred to as "allovehicles"), which is set forth in the following diagram. We will also refer to the "traffic-lane" to indicate the right-most lane of freeway travel (assuming the standard right-side entrance ramp) and into which the merge will be executed; we refer to the "merge-lane" as the lane from which the merge occurs, which expires at some critical forward longitudinal distance.

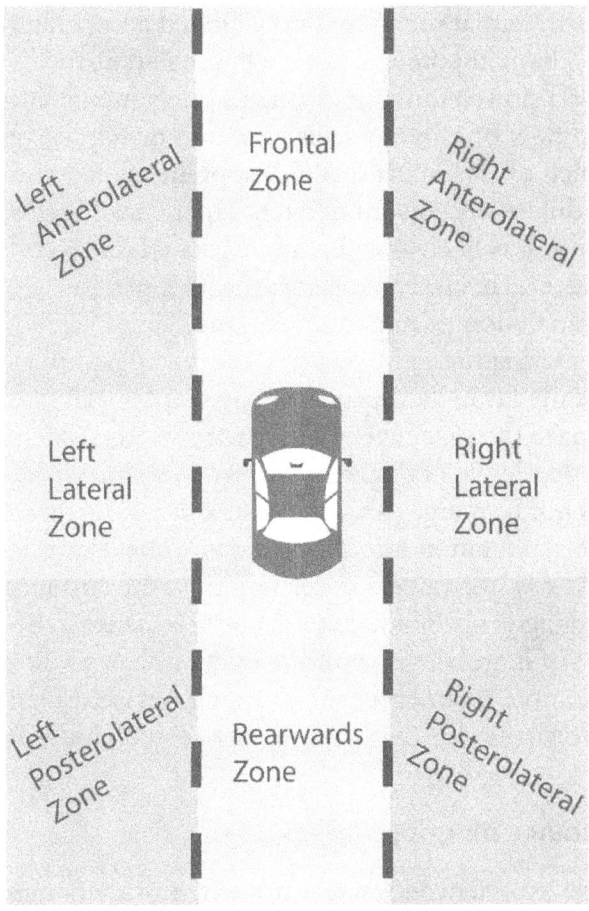

Figure 5– Exovehicular spatial zones to which we heavily refer throughout this book

Highway entrance merging psychology

Introductory driver education courses typically tend to suggest that merging on and off of the highway represents the most intricate and potentially dangerous part of highway driving, with easy-going, smooth-sailing, highway-speed-cruising to occupy the interstitial travelling portion once on the road. While this entire book may be taken as direct proof of the overall falsity of that attitude (or at least its status as a gross exaggeration), the quaint aphorism still suffices well to demonstrate that merging onto a limited access highway carries with it a basic theoretical safety challenge (i.e., the requirement of a slower-moving vehicle to safely merge into a highway-speed flow of moving vehicles and to match its speed thereunto) which causes much fear and apprehension among first time highway drivers. As any moderately experienced highway driver may attest, it is likely this fear itself which leads to problems in merging under difficult circumstances, with a nervously over-conservative estimation of minimum entrance speed scaring novice drivers from entering the right lane (if a car is at all approaching, even if sufficiently far behind), and thereby stopping all highway ingress as to make the maneuver even harder and less safe (since the car must now decelerate perhaps all the way to a stop, since its driver decided not to merge, which only lengthens the distance required for re-acceleration into the highway). That is not to say that some situations will not call for deceleration on the entrance ramp when safe merging is not possible or is not forecasted to be possible at the moment of ingress by a sound predictive analysis; however, we only seek to note that nervousness among novice drivers has had the tendency to create this over-conservative estimation effect.

Highway entrance merging phases

The moderately experienced freeway driver is already familiar with the general procedural outline of the merging operation, to an extensive or perhaps complete degree, and so we will not likely show in this section some sort of revolutionizing and unconventional merging strategy; however, we will break down the fine details of the traditional procedure and highlight its finer constituent areas in which the professional driver has superior knowledge and awareness, which may itself have the effect of seeming to be "revolutionizing" compared the often ill-informed, dangerous, and unaware merging behaviors of the less-experienced driver. We define the traditional merging process as a three-step consecutive sequence, which is spatially defined along the vehicle's path-of-travel:

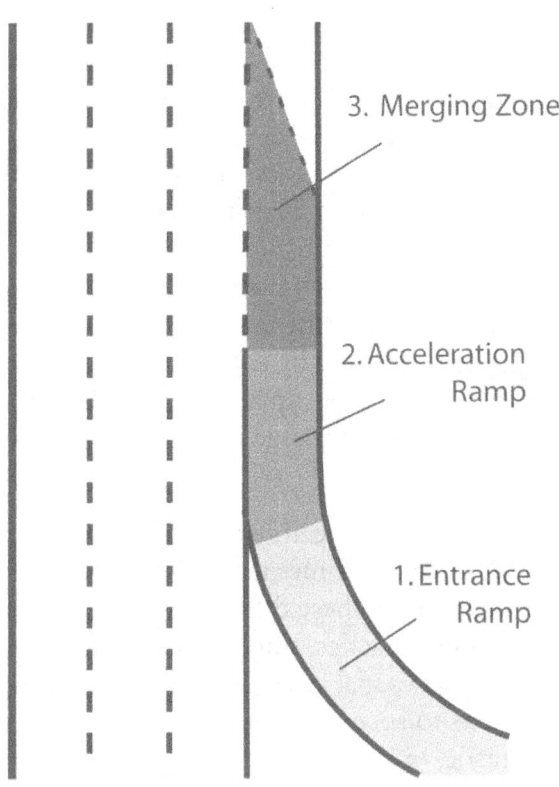

Figure 6 – An approximate graphical shading of a simplified, idealized highway entrance ramp demonstrates the relative demarcations between the three zones.

Chapter 4: Highway Entrance Merging Procedures

1. The entrance ramp which interfaces with the road from which the vehicle enters the highway (and which has likely contained the vehicle in a much slower speed range than that which will be achieved during the acceleration required for merging);

2. The acceleration zone, after speed and/or visibility limitations from road curvature during the entrance ramp stage have been passed, and in which the vehicle accelerates to highway speed while simultaneously balancing spatial information to inform the final stage; and

3. The merging zone, in which the vehicle must find a gap in lateral traffic and execute the actual lane switch maneuver, and which is characterized by some sort of fixed end point in which the merging lane expires, before which the vehicles thereon must necessarily merge into the flow of freeway traffic.

Differing geometric layouts of the above three road structures are bound to alter the comparative times in which the vehicle spends in any given one of these stages; these differences have a direct impact on appropriate selection of tactics, since circumstances may vary as to how challenging visual spatial awareness of the traffic to be merged into may be, as to speed regulation obligations in any stages due to curvature, traffic, or other factors, and as to the length of the road which is given to the driver in stages two and three. The extreme case of difficult road-geometry for merging would involve a sharply turning entrance ramp (limiting speed and preventing highway visibility until a delayed time), a very short acceleration zone, and a short or non-existent merging zone (depending on where one subjectively demarcates the two) – and great variability in these standards persist throughout the American interstate network. For one extreme example, the I-45 southbound entrance ramp from Allen Parkway in Houston, TX affords the driver a mere 315ft length of merging lane distance, until it fully returns to the original narrowness of I-45 South's left lane, having afforded the driver an even shorter 280ft of acceleration lane distance on which to get up to highway speed. Entrance ramps at high-volume interchanges which were originally designed to expect greater traffic levels may grace the driver with a nearly effortless task; we may take the I-95 westbound to I-93 northbound on-ramp in Reading, MA as an example of this extreme end of the spectrum, affording the driver 420ft of straight-line acceleration-zone distance and a whopping 1,575ft long merging lane (not to mention the full clearing of interstitial flora and vegetation, affording great visibility, and a gracefully double-bended diamond-intersection curve, as opposed to a harshly angular loop which any freeway driver is likely to encounter in a memorable percentage of other locations). In reality, the professional driver will most often navigate merging situations somewhere in between these two extremes, however he or she must always expect and be prepared for the most challenging conditions in order to exercise the greatest optimization benefits if possible, and at the very least, to execute a safe and successful merge.

Preparatory factors

Let us start with the typical, one-lane, curving entrance ramp which straightens out into an acceleration lane semi-parallel to the highway, which itself ultimately merges into the right lane of the freeway (we will consider the manifold variations which may alter this exemplary and over-simplified description, but for the moment it will be used as a descriptive introduction to tactical maneuvering while entering the freeway). The desire of any professional freeway driver before merging is to obtain spatial information concerning the flow of traffic and individual vehicles into which the driver's vehicle must merge – for as long and as actionable a time before actually executing the lane merge maneuver. This essentially boils down to making predictive analyses based on the flow of traffic as to where will be the area most conducive to merging. We will detail the specifics on how to conduct that analysis, but for the moment, we only consider that vision of the traffic is necessary for this process, and that its success is positively increased by a longer pre-merge duration of freeway traffic visibility from the on-ramp (since the predictive analyses which seek to establish an intended merging zone will become more and more certain as the behavior of traffic-lane vehicles becomes more evident with continued visual observation, and even more so, as the temporal range of the prediction becomes more and more proximate, since the vehicle is travelling closer and closer to the merging zone).

This basic understanding has led us to consider the first inter-competing factor while merging: optimal speed. It is clear from the above that driving more slowly on the entrance ramp would be beneficial, since the period of visual observation of traffic is longer. But on the other hand, the vehicle must at some point accelerate to highway speed, which is likely necessitated to be done on the acceleration ramp and not before, given the speed-limiting effects of entrance ramp curvature. Furthermore, even the most comprehensive and immediate study of traffic-lane traffic is entirely irrelevant if the predicted gaps in traffic have travelled 500ft in front of and away from the vehicle, since it is going that much more slowly than the traffic on the highway. This reveals two considerations: (1) that the slower the merging vehicle is travelling on the entrance ramp (relative to the freeway flow of traffic), the more rear-wards (relative to the actual freeway) must be the interest in spatial awareness for analyzing potential openings in the traffic, and (2) that driving faster on the acceleration ramp benefits the immediacy and actionability of merging-lane traffic analyses, since any identified gaps in traffic are staying far closer to the merging vehicle due to their comparatively similar speeds (since the merging driver is going more quickly as to almost match that of the highway speed), with the added benefit of transitioning the lateral spatial awareness focus more frontward, which will free up head-checking and/or mirror checking resources in the sensory input control loop. However we already established that driving faster on the highway entrance ramp necessarily engenders an abbreviated traffic analysis period, and far more riskily, if the traffic analysis indicates that there is indeed no present gap into which the vehicle can merge, then the driver must decelerate back to comparative slowness in order to wait for and find a gap, which could risk a rear-end collision from an accelerating driver behind, which is still limited by some sort of impeding termination of the merge-lane, and which brings us back to the aforementioned detriments of driving slowly on the acceleration ramp. We have up to this point followed a seemingly nonsensical circle of mutually dependent factors, some calling for increases in entrance-ramp speed, and some calling for corresponding decreases — and we have thereby demonstrated the quintessentially multivariate nature of this precise driving maneuver of freeway merging. The key to the professional driver's understanding is that some form of ideal balance of these factors, in different segments of time, yields the best overall outcome, and that is what we will seek to optimize in this chapter.

Two general, high-level considerations should be noted: firstly, the present discussion applies to the (perhaps uncommon) occurrence of the most challenge co-presence of dense and fast-moving traffic to merge into from the merging lane. In reality, congestion effects accordingly decrease the speed of traffic flow when following distance is lower (which reflects drivers' safe instinct to follow the basic speed rule): that is to say, it may be the case that high traffic conditions will cause very small gaps between vehicles, but then a resulting decrease in speed will ease the merging driver's task by allowing more time to spatially analyze his or her points of lane ingress, and to signal his or her decided merging maneuver to the comprehension of the driver in front of whom the merging driver is merging (i.e., the posterolateral driver, in our terminology established above). On the other hand, if the speed of the traffic flow is high (which would presumably create additional difficulty in accelerating to a matched speed and merging into a gap), the compensating effect will be an increase in following distance, which allows accordingly easier merging given the large space in between travelling vehicles into which a merging vehicle may merge. Each extreme carries its own set of priorities and considerations; in the slow-moving, bumper-to-bumper traffic case, an emphasis must be placed on turn signaling and confirming the intentions of the proximate driver to make appropriate room for the driver's merging vehicle, which is the result of a basic predictive analysis of vehicle behavior (which we will detail in a bit). Essentially, this case would have entailed confirming that the other driver is not in a complete state of inattention to the road, during which he or she could fail to notice the driver's having merged in front of them, and continue at a slow speed without checking their path-of-travel (thinking it to be sufficiently clear because of their inattention) and thereby risking a rear-end collision. In practical terms, this is not a serious safety risk due to the low speeds involved but is indeed and significant economic, time, vehicular, fuel-efficiency, time-efficiency (and of course, at any rate, safety) sub-optimality. The other extreme case is potentially more dangerous: if merging into a seemingly wide open gap between two fast-moving vehicles under light traffic conditions, one must ensure that the lateral merging motion into whichever lane does not coincide with a driver on the distant lane's merging into that same lane – which clearly would result in a lateral collision (and a particularly ominous consequent situation for the vehicle directly behind the two vehicles which have just laterally collided in front of it as a result of concurrently merging into the same lane). These lateral collisions are usually more dangerous than low-speed, rear-end, "fender-bender" collisions pertaining to high traffic situations, due to (1) the potentially greater impact speed (exacerbated by the vehicles' opposing – rather than co-directional – vector of motion), (2) the heightened likelihood that the merging driver (the one entering the freeway) will be more assertive and less-cautious in the lane switch, thinking that the job is done once the gap is cleared for entry (unlike the constantly cautious mental state brought about by slow, traffic-congested driving), and (3) (especially for the driver on the right, for right driving countries) the lesser force-cushioning capabilities of the vehicle in a lateral collision versus that of a collision along the front-rear axis of the vehicle. This is all to state the fact that merging drivers into the freeway must not only confirm the vacancy of the space in the lane into which they intend to merge, but must also maintain full spatial awareness of their surroundings with a strategic priority on the next lane over, adjacent to the traffic-lane, in which an unsuspecting driver could be merging into the very same spot which the other merger is currently undertaking[1].

We will review the dynamics of lane-changes and safety precautions thereabout, in detail, in a later section – in here, we only intend to underscore the two sets of unique considerations to each extreme of traffic conditions under merging: light and fast, and heavy and slow. We ignore, of course, the condition of no vehicles being present whatsoever, such is likely in rural areas or late at night in areas of less-than-appreciable population, but in this instance there are little to no relevant tactics as the task would pose no difficulty whatsoever. The matter at hand, in fact, is whatever is the relative absence of the two aforementioned compensating factors – that is, the degree to which the traffic to be merged into is both *fast* and *dense* (two factors, as we have shown above, which typically oppose each other and are inversely proportional): that is, the measure of how challenging a successful merge is going to be, and of how increasingly important our specific tactical model for merging will be to ensure the optimum response given all (strategically optimized) sensory input data. Let us call this "*fast* and *dense*" measurement the "merging lane risk coefficient" and let it be defined as the speed of the traffic flow (of the lane into which the driver is seeking to merge – typically the right lane of the freeway) divided by the average following distance of said traffic flow – the higher the speed or shorter the average following distance, the greater difficulty the merging vehicle will have. Situations in which the highest merging lane risk coefficients are to be found will be those in which travel priority is higher, as it is esteemed by the average consensus of drivers constituting the traffic flow: high-volume, high-speed rush hour traffic in the morning and later afternoon around large cities will increase this risk accordingly. (This is a common phenomenon in cities along the East Coast of the

---

[1] This circumstance could lead to the rare situation, discussed in Chapter 8, in which two vehicles are concomitantly merging into the same lane and same lane position from both opposite, adjacent lanes. See the "Passing on the right" subsection of the "General passing" header, Chapter 8.

USA – it is an unwritten social norm to travel approximately between 68mph and 74mph in posted 55mph sections of, for instance, I-95 S into Philadelphia or I-93 S into Boston, in the morning hours, whereas drivers would never exceed the speed limit by the same absolute or relative margin on a 65mph at 11pm at night, when and where ticket risk is much higher, and collective driving priority much lower.) When traffic-density increases significantly enough even more, starting from this worst condition, the merging risk will actually decrease in our theory (because of the slower average speed and easier merging opportunities), and accordingly, when the traffic frees and speeds up, the merging risk should also drop in accordance with the resulting following distance increase. The professional driver will be familiar with the specific trends in these phenomena in his or her area when possible, and will always perform an expert, subjective analysis of the merging lane risk coefficient while entering the freeway to inform a preparatory expectation as to the difficulty of the upcoming successful merging task.

The second high-level consideration which should be noted is that, wholly as a tendency and never as a rule, more experienced and professional drivers will tend to accelerate faster on the acceleration ramp and enter with more aggressive speeds (and especially those with a fine motor control of the vehicle's positioning, and those who operate smaller, more agile vehicles), since need for decreasing speed by means of using the brakes can be more quickly achieved than that of a sudden need to increase speed by means of the accelerator. (That is, brakes are almost always more immediately responsive than the accelerator.) Clearly, a finer and more agile car will have increased ability to rapidly alter speed, as would behoove any challenging merging situation, in both decelerative and accelerative capacity. However the energy inefficiency of this approach must be balanced (relying on a high probability that momentum energy will be wasted into sudden friction produced by the brakes) with its performance advantages (and by the lessened amount of viable merging opportunities to be statistically encountered by overtaking a given stretch of valuable, fast-expiring merging-lane distance at a comparatively higher speed). At any rate, we will arrive at proper speed optimization while merging into the freeway by the ground-up construction of a tactical model, and only seek to mention this tendency as just that – a remark on a *tendency* – rather than to arbitrarily assert that every condition will call for maximum acceleration and then according deceleration into the first available gap in traffic, to precede merging, as of course each particular situation will call for its own unique response, as we shall see.

In the following discussions which constitute our tactical model for highway entrance merging, we will refer to "the driver", "the merging vehicle", "the professional driver", and "the merger" synonymously to denote the point of reference of the reader (the driver) who is entering and needing to merge into the highway. The "frontal merging vehicle" or "frontal merger" will refer to the vehicle in front of the driver who is also entering the highway and who will merge before the driver (in all standard circumstances), being further in front. The "traffic lane" or "flow of traffic" will refer to the lane of the highway into which the merging lane ends (typically the right-lane with vehicles entering from the right). The "traffic-lane vehicles" will refer to the relevant vehicles constituting geometric obstructions in the traffic-lane, which the driver must deal with in facilitating safe entrance into the traffic lane (and which may be further specified as the "frontal" and "rearwards" traffic-lane vehicles relative to the area into which the driver intends to merge, or, respectively, as the "anterolateral" and "posterolateral" vehicles, relative to the driver's merging-lane position itself). The "merging gap" or "traffic-lane gap" shall define the chosen interstitial distance between two vehicles in the traffic-lane into which the driver intends to merge.

Entrance ramp procedure

It would behoove the simplicity of our tactical model for highway merging to assume that the spot at which the entrance ramp stops curving (and bends towards becoming fully straight) is also the same spot at which visibility of the traffic flow beside the merging lane first becomes visible to the driver. In reality, this may very often be a quite false assumption. Speed of course is limited by the entrance ramp's radius of curvature, and so there will be little to no prospect of accelerating to match highway speed until the acceleration zone is reached (and if the traffic flow is slow enough to render that statement false, then there is no motive to begin with for greater speed). Therefore our definition of the entrance ramp stage, for purposes of discussion, will set the boundary with the acceleration zone at the point at which the road straightens as to make possible acceleration up to highway speed. If visibility of the relevant flow of freeway traffic becomes partially or fully visible before this time, then the only difference in the professional driver's behaviors during this stage will be a gradually increasing visual scanning priority of the traffic flow relative to the other visual regions for processing in the control loop – namely, monitoring road curvature for steering and speed-regulation response, and monitoring other potential vehicles within the driver's path-of-travel on the entrance ramp.

By far the most (and perhaps only) noteworthy tactic a professional driver can achieve during this rather conceptually straight-forward (however geometrically curved) stage is to create a large following distance between the vehicle and any frontal vehicle. This frontal vehicle may not exist, in which case this tactic does not apply, however it will frequently be the case that a professional driver must enter the freeway entrance ramp at some sort of traffic-light-regulated intersection and that a timed flow of vehicles will all be entering the freeway in succession – in which case this optimization holds great merit for all but the driver who first enters the entrance ramp. In order to demonstrate the potential benefit of a large following distance (more than may normally be appropriated for basic safety margins in case of rapid deceleration of the frontal vehicle) while merging onto a freeway, is it necessary to temporarily depart from our chronological progressive and to think of the end of the process when the driver's vehicle is in the merging lane ready to make the decided lane switch into the freeway: conducting this process with an overly-proximate vehicle in front may constitute any of the following safety risks or suboptimalities:

1. Heightened risk of rear-end collision due to the overall higher expected speed variability of the vehicle in front (who may sense the need to brake suddenly in order to slow his or her vehicle to an achievable merging speed into a gap in traffic quickly noticed on the side) – and the more-than-typical danger of such rear-end collisions, due to the approaching expiration of the merging lane and remaining necessity to merge back into the fast traffic for finding a wide-enough breakdown lane down the freeway – a new post-accident merging requirement many times more difficult than the original merging requirement, due to the lowered speeds associated with vehicular collision accidents;

2. The above, but from a sudden deceleration of the driver in front pertaining to his or her failure to execute a successful merge, and needing to slow as to not drive off the road whereupon the merging lane may soon end;

3. The tendency for travelers in the being-merged-into traffic-lane (usually the right) to slow down upon lateral sight of a merging driver, which makes room for that merging driver who is in front of the present driver – the present driver who failed to create a large enough following distance between his or her vehicle and the vehicle merging in front – the present driver who now has more limited merging opportunities since the slowing down of vehicles behind the area into which the foremost merger is merging creates tighter traffic in the lateral region of the present driver, limiting merging opportunities (in other words, the room made for the merging vehicle in front of the present driver necessarily translates into less room for the present driver's merging on his or her side, since those vehicles have slowed

to accommodate the merger in front of the present driver, bring themselves longitudinally into an obstructive lateral position for the present driver);

4. The lessened reaction time afforded to the driver if the merging driver in front does collide with the flow of traffic while executing his or her merging maneuver, which could very quickly cause a pile-up of related accidents over the collision area (located in between zones of potentially great speed differential), and which could therefore trap the too-closely-following, merging driver in an accident situation of extremely difficult evasive potential;

5. The decreased capacity to rapidly accelerate (in an attempt to match traffic-flow speed as part of a merging execution attempt) in the merging lane without dangerously compromising the safety margin following distance between the merging driver and the one in front (thereby also exacerbating the first enumerated risk); and

6. General risks concerning and healthy discomfort with a lack of liberal safety margins in a region which is already precarious, due to a potentially large gradient in traffic flow speeds between the merging lane and the interfacing highway travel lane.

The professional driver therefore recognizes that the first and perhaps largest tactical optimization which can be made to freeway merging procedure is the creation and assurance of copious frontal following distance. This begs the question, what is the optimal method of creating and ensuring this distance? Multivariate factors which determine an according emphasis on speed necessity during the respective phases of merging (many of which we have already alluded to) will adjust the professional driver's sage assessment of these necessities balanced against the benefits of increased following distance – but as an applicable general rule – it is almost *always* advantageous to create the extension in following distance as early as possible in the merging process, during stage one (the entrance ramp) in which higher speed is least likely to be necessary (and with the probabilistically higher areas of high-speed-necessity being optimally desired to coincide with the areas in which the driver has already established copious following distance, such that the potential accelerations will be of higher safety and possibility). With a copious and permissive following distance already having been established by the time the vehicle enters stage two (the acceleration phase) or stage three (the merging lane) of the merging process, then he or she is afforded the extra space in which to accelerate if it is determined that such acceleration is optimal for securing longitudinal parallelism with an observed and/or predicted gap in the flow of traffic into which the driver will execute the final merging maneuver. Had the driver not established this permissive and safe extra margin of frontal following distance, he or she may not have had the opportunity to accelerate to such a relative longitudinal position to the freeway flow of traffic (and, at the very least, not without much more risk) – and at that, even, there are still equal or greater chances for the ease of procuring such a merging gap (due to the frontal-merger localized congestion effect mentioned in the third enumerated point in the list above) under a relative spatial positioning of further distance away behind from the merging vehicle in front.

This optimization is ideally executed in the very beginning of entrance onto the entrance ramp, since if one can facilitate the development of the aforesaid large following distance between the highway-entering driver and the highway-entering vehicle in front of the driver by means of slower acceleration, rather than by decelerative braking, ameliorated fuel-efficiency is gained by the comparative lack of needing to waste momentum energy as frictional loss in the brakes. It may not always be possible to create the merging frontal space buffer in this way, especially if traffic levels are congested enough as to cause an abnormally slowed flow on the on-ramp. We will discuss the generalities of following distance, progressing into finer tactics, in a later section – a discussion which is transferable to that of following distance on the entrance ramp. The other present factor which is called into question, however, is that of rearward following distance on the entrance ramp. If one of our largest justifications for increasing frontal following distance on the entrance ramp (first stage) was the increased accelerative potential for the latter two stages, not-otherwise-available in closer following-distance circumstances, then would not the same hold true for *decelerative* rearwards buffer distance pertaining to the vehicular space buffer between the driver and the vehicle *behind* as well? We answer in the affirmative, since the increased safety margin logic holds true for both the vehicle's frontal path-of-travel and rearwards travelled-path. However the emphasis as it concerns the highway-entering driver is and must be on first maintaining frontal buffer distance since it is by acceleration through this distance that a balanced rearwards space gap can be created: and that is the second highway-merging tactic which we list in our model. To clarify:

1. If there are no vehicles in front of the driver, proceed with the remainder of highway merging procedure.

2. If there is a frontal merging vehicle on the entrance ramp, create increased frontal following distance buffer.

3. Then, once copious frontal buffer distance has been created, and if there is a rear following vehicle on the entrance ramp (information which proper spatial awareness procedure has already prioritatively investigated prior to, or immediately during, entering the entrance ramp), accelerate as to lengthen the distance buffer between the vehicle and the following vehicle behind.

The professional driver must balance the timing and accelerative or decelerative intensity of both operations #2 and #3 from the above such that his or her vehicle, by the time of arriving in the acceleration and especially merging zones, is positioned optimally between the vehicle to the front and the vehicle from behind such that there is ample safety buffer distance between the vehicle and both zones, in order to afford safety in the vehicle's potential need to accelerate or decelerate rapidly in order to perform the merge (keeping in mind that our tactical model for highway entrance merging assumes the most challenging possible conditions – a high "merging lane risk coefficient", as we defined above – and in many cases the afforded safety margins will be entirely sufficient). "Positioned optimally" does not necessarily mean in the dead linear middle between the frontal vehicle and the rear vehicle – this determination must arise from a prediction on whether rapid acceleration or rapid deceleration is more likely to be necessary in the merging zone. If it is determined for whatever reason (that, for instance, the traffic on the highway is going very quickly compared to the speed which it seems may be feasible under present circumstances in the acceleration zone) that rapid acceleration will be more probably needed than rapid deceleration in the merging zone, then the professional driver should adjust his or her interstitial position between the frontal and rear vehicle on the entrance ramp (and finalizing these adjustments in the acceleration zone) so that it is somewhat closer towards the rear vehicle, since his or her assessment that rapid acceleration may be more likely to occur than rapid deceleration places a higher predictive risk on a frontal collision with the frontal vehicle than being rear-end-collided by the rear vehicle. Conversely, if the professional driver determines for whatever reason (for instance, that the speed of the traffic flow on the highway is actually slowing and that he or she is already going quite fast enough on the entrance ramp and acceleration zone to match – or perhaps even exceed – the present average highway speed) that rapid deceleration in the merging lane will be slightly more likely than rapid acceleration, accordingly he or she should adjust the vehicle's interstitial position between the front and rear vehicle such that it is slightly closer to the frontal vehicle, anticipating a higher risk of being rear-end-collided than to be a rear-end-collider (we shall note, however, that decreasing frontal following distance is generally frowned upon for good reasons which exist outside of this very limited, binary spatial analysis we perform here – such as the legal responsibility of rear-ending versus the near-universal legal irresponsibility of being rear-ended – if these considerations are relevant to the professional driver's overall highway strategy, then we recommend attenuating the present intervehicular buffer distance optimization adjustment in the case of moving closer to the front vehicle[2]).

The hereunto unaddressed and fourth possibility is that there is no frontal merging vehicle on the entrance ramp but there is a rearwards vehicle: in this case the driver may apply the same above technique, however without having to worry at all about maintaining a frontal following distance. Instead, the task will be basic speed regulation on the entrance ramp such that the ensuing acceleration will be sufficient enough to separate the vehicle and the vehicle behind for the establishment of beneficial safety margin space to improve safety for both drivers. Clearly, if the vehicle is heavy and underpowered, and if the rear vehicle is agile, light, and driven by an unsafe driver who is ignorant of the universal benefits of allowing for greater frontal following distances, then in this worst case, the driver is simply limited in equipment and physical capacity to instill a safe following distance in the rear of his or her vehicle. This would only become a problem in extreme cases of vehicle disparity and rear-driver insanity – if possible, a predictive analysis of relative vehicle acceleration ability on the road before entering the entrance ramp could potentially benefit this situation (which is already quite the stretch). Practically speaking, the most useful thing which may be learned from pondering this hypothetical is the fully extensive optimization benefit of being the only driver on the entrance ramp. A practical situation in which this knowledge may come in hand is

---

[2] Reference should be made to our Chapter 5 discussion of the "whole intervehicular isolane space" and the nearly invariable safety optimization requirement of prioritizing frontal versus rearwards following distance. See the "longitudinal-axis safety margin and following distance optimization" heading in Chapter 5.

when entering the highway by means of a timed-light-controlled intersection – and predicting challenging merging circumstances – and furthermore being caught in an edgy stale-yellow-turn signal; it is in this case known to the professional driver that being the only (or at least, the first) driver entering the ramp is beneficial for safety and successful merging, and he or she may therefore be more moved to wait for the next iteration of the light than to "cut it close" only to enter the freeway with everyone else (clearly assuming there are a plurality of drivers entering the ramp). In most cases, maintaining proper following distance between the rear and front vehicles (if any) on the entrance ramp will be a largely straightforward task, uncomplicated by the nuanced and unlikely hypotheticals which we have posed in this last section. The three step sub-procedure above stands as the first significant establishment in our tactical model for freeway entrance merging with which the professional driver is thoroughly competent, reaping the benefits of increased safety, merging facility, and perhaps even fuel-efficiency due to the decreased braking necessity inherent to larger following distances. It should also be noted that time cost is minimal to non-existent by means of this tactic, since the vehicle's motion is necessarily limited by that of any front merging driver's position anyway (we are assuming the simple, common case of a single-lane entrance ramp wherein passing is neither legal nor safely possible). A microscopically minimal time-cost may be associated with the frontal vehicle's going slightly slower than it would were the driver being pressured by a tailgating, forcing vehicle to drive faster, thereby speeding up the tailgater's frontal vehicular position constraint – however this small time-cost is more accurately considered a remnant of avoiding reckless and irresponsible driving practices, must less a valid criticism of our tactical model for increasing following distance on the entrance ramp in preparation for a merge.

Acceleration zone and merging lane procedure

We now turn our attention to the highway entrance merging stage in which the entrance ramp is geometrically straightened as to provide a clear path of acceleration over which the driver's vehicle must be brought up to highway speed. In some varieties of entrance ramp design, this zone may begin immediately once the driver has entered the entrance ramp, in which case the formerly discussed technique of establishing frontal and rearwards following distance buffers is simultaneously relevant to this section. In fact, even if the entrance ramp is designed with a large and identifiable rotational section which precedes the acceleration zone, the driver may still be able to widen the aforementioned distance gaps by careful speed manipulation (essentially, this section will discuss the tasks and procedures *typically associated* with this later stage in highway entrance merging but certainly not canonically fastened to a black-and-white, linear conception of highway entrance merging – since all of the discussed factors may be co-relevant and inter-dependent, to a degree, and must be at times simultaneously handled by the driver). This complex balancing of multivariate tasks – a property which distinguishes highway entrance merging and freeway driving as a whole – becomes much more evident in this crucial state of highway entrance merging.

Speed-adjustment feedback loop

Given that the purpose of the acceleration lane is to facilitate the coming to speed which will most safely and feasibly enable the final merging procedure, it is a justified simplification to state that the responsive processes which are executed in this phase simply seek to adjust the driver's perception of how speed should be changed (faster or slower), by how much, and how quickly, in preparation for the merging lane. These determinations derive from continually perceived reasons to speed up or slow down accordingly (a complex determination influenced by a host of variables), and continually flowing from a feedback loop of optimized perceptive information (e.g. looking at forward at the path-of-travel to guard against frontal collisions, looking through the side window to gain understanding of traffic pattern, speed, and potential merging possibilities, executing behavioral prediction analyses on relevant vehicles, and, later on, looking in mirrors in the merging lane phase). We will break down the complex process by defining the individual, constituent sources of perceptive feedback for this continuous process, so that the relative priorities and necessities of each can be understood by the driver in order to ensure an optimal flow of sensory ingress which will enable the best decisions as it pertains to speed regulation in the acceleration zone of highway entrance merging, in order to ensure a safe and successful merge.

Risk analysis

In this chapter's introduction, we already hinted as to the importance of risk analysis: firstly, knowing when a relatively lesser or greater need for utmost care to safety is required can allow the driver to balance an appropriate and according interest in other optimization benefits, and secondly, proper risk analysis identifies areas of spatial interest which will be assigned higher or lower priorities according to the situations which merit them (e.g., if there is no traffic whatsoever on the highway into which the driver is merging, then clearly a far greater visual scanning emphasis on the vehicle in front on the entrance ramp occupies a greater priority than if repeated attention to heavy traffic were needed with the merging vehicle in front being safely and distantly removed from the vehicle). The professional driver will therefore identify the factors which contribute to this assessment, and which tend to become most immediately evident upon entering the acceleration zone of the entrance ramp.

Rear-end collisions are not uncommon for vehicles merging onto the highway (in particular, those closer to the end of the merge lane) due to the error of ignoring frontal visual attention to the merging vehicle in front due to distraction caused by monitoring the lateral traffic and a simultaneous, misfortunate deceleration of the frontal vehicle. While our tactical model for driving behavior on the initial entrance ramp phrase wholly revolved around creating a lengthened distance buffer in order to make this situation unlikely – it is still always the professional driver's responsibility to maintain constant frontal attention to his or her vehicle's path-of-travel – and so we identify the first information source of our risk analysis procedure as the frontal following distance between the driver and the vehicle (if any) in front of the driver. Clearly, the closer this distance, the more attention must be appropriated towards frontal spatial awareness (and, if possible under the potentially conflicting acceleration directives produced by the need to get up to highway speed – decelerating to lengthen this distance).

The second input to the risk analysis process is a probabilistic analysis that rapid deceleration will be more likely due to a profiling of the vehicles in front (if visible). Large/long trucks merging into the highway in front, for instance, must prompt a heightened sense that deceleration may be necessary in the acceleration zone, since these large vehicles may need to (in the most extreme case) come to a complete stop until a suitable gap in traffic is found. Larger and less agile vehicles such as SUVs and minivans also satisfy this criteria to a proportionally smaller extent. Monitoring and profiling the types of vehicles in front of the driver is therefore, in fact, largely pertinent to the initial entrance ramp phase, in which rotational curvature on the ramp may provide otherwise-obscured visibility to these vehicles, and in which concurrent visual scanning and processing demands for other tasks are not as great. On the other extreme, if a series of agile sports cars, spaced well apart and frontally distant from the vehicle, are seen ahead on the entrance ramp, it is probabilistically more optimal to devote marginally more visual scanning attention to lateral vision of the traffic flow on the highway – where it is more likely to yield safety-significant information.

Thirdly, an understanding of the tolerances granted by the physical structure of the merging lane and breakdown lane will greatly aid in the assignment of proper visual scanning regional priorities during the acceleration zone. On one extreme, if the professional driver has a familiar and certain foreknowledge that the merging lane is extremely long, or that the breakdown lane beyond the merging lane is very wide as to be sufficient for travel in the (very unlikely) case that an opportunity for a safe merge does not ever present itself, or a combination of these – then a higher emphasis on attention to the frontal zone of the vehicle's path-of-travel must be appropriated, since the likelihood that a potentially unsafe situation as a result of a failed merging (colliding with the road barrier at the end of the merging lane, needing to stop at the end of the merging lane which could prompt a rear-end collision or – at the very least – an even more precarious and difficult second attempt at merging, etc.) would drastically fall in comparison to the probability that a frontal collision with another merging driver may occur, because of the geometric liberality of the road construction which lowers the former collision likelihood to slim-to-none. Some highway entrance ramp merging setups, however, are very precariously structured and indeed may lead to an unsafe situation if a successful merge is not executed before the termination of the merging lane, however unlikely that may be. Therefore the professional driver who lacks foreknowledge of the road safety margins and merging lane length at the merge itself should always assume the worst possible scenario and, as far as it concerns this variable in the risk analysis, assign an accordingly higher priority to lateral spatial awareness towards the flow of traffic on the highway in order to ensure that the likelihood of missing a safe merging maneuver is diminished.

Spatial awareness model

The nature of the tasks which must be performed on the acceleration zone of the highway entrance ramp is such that some situation-specific adjustments to our general spatial awareness model should be made. During the acceleration lane phase of highway entrance merging (or, perhaps not concurrent to this, whenever line-of-sight vision opens up to the flow of traffic into which the driver must merge), the pressing spatial-awareness need to examine and analyze the flow of highway traffic must necessarily be balanced with the standard and necessary attention to the vehicle's frontal path-of-travel as is exigent and required in all situations (in the preceding sections, we detailed a risk analysis procedure which determines to what degree this focus should be given). As it applies to the head and eye mechanics of balancing these two competing visual scanning necessities, we may identify three different general zones between which the driver's vision must switch during freeway entrance merging: (1) the frontal line-of-sight vision through the windshield, (2) lateral traffic flow line-of-sight vision by partially rotated eye/head glances through the driver's side window (or passenger side windows, in the uncommon case of merging from the left), and, especially later on in the merging lane phase, (3) usage of mirror/head-checking proximate lateral and posterolateral spatial awareness methods (detailed extensively in the prior chapter) for obtaining information about rearwards traffic-flow-lane spatial information when the angularity of the merging lane approaches that of full highway-parallelism (as it prepares to end) and zone #2 no longer affords this information. Zones #2 and #3 are relatively easily switched between, however switching visual interest between zone #1 and zone #2 (or between zone #1 and zone #3, especially if spatial interpretations indicate that head-checking is required) may be more costly. Therefore, especially when nearing the merging maneuver at which point visual zone #3 becomes of proportionally higher significance than that of zone #2, it is geometrically optimal to group #2 and #3 together (in alternations between side mirror-image-viewing and line-of-sight vision outside the side window) with interstitial returning head movements to the windshield of the vehicle in order to minimize the amount of wasted time spent changing sight between the three zones. When eye rotation is combined with head movement, as it is recommended in our aforedescribed tactical model for spatial awareness, the time cost of the scanning maneuver is accordingly diminished (this is especially true when the only appreciable safety risk against which looking forward is intended to guard is overly-proximate distance to the frontwards vehicle whose rearmost physical extent on one side is almost guaranteed to be of equal forward/backward distance from the driver's vehicle as that of its other side (assuming relative parity between the two vehicles in interlane position) – in other words, the professional driver whose visual attention is caught between lateral, traffic-flow-lane visual attention and basic path-of-travel safety-checking frontward glances of the vehicle in front only needs to rotate his or her head and eyes to zone #1 from zones #2 and #3 enough to see the left-most (or right-most, if merging from the left) edge of the frontal vehicle, since the physical, longitudinal distance to that edge is almost certainly guaranteed to be the same effectual longitudinal distance to any other point on the rear-end of the frontal vehicle, since all vehicles are transversely symmetrical). Grouping together visual scanning of zones #2 and #3 (when they are both necessary) during mature states in the merging process in which head-check maneuvers become necessary also capitalizes on the natural benefit that eye-head position while examining zone #2 lies directly along the head-check eye-focus rotation path which travels from the side mirror to the blind zone during the execution of such a proximate lateral spatial investigation (which we classified as zone #3 – or "method #3" as it perhaps would be better defined, since this process involves potentially executing a head-check on top of mirror glancing).

General acceleration-incentivizing factors

It should seem apparent from this discussion that, all other things being equal, it is beneficial to achieve highway speeds on the acceleration ramp sooner rather than later, since the areas of visual investigation in the flow of traffic will then travel along with the driver for his or her potential merging once the merging lane is reached – whereas visual investigation of the flow of traffic before reaching appreciable highway-speeds serves no other purpose than that of general qualitative risk analysis, since any spatial information gained about the placement of allovehicles in the traffic flow will be irrelevant by the time the driver longitudinally reaches the merging zone in this case. This is a common mistake observed among nervous beginner drivers who slowly and cautiously traverse the acceleration zone and study the patterns of the (by far faster travelling) flow of traffic, hoping to find a gracious merging gap, whereas in reality such sudden fortuitous gaps in traffic are unlikely to occur under challenging conditions, and also whereas the professional driver understands that achieving highway speeds on the acceleration ramp will be necessary anyways for the execution of a successful merge. This reasoning corroborates our aforesaid theory that more experienced drivers will exhibit a tendency to even over-accelerate on the ramp and may even at times then *decelerate* slightly into their chosen merging opportunities. If we hypothetically forget about the potential existence of frontwards merging vehicles and about the less-safe termination of the merging lane while travelling at higher speeds, then this method has no inherent detriments (other than that of fuel inefficiency) than that of the same marginal amount of *acceleration* into a chosen gap (and in fact may be superior, again barring the excepted factors above, due to a highway travelers' greater statistical probability of seeing an adjacent-lane anterolateral vehicle as opposed to that of posterolateral vehicle on their side but to their back, where blind spots exist).

Behavior-predictive observational analysis

As the driver continues into the merging lane zone, having achieved highway speeds or speeds very close to it, the task of finding, choosing, and entering a sufficient gap in the flow of traffic into which the merge will be executed involves making predictive analyses concerning the future viability of such opportunities. This is clearly prerequisite to an optimal highway entrance merging tactical model since precious distance on the finite-length merging zone may be wasted if the driver accelerates only to attempt to merge into a gap which becomes inviable for merging, and on the other hand, less distance on the merging lane is required if a preparatory acceleration or deceleration correctly predicts the continued or becoming viability of a certain traffic-flow-gap merging opportunity. It is seen through this example that it is always desirable to merge safely as soon as possible when in the merging lane zone, in order to avoid potential risks associated with staying in the merging lane (front-end or rear-end collisions with other merging vehicles due to sudden braking/acceleration, reaching termination of the merging lane, etc.) and also in order to afford greater distance for additional merging opportunities if the attempted one suddenly must be aborted due to an unpredicted event, such as an aggressive traffic-lane driver suddenly accelerating to cut off the merger's opportunity and divert him or her to other potential gaps behind the aggressive vehicle. As even the mediocre highway driver knows, it is those vehicles who are already travelling in the freeway who have the right of way – and *not* those who are merging (it is therefore always the entrance merger's responsibility to find and safely enter a spot in which to merge – it is never the responsibility of a highway-traveler to surrender such a space).

Predictive analysis of spatial and perceptual information about other vehicles gained by visual scanning allows the driver to make probabilistic guesses as to the future positioning and velocity of the vehicles in interest, which aids the merging opportunity selection process by adding according speed control incentives for acceleration, speed maintenance, or declaration as the situation requires. Allovehicular behavior prediction analysis is a large topic in this book which the professional driver will use regularly in his or her freeway driving, and is accordingly developed in detail throughout later sections – however, here, we will only focus on the specific subcategories of this analysis process which are informative to highway entrance merging – that is (almost exclusively), a probabilistic assessment of whether or not a given vehicle is likely to speed up or slow down. We define two classes of vehicles of interest to the merging-driver: those in front of the vehicle on the acceleration/merging lane itself, and those already in the highway flow of traffic into which the driver will merge.

Frontal merging vehicles

Behavioral predictive analysis of the merging vehicles in front is proportionally more relevant when the success of having established a large following distance is lower (such that the results of such an analysis may appropriately divert more visual scanning attention to the frontal regions of the vehicle if necessary). Directional signal activation and drifting interlane position towards the traffic lane obviously indicate that the frontal merging vehicle is preparing or beginning to execute a merge – insofar as visual scanning resources permit (and according to the immediacy of information pertaining to the frontal vehicle – which is virtually zero if it is sufficiently distant in front), the professional driver should briefly check the size of the gap into which the frontal driver appears to be merging in order to derive the useful behavior prediction: is the traffic gap of sufficient longitudinal size so that the frontal merger will have no trouble in executing the ultimate lane-switch maneuver? If so, then he or she is likely in the process of merging (or very soon about to commence) which will: (1) free up frontal merging-lane space for the driver, making any called-for acceleration more feasible, and (2) will likely cause the traffic-lane vehicle in front of whom the frontal vehicle has just merged to slow down in order to restore the following distance which has just been cut short by the vehicle which has just merged into said gap (if these events are close enough to the driver, the aforesaid anterolateral vehicle's predicted deceleration may cause the narrowing of traffic gaps which are lateral to the driver, since the decelerating traffic-lane driver may his or herself be the frontal demarcation of the gap to the side of the driver, or may otherwise cause the next-following and even second-following (and so on) traffic-lane vehicle to decelerate accordingly, which could propagate back to the merging driver's lateral merging region of interest if distances are sufficiently proximate). Returning our attention back to the traffic-lane space margins beside the merging frontal vehicle: is the nearest feasible gap into which the frontal vehicle could merge appreciably in front of or behind the frontal vehicle? If so, an according deceleration or acceleration of the frontal driver should be anticipated, which may hold the following relevant consequences: (1) most obviously, an anticipated deceleration of the frontal vehicle calls for increased attention to frontal spatial awareness in order to avoid a collision, insofar as the frontal vehicle is close enough to warrant such concerns; (2) traffic-lane vehicles whose drivers are either oblivious or otherwise preoccupied such as to not have noticed the merging vehicle may instinctively decelerate if they notice an attempting-to-merge vehicle accelerate ahead of them to their side, knowing that it will eventually need to merge due to the merging-lane's impending expiration – a frontal-traffic-lane-vehicle deceleration which holds the same potential consequences as described above (note that the consequent incentive here for the driver may be to *decelerate* due to this factor – as opposed to the more instinctual *acceleration* response inherent to seeing the frontal driver accelerate and therefore widen following distance); and (3) if the frontal driver does accelerate in an attempt to make a merge of questionable safety distance margin in between the two traffic-lane vehicles, a proceeding (and perhaps quite rapid) deceleration response from the frontal vehicle may be anticipated insofar that the relevant traffic-lane vehicle is aggressive (being more disposed to accelerate to narrow the merging gap for the merging driver as to force his or her abortion of the maneuver rather than to obsequiously (and perhaps dangerously) decelerate in order to allow the merger to perform the questionable merge) and insofar that the traffic gap is seen to be dangerously narrow in the first place.

Lateral traffic-lane vehicles

Behavior-predictive analysis of the lateral traffic-lane vehicles is not only relevant to the discussion above, concerning that of the frontal merging driver, but is also clearly crucial to the final merging tactic of the professional driver him or herself. Once a potential merging gap and the vehicles constituting the rear and frontal boundaries thereof are identified, visual scanning interest on both of these vehicles should be increased (especially if the gap – though being the safest and widest visible opportunity – is still not optimally wide) for the appropriation of information which may lead to a more accurate predictive analysis of their future speed, and therefore, a to final decision as to whether or not to merge, and when, and by what speed adjustments. The most simple and immediate constituent to this analysis is current change in speed – either vehicle could be accelerating, maintaining speed, or decelerating such that the merging-potential space gap between the two is stable, growing, or shrinking. This instantaneous velocity analysis can be executed in under one second of visual attention on either vehicle. Less straightforward and more behavioral factors, however, must be analyzed in order to predict the higher degree of this speed analysis – that is, not of what is the present acceleration of each vehicle which will affect a change in *relative* speed between the two vehicles (and thereby the short-term change in their gap distance) – but rather, the derivative of *that* analysis, of what the *trend* in acceleration is which will determine the *trend* in the change of relative distance between the two vehicles which will be relevant for the merging maneuver, since the gap space may be changing as the driver executes the merge. It is this degree which is relevant to the order of magnitude of time which pertains to analyzing and determining merging opportunities, typically in the ballpark of 1.5 to 5 seconds. The relevant behavioral observations for *this* analysis, then, are as follows: (1) interlane position, (2) speed response trend, (3) human driver profiling, and (4) situational profiling.

Is the traffic-lane vehicle off the lateral lane center as to be too far to the right or left in their lane? This may indicate that a corrective gesture is about to be carried out, which may affect safety margins during the execution of a merge. Is the traffic-lane vehicle's interlane position highly variable, as to suggest that the driver may be impaired either by substance use or manual electronic device operation? This should cause the professional driver to require heightened safety buffer margins before merging to compensate for the resulting lessened confidence that the traffic-lane driver will safely respond to a lateral merging driver entering his or her lane in front (note that this specific indication applies mostly to the traffic-lane vehicle at the rear of the gap but however is also relevant to the one at the front of the gap, since a distracted frontal traffic-lane driver may be anticipated to have a higher likelihood of needing to decelerate rapidly due to narrowing frontal following distance which went unsafely ignored during whatever period of distraction). After the merging driver makes merge-assertive indications that he or she will attempt to merge (detailed in the following section), how does the proximate traffic-lane driver respond as it pertains to their speed response trend? If the traffic-lane driver obsequiously slows down, a fast-expiring impulse to execute the merge should be considered and taken if the overall safety margins are sufficient (since the enlarged gap which the polite traffic-lane driver made may not remain for much longer at its presently widened state). Does the traffic-lane driver show no indication whatsoever of having noticed the assertiveness attempts? This should prompt a lessened trust in the traffic-lane driver's spatial awareness capacity and an increased margin of necessary safety buffer distances. Does the traffic-lane driver quickly notice and accelerate to cut off the merge attempt? This indicates that, although the driver is generally aware, he or she has a higher sense of urgency and speed-necessity, and that making the merging in front of this aggressive driver is not likely to be a wise or even feasible maneuver.

If possible under the circumstances of visibility, human driver profiling (and even interaction) can aid greatly in this process. If assertive eye contact can be made with the aware traffic-lane driver, this will confirm a mutual understanding of the merging attempt and will heighten the probability that the traffic-lane driver will adjust speed to aid the merging driver (and, at the very least, will almost always cause the traffic-lane driver to declare some sort of response to the merging assertion – even if it is declaring a useful unwillingness to accept the merging driver by accelerating, making infeasible the frontal merging gap, and saving the merging driver some time in making the determination to abort that particular potential merging opportunity which would otherwise have taken longer to determine). Visual information about the driver and the statistical profiling thereof can also be of aid in close-call situations when a determination must be made as to whether the merging driver must accelerate and assert his or her vehicle into the space with the intended response that the rearwards traffic-lane driver will slow down and permit greater room for this maneuver, or whether the merging driver must him or herself decelerate in order to attempt merging behind the current posterolateral or lateral vehicle due to an assessment that the driver would not have likely decelerated to give sufficient space, given the size and condition of the merging gap. In this manner, visible human features of the driver which indicate higher probabilistic acquiescence to the merge assertion include: senility, jovial facial expressions, and casual clothing. Human factors which probabilistically tend to suggest that the driver is less likely to be acquiescent to a merge assertion include: youth, male gender, athleticism, appearing straight-faced and competitively focused to driving, and more formal clothing which may indicate that the driver is *en route* to professional activities (therefore likely to perceive his or her driving as high-priority and time sensitive). Traffic-lane drivers who are holding a phone to their ears may indicate that they are multitasking due to time constraints (i.e., higher self-perceived driving urgency) or may have a precognitive, "careful" mindset of driving to compensate for the increased risks associated with phone usage (i.e., more likely to be polite) and so this observation is not as clearly indicative as the others. We clarify that in no way do we mean to assert that an individual is automatically categorized into a certain set of behaviors given their applicability to any broad categories of the former two lists, but only mean to assert that the higher likelihood is that individuals resembling the enumerated characteristics will exhibit the corresponding behaviors – which is a useful tool for making split-second merging decisions in which all other factors seem to balance even (keeping in mind, of course, that obtaining such direct visual sight of the driver's personage in the way described herein is quite difficult and rare to begin with). Some of the constituents of our list are strongly substantiated by scientific research, such as that young male drivers are the most aggressive, found by Parry (1968)[3], and others are a product of experience and sound inference. At any rate, these observational human factors should not be isolated alone but taken in conjunction with situational analysis to form a more accurate prediction of traffic-lane driver behavior in response to the merging driver's merge attempt. Is the 28-year-old male traffic-lane driver already speeding at 75mph at 7:45am on Monday morning headed into a major city wearing a business suit and driving a Mercedes? This situational analysis would clearly represent to the

---

[3] Parry, M., 1968. *Aggression on the Road.* London: Tavistock.

professional driver that the traffic-lane driver in question is less likely than normal to slow down and acquiesce to a merging driver, he having the right-of-way, since it certainly seems as though the traffic-lane driver has a high sense of urgency, likely being *en route* to professional activities. Does the merging driver witness in his or her lateral merging region a bumper-stickered Subaru filled with three children and one driving mother who seems to be singing along to an unknown musical radio selection and who makes smiling eye contact with the merging driver on Saturday afternoon travelling 62mph in a 65mph zone? On this extreme end of the present spectrum, the merging driver may assume that the necessity of aborting the present merging assertion into a sufficiently safe gap would not be as high, since the human and situational analysis of the traffic-lane driver in question seems to indicate a high likelihood that the traffic-lane driver would not aggressively accelerate into the gap as to necessitate the abortion of the merge attempt. With traffic-lane-travelling merge-obstructive vehicles of particular length, such as trucks, a predictive behavioral analysis must be made quickly due to the increased distance of merging lane which must be overtaken before the decided deceleration or acceleration has its effect for long enough so that the obstructive truck is either sufficiently forward or rearwards relative to the merging as to render new merging opportunities for the merging driver – which altogether increases the time-urgency of making such a safe successive merge due to the more-quickly-expiring merge lane ending ahead.

Action and assertiveness signaling

The professional driver who must merge into the highway (under the most-difficult circumstances we are assuming in this present discussion) is able to elicit a higher statistical cooperation rate from the travelling traffic-lane drivers if assertiveness and appearance to be about to execute a merge are brought to the attention of the relevant traffic-flow drivers. As in all things, appropriate balance must be decided: the professional driver would not dangerously swerve uncomfortably close into a tight following gap between two traffic-lane vehicles in order to try to compel the rear driver into decelerating and widening the gap by fear of collision – thereby risking collision itself or the creation of road-rage situations. However, on the other extreme, the merging driver must demonstrate some healthy amount of confident assertiveness in difficult merging situations or else he or she will face more dangerous outcomes pertaining to never having executed the merge before the merging lane comes to a precarious end, forcing the merger either to slow down or become even more aggressive in pursuing the present merging opportunity (both very dangerous). Therefore the professional driver must decide on the appropriately balanced amount of assertiveness to demonstrate in his or her vehicular body language and then execute according to the following methods.

A vehicle's directional signals (or "turn-signals", or "directionals", or even more colloquially, "blinkers") are the most obvious and necessary component of this signaling process. We contend that the merge-direction directional signal should be activated for the entire course of travel on the merging lane (and even perhaps starting at the end of the acceleration lane) – the entirety of the distance in which the driver is seeking for merging opportunities. This probabilistically maximizes the chance that the relevant traffic-lane vehicle which will come to pertain to the decided merging maneuver will see the merging vehicle and causes an overall more alerted, cooperative lateral traffic-lane by asserting the intentions for the merge. The driver should *not* wait until a specific merging gap is found and merging maneuver undertaken to activate the relevant directional signal – this is a *common* error among inexperienced drivers and even some more experienced drivers who either never paused to consider the logic of this misbehavior or who bear characteristically perverted highway driving philosophies. The merging signal should be activated for the entire course of the merging lane: for if a traffic-lane vehicle does not notice the merging vehicle even with the directional signal activated, then it certainly would not have been noticed without the additional visual stimulus and therefore nothing is lost by the activation of the directional signal. Furthermore, if the traffic-lane vehicle does see the vehicle and perceives the vehicle as being about to merge as a result of its assertive activation of the directional signal, then this vehicle will be compelled to clarify in short time its willingness to assist the merger by aiding the formation of a viable gap, or its persistence to disallow the merge into its frontal space. Either case assists the merging driver – if the traffic-lane vehicle above is passed or never reached by the merging driver, his or her having noticed

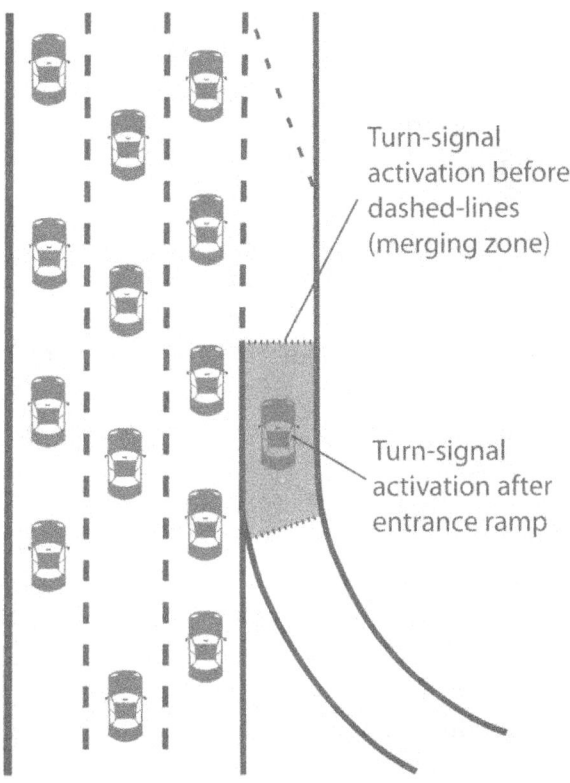

Figure 7 – A shaded graphical demonstration of turn-signal activation on the entrance ramp; the professional driver never delays such merge-intention declaration until a final maneuver is underway

the directional signal of the merging vehicle is completely irrelevant to the merging driver (again, there is no loss). If however a traffic-lane vehicle who is either in front of or behind the interstitial gap into which the merge will be executed notices the merging driver earlier than otherwise would have occurred were not his or her directional signal activated, this clearly would benefit the merging driver by making his or her presence more immediately known so that the relevant traffic-lane vehicles have more time to adjust their safety margins and following distances to ensure the safety of the merge (as the collision of the merging vehicle as a result of the merge necessarily entails collision with one of these traffic-lane vehicles – a mutually undesirable outcome). An absurd objection to this reasoning may argue that, by strategically delaying or entirely omitting the activation of the directional signal, the merging driver may surreptitiously "sneak" into an area which the aggressive traffic-lane drivers would have otherwise adjusted their speed to render impossible. We reply to this absurd objection that the avoidance of collision is a mutually beneficial interest for both traffic-lane and merging vehicles, and that therefore in no event should communicative declaration of the merge be minimized in an attempt to alter traffic-lane-driver behavior. Safety is of paramount importance while merging, and all other competing optimizations during this phase are almost wholly irrelevant due to the relative temporal insignificance of the (potentially dangerous) one-time-per-trip execution of an entrance merge compared to the much larger and far more impactful time spent actually driving on the highway, when long-term secondary optimizations hold more significance. The professional driver always ensures that the vehicle's corresponding directional signal is activated from the beginning of the merge lane until the end of the merge (or even afterwards if subsequent lane switches are intent).

Merge-intent-declaring assertiveness may also be achieved by maximizing (if possible) the time spent travelling parallel to a stable entrance gap in the traffic-lane-flow (and even slightly ahead of the region into which a gradual pre-merge deceleration is executed). This temporally maximizes the opportunities which the rearwards traffic-lane driver has to spot the merging vehicle and accordingly decelerate as to expand the merging gap. This optimization may be difficult to perform under challenging merging circumstances due to more stringent time requirements, but insofar as it is possible, it is always advantageous to impart as much visual lead warning time as possible to the relevant traffic-lane driver such that the according safety margins can be mutually established among the drivers executing and surrounding the merge. Visual scanning is of particular importance during this phase, since the rear vehicle may aggressively respond to shut the merging gap by accelerating (an aggressive behavior better found to exist before the merge is attempted rather than during). We may take the opposite of this merge-assertion method of quickly accelerating up to a traffic-lane vehicle and cutting it off in a quick and tight merge into their frontal following distance, affording them only a handful of moments to react and guess as to the merging vehicle's future path, which may reflexively prompt a whole host of potentially dangerous behaviors on the part of the nervous traffic-lane driver (such as rapid acceleration, rapid deceleration, or unchecked swerving away from the merging lane which may risk a lateral collision with the second lane) – by parallel example to this dangerous setup, the professional driver's ability to secure and temporarily co-follow a stable merging spot, ensuring its safety before merging, will always ensure the greatest safety for both the merging and traffic-lane travelling parties. During this pre-merge stage of travelling to the side of the chosen traffic gap for a moment or two, drifting interlane position closer to the gap will of course signal that the merge is not only intended but underway to any watching traffic-lane drivers. This of course should never be done if safety margins are insufficient to begin with, but an initial drift motion of no more than one second preceding the full execution of a merging maneuver may endeavor to clarify the finality and impeding execution of the decided merge operation.

Merge execution tactics

Our "no more than one second" qualification in the paragraph above derives from the first and foremost tactical necessity of merge execution dynamics: that once a safe, declared, and acknowledged merge is established, it should be quickly and precisely executed – not slowly drawn out over the course of the remaining distance of the merging lane but swiftly achieved in one fluid motion. We have hereunto described the tactical process of scanning and optimally choosing a traffic-flow gap into which to merge, and the driver has achieved isotachic parallelism with this gap in the merging lane at this stage in our chronological description of the merging process. In preparation for the turning maneuver which will physically merge the vehicle fully within the constraints of the traffic lane, the professional driver will execute one confirmative frontal visual scan before executing the merging turn (as to free up lateral and rearwards visual scanning resources which will be most necessary during the merge, especially the initial part). The optimal speed of the merge will transition the vehicle into the gap as quickly as possible (for the aforementioned reasons) without approaching such an extreme degree of "jerking" as would interrupt constant vehicular frictional traction between the tires and the road (an unrealistic problem at speeds appreciably below highway maximum) and as may frighten the rearwards traffic-lane driver who must accordingly decelerate to restore a following distance equal to that which they had been maintaining before the merge. In practice, this properly balanced speed of the merge execution will be faster than that which the average driver is accustomed to executing, since the professional driver understands the dangers of prolonging a merge execution for too long and is also able to control the vehicle dynamically with rehearsed comfort and firm steering-wheel grip. Obviously, the faster one is travelling, the smaller will be the necessary angular adjustment of the wheel and the opposite corrective returning rotation gesture (we will discuss vehicular interface dynamics in detail in a future section). The increased sensitivity, therefore, of the steering wheel at higher speeds when executing the merge necessitates an accordingly strengthened and intent hand grip on the wheel such that the precise steering speed and margins for the merge may be executed. Insofar as additional lane switches are not being sought by the driver (and perhaps so, momentarily, even then), it is the immediate task of the having-merged driver to attend to the frontal and rearwards following distances between the two enclosing vehicles and balance them accordingly (or with minor adjustments, if the results of the formerly executed behavior-predictive analysis of one certain vehicle relative to the other so warrant).

Merge abortion and/or total failure

In the unforeseen event that an aggressive and/or impaired traffic-lane driver begins to dangerously accelerate into the merging gap during the merge execution, or that of deceleration from the frontal vehicle (which is far more likely to be unintentional), then the professional driver must abort the merge if the safety margin distances are such that a collision would occur were the merging motion to be continued. This possibility explains two of our prior tactical necessities of the professional driver: (1) that he or she should execute a frontal path-of-travel visual scanning check prior to the merge maneuver as to free up lateral and rearwards scanning resources (i.e. watching the vehicles surrounding the selected merging gap in the traffic lane) in the lateral and posterolateral regions in order to check for such erratic traffic-lane-vehicle behavior which would warrant the immediate abortion of the merge, and (2) that the merge, once safely appropriated with sufficient distance buffers and declared through traffic-lane-driver signaling, should be executed quickly so that any other vehicle still in the merging lane does not have time to accelerate or decelerate under the assumption that the merging driver will be "out of the way" in mere moments (seeing him or her begin to execute the merge), such that the merging driver who suddenly needs to abort the merge finds his or herself "boxed in" between the two and precariously narrowing lanes – with there being vehicles on either side which would cause a lateral collision. In other words, if the merging driver fails to swiftly execute the maneuver yet draws out the lateral merging motion for longer than is optimal, this not only increases the temporal plenitude of opportunities by which the safe-designated merging gap could narrow beyond critical safety limits, but also increases the sense of security to the other (and almost always, rearwards and following) merging-lane drivers who will assume the merging vehicle to be clear of the merging lane in moments once it fully goes into the traffic-lane – which could prompt acceleration of a following merging-lane driver or even, in an extreme case, an attempt at passing on the merging lane – both actions which increase the risk of colliding with another merging-lane vehicle if indeed a merging driver must abort the merge due to an erratic, sudden circumstance on the other side, being caught between two areas of unavoidable collision. We recapitulate that the method by which the professional driver will avoid this situation is ensuring a safe, sufficient merging gap distance before attempting the merge, using the strategic signaling strategies documented above for maximizing the probability of traffic-lane driver cooperation, and most relevantly, by executing the merge maneuver with dexterous celerity.

In any event, we now seek to document the optimum tactical response if indeed the professional driver, for whatever reason, does find himself or herself in a merge-abortion situation. The opposite directional signal should immediately be switched on and the horn straightaway sounded – even before visual scanning of the circumstances of the merging lane – in order to maximize probability that any encroaching merging lane drivers will notice the corrective gesture and make room accordingly. Unlike some near-accident situations when sounding the horn could potentially have a deleterious effect of alarming a driver to an irrational braking action, the likelihood in this instance is far greater that the auditory alert will only help the other merging drivers notice the attempted re-entrance of the failed merger, since the traffic-lane drivers, however startled or alarmed, are already in some capacity executing some accelerative or decelerative behavior as to warrant the necessity of the merging abortion, and therefore their reactions are more or less irrelevant. After immediately activating these external attention-attracting signaling devices, the driver must quickly shift spatial awareness scanning priority to the rear and lateral region on the other, merging-lane side to ensure that, in fact, there are no vehicles against which a collision will occur once the corrective gesture is completed. The present description has become increasingly complex, hypothetical, and extraordinarily unlikely to occur – again, we only seek to detail the most challenging situation. However the necessary abortion of a suddenly-dangerous though already-undertaken merging attempt may be expected to occur a few times throughout the course of the professional driver's career, in which the necessity of ensuring that another (and potentially worse) accident resulting from the corrective maneuver is important to describe, no matter how improbable.

Utter failure to execute a merge before the gradual termination of the merging lane reaches a critical point is virtually guaranteed never to occur as long as the proper process, documented above, is followed. Traffic engineers carefully design freeway entrance structures so that plenty of opportunities are afforded, as coming to a full stop at the end of a merging lane represents a massive safety risk to the driver and to the vehicles behind the driver, not to mention an extremely fuel-inefficient waste of momentum energy by means of the necessary reacceleration to highway speed which must at some point occur. Accelerating from a stop to a speed at which safely merging into the highway becomes possible requires a large distance (depending on vehicle) – a traffic gap which may be completely impossible to obtain in realistic traffic conditions. A full appreciation of the risks associated with coming to a full stop on the merging lane will inform the knowledgeable driver as to the optimum assertiveness which he or she must assert on the merging lane; more times than not, being more confident and therefore obtaining a safe merging opportunity will be less risky than coming to a full stop on the merging lane. But in the worst case, should it occur, the driver should examine the geometry of the breakdown lane (to see if potential evasion of the area is possible for delayed reacceleration) and simply wait for a sufficiently wide traffic gap to materialize before reacceleration to highway speeds and merging is accomplished.

Weave lanes

In some precarious traffic setups known as "weave lanes", the lane designated for highway entrance merging is the same lane into which exiting vehicles merge, leading to the next exit instead of terminating into the right-most (or left-most) highway lane. The professional driver understands the technical and practical fact that drivers exiting the freeway have the right of way, and that vehicles merging onto the freeway must yield to those exiting vehicles. These vehicles may be travelling at excessive speed and may entirely omit directional signal activation; therefore, although driver foreknowledge that the merging lane is also a weave lane would certainly prompt heightened attention and spatial awareness to these potential vehicles, it may not always be known to the driver whether or not the merging lane is a weave lane or not.

Highway entrance merging in unfamiliar areas, therefore, must always prompt an addition to the merging-zone-entrance initial risk analysis which analyzes the condition of rear-lateral traffic-lane drivers (and even the lanes beyond that) and which scans for behavioral signs which indicate the existence of an exiting driver, such as deceleration or directional usage – if the lane does in fact turn out to be a weave lane. Due to the added merge execution risk inherent to weave lanes by virtue of the dynamic addition of traffic-lane vehicles potentially merging *themselves* into the lane of the *merger*, and also due to massively smaller safety risk of failing to execute a merge whatsoever (since the driver would simply continue off the exit to which the merging lane leads), therefore highway entrance merging behavior on weave lanes should be characteristically more conservative and demanding of greater safety margins and clearance buffers than that of traditional merging lanes.

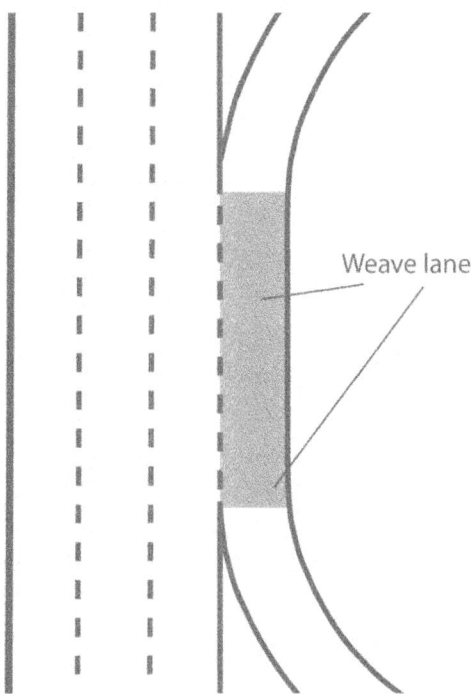

Figure 8 – A weave lane, which further necessitates comprehensive lateral spatial awareness attention during merging, since intrafreeway vehicles may be merging into the same merging lane for highway exiting; merge assertiveness is therefore to be lessened due to the safe evasive opportunity afforded by the exit in case a successful merge is not conducted by the end of the lane.

Multi-lane ramps

We hereunto constrained our tactical model in its explanation and theoretical justification to the most common and traditional setting of a single-lane, limited-access, one-way entrance ramp. Some high-volume highway entrance structures comprise of multiple entrance ramp lanes between which lane-switching is possible. In these cases, the traffic engineers have certainly not terminated both or however many entrance lanes with the same sudden sharpness as that of a single expiring merge lane – they are gradually tapered to end in succession, at worst, and may even persist for a sizeable section through a henceforth-widened highway. In the first case, the termination of whichever right-most (or left-most) lane would involve the same tactical model which we described in the traditional case above, since the expiring entrance ramp lane would functionally identify with the merging lane, and the inner, persisting entrance ramp lane would functionally identify, for all tactical purposes, as an exact analogy to the traffic-lane into which a driver in the ending lane must merge. However there are of course additional complexities with regards to merging or *switching* between the *other* lanes, be it between the innermost of the entrance ramp and the existing highway lanes, or be it even between only the existing highway lanes. This prospect is surrounded by a different and far wider array of tactical considerations, warranting therefore an entirely separate tactical model and appropriately transitioning our discussion into that of general lane optimization.

CHAPTER 5

Lane Optimization

The entirety of the professional driver's actions on the highway ultimately seek to establish nothing other than lateral positioning of the vehicle (excepting that of longitudinal speed control), which fundamentally places the present topic of lane optimization and control at the central crux of our comprehensive discussion on advanced freeway driving tactics. Having established proper spatial awareness technique to be executed at all times, and having established a detailed model for highway entrance procedures, we now progress to the details of substantive safety and optimization tactics on the freeway itself.

General factors

From solely a safety perspective, it is desirable never to have to switch lanes in the course of travel on the freeway. This laconic sentiment is often expressed in driver's education courses (with overly simplified exhortations to "minimize lane switches") and is even reflected in the statutory bodies of some jurisdictions which enable traffic enforcement officers to cite "excessive lane changing" (or elsewhere, more narrowly, "improper lane change") as a finable offense under the umbrella of reckless and aggressive driving behaviors. The general sentiments which favor lane maintenance are sound, as making a lane change necessarily involves the risk that a lateral collision will occur if spatial awareness technique is not properly executed to comprehensively check and clear not only the vehicle's external blind-spot regions, but also the behavioral characteristics of any surrounding vehicles or objects which could lead to a collision during or even after the unwise lane switch. However it is also incontrovertible that safety optimization – even altogether collision avoidance – is possible from occasional lane changes, not to mention the (perhaps even greater) array of non-safety-related optimizations which can be rendered by proper selection and switching of vehicular travel lane. Our tactical model for lateral positioning on the highway, with respect to the marked lanes, will therefore provide instruction as to the most optimal choices given a comprehensive analysis of the driving situation – with differences in high-level driver strategy bearing large consequences on whether or not (and where, and when, and to what degree) the following optimizations will be made. This overall analysis of continuous *lateral position* versus that of the constrained, discrete *lane position* reflects the reality of the dynamics between vehicle and freeway: the adherence to lane markings is merely an artificial, high-level control task which the professional driver executes continuously, however he or she is able to adjust the lateral positioning of the vehicle to whatever margin of lateral distance he or she wishes regardless of lane markings; the fluid nature of vehicular traffic as it pertains to this fact mandates that the present tactical model for spatial freeway maneuvering may also incorporate control of *interlane position*, which we define as the interior range of lateral positionings a vehicle is able to occupy inside a lane. Some rare and extreme conditions (other than brief moments while executing lane switches themselves) will call for temporary driving completely out of lane – that is, constrained to no single lane whatsoever. Due to the interlinked nature of all the factors which dictate proper interlane position (which is almost always dead-centered along the middle of the lane, equidistant to both lane edges), we will discuss it when relevant in each situational topic rather than unnaturally forcing all of these interlinked (and unavoidably repeated, as it would be) factors into one reserved section concerning interlane position. An understanding of the dynamics of the lane switch maneuver can, however, be discussed in a singular preparatory section as an understanding thereof will be necessary for full appreciation of our manifold lane optimization topics. We will therefore proceed with this prerequisite discussion first, before transitioning focus to the individual lane optimization tactics which the professional driver executes.

Lane-switch maneuver dynamics

An understanding of the particular dynamics of a lane switch is necessary for the professional driver as it pertains to the aspiration of achieving optimizations in lane position. We will not bore the reader with an unnecessary chronological account of each successive detail on how to execute a basic lane switch; this book assumes an already moderate-to-advanced reader driving skill level, and even the advanced methods of comprehensive spatial awareness which must be executed before a lane switch we have already discussed. Proper safety clearances and blind-zone checks for a given lane switch are assumed to have been already secured, and our interests in the physical dynamics of the maneuver begin with initial steering wheel heading-corrective adjustment itself.

Lateral speed

Lane switches can either be conducted abruptly, with a large rotational adjustment to the steering wheel angle and following corrective readjustment, or very gradually by altering the steering wheel angle by fractions of a degree over an extended period of time. This of course determines the lateral speed of the vehicle and the time which the lane change maneuver will take. It is generally desirable to be swift and immediate with lane changes, as to avoid the dangers of slowly "hanging out" between lanes as described formerly in our tactical model for highway entrance merging. However different circumstances will call for accordingly adjusted lateral speed in executing a lane switch, as will be evident in our discussions on each category of lane optimization by the relative priority given to a particular lane switch situation. What can and should be generally known, however, is the geometric optimality of very slow lane changes – whether by fuel-efficiency (lower speed required for same travelling distance), by time-to-destination minimization (greater forward position holding speed constant, due to the smaller distance travelled), by speeding-risk minimization (lower required speed holding distance constant), or by improved vehicle control (less sudden lateral weight transfer between sides of tires, decreasing lateral instability – which is very important for tall and high profile vehicles). These four interrelated optimization factors can and should be selectively optimized according to their individual priorities given the situation, and all stem from the same basic geometric explanation: the shortest distance between two

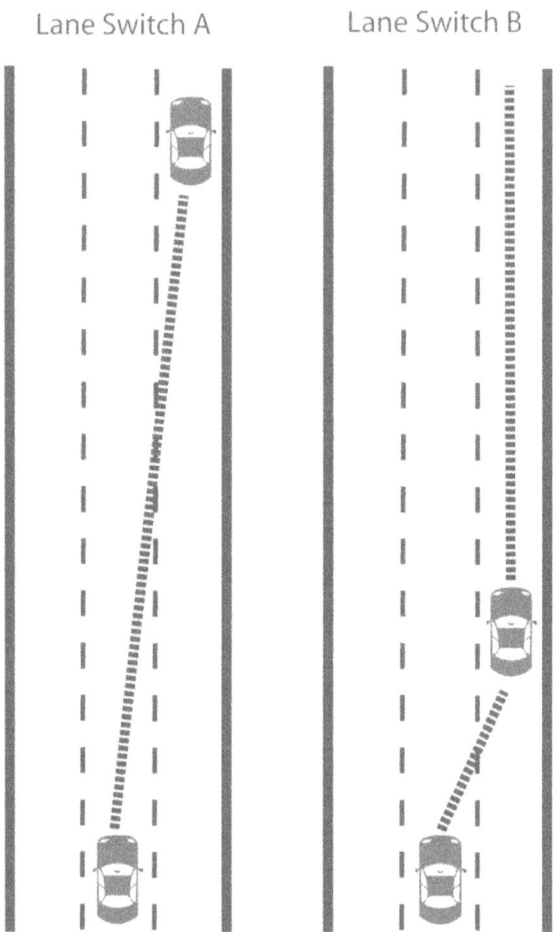

Lane switch A results in marginally lower travel distance than that of B, however undesirably lengthens the out-of-lane travel period.

Figure 9 – Two different lane-switch lateral position profiles, the first of which demonstrates slower lateral speed

points is a straight line, and the slower a lane change is taken, the more closely the vehicle's path-of-travel resembles a line.

Let us take, for example, two extreme cases to illustrate this phenomenon: were the driver to extensively and rapidly adjust the angle of the steering wheel as to cause a very quick lateral motion into the next lane (assuming, for example, that the maneuver is executed fully over only 30 feet of frontward distance) and then continue for 100 feet in said lane, the path of the vehicle over this 130 foot long stretch of highway would resemble a zigzagged, diagonal line through the first 30 feet and a straight line thereafter. If one were to draw a line from the initial position of the vehicle to the final position of the vehicle after the 130 feet of travel (as would resemble the path of a laterally slow, extended lane switch), this line would clearly represent a shorter distance since it is the most direct path between the initial and final positions of the vehicle, un-extended by ragged "zigzag" protrusions engendered by the more-abrupt lane switch. It is no surprise, however, that this theoretical efficiency optimization generally runs opposed to that which is more safe, since safety is commonly at odds with other (more tangibly economic) optimization factors as we have seen and will continue to see throughout this book. However, knowledge of this phenomenon will enable its inclusion into the following topics of lane optimization, such that it may be taken advantage of when and to the degree that safety is not compromised. Still, it is at best a moderate effect and only holds much if any tactical relevance in situations of highly demanding driving requirement, long distance, and/or greater prevalence of lane switch frequency.

Lateral acceleration profile

The professional driver is also aware of the different *lane switch acceleration profiles* which he or she may find suitable for the situation, which we define as the pattern in or profile of lateral speed throughout the entire course of the lane switch maneuver. The acceleration profile only refers to the relative timing of the applications of the changes in lateral speed and does not itself have anything to do with lateral speed; it is possible to execute a fast lane switch with a gradual acceleration profile and the inverse (a slow lane switch with an abrupt acceleration profile). The most generally safe lane switch acceleration profile, holding the overall time and speed of the maneuver constant, introduces a slight gradual heading change, mostly in order to make visual alert of the lane switch to surrounding drivers, before taking the steering wheel angle sweep to its maximum extent and then correctively adjusting the wheel to revert heading back to twelve o'clock. Evasive situations generally call for the opposite, as an immediate change in lateral position is needed and with the gradual, surrounding vehicle visual scanning stage occurring at the end of the corrective steering gesture (i.e., easing into the new position), as all evasive and defensive maneuvers of this variety naturally involve a present exigency to move out from one risky position and into another which may also be risky due to unseen vehicles – and therefore a relative amount of slowness (to whatever degree possible) is desirable in this latter phase of the defensive maneuver in order to scan for surrounding vehicles again and to afford greater opportunity for the vehicle itself to be seen by other drivers. Furthermore, if fuel-efficiency is of great concern, a more gradual lane switch acceleration profile will be beneficial to the ends of minimizing friction losses in the tires associated with rapid and sudden movements, a factor which is, however, negligible at low speed and even otherwise quite minimal.

Directional signal usage

Directional signal usage embodies a key part of the psychological dynamics of the lane switch maneuver as it concerns the awareness and response of surrounding drivers. While the common driver embraces a narrow and often begrudging view of directional signal usage, the professional driver adopts an expansive vision concerning directional signals and their usage as general *psychological stimulus instruments* to the surrounding allovehicular drivers, not constrained by the solely academic canonizations of when they are to be activated and when they are to be off, to the ends of influencing other drivers' behavior so that it is beneficial to the professional driver in any way (most importantly, to his or her safety). This describes the role of directional signal usage in our tactical model and as such we eschew any and all hard-fast rules concerning directional signal usage, such that, in the present context, they be activated before and for the duration of any lane switch. In practice, however, it is extraordinarily difficult to conceive of a lane switching situation in which the professional driver will not properly use directional signals as such – and so perhaps our unconstrained, expansive vision concerning the role and usage of directional signals should only serve to widen the driver's appreciation of circumstances in which they are useful: which is always for simple lane switches, and potentially so also in other situations (most vehicles' "hazard lights" feature, for instance, will flash the same lights used for the directional signals, showing their multifaceted purposefulness). We will find that careful and strategic usage of directional signals in certain situations can improve safety and overall driving outcomes; however basic directional signal activation long prior to and during the execution of a lane switch is a basic necessity which the reader is already assumed to understand.

Lane switch abortion

The abortion of a regular freeway lane switch is largely similar to its analogue in the process of highway entrance merging, as we discussed above. However there are many formal differences to it than that of the former: (1) general freeway lane switch abortions are typically associated with a comparatively lower-risk, higher-safety-clearance environment than that of the former, due to the usual lack of momentary driver tension and an expiring merging lane from which one *must* merge (with most regular freeway merges being voluntary), (2) the theoretical possibility for the driver exists to evade the new lane (out from which there is suddenly a safety impetus to move) by means of switching *even further* into the lane beyond that of the new lane, if spatial awareness clearances indicate that safer and more liberal vehicular distance margins exist on the other side, and if the driver is already far enough into the immediately-dangerous lane to escape just as quickly as if reverting heading to the original lane (not at all unlikely due to the lack of needing to reverse the direction of the vehicle's lateral inertia in such a case), (3) drivers are less likely to be aware and not in a state of being preoccupied with safety checks (which is hopefully the case at least in merging zones), (4) directional use and overall visual indication of the lane-returning (or otherwise evasive-refuge-entering) maneuver is more important, since merging-lane highway entrance drivers are simply looking to merge whereas travelers on the highway are often seeking to optimize speed and following distance and to accelerate into newfound extensions in following distance when possible (such as when a vehicle merges or begins to merge into a new lane, freeing up space for the rearward vehicle's acceleration), which is clearly a dangerous and potentially collisional circumstance for the driver who is aborting the lane switch and likely seeking reentrance into the first lane. Careful consideration must therefore be made by the professional driver of the dangers associated with lane switch abortion in circumstances when it seems beneficial – continuously scanning one's surroundings with proper spatial awareness protocol will enable a sound decision to be made as to whether it is more dangerous to not abort and remain in the (for whatever reason) dangerous lane, or to abort the maneuver and enter (or re-enter) another potentially collisional zone.

Geometric economy: the curve-distance interlane disparity effect

For the intensive purposes of the professional driver, freeways cannot be oversimplified into a mere sequence of one-dimensional line segments into which they are often theoretically simplified for the purposes of distance calculation and conceptual navigation (such as is purported by mile marker signs' conceptual connotation of solely linear distance). Such simplifications of an entire two (or even three) dimensional highway surface topology are derived from the center line equidistant to either edge of the road – a valid approximation. However it is obvious that vehicles do not travel in just one line, nor even over the direct center line of the highway in most cases; spatial freeway distance factors to the professional driver must account for the two-dimensional (at least) forward *and* lateral field of space through which the vehicle may be maneuvered. This theoretical acknowledgement opens the field to a host of geometric path-of-travel optimizations which can augment efficiency in any of the interrelated ways by seeking the best approximation of a straight line through a given stretch of highway length. Naturally, a simple and unitary curve would require less travelling distance for the vehicle when the vehicle's path-of-travel stays in the lane closest to the inner bend of the curve, whereas a longer geometric path-of-travel would be necessary to achieve the same longitudinal position relative to the linear distance (i.e., central line) measurement of the highway when following the outer path. This relationship is due to the basic mathematics of circles: as radius increases, so does the circumference by a certain constant linear coefficient (pi). However in many situations, it is only the linear, "one-dimensional", forward travelling distance on the highway gone (i.e. relative to the measured mile marker, which itself is relative to the center line) which is of any importance, since exits (the destination of every freeway driver) exist at discrete and constant linear distance intervals. There is therefore a true and disparate travelling distance difference between the vehicle in the inner-curve lane and the vehicle in the outer-curve lane in the case of a simple curve, holding all other factors constant. This concept is conceptually identical to the "staggered start" arrangement of Olympic track athletic events: the athletes occupying an outer lane position have a greater distance to travel relative to the linearly-constant, straight, and perpendicular line which demarcates the end of the course (as we would liken to the nature of the placing of highway exit off-ramps). Our prior explanation of the geometric optimality of slow lane switches also follows for similar reasons. This concept, which we will name the "curve-distance interlane disparity effect", is extraordinarily relevant to our ensuing discussions in two general categories: (1) firstly, due to the prospect of performing Pareto geometric optimizations by safely following a path-of-travel of shorter distance (thereby requiring less speed holding arrival time constant, enabling faster arrival time holding speed constant, and generally increasing fuel-efficiency due to smaller travelling distance – notwithstanding the marginally greater rotational G-forces and any of their minimal effects on tire-road-surface friction), and (2) secondly, due to the intervehicular dynamical effects of passing and in-lane-travelling vehicles whose relative positions on the highway are thrown off by such curvatures when speed is held constant, holding large consequences in predictive behavior analysis, speed optimization, and lane

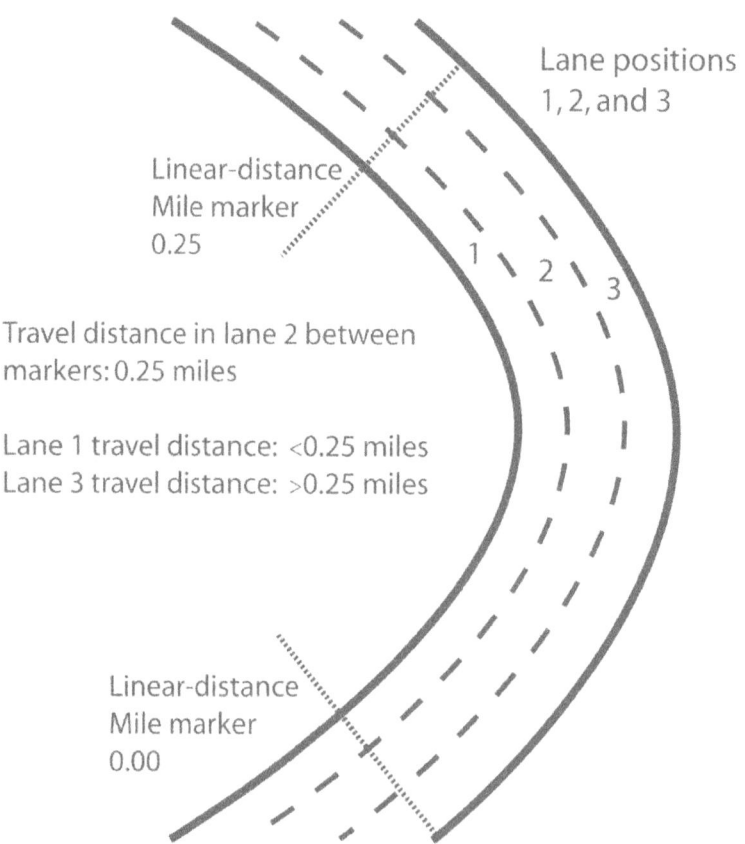

Figure 10 – *A geometric visualization of the curve-distance interlane disparity effect*

optimization[1]. We shall reserve examination of the effects in the second category for our later discussion on intervehicular dynamics; herein we will concern ourselves only with the first category: geometric distance optimization of the curve-distance interlane disparity effect.

As with many optimizations, a deterring safety cost may be associated with the optimization's implementation if the situation is not appropriate or permitting; we repeat that optimizations which also constitute safety risks are themselves less-optimal than they are in raw theory due to the sub-optimality in every measure of vehicular collision (and this is true insofar as driver skill estimated to be insufficient to safely execute whichever technique in the present circumstances); the reverse also holds true usually: that economic optimizations, by themselves and theoretically without any associated safety cost, would in fact constitute safety optimizations since the quickening of destination arrival (holding all other variables, such as speed, constant) equates to less time spent on the highway and therefore lowered risk that a collision will occur. These two theoretical extremes however each lie on absolute poles of highly theoretical and minimally realistic constraints: the first constraint being that the arrangement of vehicles will make it impossible to execute the optimization without incurring safety risks, and the second theoretical constraint being that safety is prioritized to the extent that marginally faster time-to-arrival constitutes an appreciable decrease in collision risk. In reality, there will be many situations in which geometric optimization can be used safely but with neither great risk nor great benefit as it pertains to safety. We therefore only serve to clarify with this present theoretical tangent that geometric optimization of the vehicle's path-of-travel for the curve-distance interlane disparity effect should only be done in cases where it is safe (i.e., low traffic-density to a total void of allovehicular drivers altogether), since in only those situations is it optimal when the inherent preferentiality of avoiding

---

[1] For a discussion on the intervehicular dynamics of the curve-distance interlane disparity effect, see the "Road Curvature" section in Chapter 8.

lane switches is considered. The safety analysis of a geometric curve-distance optimization technique will compare the vehicle's path-of-travel without the adjustment to that of the adjustment added and will use spatial awareness information to estimate the risk of collision associated with changing the path-of-travel in the desired manner.

If it is 3am in the morning, completely dark outside, the professional driver being entirely alone on a curvy highway, beginning a long 120 mile trip on this same freeway, and there being no left lane travel restriction (as we will discuss later) nor any other deterring factor, and the highway curving to the left – then in this hypothetically extreme case, it would betoken a sizeable mark of ignorance to travel in the center or right lane when large geometric distance optimization could be obtained by left lane travel, since that is the lane most closely approximating a straight line (the inner curve) – the shortest distance – in this case (for our solely illustrative purposes, the fact that this absurd example freeway would seem to curve inwards in a never-ending spiral must be ignored) . There is no safety cost (other than very fine and minimal variables which we will omit from this exemplary hypothetical) since the freeway is devoid of other drivers which would enable a vehicular collision during lane switching. If the driver's destination exit were a rare left lane exit, this optimization would be even more sensible due to the lack of needing to thereafter waste lateral distance spent transitioning into the geometrically optimal lane. In this way, the professional driver must be aware of the inherent distance optimization cost of lateral travel in the freeway (as we already discussed) – but if the upcoming curvature of the freeway is extended, repeated, and long enough to overcome that initial expense, then the lane switch is justified in this constrained hypothetical. In this way, lane switches on the highway function as one-time, up-front costs in order to accrue a continuous, compounding optimization benefit throughout subsequent travel in the new lane (of shorter distance, in this case) which, integrated over the time of travel in the new lane, hopefully outweighs the cost of the initial lane switch. As a general and far more practical rule, if vehicles are anywhere in the vicinity, the safety cost of a lane switch would likely outweigh any such geometric curve optimization due to inherent collision risks to lateral motion within a fluid stream of vehicular traffic. We also see that the professional driver who has precise foreknowledge of the highway will be the one most able to drive optimally: if a driver unwisely goes through the hassle of switching lanes in order to get on the inner edge for an upcoming curve, only to find that the curve again reverses in the opposite direction after the first curve, then he or she may regret the maneuver as a wasteful and potentially risky lane switch maneuver for little to no optimization benefit (especially if traffic conditions would make it difficult to get out of this initial lane, which will soon become the least optimal and longest lane upon the advent of the second and opposite curve). This should remind the professional driver that the curve-distance interlane disparity effect is defined for any two forward-distance points on the freeway and must therefore be evaluated holistically in some situations: if the road curves in one direction and immediately thereafter recurves into the opposite direction, then the three lane switches necessary throughout the course of the two curves to follow their inner edges (assuming that the vehicle enters the setup in the center lane) is not likely to be safely possible (that is, of possible safety as would warrant the optimization in the first place), and therefore staying in the center lane throughout the setup and doing nothing with regards to the effect is in fact better than switching into the first inner lane and then being stuck in that lane, so that the second curve would be equally lengthened as the first shortened, since the latter involves a safety cost of lane-switching (not to mention greater inertial strains and heightened driver attention requirement to path-of-travel, steering feedback) whereas the former does not and is equal in travelling distance to the latter. A professional driver therefore understands the proper and occasional role of optimizing the curve-distance interlane disparity effect and is not found being caught in

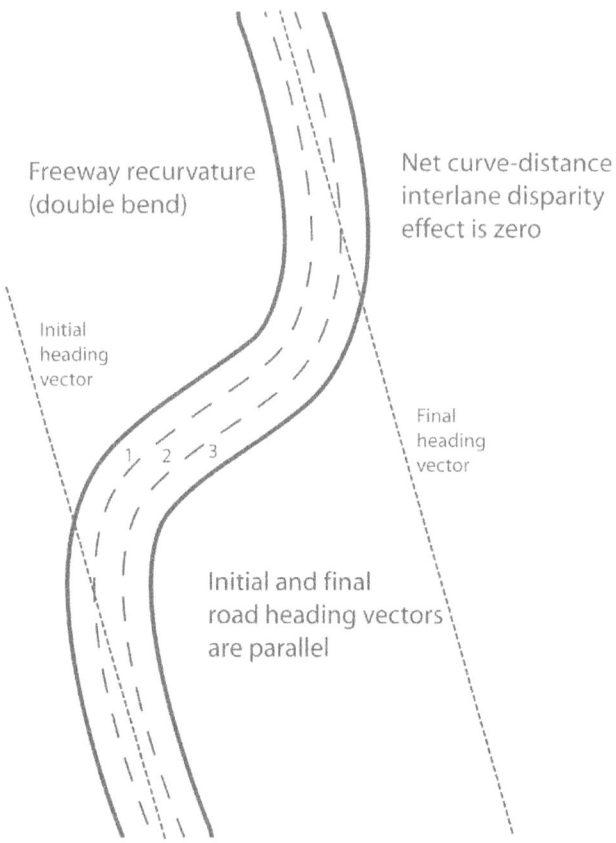

Figure 11 – Potential negation of the curve-distance interlane disparity effect from two symmetrically opposite curves

situations wherein safety and even the intended optimization itself are compromised due to an overactive excitement to "hug the inner curves" and presumably execute the optimization. However a theoretical understanding of these different effects is necessary, since if for some reason the professional driver's high-level strategy legitimately called for high-urgency, time-sensitive driving, with a decreased emphasis on safety, then he or she would certain be more aggressive with lane switches aimed towards the shortest and most direct linear distances on the freeway. However this is neither a standard situation nor the regular manner by which the professional driver drives; optimization of the curve-distance interlane disparity effect should be reserved for obvious situations in which a safe lane switch can be made to follow a substantially shorter and extended inner curve rather than following the longer and therefore suboptimal unadjusted path-of-travel of the vehicle.

Optimization of the curve-distance interlane disparity effect should on absolutely no (or only in extremely rare) circumstance have an impact on interlane position, as one may creatively think by observing the inherent relevance of lateral positioning to the act of steering into the shortest path. This is especially true for travel on inner freeway lanes, on which it is not such that a vehicle-free zone is mostly guaranteed to exist on the edge to which the hypothetical interlane adjustment would attract the vehicle, as there is usually on the right-most or (especially) left-most lane depending on direction of curvature respectively, and also on which the marginal curvature-shortening benefit of such an interlane adjustment is not even as high to begin with, due to the larger radius of curvature. Clearly, off-center interlane position in such a lane would dangerously narrow the lateral distance buffer between the vehicle and any other vehicles travelling in the adjacent lane, or which may come to pass the vehicle on the relevant side[2] (that is not to nullify the entire topic of interlane position altogether by mandating unequivocal obedience to the direct center line of the lane of travel – as we shall see, there are rare cases in which the benefits of slight lateral interlane adjustment outweigh the costs – however this is by and large not one of those cases). If a driver's high-level strategic reason for using the freeway were of such a speed-urgency as to overcome the small safety cost of narrowed lateral safety margins, then he or

---

[2] See Chapter 12, accident situation #5 which demonstrates the circumstance of lateral allovehicle lane-switch attempt, which would massively augment the likelihood of collision if the reference driver's interlane position were off-centered into the dangerous zone, let alone evasively moved away from it.

she would have most certainly maneuvered the vehicle into the optimal non-inner lane around the curve in which lateral vehicular proximity would not be a concern. However even on the right-most or left-most lane in the inner-curve of a bend, it is still unwise to adjust interlane position precariously towards the inner portion due to the risks of: (1) slippery road conditions risking loss of vehicular traction with and possible sliding off of the freeway surface[3], (2) decreased ability to evade any obstructive objects which may be lying in the breakdown lane or the left curb – an effect exacerbated by the decreased time afforded to the driver in which to react to such threats, given the tight curvature, (3) affording vehicles in the next outer lane (or even aggressive passing vehicles behind in the same lane) a greater lateral buffer with which to be aggressive and disrespectful of the proper lane boundaries, which could lead to the curve-hugging driver's inability to restore proper, centered interlane position if other factors come to suddenly require it, (4) friction-related fuel-efficiency detriments associated with potential shoulder grooving, and (5) potential friction-related tire slippage fuel-efficiency detriments associated with the greater rotational inertial forces applied to the tires of the vehicle, hugging such a curve at such speed (and not to mention the resulting dynamical effects). Freeway curvature radii are designed by traffic engineers in keeping with the reasonable expectations of speed and lateral position inherent to the design of the highway, which entails a general obedience to the speed limit and adherence to the center of one's lane. Optimization of the curve-distance interlane disparity effect is already an undertaking which only promises non-negligible results during trips of sufficient length, higher than average arrival-time pressures, high variations in road curvature, and a relatively sparse freeway in which the potentially frequent required lane switches can be executed without constantly risking collision; therefore, pushing what is already a mostly-negligible effect to the degree of perverting properly centered interlane positon is a behavior almost always

---

[3] This road-departure hazard could occur from "oversteer" (discussed in Chapter 10) or even by an erratic lane-switch acceleration profile if surface conditions are slippery enough. See Chapter 12, accident situation #11.

guaranteed to produce a greater safety cost than geometric optimization. The professional driver must therefore balance accordingly all of these factors while optimizing the curve-distance interlane disparity effect in accordance with his or her personal freeway driving strategy to achieve the subjectively optimal outcome as it concerns this one particular effect.

Longitudinal-axis safety margin and following distance optimization

In our former discussion of highway entrance merging, we proved that maintaining large following distances extending out from the fore and aft of the vehicle massively improves safety and increases opportunities for optimization. We shall refer to these zones more generally as "longitudinal-axis safety margins", since such gaps of intervehicular space are advantageous both from behind and to the front of the vehicle (with the term "following distance" tending to suggest only that of these two which lies in front of the vehicle). The term "longitudinal-axis" denotes the front-back axis of the vehicle relative to the forward motion of the vehicle's path-of-travel, as we will distinguish from "lateral" safety margins to be discussed in a future section. Longitudinal intervehicular distance buffers are critical for safety and optimization on the freeway just as they are on the merging lane for the most simple reason that more reaction time is afforded to the driver and to the driver behind in the case that there is need to respond to (or originally perform) a sudden deceleration, and also since there is more distance through which to carry that deceleration. Generous following distances on the highway also create the potential to make the task of lane optimization much easier by widening the possible opportunities for safe lane switches; as we discussed formerly with highway entrance merging, merging into a different lane may necessitate fine adjustments to speed which are not safe unless longitudinal safety buffers afford sufficient distances to the forward and rearward vehicles as to not engender a collision risk. In the case of insufficient longitudinal safety buffers, lane optimizations which would otherwise be beneficial may be impossible to carry out without suffering a greater safety cost than is the magnitude of the intended optimization benefit, and so the likelihood of suboptimal situations is correlated with a lack of sufficient following distances. Minimal frontal following distance also constitutes a general impediment to spatial awareness, as a greater angular percentage of the frontal windshield view is overtaken by the rear end of the frontal vehicle when following distance is decreased (in the case of larger frontal vehicles, even greater attention should be paid to this effect).

For all of these reasons, there is a great incentivizing factor to the driver of switching into a lane of greater following distance than that of the present lane of travel. This is the mechanism by which highway traffic behaves as a fluid and generally tends to even out regions of "pressure" (close vehicles) differential – in the extreme example, one lane is packed with cars and the adjacent lane is entirely free, which will cause drivers to merge into the free lane perhaps even until that lane itself contains a higher vehicle traffic density, which would then prompt some drivers to return to the first lane and so on until there is a general parity between the traffic densities of the two lanes. This is the most efficient manner of vehicular travel on the freeway, since it distributes and uses all of the available lane space instead of a certain subsection, and since higher space margins usually translate into higher travel speeds due to the increased stopping distance (i.e., the highest speed at which a driver may maintain adherence to the basic speed rule is greater)[4]. What the professional driver must therefore be aware of, however, is that if a particularly obvious and advantageous lane switch opportunity comes about in the simple light of increased following distance relative to that of the current lane, then it is also highly likely that other vehicles, both behind and (more relevantly) in front, will also execute such lane switches. It is therefore unwise to switch into the freer lane and rapidly accelerate to take advantage of the

---

[4] We discuss the basic speed rule in Chapter 6, under the "Determination of the freeway-vacant ideal travel speed" section.

increased following space, since other drivers in the old, denser lane may also be attempting the same switch, and since it only takes one incompetent driver (who fails to see the approaching vehicle, perhaps in his or her blind spot, and who may also fail to declare the lane switch with directional signals) to cause an accident. The professional driver must therefore take great care in any situations in which there is an appreciable speed differential between that of the travelling vehicle and that of the vehicles in any adjacent lane, since this difference in speed is what therefore can cause accidents to occur. Expecting to hold speed constant is therefore necessary to rightly declare following-distance-optimizing lane switches to be beneficial in the vast majority of circumstances. Once the new lane position is securely obtained, and if there is a need for such speed to begin with, then the driver may carefully and slowly accelerate in the new lane with an increased spatial awareness emphasis on potentially merging drivers from the adjacent lane – however most of the time, these types of following distance optimizing lane switches will procure increases in frontal following distance to the degree that much acceleration will not be safe, possible, or even needed, as the forwards position of the vehicle is still theoretically limited to the position of the travelling vehicle in front. This very point is emphasized in the mind of a professional driver, as altering relative distance behind a frontal vehicle, whose position is already a limiting factor to the driving vehicle's position, only constitutes a constant distance difference and is completely overshadowed by even small differences in speed – a variable which is integrated into distance – and as such, inconsequential absolute position-altering (relative to the frontal vehicle) will almost always pose much greater safety consequences than that of arrival-time consequences, assuming that the two vehicles are generally close enough as to need to travel at equal speeds. A 50 foot increase in following distance, for illustration, as a result of switching into a new lane yields a far greater and more impactful safety benefit than would be gained for arrival time optimization from a mere 50-feet-closer-to-destination benefit caused by accelerating accordingly in the new and slightly more open lane. It is therefore almost always wisest to take the safety benefit of maintaining the increased following distance in the new lane than the short-lived (and entirely reversible) forward position optimization by accelerating in the new lane to match whatever was the former following distance. If the next isolane frontal vehicle is a quarter of a mile down the freeway, on the other hand, then clearly one may safely accelerate to a more optimal speed in order to optimize arrival-to-destination time – however if the traffic on the highway were this sparse, the driver would have likely already been travelling at the desired speed to begin with. This also should illustrate that right lane travel in sparse traffic conditions in any form behind a proximate vehicle is suboptimal, since their deceleration in this lane is to be expected at some point in time when they prepare to enter the exit ramp: whereas the left and middle lane traveler would be much more wont to switch out of their lane and enter the right lane (or even better, the approaching exit lane, if any) before beginning the exit-preparatory deceleration.

We should also attend to the theoretical situation in which the second lane over to one side from the driver's present lane affords a more attractively large following distance buffer, however the lane in between (which would necessarily need to be traversed in order to reach the desired lane) presents circumstances of equal or worse following distance than that of the present lane of travel. On the surface of this situation, it seems that it may be wise to undergo a one-time, temporary safety cost in order to induce a longer-lasting lane travel circumstance in which the overall and enduring safety risk is much lower than that of the present, due to the increased following distance in the desired second-over lane. But in general, switching to lanes with tight merging gap margins (i.e., the short following distance of the immediately adjacent lane in this hypothetical) is even worse and more dangerous than just travelling in them, since the drivers in such a lane are likely attending to their own speed relative to the vehicle in front and are not being overly aware of other vehicles from the side which could be trying to merge into their front. The frontal driver in the new lane could decelerate (for whatever reason) and cause the merging vehicle to rear-end collide since the merging vehicle is spending thin spatial awareness resources on lateral scanning and may not even be able to decelerate him or herself without creating an identical situation for the driver behind. Clearly, this worrisome analysis applies exponentially more to lane switches of tight margins; if the adjacent lane is sufficiently sparse, then it may very well be optimal for the driver (going back to our present hypothetical) to cross the adjacent lane in order to merge into the most optimal second lane over from the original lane of travel. The desire to do so will, of course, be driven by the speed-urgency of the driver's destination and the degree to which the freer lane promises a larger following distance (keeping in mind that, if this figure is so comparatively large, it is likely to be soon "evened-out" by other drivers merging into the space). It is usually necessary, however, in this case, to execute a single lane merge into the interstitial lane, reconfirm safety margins and spatial awareness checks, and *then* to carefully execute a second lane switch into the destination lane – rather than crossing the two lanes from the first in one fast and dangerous motion, with one unitary lateral acceleration profile, which may risk collision from a potentially faster-travelling posterolateral vehicle from behind in the destination lane, which may not have been visible from the initial lane due to line-of-sight visual obstruction by a vehicle travelling in the interstitial lane. Multi-lane lane switches should therefore always be taken carefully and one at a time, unless if the entire relevant area of the highway is visually scanned and spatially guaranteed to be free of all allovehicular presence (in which case getting out of the way of the original-lane vehicles in one quick motion is actually beneficial). This situation is often encountered after the reopening of closed lanes, such as after passing an accident or road work, or when entering the highway (with the left or middle lane selected as the lane of travel) under very low traffic conditions. We do recommend keeping directional signals activated throughout the entire maneuver, however, for as long as there is an intention to merge into the next lane (keeping them on only serves to make the surrounding vehicles more tolerant and aware of the planned maneuver, which, as we already explained, constitutes no safety loss if the switch is aborted but does indeed constitute a safety gain if the lane switch comes to be executed).

Up unto this point we have concerned ourselves simply and solely with optimization of the frontal following distance, however this is only one component of the general longitudinal-axis distance gap which exists between the two closest vehicles to the fore-end and, oppositely, the aft-end of the vehicle in the lane of travel; there are of course safety benefits and subtle intervehicular dynamical ramifications pertaining to the lengthening of the rearwards distance buffer as well. What complicates this second factor is that it is intimately interlinked with the first and primary factor of *frontal* following distance: if the driver accelerates, he or she narrows frontal following distance by *lengthening* rearwards following distance, and on the other hand, if the driver decelerates, he or she lengthens frontal following distance at the expense of *shortening* that of rearwards safety buffer distance. We must therefore take the separate concepts of frontal and rearwards following distance and unify them into a singular "whole intervehicular isolane space" concept which considers the *whole space* between the rearwards vehicle and the frontwards vehicle and leaves the professional driver to optimize the relative proportions of frontal following distance to rearwards following distance (which together constitute the whole space). In the most basic of circumstances, it would seem evident to the novice driver that an even balance of 50% rearwards and 50% frontal following distances should be assigned by the vehicle's interstitial position – that it is to be in the exact middle of the two surrounding forward and rearward vehicles – but however certain circumstances may call for certain optimal adjustments that would interrupt the even balance of this proportion (in an extreme example, if the driver were safely following a frontal vehicle 700 feet away at equal and ideal speed, with the nearest rearwards driver being 2,300 feet behind the driver, then clearly there is no need to decrease speed in order to ensure a full and balanced 1,500 feet of following distance in between each vehicle since the safety margins

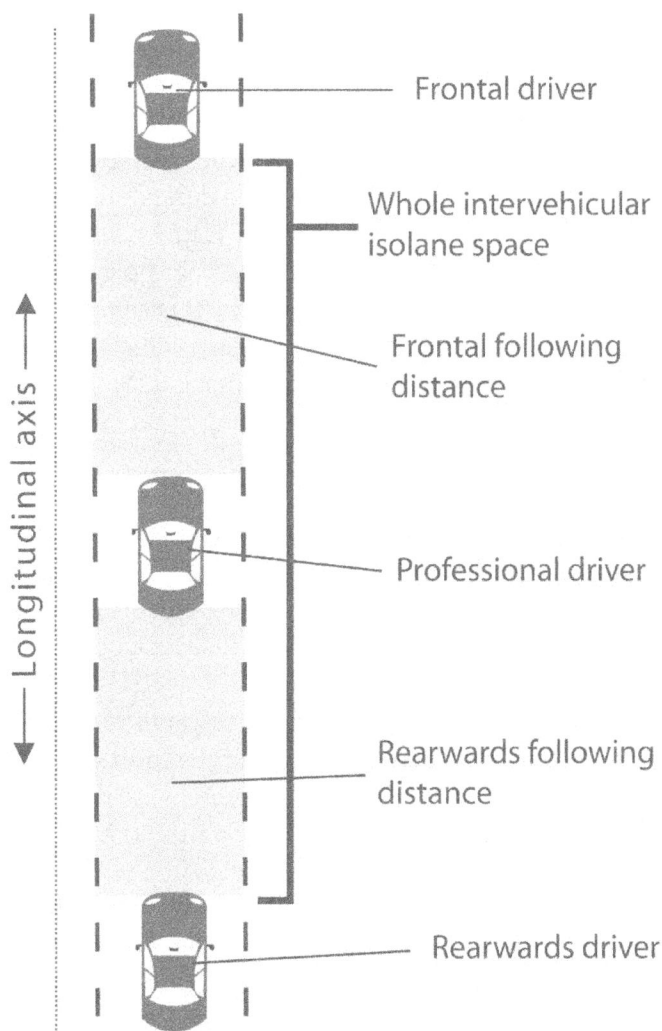

Figure 12 – The whole intervehicular isolane space, longitudinally divided into its two constituent frontal and rearwards following distances

are already plentifully extensive). In general, a greater relative emphasis on and proportional balance to *frontal* following distance is appropriate for the following reasons:

1. The driver of the vehicle who rear-end collides the frontal vehicle is almost always responsible in the legal sense;

2. Frontal collisions of equal force are potentially more dangerous to the driver than that of being rear-end collided, since the typical nature of most vehicle designs is that there is more cushioning distance of vehicle frame behind the driver and to the rear than that of his or her position to the front (however we very cautiously make this statement, which may not always hold true for every vehicle, due to vast differences in impact safety systems and the generally greater amount of momentum-insulating mass constituted by the engine components to the front);

3. Greater frontal following distance in the case of the rapid deceleration of the frontal vehicle may afford lateral escape opportunities that would not otherwise be possible were specifically-frontal following distance insufficient;

4. The rearward driver is highly likely to respond to a decreased following distance caused by driver deceleration with his or her own deceleration, widening the overall whole intervehicular isolane space – whereas on the other hand, the frontal travelling vehicle, if more closely approached, is not at all likely (or safely able) to compensate by accelerating to restore the safety buffer since highway drivers spend most of their time looking ahead instead of monitoring following vehicles in the rearview mirror;

5. Greater distance from airborne debris associated with a collision which may occur in front of the vehicle, which could pose sizeable safety hazards even if the provisions stated in reason #3 are sufficient to allow successful evasion of the disabled vehicles themselves; and

6. Vehicles from any lateral lane which may be potentially seeking to merge into the lane of travel (thereby cutting off safety buffer space and shortening the whole intervehicular isolane space) are probably more watchful of the posterolateral vehicle's frontal acceleration, and more hesitant to make the lane switch because of this possibility, than that of being careful about the potential *deceleration* of an *antero*lateral travelling vehicle – i.e., the probability of such other vehicles' merging into spans of frontal or rearwards following distance is lower therefore if frontal distance is greater (more merge-deterring, due to greater tendency to fear acceleration) than if rearward distance is greater (more merge-inviting, due to lesser tendency to fear deceleration).

Relative prioritization of the frontal following zone is called for in any situation in which the vehicle's stopping distance is increased, such as would result from hydrometeor-induced wetness or any otherwise slippery material covering the surface of the freeway. In some unique situations, greater relative prioritization of the rearwards distance buffer may be in order. If behavioral analysis indicates that more rearward relative longitudinal position would bring the vehicle closer to a vehicle observed to exhibit dangerous road-rage or substance-impairment symptoms, then a modest frontal following distance of basic, safe dimensions will do well to keep the driver away from the areas of potentially greater risk. If a lane switch is intended to be executed in a more-forward-than-desirable longitudinal position within the whole intervehicular isolane space, due to a lack of merging opportunities in the posterolateral region, then a momentary and signaling travel period parallel to the intended merging region (with directional signals already activated) is beneficial to warn the relevant drivers of the impending merge, as opposed to speeding up to the gap zone and quickly executing the merge having only just exited the blind spot of the vehicle to be merged in front of. However great care must be taken in this situation to ensure sufficient basic following distance to the frontal vehicle, as adjustments to speed in preparation for a merge (and while paying most spatial attention to the lateral rather than frontal areas of the vehicle) can cause the driver to lose focus of the driver in front, risking a frontal rear-ending collision if the frontal vehicle decelerates before the driver escapes the lane by means of the lane switch. If such a lane switch is necessary in the first place under tighter longitudinal distance buffers, then it is likely wise to attempt to create an increase in frontal following distance first before attempting the lane switch. This transitions our discussion nicely into another very relevant topic related to the "whole intervehicular isolane space" concept, which concerns actionable tactics to change the total length of the space itself and the potential ramifications of doing so.

Our initial lane-optimization example of simply switching into a lane with greater frontal following distance serves as a useful tool for general and initial lane switch optimization analysis, however the professional driver must holistically evaluate effects on the entire "whole intervehicular isolane space". That is to say, by the illustrative example of an extreme situation, that if a potential lane switch would afford 10 extra feet of frontal following distance, but minimizing rearwards following distance by 100 feet, this is unlikely to be a justified lane switch since the whole space between the rearward and frontal vehicle is minimized; in this case, an increase in frontal following distance could be obtained merely by decelerating in the present lane of travel and thereby converting some of the extra and less-necessary rearwards following distance into much needed frontal following distance (in this example, there is an extreme disparity in their relative balance with 10 feet in front and 100 feet behind). In the same way, on the other hand, if a potential lane switch affords no improvement or even a slight *reduction* in frontal following distance, but which would also place the vehicle much farther in front of the new rearwards vehicle, then the lane switch may very well indeed be justified since *whole intervehicular isolane space* is enlarged, and therefore a subsequent deceleration in the new lane would appropriately balance each frontal and rearwards following distance zone – having optimally extended both zones as opposed to remaining in the first lane and being stuck with a shorter following distance. We should warn against the extreme case of this maneuver, however: as there are always inherent risks to switching lanes in the first place, it must be sensibly judged by the professional driver that the intended benefit of the increased safety margins as a result of the lane switch does in fact outweigh the inherent collision risk of executing the lane switch in the first place. Therefore, if it is impossible to merge into the otherwise-desirable lane without maintaining a basic, healthy margin of frontal following distance to the anterolateral vehicle, then the maneuver should not be executed (regardless of the potential increase in whole intervehicular isolane space per the increased rearwards distance) due to the heavy collision risk of merging that closely behind a vehicle, which would outweigh the safety margin optimization benefit. In this case, if following distance margins in the present lane allow, it may be optimal to decelerate in the present lane in order to get sufficiently behind the anterolateral vehicle such that the beneficial lane switch can be made without incurring a safety cost greater than that of the lane optimization benefit. As in any case of deceleration in the whole intervehicular isolane space, additional spatial awareness attention must be momentarily given to the vehicle behind to ensure that the rearwards safety margin does not dwindle below critical minimum levels.

Changes in either region of frontal or rearwards following distance can induce impactful intervehicular effects. The most relevant and basic of these is the increased likelihood that vehicles on either side of the frontal or rearwards intervehicular space gap will merge into the gap when it is larger and increasing; this redefines the frontal or rearward vehicle accordingly (depending on where they merge) to the driver and therefore cuts off either frontal or rearward following distance at a closer point, prompting the driver's deceleration (in response to a frontally merging vehicle) or *slight* acceleration (in response to a rearwards merging vehicle – and only perhaps even at that, due to the aforementioned priority of frontal versus rearwards following distance) in order to restore the proper relative proportional balances of rearwards to frontwards following distance. When the whole intervehicular isolane space in shortened in this manner, the proportional balance of frontward vs. rearward following distance will likely itself change (especially under tighter safety margins) and should almost always grant a greater proportional share of space to the frontal region than to the rearwards region, since the scarcity of distance resources serves to highlight which of the two spaces is more critical – the frontal. Regardless of this balance, it is clearly optimal to travel inside an altogether larger intervehicular isolane space, which is cut short when other vehicles merge immediately in front of or behind the driver's vehicle. We then may seem to arrive at a paradoxical conclusion that increasing following distance may not always be optimal, since it may induce a foreign lane traveler to switch in front of the vehicle and reduce following distance to less than that which it would have been were the original following distance maintained (and the would-have-merged vehicle in front therefore made to stay in his or her own lane). We respond to this tragically complicated inconsistency with the following dicta:

1. This issue is almost exclusively a factor of any substantial relevance only in high-traffic, low-speed conditions. We will discuss this special set of conditions in a future section, however here we will state that careful attention to potential frontally merging allovehicles and safe deceleration after such merges are made is a safety prioritization task which is unlikely to have any appreciably negative impact on arrival time, due to the already slow conditions of freeway travel.

2. It is certainly conceivable, in theory, that under certain speed and following distance circumstances, it would be better for the professional driver *not* to increase frontal following distance to an otherwise more optimal degree due to the heightened likelihood of an anterolateral vehicle merging into the frontal zone, and of being left with even lesser frontal following distance. However, it is extremely unlikely that there will not be enough rearwards space for safe deceleration and restoration of the frontal distance after the

other vehicle's merge since, were there not, there would probably also be insufficient space for the merge to occur in the first place, or the driver was massively failing to institute a proper relative balance of frontal versus rearwards proportional space in the whole intervehicular isolane space.

3. As we stated before, vehicles merging into regions of high vehicular density to low vehicular density is the natural mechanism by which highway traffic evenly distributes itself in a fluid fashion to make maximum economy of the available space. When safety margins are lower due to higher traffic density (as would be the present trend for the driver in question, who is having an anterolateral vehicle merge into his or her frontal following distance), global traffic speed will be naturally lowered, and the initial frontal following distance requirements will be accordingly lowered.

4. If all drivers were to shut out globally optimal lane switches by (perhaps dangerously) insisting a more proximate following distance to the frontal vehicle, then the natural process described above would be more difficult, slower, and more dangerous to occur. It may therefore be taken as an example of reciprocal altruism not to close out the merge-volitional anterolateral driver in the hopes that the establishment of this global standard will benefit the driver when such lane switches are optimal for him or herself.

5. If the driver does maintain overly proximate following distance to the frontal driver, his or her perception of what constitutes the maximum following distance necessary to dissuade the anterolateral merger from making the lane switch may not accord with that of the merge-volitional driver if he or she is aggressive, in a particular high-urgency driving situation, or under the effects of substance impairment. Therefore, an even more dangerous situation may be created in which the anterolateral driver persists with

the merge into the unnecessarily tight safety margins created by the stubborn present driver; in this case, the unnecessary stubbornness and aggressiveness of both drivers combine to create a mutually suboptimal situation in which collision risk is greater for both vehicles – not to mention the third, originally frontal, and perhaps entirely ignorant vehicle in the present lane in front (the vehicle anterolateral to the merging vehicle), who may instinctively decelerate if horns are sounded from one of the combative vehicles behind, which would certainly lead to a high collision risk involving two or all of the vehicles, one of which was entirely innocent and unaware of the goings on behind.

We therefore conclude that it is generally optimal to eschew consideration of potential merging vehicles which would not otherwise enter such enlarged frontal following distance, and to continue with longitudinal-axis safety margin optimization as one would. If a merging vehicle is detected in front, the professional driver will respond with the standard reactive procedures of decelerative readjustment to the optimal safety margins given the new shortened intervehicular isolane space. The likelihood of such frontal merging vehicles is of course proportional not only to the viability of the frontal following distance itself, but also the traffic density and following distance conditions of the side-lane vehicles themselves. Clearly, if the lane to the side is far denser than that of the present lane, a frontal merging vehicle can be predictively anticipated. Conversely, if a lateral lane's vehicular traffic density is *lower* than that of the present lane, then it may be the driver him or herself who will be seeking to execute a following distance optimizing lane switch.

Our discussion of following distances has hereunto omitted reference to quantitative distance figures which are appropriate and desirable at a given speed; our qualitative analysis, however, is more useful since the professional driver will need to respond to changing situation with following distance adjustments of too great a potential variety to numerically quantify – if even possible to begin with. It is important for the driver to understand the general principles surrounding lane optimization for following distance and the ideal relative balances of frontwards versus rearwards distance instead of attempting to develop a structured table of memorized distances and balancing coefficients – driving humans are not computers, and as such they do much better in applying learned principles to established instinctive responses than trying to execute numerical approximations of rapidly-changing distance values. Numerical attention to time, however, removes the complicated integral relation of speed and distance and makes such quantitative processes more feasible to the common driver; the "two-second" rule is therefore often touted (in a general, non-freeway-specific context) as a minimum safety threshold of following distance (that is, that two seconds should elapse before the absolute forward position of the frontal driver is reached by that of the driver's own vehicle). The professional driver's assessment of proper quantitative frontal following distance, however, is not limited to such trite and generalized aphorisms which completely exclude the necessary consideration of other factors which may in fact greatly lengthen the minimum two-second following distance (such as the anticipation of rapid deceleration or slippery road conditions). There is therefore little use in categorizing every possible combination of factors into precise situational minimum following distance times – since the mental resources needed for such enormous categorization and memorization would vastly exceed that which is needed for a simple and informed qualitative analysis of the need for increased frontal following distance, using instinctive driving experience as a starting point.

Longitudinal-axis safety margin and following distance optimization by means of attention to frontal following space and by means of executing beneficial lane switches holds the potential (in one of the largest ways which is discussed in this book) to avoid vehicular accidents and to increase the viability of other speed and/or fuel-efficiency optimizations which would not have otherwise been possible under conditions of suboptimal safety margins. The implications of this field of concepts and optimization potentialities will hold a heavy continued relevance throughout the remainder of our discussion on lane optimization and on freeway spatial maneuvering as a whole.

Predictive deceleration and collision zone avoidance

Premonitory identification of frontal regions of impending rapid deceleration or even collision give way to a wide array of optimizations which the professional driver can perform to: (1) reduce crash risk, (2) decelerate in a more optimal manner if deceleration will be necessary anyway, and (3) maximize arrival-time economy and fuel-efficiency by eliminating or attenuating the need for momentum-wasteful deceleration by altogether escaping the frontal region in question by evasively switching into another lane (which therefore loosely classifies this topic as an appropriate discussion for our lane optimization chapter, however it is heavily interlinked with speed optimization which we will discuss in a future section). These optimizations can be broken down into two constituent discussions: that of predictive identification of high-risk frontal deceleration zones, and that of proper response to them.

A good share of accidents on the highway occur due to driver failure to execute the current task of deceleration zone identification (let alone prediction) and subsequent rear-end collision caused by delayed deceleration of the driver's own vehicle. The most common cause for such rapid and negative speed differentials is encountering a sudden zone of severely slowed or altogether halted traffic due to an accident, road work, or lane closures of any cause. High level strategic factors which we already discussed (such as the driver's attention to traffic information devices) may do well to provide a supplementary sense of anticipation for such factors; however, in the tactical sense, methods of predicting and identifying such regions of rapid deceleration must come from and only from spatial awareness information, since strategic information sources such as web-enabled traffic devices will never be able to encapsulate the tactical, present reality of those conditions to which the professional driver must respond on the road. Forwards path-of-travel scanning will identify regions of slowed or entirely halted traffic ahead, however road curvature, road inclination, and frontal vehicle proximity (to whatever degree those factors are present) will each contribute to a difficulty or even complete impossibility with regards to procuring long-range path-of-travel visual scanning feedback. In these situations, a heightened sense of risk must accompany frontal following distance length assignment due to the possibility of encountering rapid traffic-related deceleration without prior visual indication. In some limited situations, altering interlane position to either side of the frontal vehicle for increased visibility to the traffic down the road may be beneficial if no lateral lane vehicles are present as to make the interlane position adjustment potentially dangerous – however this represents only a small and temporary optimization in the face of continued and potentially greater risk associated with vehicular interlane adjustment as would decenter the driver's vehicle from the middle of the travel lane (we will discuss visibility related lane optimization in depth in a subsequent section). The prevailing reality is that many traffic situations will obscure long-range frontal path-of-travel visual scanning and must therefore engender a heightened sense that rapid deceleration may soon occur in the frontal vehicle, prompting an according extension in following distance if possible. The second field of predictive strategies for frontal zone deceleration concerns lane switch related collisions which may occur either in front of the frontal vehicle or (in a manner easier to identify) behind the frontal vehicle and therefore into the immediate frontal zone of the driver's following distance. In the first case, an anterolateral vehicle travelling in either lane adjacent to the present lane of travel may attempt a lane switch without noticing the other vehicle in his or her blind spot, or may successfully complete the lane switch in front of the frontal vehicle and then decelerate for whatever reason, causing a rear-end collision between the two frontal, isolane vehicles due to the momentarily lessened following distance which resulted from the lane switch (and which probably was unwisely short for such a lane switch to begin with). Collisions such as these, occurring in front of the present driver, clearly pose an additional safety risk to him or her since the collided vehicles are likely to slow down after collision (or perhaps are forced to because of engine disability, in the case of more serious accidents) and may otherwise cast flying objects of debris into the airspace soon to be occupied by the driver's windshield. The driver must take any sign of a lane switch involving the frontal vehicle, therefore, as a predictive indicator that a collision may occur – and must therefore attempt to lengthen following distance (or, ideally, facilitate a safe evasive lane switch away from the zone) whenever he or she notices the activated directional signals of an anterolateral driver indicating that a lane switch is planned involving the frontal vehicle. The same is even more true and relevant for lane switches which occur behind the frontal vehicle – not only for their closer forward proximity to the driver's vehicle, but also for the heightened likelihood of a rear-end collision between the two frontal vehicles resulting from a momentarily panicked or otherwise caused-to-decelerate original frontal driver upon noticing the rapid, aggressive, and perhaps alarming merge of the merging driver in their rear-view or passenger side mirror (which can distort perceptions of forward proximity, as we have seen). Therefore, *especially* in cases of seeming anterolateral vehicle lane switches involving the frontal vehicle by virtue of their destination *behind* the frontal vehicle, it is critical for the professional driver to anticipate the possibility of such collisions by deceleration and by active seeking for evasive opportunities to escape from the lane if necessary.

The soundest escape measure in the event that a rapid frontal deceleration occurs is to already have lengthened following distance and to have already scanned for lane switch opportunities by predictive anticipation. The professional driver must always scan the behaviors of anterolateral vehicles for indications that a lane switch among them and the frontal vehicle may occur; then, immediately, responsive deceleration and active lateral scanning should be initiated to evaluate the prospect of switching into an evasive lateral lane if necessary. If there is not any safety-margin dissuasion to executing a lateral lane switch, in the event of a declared lane switch intention of an anterolateral driver, then there is absolutely no reason not to execute the lane switch in order to premonitorily evade the frontal zone which could soon become rapidly decelerative. This is not to say that every other highway driver is incapable of executing a safe lane switch without sizeable risk that a collision will occur, but rather to suggest that a free and open lane switch opportunity in this case would only serve to minimize whatever potential collision risk there is to the lane switch occurring in front of the driver. It may not always be the case, however, that the permissive safety-margins of such an evasive lane switch maneuver warrant the professional driver's already having been in that new lane for two reasons: firstly, even given two potential lanes of equal frontal following distance, the professional driver would choose the one in which a frontal driver is merging *out of* instead of *into*, due to the likely positioning of any lane-switch-related accident; secondly, if the frontal following distance parameters of both lanes were otherwise completely sufficient for basic safety, then there is no need to merge into the other lane which may afford a slightly greater following distance, since lane switching (as we stated at the beginning of this chapter) should generally be minimized and only executed when the benefits of such a maneuver would substantially overcome the relative costs of not staying in the present lane. It is therefore appropriate to increase emphasis on lateral spatial awareness scanning in the event that a merge is seen to be about to take place involving the frontal vehicle, since the inherent risk that this may create a dangerous collision warrants the exploration of lane switches which may be at worst evasive maneuvers to an observed frontal collision, and at best (and most commonly), predictive optimizations which put the driver in a much better responsive position if a collision does occur, and in no worse position in the overwhelming likelihood that the anterolateral driver's merge ends successfully. At this, still, the having-merged status of the anterolateral driver, potentially freeing up a merging

156

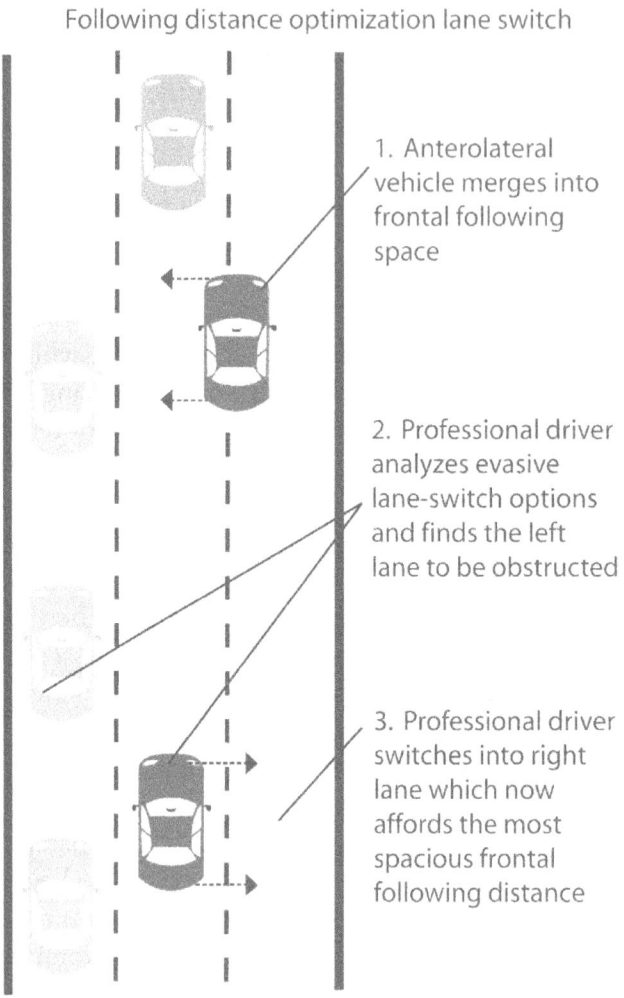

Figure 13 – The professional driver responds to changing frontal following distance spaces by executing optimal lane switches which increase safety margins for collision avoidance.

gap in his or her original lane, and combined with the decreased following distance at any rate to be encountered upon the merge of this vehicle in the driver's original lane, may indeed (in some conditions) create a situation in which lane switching into the old lane of the having-merged driver would be done a few seconds thereafter anyways as a general longitudinal-axis safety optimizing lane switch.

Returning to the far more likely frontal vehicle deceleration cause of coming upon suddenly slow or halted traffic, lane optimization can also serve in some cases to increase the efficiency of the inevitable deceleration to the new slow (or even fully stopped) traffic speed which must be achieved anyway before some rapidly approaching point. Deceleration from one given speed to another given speed is always more efficiently and safely conducted when the distance over which the deceleration occurs is greater, for the following reasons: (1) it is safer due to the decreased suddenness with which brakes must be applied, decreasing risk of a rear-end collision with an inattentive rearwards vehicle; (2) it is more efficient due to the greater potential that a gradual decrease in vehicle's momentum may be at least initially sufficient for facilitating the first part of the deceleration instead of wasting the having been spent energy as friction in the brakes – energy that was actively spent propelling the vehicle to the more forward position preceding brake usage (in the short stopping distance case) as opposed to the long prior termination in accelerative energy expenditure as the vehicle enters the long and gradual deceleration stopping distance (in the alternative and optimum case); (3) it is more efficient due to decreased wear on brakes and decreased inertial stress on other internal components of the vehicle related to rapid deceleration; and (4) it is more efficient and more safe due to the greater time in which the professional driver will have to evaluate the potentially variable end position at which the final lowered speed must be attained. For all of these reasons, if a free and open lane of greater following distance runs next to the driver's current lane, and with the visible expectation of traffic-related deceleration necessity, then it will be optimal and justified for the driver to switch into the open lane which affords a longer deceleration distance as opposed to that of the shortened frontal safety margin in the original lane. Care, however, must be taken as it regards anterolateral vehicles in the original lane who may merge into the freer lane through which deceleration is being carried out.

Lane closure and obstructive object avoidance

The necessity of continuously scanning the entirety of the vehicle's frontal path-of-travel for the plethora of potential obstructions which would require responsive driver action is considered a basic freeway driving skill and needs not to be formally justified in this discussion. This discussion, while not as profound or vivacious as our prior discussion concerning such insightful intricacies of frontal versus rearwards following distance balancing and their interrelated effects, still duly merits its share of attention as areas of higher predicted obstructive object likelihood would certainly evince a preference to travel in a safer lane – a consideration to be balanced against all of the other described lane-optimization effects (as it is with each of these sections). It is unfortunate that the left-most lane of the freeway, often the most optimal for long-distance travel under certain sets of parameters (and invariably the highest-speed) is also the lane in which there is likely the greatest chance of physically obstructive (i.e. lane-space intruding) objects, due to its being an edge of the highway (therefore being one of two resting places for dispelled intrafreeway ejecta) and, in comparison to the right lane edge, due to its typically having far narrower of an interstitial lane-edge-to-highway-edge space – as opposed to the right edge of the right lane, which is typically afforded an appreciably wider breakdown lane into which any debris may rest farther from the driving lane portion of the highway. If wind is of substantial magnitude and is perpendicular to the highway travel vector, special attention to the leeward edge of the highway must be taken (and even more so in the case of the existence of a median or rail-guard structure, which could potentially trap airborne debris) – although the windward-edge driver must also take inventory of the human and floral structures windward to his or her edge from which a strong wind could cast debris of any sort. (The existence of the wind parameter, therefore, is less of a left versus right prioritizing consideration, but rather a consideration which should unilaterally heighten attention to debris avoidance factors.) During and after periods of road-work in windy conditions, the standardized orange traffic safety drums (also called "barrels") may be toppled over and even rolled into the lane of traffic if winds are strong enough (this phenomenon is more familiar to drivers in areas which are distinguished simultaneously by both high human development (to warrant extensive use of such traffic devices) and by high average wind speed or high climatological frequency of strong-wind conditions, for example, areas such as coastal New England and Nova Scotia during the winter and shoulder seasons which satisfy both risk parameters above).

So far we have examined conditions which may make the edges of either side-lane more dangerous as it concerns the likelihood of encountering obstructive debris than in the center lane(s). However, sudden debris-reaction anticipation is necessary in every lane, and in every lane there exists an analyzable probability which would indicate the safest lane by this metric with which a holistic consideration of lane choice can be made. In non-winter times of year, or in above-freezing climates, the two most likely predictive indications of interior-lane debris response are: (1) vehicles carrying loose and/or uncovered materials either attached above or behind the vehicle, or in the basin of a pickup-truck, and (2) debris resulting from a vehicular collision (which we have already discussed). In hiemal climates, an even greater danger exists in the form of frozen hydrometeoric accretion and/or accumulation on the top surface of the vehicle (or any combination of these), which could attach to the roof of a frontward vehicle and fall off with great inertial force into the windshield of a following driver. A layer of ice accretion on top of snow accumulation can exacerbate the risks associated with this debris factor, both holding in place the frozen mass until high wind-resistance (and therefore speed, and therefore the potential danger of falling ice) is sufficient to prompt its dislodging, and also attaching the heavy mass of the snow to the sharp, hard, and qualitatively piercing ice which would represent potentially catastrophic news for the following driver in the worst circumstance. Although full penetration of windshields is generally impossible in the absence of significantly higher forces, still, a cracked windshield creates an equally disastrous and unsafe situation for the utter ruining of the driver's frontal spatial awareness visual scanning ability. The professional driver driving in a hibernal climate zone is therefore always aware of the meteorological conditions which occurred prior to driving and keeps a close eye on the roofs of frontal vehicles – giving heed to the probabilistic safety optimization of switching out of a lane in which travel behind a potentially lethal ice-cadence situation is possible. Special evasive attention should be given to tall trucks in climatological and meteorological contexts in which this potential crisis is possible, for three reasons: (1) large semi-trucks simply support a larger top surface area, thereby increasing the amount of potential snow and ice which could fall onto the following driver's windshield; (2) the height from which the debris would fall is above that of regular allovehicles, thereby increasing the gravitational potential energy which will contribute to the exertion of an even greater impact force on the windshield of the following vehicle than if the veritable avalanche were to originate from the top of a shorter vehicle; (3) the increased angular difficulty of visually detecting such snow or ice accumulations on the top surface of a truck, due to its increased height (in this light, it is possible that the rear, visible top surface edge of the truck may be seen to be snow-and-ice-free, while in reality there exists plenty of accumulation over the invisible surface areas of the truck's more-frontal top surfaces); and (4) the aerodynamically boxy design of semi-trucks may enable such accumulations to stay on for longer than would be possible with regular passenger vehicles, thereby causing a greater likelihood for the deposition of such accumulations to occur on a length of road of higher travel speed and of longer travel time (a description fitting for nothing other than the freeway), whereas the more aerodynamic regular passenger vehicles would be more likely to have deposited their top surface winter accumulations before entering the highway while travelling at a lower speed. For all of these reasons, the professional driver is particularly hesitant to drive behind trucks in the winter (that is, without at least a healthy following distance) and will desire to optimize lane choice accordingly.

Lane closures pertaining to accident emergency response and general road construction constitute a special class obstructive-object likelihood lane-profiling situations in that (1) they are intentional human obstructions of regulated temporality, (2) they therefore are constructed with the intention that approaching drivers will need to be signaled to perform a lane switch (typically prompting the erection of amply fore-distant warning signs before the necessary switch), and (3) that travel in the obstructed lane is wholly impossible, as opposed to being a conditional dissuading factor towards travel in that lane which may be outweighed by other factors. The first two factors enumerated above generally classify temporary lane closures as posing a lesser general risk than that of obstructive, foreign errata which may violate the spatial extents of the vehicle's path-of-travel – however special attention must be paid to their existence in order to optimize execution of the lane switch and also to prepare in time for the deceleration which they will almost always require. Road work related lane closures are almost always held on one or more side lanes of the freeway – however in rare construction situations (such as MassDOT's 2012 reconstruction of the I-495/Rt.3 junction in the Boston metropolitan area), the flow of highway traffic may be diverted into two laterally disjunct lanes bisected by the construction work. In this case, common sense indicates that the more sparse and wide lane should be chosen (a choice to be promptly indicated by activating the appropriate directional signal) – since the previous factors controlling optimal lane position are probably altered, in most or in whole, by the new and extremely different layout of traffic. These construction areas (and also lateral lane closures) necessarily include some sort of physical demarcation which typically constitutes the nearest physical obstructive object to the vehicle. In case of loose traffic drums, special increases to following distance must be made due to the possibility of the frontal driver colliding with one of these structures on the side (especially if they indicate signs of inebriation or road-rage) and therefore executing a rapid decelerative braking in panicked response to their driving malfeasance. Solid and continuous structures such as concrete traffic median blocks typically exude a stronger and more severe sense of border avoidance priority – however lateral/anterolateral collision with a tight lane-closure periphery structure could always occur, and therefore travelling in such areas of artificially heightened traffic density should prompt an increase in following distance proportional to the speed of the traffic (with higher speeds against such tight boundaries being more dangerous). Returning to the other and more simple case of one-side highway lane closures' diverting traffic to the other side of the highway, general deference to our previously discussed proper merging procedure under stressful traffic circumstances should be made as one executes the necessary lane switch. The optimization potential here is to already have been in any of the continuing lanes in order to avoid the lane switch, which improves both safety, speed, and fuel-efficiency in the ways which we have already shown. Executing this optimization requires earlier foreknowledge of the impending lane closure merge in reference to the other drivers, which may be obtained by (1) superior long-range frontal path-of-travel scanning technique and prevalence, seeking for electronic signs (often illuminated with a large arrow pointing in the direction of the merge) declaring the upcoming closure, consequent frontal traffic patterns, and/or the lane closure structures themselves, (2) driver foreknowledge of the present road work schedules affecting the present freeway, of particular consideration at night, and (3) strategic incorporations of tertiary source traffic data including live accident report data streams and/or pre-drive investigation as to road work conditions that are ongoing and planned for the time and length of planned freeway travel. Care must be taken that visual attention costs in executing any of the three above lane-closure anticipation methods do not outweigh that which the benefit of executing the necessary lane switch (if any) earlier promises: in almost all cases, even if the driver were to remain in the expiring lane for much distance, he or she would be able to merge into the narrowed flow of traffic with relative safety and ease if following the proper procedures for doing so which we outlined in the previous chapter.

The remaining critical concept to explain as it regards the obstructive object avoidance lane optimization is the necessity of factoring in an analysis of the viability of lateral escape margins should a merge into a lane more distant from an approaching hazard become necessary. For this purpose, we return to the "merging lane risk coefficient" terminology which we established in the previous chapter as a means of quickly and subjectively qualifying the level of difficulty which the lane in question would pose to the driver travelling in the next lane over who wishes to merge into the lane in question. If a relative parity in other lane optimization factors is lending particular relevance to the present obstructive object avoidance optimization, or if an overall heightened likelihood of encountering obstructive and potentially dangerous errata on the freeway accomplishes the same, then a particular emphasis must be given in determining each lane's relative safety to the condition of the "merging lane risk coefficient" (how difficult it would be to merge) of the lane into which a driver would theoretically escape in order to avoid a sudden obstructive object (typically this would refer to the traffic density of the lane to the right of the left-most lane, if we are considering the safety of travelling in the left-most left, or to the traffic density of the lane to the left of the right-most lane, if we are considering the safety of the travelling in the right-most lane). If it is judged, for instance, that whatever current conditions are combining as to make the right lane slightly more probable than the left to contain dangerous, obstructive errata – but that the lateral escape possibilities in the right lane *by far* outweigh that of those in left-lane travel – then in this (highly unlikely and solely academic) example, the professional driver favors travel in the right lane versus the left lane, ignoring of course all other constituent (and likely far more relevant) factors in the lane optimization process. Due to the general tendency of traffic to evenly distribute over a given area of highway space, however, this effect is somewhat minimal: the lane optimization question as it pertains to obstructive object avoidance will most usually ask whether or not there is any substantial likelihood for a hazard in a given lane, and if so, will suggest avoiding travel in the lane regardless of the merging lane risk coefficient of either of the surrounding escape lanes (since the risk of properly merging out of a potentially dangerous lane, for instance in which the driver would be travelling in front of a semi-truck travelling at 65mph and covered in 6 inches of granular snow which is itself loosely held in place by a thin 1/8 inch coating of ice accretion, would be minimal compared to the risk of remaining in this lane, in the case of a rather extreme example).

Lane designation compliance

It may be keenly noticed that we have insofar omitted much of any reference to the regulatory and legal traffic rules which govern freeway travel, as they are indeed of significant tactical relevance to the professional driver (as we shall see in future sections). The most obvious and well-known manner in which this statement holds true concerns speed limits and their role in speed optimization, which is an absolutely enormous factor for the professional driver's consideration which we will investigate in depth in the following chapter. In this section, we only seek describe that speed limits are not the sole means by which traffic rules regulate highway travel: lane choice itself is informed by various regulatory designations which vary from state to state and country to country. We will save a more elaborate philosophical discussion on whether or not it is the responsibility of the professional driver to obey traffic laws in the sense of a categorical imperative for a later discussion; no matter what the reader's persuasions are concerning that question, it is incontrovertible that being pulled over by a traffic enforcement officer is suboptimal and should be endeavored to be avoided, since it is (1) fuel-inefficient due to the need of cancelling established vehicular momentum by wastefully decelerating to a stop, and then needing to reaccelerate to highway speed (an overall vastly increased energy expenditure per unit distance than that of uninterrupted travel), (2) arrival-time inefficient due to the obvious delay and added time expenditure, (3) economically inefficient due to the opportunity costs of both law enforcement and driver spent time,

(4) risky from a safety perspective due to the likely necessity of executing lane changes in order to get over to the right-side breakdown lane, (4) of decreasing frontal visual scanning spatial awareness interest due to the distraction of the officer in the rear-view mirror, and (5) of needing to re-accelerate under potentially difficult traffic circumstances after the stop is finished, and (6) especially risky for non-professional drivers in that they may afterwards overcompensate any sort of corrective, over-conservative driving behavior (such as travelling 50mph in a flow of 72mph traffic, creating a large and potentially dangerous space-speed differential) or in that they are psychologically unable to continue in driving without distracted mental attention to the cyclical "control loop" of highway information processing (these last enumerated factors of course will not hold true for the professional driver). If the reader is him or herself a law enforcement officer, then lane designation compliance will clearly not constitute much or any of an impactful factor in tactical lane-optimization decision making, due to the non-existence of the aforementioned sub-optimalities (we recapitulate that this statement is constrained to the purely *tactical* sense – such officers may be influenced by certain high-level strategic factors such as obedience to the same traffic rules which they enforce, however that consideration is exterior to our solely tactical scope of focus). The professional driver will always be aware pre-drive of the lane designation measures which are in effect for the jurisdictions in which he or she will be driving. It should be noted that traffic-law enforcement stops due to solely lane-designation noncompliance is excessively rare (except for extremely explicit cases, such as HOV lane prerequisite noncompliance). What we are primarily concerned with here, then, is travel in the left-most lane of the highway – which is sometimes reserved for passing only (called a "passing lane" in North American terminology or an "overtaking lane" in Britain). It is the knowledge of even a novice freeway driver that the left lane of a three or four lane freeway is often the best for long-distance travel as the average speed tends to be highest in this lane (and therefore the most time-efficient), assuming that the driver's decided appropriate speed is still possible

in traffic-flow conditions of the left lane (we will discuss potential discrepancies in left-lane traffic flow speed in a future section). Traffic enforcement officers, however, are known to use left-lane passing-only designations as justifiable excuses for executing a stop in the case that other concerning behavior is witnessed, such as variable interlane position which may indicate an impaired driver – however this of course does not pertain to our present description of the professional driver, and so we can conclude that the risk of being pulled over for illegally travelling in a passing-only left lane is generally lower than that for speeding. Great regional variations exist in this enforcement; the slow left-lane travelling driver in Texas (where permanent "Left Lane For Passing Only" signs are common) would be taking greater risk than in Massachusetts, where permanent signs to this effect are few to none, and where it is technically illegal though wholly an accepted social norm (though not unless travelling at the speed of the flow of traffic). Some other US states, such as Virginia and Maryland, categorically permit left-lane travel as long as the vehicle is going at least as fast as the speed limit, and others, such as New Hampshire and Connecticut, permit left-lane travel on the condition that speed is matched to that of the flow of traffic. Another small yet notable safety peculiarity regarding the left-lane is that, in the rare though occasionally certain case of wrong-way drivers (indicating the type of uninformed and likely insecure driver as to be driving on their sense of right to begin with), it is likely that they will be travelling in the left-lane which would risk a precarious head-on collision if evasion opportunities are limited, a point which is sometimes used as justification for left-lane passing-only regulations. In this light (of the left lane being reserved for passing only), the middle lane is commonly viewed as the travel lane and the right lane reserved for slow vehicles and/or those exiting the highway (and regardless of formal regulation, this is often taught as the ideal recommendable model). Regardless of their efficacy and intent, the professional driver is aware of these regulations and the potential risks of travelling in the left-most lane when it is reserved for passing only.

Visibility optimization

A general conspectus of the possible spatial-positioning-related visibility optimizations persuasively demonstrates the primacy of simple following distance increases and their supreme potential in creating more auspicious visibility circumstances for the professional driver's spatial awareness scanning ease. We have already commented on this phenomenon in a simple and passing manner, when we remarked that the more narrow the space is between the driver and a frontal vehicle, the greater angular proportion of the frontal windshield view is obstructed by the physical structure of the frontal vehicle. This phenomenon also applies to rear following distance and effects on the surface area occupation of the center mirror (although to a less meaningful extent) – and even perhaps to side mirror coverage in consideration of rearwards and lateral space gaps (and with this mode relegated to, of course, an even lesser degree of meaningfulness). Still, the effect is of consequential significance in the light of frontal path-of-travel viewing, and it typically constitutes an incentive to increase following distance concordant with that of the many other reasons of doing so which we have explored. However, as it pertains to lane optimization (which the aforementioned does not), optimum visibility conditions can be obtained by (1) travelling in the area of least vehicular density and (2) making advantageous use of highway curvature. Let us quickly address and dismiss method #1 so that we may focus on the more consequential second method: other optimization benefits already having been discussed (such as arrival-time optimization, by means of possible acceleration to optimal speed, or general collision avoidance by maintenance of sufficient safety distance margins) suggest to the professional driver that areas of lesser vehicular density are superior to those of greater vehicular density, with the added benefit of greater circumspective visibility being a natural result of the freer space afforded by such open environments. Finer effects on path-of-travel and allovehicular visibility proceed from lateral lane position around a curve in the highway: given two isotachic vehicles following a bend, and assuming that human or floral structures on the left side of the highway limit path-of-travel forward scanning vision to the line-of-sight which traverses only frontal road surface, and assuming the present curve bends to the left, then the left-lane traveler will have less stopping time in which to react to a potential hazard than the right lane driver, with the hypothetical frontal hazards in each lane occupying equal forward positions (since the inner curvature of the left lane shortens the distance to the same relative forward position compared to that of the outer right lane). The significance of this constrained example is that the right lane driver will have vision of the left-lane traveler's frontal hazard earlier than the left-lane driver (even though the two are at equal forward positions) since the right lane traveler has a wider angular view of the entire proceeding highway surface area, whereas that of the left-lane (inner curve) driver is somewhat cutoff by the tightness of the inner curve. This theoretical visibility optimization (of being in the outer lane at curves) opposes that of the geometric inner-curve-following optimization which we first discussed in this section, and must therefore be balanced accordingly, with greater emphasis on speed and indifference to fuel-efficiency and arrival-time lending favor to travel around the outer lane of the curve.

Lateral safety clearance optimization

As it concerns optimal lane choice, we have hereunto given a substantial amount of attention to longitudinal-axis distance clearance margins and reserved that of lateral safety clearances for the present discussion. Clearly, advantages inherent to wider lateral safety buffers promise similar benefits as do those of frontal and rearwards following distance gaps, but which are more pointedly directed towards safety and which do not have quite as extensively dual an application in creating optimization opportunities as that of the latter. The significance of such lateral safety factors cannot be underappreciated, however, since lateral collisions pose the particular dangerous which we described towards the beginning of our discussion on highway entrance merging. Allovehicular width is a simple and effective metric of lateral collision risk when comparing two or more lanes in the light of the present factor: in the event that the driver must travel beside a vehicle in a bordering lane (which of course is a constraint which optimally does not exist, however likely will be unavoidable in anything greater than moderate traffic conditions), it is preferable to travel alongside vehicles of narrower width due to the greater lateral safety clearance which affords more evasive interlane position opportunities. Since semi-trucks are usually prohibited from travelling in the left lane, on a four-lane controlled-access freeway, this factor alone would preferentially favor travel in the left or second-to-left lane due to the heightened likelihood of avoiding lateral travel alongside a wide truck (this analysis also elucidates the analytical method of holistically evaluating the probabilistic vehicle widths of an entire lane, since differences in speed between the chosen travel lane and the evaluated lane will cause a plurality of vehicles to pass laterally on either side – and so an individual analysis of vehicle widths in a bordering lane is only meaningful (or even feasible) under conditions of reasonable speed-parity between the two lanes, in which the widths of noted vehicles are more likely to maintain more than momentary relevance). This naturally induces the question of interlane position and its place in ensuring proper lateral safety clearance; it is a somewhat extreme position to state that lateral interlane position in response to surrounding vehicles on either side is a dynamic relationship completely analogous to that of longitudinal-axis safety margin balancing between the frontal following and rearwards vehicle: however the similarities and differences between the two should be analyzed. Firstly, routine optimization and general care towards the vehicle's interstitial position in the intervehicular isolane space (i.e., between the rearwards and frontal vehicles) is not subject the painted geometric lane-marking constraints in which the driver is expected to limit his or her path-of-travel as is that of lateral interlane position. The second reason why the longitudinal dynamics are not equally translatable to that of the perpendicular is that interlane position should ideally remain constant – fixed along the middle, center line of the present lane – rather than that of following distance proportions, which can change precipitously and for many good reasons already discussed, requiring at times acceleration and deceleration in the longitudinal sense. The relevant similarity between the two, of course, is the professional driver's responsibility to avoid collisions in the case that a safety margin on either opposite lateral or longitudinal side becomes precipitously tight and impeding collision is risked if corrective action is not taken. We therefore concede that, as a matter of basic safety necessity, some situations may warrant extended off-center interlane position if this adjustment is necessary to restore even and safe lateral distance margins between the two parallel vehicles. (If the vehicle is unconstrained on one side, then of course he or she would switch into the lane – we are concerned here with the constrained case in which that is not possible.) Any such tight situations, caused by wide vehicles, improper allovehicular lane position, or a combination of these, of course will prompt a safety exigency to exit the area by means of the acceleration or deceleration necessary to longitudinally escape the scenario and, if needed, merge into another lane as an evasive maneuver – however this is a topic for our following discussion on intervehicular dynamics. As it concerns lane position, the necessary safety adjustments should be made in the case of an encroaching side driver in order to even the safety margins, and then immediate intervehicular signaling with directional signal activation in the direction of the desired escape lane (to prompt, in any bit of fortune, the obstructive driver on that side to notice the errant driver two lanes over and make room for the endangered middle driver who desires to evade the situation) and with horn sounding. This response procedure assumes that the offending sideways driver has no reason to be out of proper, centered interlane position and has full ability to return (likely the result of electronic device operative distraction, substance use effects, or mental conditions of high fatigue). Some naturally constrictive situations, such as lane-closure related narrowing of overall lane width, will evince tighter lateral safety margins in which corrective response would neither be appropriate nor fruitful for any cause; an organic decrease in forward speed should accompany these situations in order to compensate for the concerning diminution of lateral safety clearances. Returning focus to standard highway conditions, left-lane travelers must be especially aware of inebriated, enraged, or fatigued drivers on their right whose driving is observed to induce disturbingly high variations in lateral vehicle position since the escape opportunities while travelling in the left-most lane are particularly limited, and in some cases may induce greater danger themselves than would a lateral collision with the concerning vehicle (such as would an icy downhill slippage into a potential tree after road departure, were the left-lane driver to over-react with left-wards steering away from the feared adjacent-lane vehicle – a tree which would collide against the vehicle at any angular combination of both the vehicle's lateral *and* (far greater) longitudinal speed, as opposed to that of a solely lateral collision with an adjacent-lane vehicle). In extreme cases such as this hypothetical, the professional driver must make a comparative decision between the dangers on each side if they are unavoidable, as a non-lethal bump on the right of the vehicle may end much more comfortably than colliding head-on into a tree or human structure at the bottom of a downhill drop-off which the overcorrecting vehicle uncontrollably launched itself into due to a combination of icy road verge surface (unheated by constant vehicular traction) and a panicked left-turning, evasion reaction to a collisionally erratic driver on the right.

Highway egress anticipation

A general and predictable trend exists throughout the linear distance of freeways (whose exits are sufficiently spaced apart and whose traffic speed and density parameters allow for more achievable lane switching) that a higher proportion of total vehicular lane switches will occur in the distance preceding an exit as the vehicles in question switch from their decided travel lane (almost always a non-right-most lane) to that of the exit lane in their attempt to exit the freeway. Under circumstances when this natural frequency in the parameter of total highway lane switches is highly correlated with approaching exits and therefore predictable (as it is usually not in stretches of highway whose exits are closely enough interspaced as to attract the average driver to initial exit-lane-seeking lane switches even before passing the exit just before their intended exit), then a general lane optimization incentive towards travel in more-left lanes is accordingly assigned due to the undesirable and potentially dangerous prospect of being caught travelling in a lane region in which there are high occurrences of perhaps-collisional lane switches (and therefore general horizontal motion perpendicular to the non-exiting vehicle's generally forward pattern of motion). In the rare case of left exits, the inverse can be stated especially when it is deemed by the professional driver's background knowledge of the exit that it is likely to be a heavy attractor of allovehicular traffic (that is, in which case, it would prompt an incentive towards travel in more-right lanes). This small optimization factor only merits consideration if the predictive analysis of the approaching exit is performed long before a majority of the referenced drivers conduct their lane switches, since late execution of the tactic could result in an even less desirable situation than that of doing nothing, if the driver thereby laterally merges his or her vehicle in a direction *opposite* to that of the prevailing horizontal pattern. Attention must also be paid to the time at which the driver him or herself seeks to exit from the highway, at which point earlier exit-lane switching promises the advantages of avoiding a potentially collisional zone of the allovehicular lane switches in the same direction, securing a merging gap space in the right-most (or, rarely, left-most) exit lane earlier and therefore more easily (due to the impending increase in traffic density in this lane), and decreasing the probability that any dangerous corrective maneuvers will need to be made in the rare event of a "close call" between the exit merge and aborting to stay on the highway (as could be caused by unpredictable situations of impaired and erratic frontal drivers while being about to exit the highway). While the professional driver must balance these benefits with those of the determined idealism of the pre-established travel lane, it should still be known that earlier merging over into the exit lane may do well to avoid otherwise dangerous situations.

Special Cases

High Occupancy Vehicle (HOV) lanes

In a former section, we had briefly touched upon the potential tactical benefits which HOV lanes afford to the professional driver: in high traffic density situations on the freeway, any such HOV lanes are likely to contain a lower traffic density and therefore are capable of affording speed and safety optimizations (1) by shortening necessary freeway travel time by increasing speed, which (2) increases safety by decreasing the amount of time spent on the freeway in which an accident could occur, and by (3) increasing longitudinal safety clearance buffers (per the definition of lower traffic density) as to afford extra reaction time to sudden frontal vehicle decelerations and to decrease therefore rear-end collision risk. While driver foreknowledge of the HOV lane's existence, its minimum passenger requirement, and its specified effective times (if any) will certainly seek to inform his or her usage of the lane if vehicular passenger plurality so qualifies, spatial attention to signs indicating these factors is still crucial for a predictive analysis concerning allovehicular HOV lane usage, which may inform lane optimization, especially if travelling on the left-most lane from where most HOV lanes begin. In other words, if a predictive analysis indicates that a left-lane traveler is not eligible for

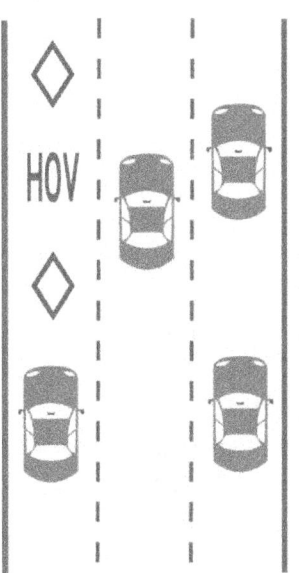

HOV lanes are often marked with white diamonds

Figure 14 – HOV lane designation

HOV lane travel yet is about to travel into an HOV lane, then the vehicle's attempt to switch lanes (or at least its greater likelihood so to do) can be anticipated. Let us assume the driver to be travelling in the second-to-left-most lane with the lateral vehicles in the left-most lane being about to enter an HOV lane some certain distance down the freeway: as a part of general lateral spatial awareness scanning (with particular emphasis lent to these vehicles when and if an HOV lane is approaching), vision is made through the windows of the lateral vehicles in question and the absence of any passengers is noted as a potential indicator that the vehicle may soon switch lanes. It would be preferable to be travelling in the lane of these potentially about-to-merge vehicles, since then they would be safety leaving the area instead of uncomfortably entering the driver's lane space: however if this were the case, obviously, the driver him or herself would be headed into the HOV lane. This optimization therefore applies to those situations in which the driver will not enter the HOV lane, but can make predictive assumptions regarding allovehicular merge probability into frontal following distance space, which may prompt an according adjustment in speed (deceleration, most likely) or a preferential switch into the next right lane (if one even exists), if all other factors between these two lanes are even. The professional driver is therefore always attentive to the existence of HOV lanes, decided as to whether traffic and passenger conditions occasion a comparative advantage in taking the HOV lane or not, and also cognizant of their habit to induce regions of preemptive HOV-lane-avoidance lane switches which are of safety and optimization concern to the vehicles in the second-to-left-most lane.

Breakdown lane

The tendency of controlled-access multi-lane freeways to maintain shoulders on either edge of disparate widths (with that of the right being wider, in right-driving countries) creates a zone in which physically viable vehicular travel may tempt drivers to enter the normally void region of unoccupied road under certain circumstances. Most commonly, the liberty of temporary breakdown lane travel is taken in high-traffic, low-speed conditions to bypass a certain amount of traffic to more quickly enter the exit lane (whereupon it begins), which is even legal in some jurisdictions within a margin of 200 feet. While this time-optimization certainly increases average vehicular speed and fuel-efficiency (due to the lesser time spent idling on the highway and time spent driving in general, and especially due to the lessened braking which would result from maintaining position in speed-variable traffic), it is unclear whether or not these benefits outweigh the natural safety hazards of occupying an area into which a proper right-most-lane traveler may need to evade for a host of different valid reasons, or into which such a travelling vehicle may merge for any invalid reason and not having conducted a lateral clearance check of the lane pre-merge (due to this driver's not suspecting anyone to be travelling in the typically off-limits breakdown lane), and risking thereby a collision with any existing traveler in the breakdown lane.. The determination of the relative safety cost of traffic-evasive, exit-lane-seeking breakdown lane usage is likely not much more than a qualification of the brevity of the maneuver's breakdown lane usage itself: however if it is particularly small, then there is unlikely any pressing necessity for its execution in the first place unless traffic is near completely halted and/or driver time urgency is of particular emphasis. The professional driver's treatment of the breakdown lane will of course depend on situation and context; some areas (such as stretches of I-93 into Boston, Massachusetts or of I-66 in Virginia leading into Washington, D.C.) explicitly open the entire breakdown lane for vehicular travel during periods of heavy traffic volume. The breakdown lane serves as a general planar evasive option in critical situations, but overall remains in standard circumstances a travel-impossible zone to the professional driver due to legal and narrow lateral spatial clearance zone risks.

Lane Optimization Conclusion

Of the two major dynamic spatiovehicular factors over which the professional driver has control, lateral (right-left-dimension) position in the highway, regulated by marked lanes, can have massive impacts on safety and optimization throughout the changing circumstances of the driver's trip on the freeway. Most of the contributing tactical discussions thereunto pertain to allovehicular factors, such as our all-important tactical model on longitudinal-axis safety clearance optimization between the frontal and rearwards isolane vehicles. Others, however, may pertain to natural and environmental factors of the road without necessary regard to the positioning of other vehicles, such as geometric optimization of the curve-distance interlane disparity effect. We shall now therefore transition the discussion topic of our tactical model for freeway spatial maneuvering to that of speed optimization – that of the forwards and backwards, longitudinal dimension – the second major spatiovehicular factor in a freeway over which the professional driver's spatial control is characteristically two-dimensional.

CHAPTER 6

Speed Optimization

The professional driver must expend his or her speed optimization efforts on two distinct categories comprising proper procedure: the first being a situational determination of *ideal* speed, and the second being careful attendance to the vehicle's speed keeping in mind the determined ideal speed and the realistic constraining factors on the freeway which may prevent that speed from being achieved. This typically refers to traffic density effects of slowing the driver's speed to below that which is ideal, however there are some extreme though conceivable situations in which situational factors would in fact constrain the professional driver to *increase* speed beyond that of the ideal. The speed optimization task will therefore require the driver to scan for viable acceleration or deceleration maneuvers (depending on the nature of the relative speed of surrounding constraints, if any) without compromising safety or efficiency in order to travel at as small a margin as possible away from the theoretical ideal speed if no traffic whatsoever were present. That is, the first aforementioned category seeks to determine the speed at which the professional driver would travel if there were absolutely no other vehicles on the freeway, and the largest component of the second category is longitudinal-axis safety margin optimization by according accelerations and decelerations – a discussion which we have already made, having been overtaken into the lane optimization chapter due to its fine interconnectedness therewith. This chapter will therefore indulge in the liberty to focus on solely speed optimization related topics which have not yet been addressed.

Determination of the freeway-vacant ideal travel speed

Developing a precursory understanding of which factors influence the ideal travel speed will establish an operational framework in which the more localized and small-scale necessary adjustments to speed will function; such adjustments throughout the course of the highway driving task will be caused, most usually, by the reality of other physically constrictive vehicles on the freeway (as a driver may not holographically "drive through" a frontal vehicle if he or she wishes to go faster) and will seek to most closely match the "freeway-vacant ideal travel speed" – the preferred speed assuming the freeway were free of vehicles under the given circumstances. Our tactical model defines two general categories – incentivizing and decentivizing – of constituent influencing factors which combine in balance to determine the freeway-vacant ideal travel speed. The incentivizing situational factors to travelling at higher relative freeway-vacant speeds are: (1) need for increased arrival-time immediateness, (2) increased likelihood that precipitously more dangerous meteorological (or otherwise visibility related) conditions are impending to the forward freeway positions that will be occupied by the vehicle, (3) large and influential likelihood that severely higher traffic density levels are impending to the same forward positions which the vehicle will in any case occupy, and (4) heightened priority of the avoidance of legal risk in the near-inconceivable event that the hereunto enumerated incentives do not effect a chosen speed exceeding that of a posted regulatory minimum speed. The decentivizing consequences to higher-speed freeway-vacant travel are: (1) decreased fuel-efficiency in almost every form of commercially available passenger vehicle, (2) higher collisional risk pertaining to obstructive object, pedestrian, or wild animal avoidance, (3) increased safety of cost of any frequent road curvature as to obstruct view potential areas of traffic buildup ahead, (4) greater mechanical wear on engine components, (5) greater potential for fuel-inefficient momentum loss and brake wear by means of necessary occasional decelerations, (6) more frequently necessary time and momentum expenditures for refueling (as it pertains to long-distance travel), which also necessitate the natural lane switch and highway re-entrance merging safety risks of exiting the highway briefly for gas, (7) increased risk associated with operating electronic devices and/or participating in any distracting activity, due to the longer comparative distance overtaken in a given amount of time at higher speed and the greater inherent stopping distance, (8) greater impairments inherent to window opening, including sound-stimulus repression by loud noise and physical irritation from aeroelastic flutter effects, (9) heightened safety risks in the presence of wet or slippery roadways, which lengthen stopping distance by proportionally greater amounts at higher speeds, and most obviously and controversially, (10) increased legal risk in being pulled over by a traffic enforcement officer for exceeding a posted speed limit. Before we qualify the constituents of these two intercompeting lists, some general and useful observations must first be made: firstly, that the raw plurality of factors is far greater in the case of *decentives* to high-speed travel, and secondly, that all but the first of the high-speed-travel *incentivizing* factors are thoroughly absurd and non-applicable in an overwhelming majority of situations. We can therefore conclude, with the exception of rare circumstances, that pressing and justified time-urgency is the only factor which merits increase in highway travel speed beyond that of the general average (which varies by region, road width, condition, and other risk factors – which traffic engineers typically do an accurate job in capturing by means of the posted speed limit), and even then, at the expense of a surmounting list of suboptimalities incurred with comparatively higher speed. It should therefore be understood by the professional driver that, beyond some margin (typically 7mph over the posted speed limit plus or minus 5mph depending on region), it will take exponential increases in time-urgency incentives to speed to yield an according linear increase in speed when balanced against the intercompeting factors; in other words, the greater the chosen speed exceeds the speed limit, a constant, marginal 1mph increase in speed yields decreasing time-optimization benefits and increasing deterrent costs enumerated in the list above. This present section will seek to impart a detailed understanding of the function and magnitude of these effects so that the professional driver can choose the optimal balancing point between factors which will dictate his or her freeway-vacant ideal travel speed.

General time-urgency and safety balancing theory

The professional driver must be able to subjectively qualify the present level of time-urgency in the freeway driving task at hand in order to strike an appropriate balance between intercompeting factors in the determination of the freeway-vacant ideal travel speed. We apply a quintessentially economic cost-benefit analysis to this determination, in which greater driver experience will enable finer precision in estimating the relative priorities of each constituent incentivizing or decentivizing factor in this determination. A fascinating piece of research by Forester et al. (1984) attempted to numerically quantify the value of human time as a function of average wage rate (time wasted by a lower speed limit) and the value of human life (lives saved, on the other hand, by a lower speed limit) in a cost-benefit efficiency analysis of the nationwide 55mph speed limit which the United States adopted in January 1974 in response to an oil embargo[1]. Unsurprisingly, they found the 55mph speed limit to be inefficient with regards to the opportunity of labor hours lost on the highway; what is interesting, however, about this form of analysis is its numerical attempt to quantify the comparative utility of increased speed and that of decreased safety, which is the fundamental subjective task of the professional driver in determining the freeway-vacant ideal travel speed. Unlike this piece of research, our tactical model is not primarily concerned with overall maximization of social efficiency parameters but instead seeks to define the ideal parameters for the *individual* professional driver – which would place an even greater emphasis on human life, since the death of the driver in a high-speed collision would betoken the opportunity cost of every single remaining hour which he or she would have lived, rather than that of the comparatively minimal

---

[1] Forester, T. H., McNown, R. F. & Singell, L. D., 1986. A cost-benefit analysis of the 55 mph speed limit. *Southern Economic Journal,* pp. 631-641.

amount of hours which would be wasted on the highway as a result of marginally slower driving (and that is without even comparing the subjective human value of living – as we may say, *enjoying* the professional driving experience – as opposed to not living those hours at all, regardless of his or her equally zero economic output between that of driving and that of being dead) that may have prevented such an accident. By this logic, we arrive to the conclusion that our wholly tactical (and therefore *individually* optimal, rather than globally optimal – or even *selfish*, as it may be put in the most negative possible light) model places an even *greater* emphasis on safety and collision-related fatality avoidance than would that of an egalitarian, social-utility maximization analysis. This is stated simply to illustrate the individual interest in assigning personal safety (and therefore with marginally lower freeway-vacant ideal travel speed) a higher priority than may seem common to the average driver, and not at all to insinuate that such responsible optimizations will not give way to a safer road for the totality of other driving individuals as well. Though not a steadfast canon of absoluteness, it is still a true general observation that the perceived marginal benefit of arrival-time optimization by increased speed is overestimated by many drivers, and that the increased risks and sub-optimalities attached to travel at marginally greater speeds above the speed limit are underestimated in the same way, as we briefly noted in our initial strategic discussion of freeway driving at the beginning of this book. The sage professional driver therefore understands the appropriate emphasis which any given sense of time-urgency should truly merit, since this is less easily quantifiable than that of the following high-speed decentivizing factors.

Fuel-efficiency factors

Under a majority of freeway posted speed limits and with almost every vehicle type, increasing speed above the posted limit (and often decreasing speed below some figure perhaps 10mph or more under the posted limit) decreases fuel-efficiency. This discussion presents an opportune moment to equip the professional driver with a basic understanding of the aerodynamic factors which massively effect vehicular dynamics and fuel-efficiency (and which will serve as the substance basis for the two following chapters). Essentially, a vehicle travelling at highway speed must be viewed aerodynamically as a stationary object positioned in a fast moving stream of fluid, such as an airplane flying against upper-level atmospheric winds. The passage of such fluid exerts a force on the vehicle (called a *drag* force) against which the vehicle must exert an equal and opposite force in order to hold acceleration constant. To establish a basis for our practical explanation of aerodynamic vehicular factors, we must consider Newton's second law of motion:

$$F = mA$$

wherein m signifies the mass of the vehicle, A the acceleration (change in velocity), and F the force. We must also consider the equation for the drag force:

$$F_d = \frac{1}{2}\rho v^2 C_d A$$

wherein ρ signifies the density of the air, v signifies the velocity of the air relative to the vehicle, C_d signifies the drag coefficient, and A signifies the frontal area of the vehicle against which the force of the wind pushes. Now in order for a vehicle to maintain constant velocity, it must exert a force against the wind equal to that of the drag force being exerted against the vehicle so that the two forces cancel, that acceleration is unchanged, and that the vehicular mass remains isotachic (at constant speed). The greater the force the engine must produce, integrated over a given time-interval, the more fuel energy must be consumed; therefore the greater the wind resistance, the more fuel must be expended on maintaining constant speed. Therefore, it is of interest to the professional driver to analyze the constituent variables of the drag equation so that the primary causes of decreased fuel-efficiency can be understood. Of the four multiplied terms which comprise the drag equation, three of them are of equal first-degree order: air density, the drag coefficient, and area. Drag coefficient and area are almost completely static during freeway travel, having been determined by the physical design of the vehicle which the driver operates; unsurprisingly, an expensive sports vehicle designed for high-speed travel, such as the Bugatti Veyron (with a top speed over 267mph), will certainly have both smaller area and a lesser drag coefficient (i.e., more aerodynamically crafted shaping) than would a large and blocky semi-truck. For quantitative comparison, the product of both drag coefficient and area (which together may be taken as one overall aerodynamic-propensity multiplier in this equation which determines drag force), called "drag area", may range from 0.47 m^2 (as in the case of 1999 Honda Insight) to 2.46 m^2 (as in the case of the 2003 Hummer H2) – the latter being 5.2 times greater than the former – which will constitute a potentially large effect in the professional driver's assessment of wind resistance severity, which will therefore inform the optimal speed point for fuel-efficiency (with greater drag force causing a slower ideal speed). Vehicle shape alone can have this large of an impact on wind resistance force.

Air density can typically be dismissed in freeway conditions due to its relative constant status, however the professional driver is aware even of this minute factor. Air density itself is defined by many variables and could change precipitously based of differences in altitude, air temperature, and humidity. Lower altitude, colder air temperature, and drier air will all effect increases in air density. The order of magnitude by which density may change under these variables in the course of the professional driver's experience is of sufficient significance for the professional driver's awareness to this factor; for instance, a driver travelling from Bangor, ME to the Canadian border on the highest speed section of Eastern America's Interstate 95 (with a 75mph posted speed limit) at 250 feet above sea level in January with -15F air temperature would press through dense 1.411kg/m^3 air, whereas one travelling on I-70 from Denver, CO through the Eisenhower Tunnel at 11,158ft above sea level (the highest point in the American Interstate Highway System) in a summer 60 degree Fahrenheit air temperature at 50% relative humidity would press through much lighter 0.796kg/m^3 air – meaning that air resistance in the former case, holding all other variables constant, would result in *almost double* (1.77 times) the wind resistance force than that of the latter, and therefore requiring an accordingly greater amount of fuel energy and engine output to hold a constant speed. Notice, however, that air density and drag area pale in comparison to the effect which *velocity* has on the drag force exerted against the vehicle, since velocity is raised to the second power in the equation, whereas the others are of first-degree order. Increasing velocity, beyond the certain optimal balancing point, will not decrease fuel-efficiency linearly but rather *exponentially*. That is, doubling speed will *quadruple* the drag force which the engine must overcome, and accordingly a fourfold increase in speed would increase the drag force which the engine must overpower by *sixteen* times. It is not scientifically nor mechanically accurate to state that this theoretically exponential increase in engine energy requirement would always translate exactly into an identical increase in fuel consumption, since the efficiency of engines at various output levels may vary according to a multitude of internal engine factors – but regardless, the geometric relationship between velocity and drag force will indeed cause largely higher increases in fuel consumption than that of whatever given increase in speed, and all the more as speed increases.

Before analyzing the high-level role of the drag force's effect in determining the fuel-efficiency optimal travel speed equilibrium, an additional qualification should be made about the nature of the (likely oversimplified) fluid dynamics model in which we applied the previous analysis. We had simplified the flow of air passing the travelling vehicle as a straight and invariable stream parallel to the instantaneous path-of-travel vector through which the vehicle is travelling, assuming that (1) the fluid mass of air is stationary relative to the road surface and that (2) therefore the only relative velocity differential between this stationary mass and that of the vehicle is created by means of solely of the vehicle's motion therethrough. The first assumption above, however, is entirely invalid under almost every circumstance due to the atmospheric existence of wind. Adding wind into the equation poses additional complications to the drag force factor of optimal fuel-efficient speed selection:

1. In the simplest case that wind direction is exactly parallel to the longitudinal axis of the vehicle, an according increase or decrease in the subjective assessment of contravehicular wind velocity can be made; in the case of wind moving with the direction of the vehicle, an according increase to the ideal fuel-efficient travel speed will be made, and the inverse.

2. Road curvature on the freeway and/or lateral wind direction to begin with will have three complicated constituent effects of: (1) increasing the effective drag area of the vehicle since the convergent wind vector will be tilted angularly away from the longitudinal axis of the vehicle, but however (2) removing a component of the necessary magnitude of the opposing engine-originating force vector (since the energy produced by the engine is necessarily constrained towards exerting a force in the direction of the vehicle's path-of-travel, due to wheel positioning) and (3) transferring an according amount of force into lateral friction between the tires of the vehicle and the road surface.

3. Predictive analysis of the above factors for the professional driver's subjective assessment of fuel-efficiency optimal travel speed is likewise complicated by multivariate factors of road curvature and changing atmospheric conditions of wind speed and direction, but for which a strategic pre-drive survey of forecasted meteorological parameters will achieve basic driver ability to assess wind effects on fuel-efficient speed selection, along with careful spatial awareness attention to the absolute cardinal heading of the vehicle's path-of-travel which may slowly and imperceptibly tilt away from the driver's initial perception if the highway is so designed with such extended curvature (such as is common

with circumurban interstate travel belts of characteristically circular geometry).

All of the discussed variables influence the magnitude of the drag force (with the greatest being the relative velocity differential between the air and the vehicle – which only matches the exact road-relative speed of the vehicle in the total absence of wind or in the case of perfect perpendicularity of the wind vector to the vehicle's longitudinal axis); there are also many other constituents to the overall road load power equation, such as passenger weight (as would affect static friction between the road and the tires – termed "rolling resistance"), tire inflation, transmission gear reduction, even engine oil viscosity (Stewart & Selby, 1977)[2], *et cetera* – however these are mostly ignorable by the professional driver since they are neither speed-related nor linked to changing circumstances on the freeway. The key point with regards to framing the utility of our discussion concerning the drag force is that we have implied the existence of some other effect which in turn *increases* fuel-efficiency with higher speed by insisting the notion of an ideal "balance point" equilibrium speed at which fuel economy is maximized. Such a factor must exist, or else the ideal fuel-efficient travel speed would be an infinitesimally small amount faster than zero miles-per-hour in order to minimize wind resistance, which is certainly not the case. The effect at hand is the simple fact that, even at zero miles-per-hour stationary vehicle speed, the engine is still running and consuming a base amount of energy to keep itself running (e.g. to power various electronic systems of the vehicle, by losing energy to pumping losses, by losing frictional energy to pistons and camshaft-valve contact, etc.). Therefore, by this effect alone, efficiency is higher the *faster* a vehicle is travelling, since the heightened output of the engine (and therefore the greater speed, and therefore the greater integrated distance-miles achieved over a given period of

---

[2] Stewart, R. M. & Selby, T. W., 1977. The relationship between oil viscosity and engine performance - a literature search. *SAE Technical Paper Series*, Volume 770372

time) makes better proportional use of the base energy loss per unit time just to keep the engine running. This concept is more communicably illustrated by analogy to the traditional economic model of production; given a firm's fixed costs (analogous to the base energy per unit time required to keep the engine running), an increase in units produced – an increased variable cost – (and analogously, an increase in engine output and therefore in distance travelled over a given distance) renders the constant fixed costs of proportionally smaller effect. Let us consider the marginal benefit of travelling 1mph greater than zero: if the engine is turned on but the vehicle is still (travelling at 0mph), it must consume an infinite amount of energy since the aforementioned base amount of energy per time must be repeatedly expended for eternity, since the vehicle will never arrive at its destination. Now let us consider that the vehicle travels 1mph: it will take very long to arrive at the final destination, but at least the amount of energy expended has been reduced from infinity to some much smaller amount. Now let us consider that the vehicle travels 100mph – it will arrive very quickly and therefore only waste energy keeping the engine active for a very short time. If the vehicle could potentially travel at 10,000mph, fuel-efficiency (in this narrow model) would be even greater, since the fixed cost of basic engine activation energy loss would only occur for a split second, and a near-whole proportion of the spent energy would go towards actually moving the vehicle instead of being wasted on akinetic losses. Therefore the phenomenon of base engine-activation energy loss suggests an ideal fuel-efficient speed of infinity, and the formerly discussed phenomenon of air drag force suggests an ideal fuel-efficient speed of zero. It may now be intuitively seen that these two opposing factors will combine to effect some ideal equilibrium speed at which fuel-efficiency is maximized, which depends on the magnitude of both opposing effects.

Quantitatively, this equilibrium fuel-efficiency-optimum speed ranges between 40mph and 60mph for the overwhelming majority of common passenger vehicles, depending on the specific balancing of all the many contributing factors which we have heretofore discussed. Clearly, to unify our prior discussions into an example of extremes, this ideal equilibrium speed would be on the far slow end for a boxy semi-truck travelling northeast on I-95 in coastal Massachusetts against a 50mph Nor'easter-induced 10-degree-Fahrenheit headwind carrying a heavy load mere feet above sea level, whereas an expensive and light sports car with one 120lbs passenger travelling eastbound on I-70 in central Colorado at 10,000 feet above sea level and aided by a warm 65-degree-Fahrenheit summer 20mph tailwind would have a remarkably high fuel-efficiency-maximizing speed (not at all that the situations for which illustrative, hypothetical extremes are well disposed in any way resemble situations in which fuel-efficiency would be of primary concern). If the professional driver frequently operates the same vehicle under an economy-emphasized highway driving strategy, it may prove worthwhile to conduct comparative experiments (for instance, between 50mph, 55mph, and 60mph travel – if possible) under normalized circumstances to discover the fuel-efficient optimum speed engendered solely by the vehicle's aerodynamic and engine efficiency design by noting the comparative fuel-usage to distance ratios of each speed. Regardless, it is beyond the scope of this book to attempt to quantify numerically, given precise quantifications of the constituent factors, what exactly the fuel-efficiency optimal speed is given every type of vehicle design and driving situation; we only seek to instill useful knowledge of (1) the general 40mph to 60mph range, (2) the overwhelmingly lower speed which fuel-efficiency optimization alone posits compared to that of posted maximum speed limits and especially that of realistic freeway traffic flow, and (3) the *exponential* nature of increasing fuel-efficiency costs incurred by travelling at speeds *linearly* above the natural equilibrium speed, which itself is almost always lower than the posted freeway speed limit.

Speed Limits and Law Enforcement

We have formerly identified the safety costs, fuel-inefficiency, potential legal costs, and generally suboptimal and undesirable consequences inherent to being pulled over by a law enforcement officer, regardless of final outcome – as is the case with any action of pulling over to a full stop onto the breakdown lane of a potentially busy and dangerous highway from which reacceleration to highway speed must occur. These particular and separate factors (separate from consideration of what behavior caused the stop or of the justice of the stop in the first place) render consideration of speed limits, road regulations, and law enforcement a legitimate and in-dismissible factor in the professional driver's determination of the freeway-vacant ideal travel speed. Before exploring these factors and their specific effects, we must take a broader step back and qualify the nature of our inherently controversial discussion in which a prevailing tactical viewpoint may seem to obfuscate common precepts (such as moral obligation to legal obedience) as may come to worry a reader who serves in a public capacity, or who is a law enforcement officer him or herself. The definition of the tactical nature of our highway spatial maneuvering model mandates that all contributing factors to the driver's task are treated objectively and from the same fresh and unbiased point of view which distinguishes any professional academic investigation, founded ultimately on objective Socratic principles. Therefore, any aphorism similar to "you may never exceed the speed limit, since it is illegal" is simply useless to the professional driver and the development of his or her tactical freeway driving model, since it (1) ignores the plain fact that the acceleration capability of passenger vehicles well-enables any driver to exceed the speed limit, an action which is therefore not relegated to an area of such metaphysical impossibility as the above so quaintly insinuates, (2) appeals to an external sense of categorically imperative morality which entirely exceeds the narrow scope of our tactical model: the consideration of *only* those factors which will best achieve the outcome of driving objectives given the driver's highway driving strategy, and (3) places this abstract and undefined moral system at a higher importance than even safety, which would be the natural prioritizing item governing the professional driver's driving even if any sort of abandonment of our narrow tactical model were to be taken (i.e., to ignore the existence of other desirable factors such as fuel-efficiency or arrival-to-destination time and their role of being balanced against safety), since, by the logic of the aphorism, even any safety-augmenting action would be unjustifiable if illegal, even to the point of lethal collision avoidance. In making these preparatory statements, we zealously seize the opportunity to point out the exciting and hopefully evident fact that the language of our discussions up unto this point in this book (such as the very preceding fuel-efficiency discussion) overwhelmingly are disposed to highlight the *costs* of speeding and the *benefits* of reasonable highway speed, and that in an honorable plurality of circumstances, it will be such that our properly applied tactical freeway driving model will insist on travel speeds at or even *below* the speed limit; this however has absolutely no effect on our professional and rational discussion to move us towards acceptance or even remote toleration of the aforementioned aphorism, since the speed-related safety and optimization principles which we have developed are derived from sound logical analysis of situational factors on the road and cost-benefit analysis of comparative, competing priorities – and not from utterly useless, illogical, and unprofessional aphorisms such as the one above which may be useful only for instruction of good general habits to teenagers or to otherwise novice drivers.

Our discussion of the present regulatory factors (and more narrowly, as it is simplified in this following section, that of the posted speed limit) therefore is abstracted to the general aforementioned safety and fuel-efficiency consequences of pulling over to stop in the breakdown lane, regardless of driver, rule, or situation, and need not concern the stereotypical cop-pulling-over-speeding-civilian image which would come to the mind of a close-minded, non-professional driver upon reading the title of this section; the speed limit regulation is only relevant due to its tendency to cause the necessity of pulling over if a law enforcement vehicle is responding to excessive speeding. This does not necessarily have to be the case, for instance if the driver him or herself is a law enforcement officer in a jurisdiction affording "speed immunity" to such officers, (i.e., if there is no risk of being pulled over), or if the driver was both wealthy and passionate about freeway driving to the extent that he or she built a freeway in his or her own unregulated private property and may therefore drive at any speed without need of paying attention to the present factor. These hypothetical situations merely by themselves do not encourage speeding nor magically imbue it with safety, however they would return the freeway-vacant ideal travel speed determination process to a far simpler and more natural balancing of general safety, time urgency, and fuel-efficiency factors with legal risk consideration having been removed from this list. For instance, we consider the driver who owns (by some amazing feat of technological achievement) a vehicle which achieves optimal gas efficiency at 130mph, and who is in a severe rush, and who is accelerating onto the center lane of an utterly void five-lane highway with seven straight miles ahead, all fully visible within the line-of-sight due to slight negative incline, with a 20mph tailwind and under ideal visibility and weather conditions. With the removal of speed-limit-related legal risk consideration, if (for instance) driving on completely private property, it may well indeed be optimal for him or her to assess a freeway-vacant ideal travel speed upwards of 90mph or 95mph, balancing the relative safety of such a speed in the (absurdly unrealistic) theoretical parameters which we have set forth and the time urgency which motivates the driver's driving. If we transition this hypothetical to that of a public freeway with a posted speed limit of 65mph, the safety and optimization risks of being pulled over for speeding (especially at such a high velocity relative to the speed limit) – which would *now* be considered – will effect a much slower freeway-vacant ideal travel speed, probably closer to 74mph or less under these same (still nearly perfect and unlikely) driving conditions, due to the added risk parameter in the overall cost-benefit analysis of making this determination. It should be noted from the extreme unrealism of this example that the posted highway speed limit frequently is indeed a reasonable speed, above which travel over 10mph should rarely or never be necessary nor optimal. What we wish to illustrate by this example is that the professional driver produces his or her own original and comprehensive determinations of freeway-vacant ideal travel speed, considering the safety and optimization consequences of the posted speed limit, whereas the posted guideline speed limit is largely an analogous attempt to define the freeway-vacant ideal travel speed for a given stretch of highway – which is impossible to capture in one constant value due to the changing nature of road conditions, visibility conditions, driver exigency, and high-level driver strategy.

At this point in our discussion of the speed limit and the effects of its enforcement on determining the freeway-vacant ideal travel speed, it seems practical to attempt to numerically quantify some approximations of ranges of typically optimal speeds which the professional driver may assess in a majority of circumstances. We repeat that these are necessarily limited to being approximations and even then are constrained to a certain authorial conception of what is most commonly encountered, as the stringency of enforcement varies greatly depending on an array of factors. Let us take the seemingly canonical example of a stretch of American Interstate Highway System freeway in a high-population area leading to and from a major city – with a posted speed limit of 65mph, copious following distance margins, unobstructed visibility, dry road traction, and with the time of day being in the early afternoon before rush hour (as would otherwise typically increase traffic density so that travel even at 65mph would not likely be possible). We also assume, of course, for the purposes of illustration, that the assessed freeway-vacant ideal travel speed is otherwise high enough such that the major constraining factor will be legal risk incumbent to exceeding the speed limit. In such 65mph areas (such as, by familiar example to many inhabitants of the American Northeast, I-84 westbound into Hartford, CT, the northern I-95 portion of the New Jersey Turnpike northbound into New York City, or the Massachusetts Turnpike on I-90 westbound into Boston before the 55mph zone), the freeway-vacant ideal travel speed is typically 71mph or 72mph. The regurgitation of a static, constant figure such as this is almost useless to the professional driver however, since a host of variable factors clearly combines to effect large situational changes in this figure (or "reductions" we should say instead of "changes", since the given example figure above assumes ideal conditions in which virtually all non-constant factors permit higher speed). Even the slightest increase in traffic density, reduction in following distance, curvature-induced limitation of frontal path-of-travel visibility, or otherwise, would instantly effect an according reduction to the above assessed speed, since the marginal safety benefit of speed reduction vastly outweighs that of the marginal cost to arrival-time (unless the professional driver, in some highly rare and questionably justified circumstance, has assigned an insurmountably exponential emphasis to arrival-time celerity due to some exigent and emergent circumstance).

Marginal analysis of speed increases: risks vs. benefits

The professional driver keenly notices the large effect of marginal changes in speeds which are generally at or above the speed limit; let us take the specific spatial, situational, and jurisdictional example proffered above, with a familiarized and instinctive understanding of the relatively uniform and commonplace tendencies of the state traffic enforcement officers in the American Northeast as of the time of this writing, and keeping in mind that this contextually narrow hypothetical is only given for the purpose of illustrative example, due to the vastly different situations which would significantly lower (or, much more rarely, heighten) the following constant figures. On a 65mph section in such a clear and auspicious environment as described in the previous paragraph, it is extraordinarily unlikely that one travelling at 71mph in the center lane under these normal circumstances would be pulled over for violating the speed limit by 9.2% or 6mph. When vehicles are pulled over at this speed, there is almost always some other valid reason which indicates to the traffic enforcement officer that the driver may be impaired (such as failure to maintain constant interlane position – swerving – and/or an accordingly disturbing pattern of erratic speed differentials), may be an otherwise aggressive driver in need of correction (such as having made a dangerous and inconsiderate lane switch, having repeatedly failed to use proper directional signals, etc.), or may be travelling in the wrong lane (such as left-lane travel in left-lane-for-passing-only jurisdictions). These errors, of course, should be foreign even to the driver of moderate skill, let alone the professional driver, and therefore we return to our example having justified that in this very narrow example and in this very certain region and under these very specific circumstances – that 71mph is a freeway-vacant ideal travel speed which does not pose much traffic-enforcement-stop risk to the driver. Now let us analyze the marginal differences in this figure with respect to simply the traffic-enforcement-stop risk factor (we already have proven the decreasing utility of increasing speed as it is suggested by every other factor other than arrival-time optimization and other than very momentary vehicular dynamical maneuvers, such as in evasive or merging situations); lowering the speed does decrease risk of being pulled over to some point at which it fact increases due to proximity to the minimum speed – however that is not desired by the combination of the other factors (unless an extreme emphasis on fuel-efficiency – such as in extreme gas shortage situations – and indifference to arrival time is appropriated, in which the safety and legal risks of travelling 45mph in a 73mph traffic flow need to be balanced and wisely considered just as that of the more common desire to speed at 81mph on a 65mph zone) and therefore attention is turned to that of the other marginal direction: an *increase* in speed beyond our example 71mph figure. Any driver with even a few years of semi-regular freeway experience notices the exponentially higher risk of a traffic-enforcement stop for every 1mph increase in speed above a certain figure (the speed limit itself, in the strictest of jurisdictions, or typically a few miles per hour over depending on standard *de facto* informal and contextual leniency). In the spatial and contextual example above for these 65mph multi-lane highways, we place the beginning of this curve at 70mph – below which the traffic-enforcement-stop risk of speeding alone is mostly negligible. Considering a speed of 76mph in comparison to that of our arbitrary 71mph reference point, an absolutely *massive* and categorically *exponential* increase in traffic-enforcement-stop risk is observed by the common-knowledge *de facto* enforcement patterns in this specific region and situational road context through a mere 5mph increase in speed. What does this 5mph marginal increase in speed achieve for the driver? Such a mere 7% increase in speed (comparing 71mph and 76mph speeds for the duration of an entire trip – notwithstanding the slower comparative average speed incumbent in the acceleration and deceleration phrases to and from the higher comparison speed, rendering the following figure a conservative understatement) over a 50 mile freeway trip decreases basic, linear freeway trip time from 42.25 minutes to 39.47 minutes – saving literally only 2.78 minutes or 167 negligible seconds – no tangible benefit in every normal circumstance whatsoever – whereas traffic-enforcement-stop risk was increased by an exponential proportion (let alone the suffering safety and fuel-efficiency factors which are almost certain to run counter to a 5mph marginal increase in speed at the 70mph range). We extend our theoretical explanation of the massively exponential marginal costs of higher speed by considering that many freeway trips will be much shorter than 50 miles; if we consider a 20 mile trip comparing the two same speeds, the simple, linear distance-over-speed difference in time-optimization by travelling at the faster 76mph speed as opposed to the more sensible 71mph speed is now only an absolutely miniscule 67 second time savings. Note also that the order of magnitude which describes the time savings of marginal increases in speed in the example above is so minor that other unforeseeable factors – such as increase in traffic, road-work related lane closure and/or lower posted speed limit, visual identification of a traffic enforcement officer, or even the fortune of the timing of traffic signals at any intersection following the driver's trip on the freeway – are all of comparable order of magnitude as to potentially render even the small (that is, utterly inconsequential) time optimization demonstrated above completely useless.

It is clear, therefore, that our analysis above of the ideal, predictable, clear, and favorable driving conditions which permit safe 71mph travel demonstrates the exponentially increasing costs to speeding above whatever upper limit situationally governs a given highway driving context. The key natures of this cost-benefit analysis are (1) decreasing marginal arrival-time optimization benefits at greater constant speed levels, (2) decreasing importance of marginally higher travel speeds for arrival-time optimizations when trips are shorter (considering proportional equality of comparative speed-increase-margins for two trips of differing length), (3) rapidly and exponentially increasing risk of traffic-enforcement stops once a certain reasonably safe speed is exceeded, and (4) the comparative pointlessness, in many cases, of even such small arrival-time optimizations due to the probabilistic existence of stochastic driving situations in the future of the driver's trip which may likely render time savings/expense consequences on the order of magnitude as to completely erase the significance of such small speed-increase time-savings – but which were likely obtained at a meaningful traffic-enforcement-stop (not to mention, safety) risk. Consideration #1 above explains the commonly observed (mostly in areas analogous to that of our hypothetical above) and seemingly illogical group-traffic phenomenon of proportionally greater speed limit exceeding in wide freeway 55mph sections (but which resemble 65mph-designed stretches of freeway) than in that of 65mph sections; it would seem to the habituated freeway driver in the major cities of the Northeast, accustomed to the customary *de facto* practices therein, that the group percentile of vehicles travelling 66mph on a 55mph-posted section of freeway (a 11mph – or 20% excess over the speed limit) would loosely accord with the same probabilistic percentile on a 65mph section of those travelling, perhaps, at 72mph or 73mph (in the former – an 8mph increase or 12.3% excess in speed limit, an approximately 8% reduction in "willingness to speed") – in other words, that 55mph zones on freeways tend to be more grossly violated than 65mph zones. This phenomenon mutually corroborates and is validated by our theoretical explanation in consideration #1 enumerated above, which states the decreasing marginal arrival-time benefit of a given excess in speed limit with higher constant speed values. To take an extreme example for illustrative purposes, consider a 30mph speed limit rural road on which travelers would commonly go 40mph – a whopping 33% percent excess of posted speed limit. If this trip is 20 miles in distance, the driver saves ten whole minutes travelling at 40mph (taking 30 minutes) as opposed to 30mph (taking 40 minutes) – i.e., the marginal benefit of speeding to time optimization is greater since the overall speeds are lower. This is decreasingly true for higher speeds, as are found on the highway. This very effect explains the 55mph/65mph speeding disparity effect noted above, since the slower speed (55mph) offers a greater marginal benefit to speeding the same amount which is factored into the global sum of freeway drivers' instinctive group behavior, whether conscious or unconscious. To further prove this point, we hold constant the time savings above of ten minutes applied to a freeway situation, in which a driver could obey the exact 65mph speed limit for the same given distance of 20 miles. This standard and legal behavior would result in an 18.46 minute trip on the freeway, using simple linear speed and distance calculations. In order to produce the same ten minute time savings as we found in the reasonable 30mph/40mph rural secondary road example at higher freeway speeds, (i.e., a ten minute reduction to 8.46 minutes), the freeway driver would have to drive at an average speed of 141.82mph. This should give a clear sense as to the mostly futile increases in speed beyond the speed limit or just over by a certain (location and context variable) amount on the freeway, due to the exponential nature of the costs associated and the miniscule benefits, a basic relationship which we have hopefully now documented *ad nauseum*.

If we control for considerations #1 and #2 enumerated above in such a way, we can however conjure a circumstance in which conservative speeding on a 55mph zone would have a non-negligible effect on arrival-time. Assuming that the other road and situational conditions are such that speeds above 65mph are safe (in which case the speed limit is likely not be as low as 55mph in the first place), and that the driver travels at 66mph on a 55mph stretch of freeway for 200 miles (a trip of such length being far from common – let alone the existence of a 55mph controlled-access highway speed limit of such a distance), 36 minutes are saved (3 hours and 2 minutes versus 3 hours and 38 minutes), which is much more reasonable and potentially impactful benefit than that of the pointless (and likely dangerous) analogous 11mph excess of a 65mph limit – however even this situation is unlikely (though feasible), and still the other factors of safety and fuel-efficiency must be balanced against the meaningful time savings. This does however corroborate our general support for the 1995 repeal of America's "National Maximum Speed Law", which capped all American freeway speed limits at 55mph from 1974 to 1987, and which repeal was found to have (at worst) "unclear" safety impacts (i.e., in our position, the economic benefits vastly outweighed the safety consequences – and some research even indicates that the increased speed limits *improved* safety – however that is heavily contested and does run contrary to basic instinctual assumptions about the nature of speed's effect on safety). Either way, we have shown that speeding over a certain amount (typically around 5mph) in sections posted greater than 55mph is an increasingly futile and risky activity. Much like our discussion on highway entrance merging, we only concern ourselves with the theoretically most difficult situation (here, in which there is a great disparity between the legal-risk pressures of the speed limit and that of the freeway-vacant ideal travel speed which would otherwise be assessed by balancing only the other factors), and that many, perhaps even a majority, of situations will not challenge the driver with quantifying this risk, since the assessed freeway-vacant ideal travel speed may already be compliant with the speed limit due to any heavy-traffic, foul-weather, or otherwise "slowing" factor which informs the professional driver's own sage determination of travel speed. The method of speed limit assignment itself usually supports this statement; in more cases than not, traffic engineers collect a sample of traffic speed data and choose the 85th percentile speed as the speed limit (by accepted convention) which only technically criminalizes the fastest 15% of drivers – however this is distorted in some freeway areas due to regulatory and political influences to cap speed at sub-85th percentile maxima, likely such as on Georgia's State Route 400, or perhaps even more risibly, on I-95's entire 55mph Pennsylvanian extent – on which the *de facto* 85th percentile traffic speed under ideal conditions far exceeds the posted speed limit, given the informal tendency to speed there, and calling into question PennDOT's justification that regular high traffic density and multiple left-side exits warrant the seemingly draconian limit. In the light of more honorable (and, therefore, contrasting) examples, some highways, such as the northernmost 110 miles of Interstate 95 from Old Town, ME to New Brunswick (75mph), afford the driver far more leniency in travelling at normal highway speeds (or slightly above) without needing to factor in an exponential increase in risk which would otherwise be present in a 65mph zone. Increasingly, of course, the other discussed factors of decreasing time-optimization, increasing comparative fuel costs, and increased stopping distance all exponentially increase and noticeably in such uncommon high-speed sections, but at least the removal of most legal risk for a certain margin may indeed effect a freeway-vacant ideal travel speed at or even a small bit greater than 75mph in this specific (and rare) case of a 75mph freeway speed limit, assuming ideal conditions, if indeed the time exigency so warrants. This uncommon ability to eschew legal risk analysis from a large part of the freeway-vacant ideal travel speed's determination is consummated at its highest and most rare form when in fact there is no official speed limit. The famous *richtgeschwindigkeit* advisory speed limit on stretches of the German Autobahn imposes no legally mandated upper limit on speed, yet only a default recommendation of 130km/h (81mph), which the legal risks of exceeding are only increased liability if a crash does occur. Yet since the professional driver is highly skilled as both to avoid crashes and to make his or her own informed determinations of freeway-vacant ideal travel speed without relying on incomprehensive constant recommendations, these certain sections of Germany's famous Autobahn system render the process of risk analysis for speed limit excess an entirely non-existent task for driver travelling on them, thus simplifying the balance of factors which will combine to effect the professional driver's assessment of proper speed while travelling on the Autobahn. For most other places in the world, however, the analytical process of legal risk assessment is at least a constituent factor to speed determination, no matter how small or great.

Situational factors of enforcement risk

In determining the freeway-vacant ideal travel speed, the professional driver performs an analysis of situational factors which dictate traffic-enforcement-stop risk in order to assign it a proper prioritative balance relative to the other factors which contribute to this determination (keeping in mind that this present topic of essentially the legal risk factor will speed-increasingly concord with every other factor in dissuading marginal increases in speed – other than that of arrival-time optimization – in almost every situation). Enforcement patterns vary by region and are often largely correlated with time of day; evening hours when drunk driving is a priority for traffic enforcement discovery are accordingly more populated with traffic enforcement personnel, as are regions surrounding routine road work and lane closures. Many such areas of road work or other temporary construction structures are occasioned by "surprise" 55mph zones (in regions which may seem fully suited to the regular 65mph posted speed limit which may normally govern such stretches) and are known to occasion many traffic stops due to increased enforcement presence, driver ignorance of the non-standard (and sometimes immediately posted without premonitory warning signs before the change) speed limit, and due to the heightened relative speeding effect naturally observed on 55mph sections compared to that of 65mph sections which we already discussed. Travel in the left lane exposes the vehicle to direct line-of-sight radar gun speed measurements by any stationary enforcement officer (hiding, for instance, in a restricted-access interchange path connecting the two directions of an interstate divided by any sort of substantial interstitial median of extensive floral or human development), especially when this lane sits on the inside of a curve as one who solely and narrowly focuses on optimizing the curve-distance interlane disparity effect would travel. The same factors may be true for the right-most lane, however it is still less generally risky than the left-most lane due to decreased average speed and decreased likelihood of its being reserved for a non-applicable driving parameter (such as (and perhaps only) that of passing-only restricted lanes). The center lane(s), if any, are therefore likely the least risky in this light. Situational factors such as "strictly enforced" signs, night-time speed limits, and routine speed traps are all known to the professional driver's consciousness insofar as pre-drive knowledge and live spatial awareness feedback are able to achieve. We will repeat our self-indemnification for the comments of this section which may seem legally subversive or discordant, as evasion of traffic enforcement and even exceeding the posted speed limit by 1mph are both activities which are technically completely illegal. We do not recommend or condone illegal behavior, however we only seek to set forth a tactical model for the behaviors of the ideal professional driver and substantiate with sound reasoning why the included recommendations are justified; if obeying this theoretically ideal tactical model for expert freeway driving (such as, in a conceivable example, going at least 66mph in a moderately heavy flow of 75mph traffic on a 65mph freeway – a completely, incontrovertibly, and wholly criminal action – the illegality of which is as evident as the arithmetic truth that 66 is greater than 65) causes illegal behavior, then we simply do not recommend being a professional driver. That is, if the ideal driving behaviors for safety and optimization, as is the focus of this book, cause one to violate civil laws concerning maximum vehicular speed on the highway, we are forced as a matter of practicality to recommend that the entire task of driving be abandoned altogether. However, if a freeway driver does wish to do that which is most optimal, and even at times that which is most safe to begin with, then he or she will most certainly exceed the speed limit by some small amount in at least some freeway circumstances – as do the vast (criminal) majority of drivers, a fact which is thoroughly documented (Mannering, 2009)[3] (Letirand & Delhomme, 2005)[4].

---

[3] Mannering, F., 2009. An empirical analysis of driver perceptions of the relationship between speed limits and safety. *Transportation Research Part F: Traffic Psychology and Behaviour,* 12(2), pp. 99-106.
[4] Letirand, F. & Delhomme, P., 2005. Speed behaviour as a choice between observing and exceeding the speed limit. *Transportation Research Part F: Traffic Psychology and Behaviour,* 8(9), pp. 481-492.

We take this opportunity to gaudily repeat the exciting fact that our objective discussions having previously been made about speed limits, in whole, *overwhelmingly* insist the massive, exponentially increasing risks and costs inherent to travel above (generally) 5mph over the speed limit in a majority of circumstances, and which seize every opportunity to highlight the usual safety, efficiency, and risk-reduction benefits of speed-limit travel speed. With this understanding, we will now continue our wholly *theoretical* discussion of what the ideal professional driver *would* do, in the interest of safety and optimization only, and ignoring all aspects of the law other than its purely tactical value as a risk-factor for inducing potential unwanted traffic-enforcement-stops – which is, of course, contrary to our (meaningless and off-topic) official dispositional statement that all traffic laws should be unequivocally obeyed in absolutely every circumstance whatsoever.

In an attempt to attenuate the seeming degree of potential conflict which exists between traffic regulations and the professional driver (which truly should be minimal, trite, and occasional – at most), we should note that posted speed limits and minimums (for instance, the common 65mph maximum 45mph minimum postings on American Interstate Highway System roads) exist invariably under the assumption of normal driving conditions; in the case of poor visibility and/or slippery highway surface, driving at 65mph may well exceed the maximum safe (or even sanely tenable) speed and therefore represents a higher ideal figure than what present circumstances would allow. Likewise, in this case, any such 45mph minimum speed would be rendered invalid as safety may dictate travel at a lower speed in such circumstances than 45mph. We state this point not to falsely insinuate that the professional driver's assessment of freeway-vacant ideal travel speed is mindlessly dictated by that of a regulatory sign (as we have set forth by example above), but only to clarify that the constituent influencing factor which speed regulations do have in this determination is not such that the law requires adherence to minimum posted speed regulations when conditions render such minimum speeds unsafe. For example, if a driver in a hibernal climate suddenly encounters a heavy snow squall, with severely limited visibility and decreased tire-pavement traction, the proper new assessment of freeway-vacant ideal travel speed would be (of course) significantly lower than that of normal conditions without regards to the speed limit, and the existence of a minimum speed limit (such as 45mph) above that of the professional driver's new assessed optimal speed would not bring about an influence to balance in the factor of the minimum speed limit, increasing the assessed new speed by whatever margin, in order to account for the risk of being "pulled over" for travelling too slowly: the law clearly states that such speed postings are *general* indicators for *ideal* road conditions, and that situational reductions may be warranted depending on poor visibility, etc. – and that they are to take precedence. The legal principle involved here is the all-inclusive supremacy of the "basic speed rule" – a curious piece of terminology to which we have specifically referred a few times already throughout this book.

Basic speed rule

Let us take a moment to explore the basic speed rule, since it is the governing principle which dictates the overarching legal requirement of any vehicle travelling on a public road and which supplements any posted speed regulation. The NHTSA's 2009 technical report on speeding-related crashes cited a whopping 45 percent incidence rate of fatal speeding-related crashes "due to ... driving too fast for conditions" (a summarization of the basic speed rule), but which indeed occurred in travel yet under the posted speed limit (Liu & Chen, 2009)[5]. The laws of various jurisdictions apply different phrasings from statue to statue, however they all share the characteristic requirement that no vehicle may be driven at a speed which is greater than that which is "prudent" or "reasonable", given the totality of situational factors which influence safety. From a casual view of this reasonable requirement, it may be seen that the

---

[5] Liu, C. & Chen, C.-L., 2009. An analysis of speeding-related crashes: Definitions and the effects of road environments. *US Department of Transportation, National Highway Traffic Safety Administration,* Volume DOT HS 811-090.

method we outline for the professional driver's assessment of freeway-vacant ideal travel speed in no way contradicts the vague "prudent" and "reasonable" descriptions set forth in the basic speed law; indeed it is very hard to think of an instance when the professional driver's own assessment of proper speed would conflict with this requirement. However in extreme cases of time-urgency, the professional driver may determine, from a high-level and strategic perspective, that the overall life expense of later arrival at a destination may outweigh the associated safety costs inherent to such faster travel – an extreme situation that is both ideally avoided and in which true time-exigency is likely to be overestimated in comparison to the associated safety risks. Our analysis of the basic speed law only serves to logically substantiate that the increasing safety risks incumbent to such behavior are also proportionally linked to increased legal risks, since the basic speed law affords no place for time-urgency or for other high-level driver strategic goals in its "prudent" and "reasonable" descriptive language.

Assured Clear Distance Ahead (ACDA)

Whether explicitly tied into the definition of a jurisdiction's basic speed law (as it frequently is) or left as a general and universal principal in accident liability proceedings, the concept of the Assured Clear Distance Ahead (ACDA) is a closely related and key concept. The ACDA, put in the most simple terms, refers to the driver's general responsibility to ensure that the vehicle may stop within the visible line-of-sight frontal range extending from the driver's eyes to the frontal maximum 20/20 vision distance, or within the frontal distance ending at the closest extent at which a potential obstruction could enter the vehicle's path-of-travel – whichever is shorter. Clearly this concept holds greater complexity in non-freeway situations, when factors such as bicyclists, pedestrians, and rural road inlets (accounting for the possibility that drivers therefrom may ignore the stop sign) would theoretically limit the ACDA under the most extreme interpretation of what may constitute a potential upcoming obstruction to the path-of-travel. But regardless, even in its more simple and predictable application on the highway, maintenance of the freeway ACDA resembles very similarly the aforementioned longitudinal-axis safety buffer optimization component of our tactical model, in that sufficient frontal stopping distance is appropriated to account for any sudden frontal obstructions (such as the rapid braking of the frontal vehicle, for whatever reason), so that frontal distance is great enough for the driver to react and brake in order to avoid a collision. The relevance of mentioning the ACDA therefore (which is *not* identical to the related component of our tactical model) is to make note of the different standards by which appropriate frontal following distance is determined; the ACDA factor is not subjectively conditioned to the considerations of many other situational driving factors as is frontal distance optimization in our tactical model, and therefore, in rare instances, the two may conflict. It is only in these cases that the ACDA would prompt an according legal-risk emphasis to adjust speed, since in the overwhelming majority of cases, the professional driver will maintain sufficient Assured Clear Distance Ahead as to satisfy the basic speed rule. Likely the most common (and at that, still rare) example of the professional driver's justified supersession of the basic speed rule is in a precarious case of highway entrance merging; as we have already discussed, there are vast safety risks associated with coming to a full stop in a merging lane, and so under the highest traffic-density and most challenging merging circumstances, it may be necessary to merge into a traffic gap of suboptimal length (and perhaps even a length in which the greatest possible ACDA would not permit the vehicle's coming to a full stop – and as such the present example follows). Likewise, subjective analysis of the collision-risk of whatever frontal object which would theoretically limit the ACDA (such as a gallinaceous bird) must be balanced against that of rear collision with an aggressive, tailgating rearwards vehicle and/or against that of the present impossibility of an evasive lane switch due to excessive traffic density in either escape lane – in which intently colliding into the misfortunate and inauspiciously located bird may be the appropriate professional driving response (and in which even a strategic, well-timed, and preparatory *increase* in speed may be optimal to increase rearwards safety buffer distance to account for the post-collision, temporary decrease in vehicular velocity, in the case of the aggressive tailgating driver) and in which the basic speed rule (intently rendering the ACDA to zero meters without compensatorily decreasing speed) would be decidedly and purposefully violated. In reality, it is only in such extreme and rare cases when application of the basic speed rule by means of ensuring sufficient Assured Clear Distance Ahead would be preferentially abandoned for a different recommendation of our tactical model, and therefore the realistic legal risk of doing so is quite small in comparison to the risks likely already at hand (of actual collision, perhaps) – and therefore the basic speed rule is in general and in almost every circumstance fully concordant with the frontal distance maintenance techniques of our tactical model (which we discussed in the previous chapter, despite speed determination's obvious relevance as well thereunto) and serves as a good general reminder about such safety practices. We only needed to address the topic in order to instill the professional driver with educated understanding of these important and pervasive legal concepts which should be known, and to briefly discuss the theoretical differences between them and the operations of our tactical model – which only diverge in extreme and unlikely circumstances. Furthermore, we are discussing currently the factors which contribute to the professional driver's assessment of freeway-vacant ideal travel speed – in which such potential disagreements between our tactical model and that of obeying the basic speed rule are even more minimized, since the major constraints of the basic speed rule involve the sort of dynamic vehicular factors which we will discuss in a later section and which limit the practical achievability of the freeway-vacant ideal travel speed on the immediate time scale (having been already determined). But as it pertains to this present discussion, the driver's ideal freeway-vacant speed would still be limited by factors as road curvature, road width, visibility conditions (hydrometeor-induced and solar-irradiance-induced), and road traction conditions (hydrometeor-induced or otherwise, be it by oil spills, leaking hydrological infrastructure, flooding, etc.). The professional driver must choose as the freeway-vacant ideal travel speed only the maximum speed (if even then so desired by a sound balancing of the other discussed contributing factors) guaranteed to ensure safe vehicular control under the present visible assessment of all these factors, unless he or she decides to make a great and conscious (and therefore, likely unwise) compromise of basic safety. What we have just stated introduces a new and significant concept in the determination of highway speed in that the existence of *changing* conditions is considered (i.e., the limiting factors summarized above are evaluated for their current visible extent to produce a determination of highway speed only for that section, after which continuous reconsiderations must be made). For instance, the enumerated factors of road surface slipperiness, curvature, and width all may change with linear distance achieved on the highway, by changing meteorological conditions, by changing road geometry, and by sudden lane-closures respectively. The same holds true for visibility conditions and virtually every exovehicular factor. This additional level of complexity – that of not only analyzing the relative balance of different factors discussed (such as time-urgency, fuel-efficiency, general safety, legal risk, etc.), but also analyzing the temporal and/or spatial *change* in these factors – naturally transitions our discussion on the determination of the freeway-vacant ideal travel speed to that of these factors' inherently variable nature.

Sectional prioritization and discretized risk analysis

Having established the general factors which dictate proper choice of speed on a theoretically empty hazardless freeway, let us now consider some intermediary factors which, in temporal size and scope, lay somewhere between the large-scale freeway-vacant ideal travel speed and that of micro-scale short-term intervehicular-dynamical speed changes. The analytical value of considering time-variable and distance-variable factors (over a fixed stretch of freeway) into the determination of speed is primarily concerned with identifying the mitigation of present factors due to more prominent future influences (e.g. changing speed limits, changing traffic congestion levels, or any changing situational conditions). For instance, if one first entering a 65mph zone must decelerate to a temporary, road-work-related 55mph zone only 1 mile ahead, is it truly worth accelerating up to 71mph – 6mph over the speed limit – only for negligible moments of arrival-time optimization due to the impending 55mph zone? Clearly, the need to decelerate anyway will add an additional fuel-inefficiency cost (by losing heat energy to the brakes likely needed to slow the vehicle from 71mph to the determined 55mph-zone travel speed), and the likelihood of increased traffic density engendered by the upcoming collision creates an additional safety cost in faster travel. Thirdly, the arrival-time benefits incurred by going 71mph on the 65mph are themselves drastically minimized since there is (in our hypothetical) only one mile of the 65mph stretch before the 55mph zone is reached, which means that an absolutely miniscule arrival-time improvement is brought about by going 71mph versus 65mph for such a short time (since the mere existence of such a 55mph zone is far more obstructive towards fast arrival anyways). Stated colloquially, our point is that in such a case, one "might as well" prioritize safety, fuel-efficiency, and attention to traffic (all aided by lower speed) due to the immutable reality that the far more impactful 55mph zone will limit the driver's ideal speed. If, on the other hand, a 65mph highway extends for a hundred miles with sparse traffic and ideal road conditions, a comparative travel speed of 71mph on a 65mph has the potential to yield far more benefits at a smaller cost. Monitoring speed limit signs is therefore an essential component of the professional driver's visual spatial awareness scanning technique, as earlier foreknowledge of such decreases (or even increases) in speed limit can afford more time to make optimal adjustments in anticipation of reaching the zone governed by the new speed limit.

Similar considerations due to differential variables such as speed limit violation risk (as elucidated in the example above) may extend to that of patterns in highway traffic density, road structure, meteorological conditions, and even the nature of subjective time-exigency itself. If it is known to the professional driver either by routine experience on a given freeway at certain times or by *in situ* traffic update data, obtained over the radio or through some internet enabled device, that an impending region of heavy traffic will create a decreased "need for speed" in time optimization on the former highway section (since arrival-time will be obstructed by the upcoming traffic anyway), then therefore the marginal arrival-time benefit of increasing speed does far less to outweigh the associated safety risks as in normal conditions (e.g. choosing between two speeds which would normally render the difference between 20 and 25 minutes-to-arrival now seem as the difference between 40 and 45 minutes, for instance, due to the unavoidable traffic delay ahead – a decreased relative time optimization benefit). Not only do such circumstances minimize the rewards to higher speed, but they also create separately increased safety costs associated with supra-speed-limit travel due to the impending (and perhaps sudden) need to decelerate upon reaching the traffic build up. In the case of narrowing road structure ahead (such as a lane reduction), the same can hold true in non-sparse traffic conditions wherein the constrained space will create lower speeds and less permissive safety margin buffers. The professional driver must also be aware of the variable nature of his or her situation of time exigency itself, since any combination of the above traffic-slowing phenomena may delay arrival time to an extent at which there are decreasing marginal returns to hastening arrival time (for a subjective strategy-level example, it may be considered far more meaningful to arrive 2.5 minutes before the begging of a meeting compared to that of 2.5 minutes thereafter than to arrive 30 minutes late compared to that of 35 minutes late – the same five minute difference which may be realized through arrival time optimization at some discrete portion of highway travel yields smaller marginal benefit when the congested discrete sections of highway travel effect a less meaningful delay anyway). This highly pertains to the driver's high-level strategic outlook for highway driving in a certain occasion, and depends entirely on specific driver need for arrival-time celerity according to individual driving circumstances.

Individual allovehicles during the highway exit phase of travel can also frequently constitute rare discretized limitations to freeway travel, which is otherwise represented by a continuous set of conditions. For instance, the freeway-exiting driver in the lane adjacent to the right-most lane must at some point lane-switch into the right-most lane (assuming a standard right-side exit) however may be constrained by a lateral or anterolateral vehicle in the destination lane. This would require an according deceleration to perform the merge into the right-most lane behind the anterolateral vehicle, or an aggressive accelerative passing of the allovehicle in order to merge in front of it. However the decreasing distance to the fixed forward position of the exit is a factor which is doubly integrated into such acceleration (with speed being the integral of acceleration, and distance being the integral of speed). Therefore, forward proximity to the exit exponentially dissuades such an aggressive passing maneuver and incentivizes decelerative merging behind the anterolateral or lateral right-most-lane vehicle. This follows the concept of our present discussion since speed is about to be lowered anyway upon exiting the highway; the marginal benefit, therefore, of aggressively accelerating to pass such an allovehicle is largely decreased, and the associated risk is largely increased due to increasing proximity to the exit, which in the most extreme case could risk collision with the exit median structure from which the exit ramp originates (if the over-aggressive and unwise passing maneuver could not be completed in time). In such situations of highway exiting and discretized allovehicle obstructions to forward position (vehicles being unable to holographically pass through other vehicles), it therefore becomes wise in this situation to decrease speed and safely merge whereas long-range, continuous, characteristic intrafreeway travel would favor the higher freeway-vacant ideal travel speed.

Variable meteorological conditions are particularly relevant to the effect described above, as they may occasion a discrete section of freeway either in the absence of or supplementarily with the other factors above. The four meteorological parameters which affect (in majority) the professional driver's tactical awareness are (1) hydrometeor-induced decreases in road-tire traction, (2) hydrometeor and/or fog induced reductions in visibility, (3) physical air-resistance effects of wind flow, and (4) cloud cover prevention or attenuation of otherwise visually-obstructive solar glare. While we will reserve a dedicated discussion concerning the general considerations which these factors should bring to the professional driver's immediate attention, a limited overview of these conditions' likelihood of being predicted during the course of freeway travel is relevant to the present topic. In the same way that knowledge of impending slow traffic would affect the driver's decision-making in the way explained above, any precognitive expectation of the enumerated conditions will accordingly diminish the marginal returns to achieving faster speed prior to the arrival of any such undesirable meteorological conditions (inverting, of course, our phrasing of the fourth factor, in which a *lack* of cloud cover may allow solar glare to challenge the professional driver's spatial awareness scanning – although this does seem to be an occurrence quite improbably predicted without specific knowledge of solar angle and of very local atmospheric conditions). The third enumerated factor, of wind drag effects over the vehicle's surface geometry, is by far the most complicated to understand clearly as the variable vectors of wind and vehicle travel themselves may change drastically (both vectors perhaps varying both in speed and direction), and so therefore a lack of precise understanding of forecast wind patterns and road curvature – a lack of extra-visual spatial knowledge to be highly likely – must effect an overall more conservative treatment of these potentially dangerous factors if high winds are generally known or predicted to be a factor for consideration. This may often be strongly correlated with localized weather and surface topography patterns in mountainous regions, prompting posted areas of "dangerous crosswinds" (such as erected warning signs indicate around mile 76 of Interstate 93 Northbound in New Hampshire) which alert cognizant drivers of the higher potential for such conditions. Therefore it would clearly represent a defeatist and purposeless attempt at arrival-time optimization to travel upwards of 70mph into or marginally before a 50mph 45-

degree (with respect the vehicle's longitudinal axis) headwind, both massively impacting fuel-efficiency if 70mph speed is maintained, with a drag force equivalent to that of regular (calm-wind) 105mph travel (the magnitude of the final wind vector being the angular sum of its two constituent vectors, $70 + \frac{\sqrt{2}}{2} \times 50 = 105$mph), dangerously impacting the lateral stability of the vehicle (with a constant 35mph lateral component wind force bearing on the vehicle), and also dangerously decreasing the maneuverability of the vehicle by increasing the lateral tire friction force necessary to counter the air resistance. While in theory a favorable wind vector direction (directly opposing the regular frontal wind drag force) may in fact improve some of these factors, it is such a capricious, unlikely, and usually unpredictable condition (perhaps along with that of changing road heading) that an emphasis on safety will interpret any present or predicted event of high wind as a potentially dangerous speed-mitigating factor to the professional driver's task of speed optimization, regardless of fine and temporary differences in its directional heading. We therefore link these considerations back into the present topic of discussion by noting its tactical similarity to that of predicted upcoming areas of slow traffic, since they decrease the benefit of any extra arrival-time optimizing speed increase and support a slower ideal speed. It is difficult to image situations other than that of pronounced topographical effects and of localized mesoscale weather phenomena in which the immediateness and variability of the wind hazard factor would be of merit in the current analysis we are performing of rapidly *changing* factors and their unique effect in lowering ideal speed before their arrival – if, of course, such challenging conditions present themselves as a mere characterizing weather condition of a given entire stretch of highway travel, then of course they are to be considered as general safety hazards to travel as would be any other mitigating factor to the determination of freeway-vacant ideal travel speed. Going back to our original list, the first and second factors are much more straightforward, requiring little explanation, in that they *always* increase the necessary frontal stopping distance – the former increasing the physical stopping distance minimum by decreased traction due to slippery conditions, and the latter increasing necessary stopping distance by decreasing the amount of afforded reaction time to a potential hazard, given the limited visibility. This should serve as a hopefully obvious reminder that basic minimum frontal stopping distance exists as a function of two contributing factors: that of vehicle brake system and tire traction physical capability, and also that of driver vision-response reaction time capability – and not solely the former, a practical reality taught in any introductory driving course.

Additional safety factors

Now that we have discussed the ideal, long-term freeway-vacant ideal travel speed, and have begun to shed light on how immediate ideal travel speeds may increasingly vary with the narrowness to which a certain spatial or temporal length is given, we will now progress onto understanding the highly immediate factors which will, on occasion, advocate departure from the determined ideal travel speed. Indeed the theoretical parameters which define our concept of the "freeway-vacant ideal travel speed", they having in their definition an utterly void highway empty of other vehicles, lacking any adverse weather or visibility conditions, and assumed to be free of physical obstructions, are rarely if ever encountered in their pure, ideal form. The professional driver must use the freeway-vacant ideal travel speed as an "attracting force" which brings actual speed closer to it when a lack of mitigating factors permits doing so. Obviously, as we have already discussed in the Lane Optimization chapter, maintenance of sufficient safety margins (in particular, the longitudinal-axis frontal/rearwards following distance buffers) is of prime importance and will often be the primary mitigating "force" in decreasing actual speed from the ideal freeway-vacant travel speed due to the necessity of maintaining safe following distance. Although this crucial and continuous task of the professional driver to maintain proper interstitial vehicular position in the "whole intervehicular isolane space" was a fitting topic for our discussion on lane optimization (due to lane switches' massive dynamical role in the concept), we may focus on a few of the related safety concepts which are inherently speed related.

We have informally described the overall danger of collision as a function of mostly traffic density up unto this point, and that therefore frontal following distance should be increased under such circumstances. While this is true, it is also relevant to demonstrate that much traffic research has indicated the *variability* of speed conditions – not necessarily concurrent to high traffic-density – as another factor highly correlated with collision risk (Aljanahi, et al., 1999)[6] (Baruya & Finch, 1994)[7] (Garber & Gadiraju, 1990)[8]. This justifies our general position that adjustments to speed on the highway are ideally minimized (being ideally unnecessary in the first place), just as we prefaced our discussion on lane optimization with the qualification that lane switching, in general, is preferably avoided unless certain benefits outweigh inherent safety risks. However, since adjustments in speed will in all likelihood need to be made during the course of freeway travel, it is always optimal for the professional driver to have additional frontal and rearwards space in which to carry forth the variation in speed so that instantaneous rates of change in speed, whether measured over fixed distance or over a fixed period of time, are minimized. In general, this decreases crash risk by the obvious physical, dynamical reason that surrounding drivers will have more time to react to the new relative positioning of the driver's vehicle and to adjust their own speed, and also by the theoretically diminished speed-differential coefficient which concerns traffic research's mathematical model correlating vehicle behavior to crash risk. In other words, from

---

[6] Aljanahi, A. A. M., Rhodes, A. H. & Metcalfe, A. V., 1999. Speed, speed limits and road traffic accidents under free flow conditions. *Accident Analysis & Prevention,* 31(1), pp. 161-168.
[7] Baruya, A. & Finch, D. J., 1994. *Investigation of traffic speeds and accidents on urban roads.* London, PTRC Education and Research Services, Ltd..
[8] Garber, N. J. & Gadiraju, R., 1990. Factors influencing speed variance and its influence on accidents. *Transportation Research Record,* Volume 1213, p. 64–71.

either perspective, this entire discussion reduces to a clearer understanding of why copious following distance margins are beneficial to safety. In the same way, the professional driver must use behavioral prediction analysis of other drivers in order to assess the likely existence of an impending change in speed of a surrounding vehicle, which we have already discussed to some extent in former sections. Here, however, we seek to instill the understanding that variations from determined freeway-vacant ideal travel speed will be necessary in order to participate in the fluid flow of traffic in the safest way possible; in the event that extraordinary emphasis is placed on time-arrival optimization, this relation still exists – however the determined freeway-vacant ideal travel speed would simply be higher, and therefore would more forcefully "attract" all choices of immediate speeds to it, with exponentially increasing safety and optimization costs, as we have demonstrated formerly.

Speed Optimization Conclusion

Our discussion of highway travel speed optimization therefore illuminates the general safety costs not only of subjectively high speeds but also of higher than necessary levels of speed *variation* around whatever average speed is chosen. Unsurprisingly, these same two characteristic speed-related safety indications hold identical effects on that of fuel-efficiency optimization and accordingly synopsize the major parts of our ensuing discussion thereabout.

CHAPTER 7

Fuel-efficiency Optimization

Our discussion of determining the freeway-vacant ideal travel speed followed a basic and necessary explanation of fuel-efficiency's most obvious and prominent causal factor: decreased air resistance gained by slower travel. Leaving the topic unexplored beyond this extent, however, would be insufficient for our comprehensive tactical model for highway spatial maneuvering, since there is a direct causal relationship between driver maneuvers and fuel-efficiency optimizations (relationships that are often interlinked with other safety and intervehicular-dynamical factors). The most basic of these, which we have shown above, is that of continued *variation* in speed – that is, more constant travel speed is usually associated with both improved safety and fuel-efficiency. Our discussion on fuel-efficiency optimization tactics, the dictates of which must always take second priority to that of safety optimization, will therefore commence with a more detailed examination on how proper control of the differential nature of speed can yield optimization benefits. We simplify the various meanings of the term "differential nature of speed" into that of an *acceleration profile* which is simply a conceptual mapping of changes in vehicular speed, regardless of however fast or slow the vehicle in question is travelling on average.

Acceleration profile effects

Since freeway speeds are greater than those of secondary roads from which a vehicle must necessarily enter a freeway, the acceleration profile of a vehicle's highway trip must at some point involve a large energy-consumptive acceleration from lower speed to freeway speed (such as is likely accomplished on the acceleration zone of a highway entrance ramp). While our discussion on highway entrance merging has analyzed the safety and intervehicular effects of this acceleration, we must also examine solely from a fuel-efficiency lens the differences between slow, gradual acceleration, moderate acceleration, and "jackrabbit", "petal-to-the-medal" acceleration maneuvers which use a high proportion of maximum engine output.

Initial acceleration to freeway speed

In most engines, low-RPM, high-gear, high-torque transmission and engine conditions (compared to that of equal vehicular speed using a higher internal engine RPM and a lower gear) is positively correlated with improved fuel-efficiency, both for diesel and (even more so) for gasoline engines. Perhaps counterintuitively, it is therefore, in general, more fuel-efficient to accelerate smoothly yet quickly rather than slowly extending the acceleration process through a more gradual distance and time. This efficiency optimization is limited in basic theory by (1) the energy-wasteful tire slippage that may occur with extreme acceleration (in addition to unwanted wear on internal components) and (2) a natural limit on engine efficiency with greater acceleration due to torque and/or RPM exceeding the optimal minimum Brake Specific Fuel Consumption (BSFC) level. The considerations of this second effect, however, are typically beyond the scope and scale in most vehicles of the quickness of accelerations likely to be performed while entering the highway, especially when practical safety considerations are applied to the professional driver's ultimate choice of acceleration intensity, and therefore the general relation of faster acceleration to increased fuel-efficiency holds true. We therefore recommend a controlled, swift, safe, and brisk acceleration to desired freeway speed (again, examining solely fuel-efficiency factors) – while rapidly upshifting gear in the case of a manual transmission vehicle (in order to maintain the higher engine torque and the lower-RPM, holding speed constant, which are associated with more fuel-efficient accelerations). We should repeat that our examination of this effect is quite limited to the theoretical vacuum of a given need to increase speed and by a given amount – in reality, of course, it is desirable lack the need to accelerate by any large margin, however it will in all standard circumstances (barring

Chapter 7: Fuel-efficiency Optimization

218

complete bumper-to-bumper traffic, or an ensuing traffic flow of most piecemeal quickening therefrom) be necessary at least once in the freeway travel task. Furthermore, situational safety factors and regular determinations such as freeway-vacant idea travel speed will limit the degree to which acceleration is performed, as clearly over-accelerating and then braking will waste much energy which could be saved simply by a marginal, reductional change in the magnitude of acceleration. The present examination, therefore, only states the narrow, controlled, and probable likelihood that accelerating from one certain speed to another over a shorter period of time is typically more fuel-efficient than that of the same acceleration conducted over a longer time-interval.

Optimal engine power vs. brake-avoidance

Once general freeway-characteristic speed is attained after highway entrance merging and initial acceleration, fuel-efficiency attention should typically switch to that of speed maintenance – chiefly obeying, of course, the most obvious rule already stated that brake usage wastefully depletes kinetic energy as friction lost for no other useful purpose and is therefore always negative from the narrow fuel-efficiency point of view (being also, obviously, critically essential to safety considerations when less immediate speed reduction tactics do not allow space margins to be sufficiently maintained in moments of instantaneous necessity). Once a view of speed-maintenance-related fuel-efficiency tactics is taken beyond that of minimizing brake usage, discussion turns to that of finding the optimum engine power level used to sustain any given maintained speed, with RPM speed being conducted through variable gear reductions in the transmission – however the quantification of this optimum level can be highly variable from engine to engine, and the driver's ability to control it to begin with is severely limited by the existence of automatic transmissions which accounted for a whopping 96.2% of new US-sold vehicles in 2010. If the professional driver is operating a manual transmission vehicle, then he or she may generally improve fuel-efficiency by opting to relatively increase gear and decrease RPM for a given speed (usually under 2500 RPM and generally a bit lower for diesel engines), thereby increasing engine torque (by the same logic as the faster-acceleration optimization explained above), yet even this trend has a lower limit which varies from engine to engine. It is therefore typically far more relevant to the professional driver seeking to optimize fuel-efficiency to be concerned with brake-usage avoidance and optimizing the constant absolute speed (which, in the light of typical highway speeds, will almost always mean minimizing it), which itself can have a much larger effect on fuel-efficiency than that which variable, unsure, and often impossible choices of isotachic gear level can create.

Maintenance of even throttle, load, and speed

Let us assume, however, the optimal engine power output level, which does vary depending on engine and circumstance, in order to qualify the energy efficiency of different methods of cruising on the freeway. Many sources, including the general attitudes recurring in this book, cite constancy of speed as a fuel-efficiency optimization relative to an acceleration profile over time of erratic changes in speed; this basic statement, however, is only generally true because of the assumed implication of *braking* and its superior negative impact (depending on extent) on fuel-efficiency than internal engine factors. What we seek to show here, however, is that a purely theoretical treatment of engine output over a stretch of variable highway circumstances does not necessarily hold constant speed as its most fuel-efficient acceleration profile. Consider the given optimal engine power output level: upon reaching the upwards slope of a hill, the speed of the vehicle would decrease holding power output constant due to the greater opposing gravitational forces; holding speed constant would necessarily *increase* engine power output beyond that which is the established, theoretical ideal point – thereby lowering fuel-efficiency. This illustrative example of an approach to the top of a hill may be extended to that of any circumstance which would increase the engine power output necessary to maintain constant speed – such as an increase in the velocity of headwind, or even decreasing air tire pressure. It may therefore seem that driving with constant throttle position, rather than with constant speed, represents the ideal fuel-efficient cruising tactic – however the relation of throttle position in most vehicles to engine output power is not exactly proportional, but rather is run through a computer (on modern vehicles) of varying function and complexity to determine the ideal engine output power. Compensation of this effect would typically, in fact, require relative modulation of even the throttle position, therefore, to maintain constant ideal engine output power at the approach of a hill or some other engine-resistive factor. It is therefore inaccurate to equate isotachic cruising with the most fuel-efficient possible cruising tactic in the strictest sense. Rather, attention to isotachic cruising generally prevents against brake usage (which may result in energy losses vastly exceeding that of the present factor engine-internal) and may *generally support* an approximate engine-power-constant output level in a manner that is tangible and simple for the driver's control – especially on flat and/or otherwise resistance-constant stretches of freeway. This explanation develops a simplistic, initial argument underlying our overwhelming support for cruise control usage – an essential weapon in the professional driver's vehicle-control tactical arsenal – to which we will devote an extensive discussion in a following section.

"Pulse-and-glide" tactic

Having characterized, however, the technically invalid nature of fuel-efficiency claims holding speed-constant cruising as the optimal cruising method, we must also explore the more extreme methods aimed at optimizing the above effect and their questionable balancing of fuel-efficiency benefits and safety consequences – a recurring theme to many of the elaborate techniques on the fringes of the fuel-efficiency optimization field. As we demonstrated above, speed gained by faster acceleration places more torque on the engine and, though of course increasing energy consumption, also increases fuel-efficiency due to a more optimal operation point on the engine's Brake Specific Fuel Consumption chart; since distance is the integral of speed, and since distance is held constant in our comparative analysis of fuel-efficiency (assuming constant freeway destination), therefore a given *distance* is more efficiently overtaken with the engine at such a higher torque level. Clearly, however, freeway speed is limited by constraining factors which make continued acceleration in this high-efficiency zone impossible. This conceptual understanding gives way to the tactic known as "pulse-and-glide" (also called "burn and coast"), in which a period of the high-efficiency fast acceleration is followed by a gradual coasting deceleration back to slower speed in which the engine is ideally off and physically detached from the drive train. This approximates chosen speed on the freeway (with an initial speed-excess phase and ensuing speed-deficit phase, compared to the chosen constant ideal speed) and theoretically limits engine usage to only the moments in which the high-efficiency, high-torque conditions are in effect – increasing therefore average gasoline efficiency compared to constant-speed cruising at less optimal engine power output levels. This technique is sound for its fuel-efficiency aim both in theory and in demonstrated actuality (though bearing far more use in slower driving situations such as secondary road suburban driving, and not primarily high-speed freeway driving) – however we strongly recommend against its usage (at least in this theoretically extreme form) due to the near-certain safety risks of increased variable speed and even more so of coasting in neutral with the drive train detached from the dead engine (also disabling therefore other features such as power-steering), limiting defensive opportunities in critical responsive circumstances which require split-second reaction to elements which would take whopping seconds to resuscitate if coasting in neutral with the engine off (which is also illegal in many jurisdictions). Therefore a more prudent and potentially viable amelioration to the raw theoretical extreme of the pulse-and-glide tactic is to coast in neutral with the engine on (affording faster engine-drive-train restoration time) or, better yet, with the transmission in gear so that defensive opportunities are not limited. In the latter, friction throughout the transmission and drivetrain components certainly will limit the effective inertial coasting distance and therefore the overall fuel-efficiency augment of this technique, however this is a necessary safety requirement to merit the likely far-inferior fuel-efficiency optimization even if this technique is to be used in the first place. Furthermore, most modern vehicles will completely shut off fuel injection during this phase of in-gear coasting (the Deceleration Fuel Cutoff or "DFCO"), which still ensures the remnant of some (and perhaps a significant amount) of fuel-efficiency optimization in the only remotely safe implementation of the pulse-and-glide technique. Even still, the generally suboptimal effects of the rapid freeway speed variation inherent to any form of the pulse-and-glide technique must inform the professional driver's decision in balancing the potential fuel-efficiency optimizations from this tactic to that of safety risk's massive concurrent correlation with potentially fuel-inefficient *and* seriously dangerous collisional outcomes.

Gravitational potential energy related methods

The nature of the pulse-and-glide tactic, taking advantage of engine output at its more optimal power levels, can be applied to the instances of variable freeway surface topography in which increases in elevation store gravitational potential energy which can later be released on the downhill part of a topological protrusion in the freeway's vertical profile. That is, maintaining constant power output on the upwards phase and then coasting on the downwards phase would mimic the same nature of the pulse-and-glide technique from the engine's perspective, which would engender the same benefits in fuel-efficiency for the same reasons. Isotachic cruising, such as is attempted by the vehicle's cruise control feature, therefore misses the optimal fuel-efficiency mark due to its inherent objective of over-accelerating on the upwards part and even braking (to slow the wasted acceleration) on the downhill part, whereas lowering speed on the uphill section (to maintain constant engine output power at the ideal level) and coasting on the way down would represent the most fuel-efficient option. As with the pulse-and-glide technique, coasting with the engine off is more efficient than coasting in neutral, and coasting in neutral is more efficient than coasting in drive with the transmission in gear – however, as we stated formerly, it is very unlikely that the professional driver would ever disengage his or her drive-train from the engine output, let alone shut off the engine, due to the massive safety consequences this would represent in limited defensive response abilities should sudden evasive acceleration become necessary. It may, however, be considered marginally safer to coast on the downhill phase of a hill on the freeway than in regular, flat pulse-and-glide operation due to the greater potential of speed that the gravitational force exerts (perhaps even *increasing* speed for a few moments during the coast), affording braking opportunities if speed needs to be reduced, rather than the solely decelerative, frictional coasting of the analogous phase of flat pulsing-and-gliding. Braking itself is a practical fuel-efficiency disadvantage of isotachic cruising over hills, since if even speed is maintained throughout the ascending of the upwards part of the hill, certainly the only way at least a portion of that energy expenditure can be recuperated is through the additional gravitational accelerative speed gained on the downwards phase – speed that is above the freeway-vacant ideal travel speed which the driver was already travelling at, and therefore speed which is likely necessary to be wastefully limited by brake usage. Maintaining constant engine load during the ascent of the hill, which would naturally constitute a gradual reduction in speed until the crest, would allow the gravitationally accelerative downwards phase to restore speed to a safe level without the usage of braking – or at least, with the usage of less braking, and/or with a reduced likelihood that braking would be necessary (certainly the lack of path-of-travel visibility which hills can create causes the unavoidable possibility that unseen frontal circumstances at the bottom of the hill, on the other side, do indeed warrant braking and deceleration – however naturally lowering speed on the upwards phase of the hill lessens the probability of needing to brake for such circumstances due to an overall reduction of speed at the crest which is comparatively maintained on the downwards, accelerative phase as opposed to that of already travelling at a faster speed on the crest of the hill). Like almost all fuel-efficiency optimizations, this hill negotiation technique brings with it potentially negative safety consequences (even if in-gear coasting is used), since the initial gravitational deceleration and descending gravitational acceleration causes a speed differential which can narrow following distance between proximate vehicles in either case (narrowing rearwards following distance in the decelerative, upwards phase and narrowing frontal following distance in the accelerative, downwards phase). It is therefore optimal for safety (assuming moderate-to-high traffic conditions in which safety gap tolerances are challenged) to maintain the presently chosen speed by slight acceleration up the hill and slight speed-maintaining braking down the hill (with a small decrease in speed, if possible, before the crest, to take into account the lack of path-of-travel visibility caused by the hill – if indeed the topological aberration is pronounced enough), which, of course, runs at odds against fuel-efficiency. Fuel-efficient negotiation of hills is therefore similar to the pulse-and-glide technique in that its potential to be safely executed is very strongly correlated with the population and density of allovehicular traffic on the given stretch of highway – perhaps safe in highly sparse traffic circumstances, and likely ignored (in large part, at least) for the better in traffic-dense circumstances when relatively minor fuel-efficiency optimizations should take a back seat to safety considerations.

Drag reduction

We have already demonstrated that the opposing drag force of air resistance causes a consequential loss of engine energy at highway speeds, and which increases exponentially with further increases in speed. Therefore, a large field of highway fuel-efficiency optimization tactics are aimed at decreasing the magnitude of this force. While lowering speed is almost always guaranteed to bear the greatest minimizing effect on air resistance drag force over any other method, there are other optimizations which can reduce the drag force in the lens of isotachic relative comparison.

Dynamical changes to the drag coefficient

The first category of these concerns changes to the vehicle's drag coefficient by altering surface characteristics. Many of these are preparatory (such as wiping off roof snow accumulations, storing cargo on the rear as opposed to the roof of the vehicle, and maintaining proper air tire pressure – all of which are excellent safety recommendations in the first place), and therefore irrelevant to the overall topic of the present discussion of highway spatial maneuvering. Therefore the largest *dynamical* factor to the vehicle's drag coefficient, mutable during driving, is usually window aperture status. As a general trend, opening windows increases the vehicle's drag coefficient and decreases, therefore, fuel-efficiency, by means of creating aerodynamic turbulence between the outdoor passing air and the still indoor air, with a relative speed difference between them in the order of 70mph (or whatever is the present travelling speed). Since this effect is therefore directly related to the speed of the vehicle relative to the still interior air, it is in large part a consideration only in the freeway context (and at regular highway speeds, at that) (Huff, et al., 2013)[1]. The phenomenon of fuel-inefficient drag increase caused by opened windows, combined with its common subjective purpose of lowering indoor air temperature to passenger-comfortable levels, has created quite the debate concerning the comparative fuel-efficiency of this cooling method to that of the other climate control option available to the professional driver: air conditioning. Operation of air conditioning compressors can create sizeable losses of engine output energy; a National Renewable Energy Laboratory (NREL) 2000 report shockingly concluded that under some extreme circumstances, "current air-conditioning systems can reduce the fuel economy of high fuel-economy vehicles by about 50% and reduce the fuel economy of today's mid-sized vehicles by more than 20%", contending that air conditioning compressor power load "can be greater than the engine power required to move a mid-sized vehicle at a constant speed of 56 km/h (35 mph)" (Farrington & Rugh,

---

[1] Huff, S., West, B. & Thomas, J., 2013. Effects of Air Conditioner Use on Real-World Fuel Economy. *SAE Technical Paper Series*, Volume 2013-01-0551.

2000)². For this reason, there have been objective attempts to quantify the comparative energy losses to air conditioning and window opening, as common sense would dictate the former only to become more fuel-efficient than the latter at and over some minimum speed at which the increased drag force caused by open-window-turbulence (which, as we stated before, is positively correlated with speed) outweighs the effect of the air conditioner's power load. As it concerns the freeway context, at or around speeds of 70mph, the distinction is likely to be minimal, since the variations in air density conditions and the vehicular aerodynamic profiles which alter this exact equivalence point tend to place the value at or just above this approximate freeway-travel-speed figure³. An illuminating 2004 SAE symposium presentation concluded that, indeed, "windows down can be a significant real impact on fuel consumption", and that SUVs in particular (i.e., higher drag to begin with) are generally far less disposed to being negatively influenced fuel-efficiency-wise by opened windows than that of Sedans (8% vs. 20%) which take on a more aerodynamic profile that can be disturbed by such window-open effects to a greater comparative degree (Hill, et al., 2004)⁴. The study also demonstrated that the balancing point is highly dependent on variable factors such as transmission gear, ambient air temperature, engine efficiency, wind velocity, and tire temperature – variability which prevents the

---

² Farrington, R. & Rugh, J., 2000. Impact of Vehicle Air Conditioning on Fuel economy, Tailpipe Emissions, and Electric Vehicle Range. *NREL Report,* October.Volume No. CP-540-28960.

³ Some sources place this optimum cross-over speed point of windows-down air conditioning usage at vastly lower speeds, such as 50mph; the exact figure of course greatly varies according to particular situational and vehicular characteristics. We only seek to note that the freeway environment is by far the most likely of any driving environment to warrant the comparative fuel-efficient usage of the air conditioning system, due to the supreme speed of air passing the windows in this context.

⁴ Hill, W., Lebut, D., Major, G. & Schenkel, F., 2004. *Affect [sic] of Windows Down on Vehicle Fuel Economy as compared to AC load.* s.l., s.n.

dictation of a simple numerical speed constant at which air conditioning becomes more fuel-efficient, since such a figure would convey a misleading sense of constancy and certainty. At highway speeds, however, our general recommendation of using air conditioning as opposed to lowering windows follows from a more holistic view of the professional driver's tactical considerations: to the degree that fuel-efficiency is a primary concern in the driver's high-level freeway driving strategy to begin with, he or she will eschew *both* types of indoor air temperature cooling, being physically conditioned to withstand the high air temperatures – and if a form of cooling must be appropriated (if, for instance, it is the plan reality that the un-adapted driver is indeed psychologically and physiologically impacted by the hot air temperatures in a negative way as to render cooling an essential safety precaution), and assuming the categorical highway speeds (in the neighborhood of 70mph) at which the efficiency of the two forms of cooling is mostly ambiguous (taking an average of all the influential variables), then the option which at least does not impose a large auditory disturbance to the driver's senses becomes preferable. At less than maximum highway speeds however, such as would likely characterize the speed of a driver maximizing fuel-efficiency to whom such factors would bear more than ordinary significance in the first place, then window-open driving with the air conditioning system turned off (at least compared to its maximum output level) is highly likely to achieve greater fuel-efficiency. Ultimate reference on the matter must be had to the particular vehicle type, aerodynamic profile, and air conditioner power requirement of the driver's specific vehicle, as well as the amount of absolute import this factor wields in his or her high-level driving strategy to begin with.

With the examination of dynamical changes to a vehicle's drag coefficient out of the way, our discussion on fuel-efficient drag reduction now turns to that of maneuvering tactics which place the vehicle in zones of decreased air flow velocity (and therefore, decreased drag force), the first of which being the rousing and memorable tactic known as "drafting". If we should even need to assign a definition to the well-known theoretical practice, we should name it the close following of another frontal (and hopefully larger) vehicle in the attempt to travel in the low air pressure zone immediately behind it which is created (i.e., a "wind-shadow") for the reduction of the drag force – using, of course, risibly neutral terms to describe what is such an obstinate affront to basic safety practices of maintaining frontal following distance, and which is therefore near to characteristic nonexistence in the mindset of the professional driver's choices for fuel-efficiency optimization; however, we will devote to it the properly full discussion and analysis which so memorably riotous a "highway driving tactic" certainly merits.

Drafting

Justification for our generally critical position on the drafting technique must not exclude full concession of the potential fuel-efficiency benefits which the practice can yield. Unofficial conceptual experiments have shown an approximate 10% reduction in fuel consumption in a four-wheeled vehicle driving 100 feet behind a large truck compared to control levels in which no frontal vehicle is present; this reduction can increase to near 40% at an absurd 10-foot travel distance behind the frontal vehicle. Large geometric volumes such as semi-trucks create an enormous slipstream behind them, which is essentially the fluid "wake" region of disturbed air through which the vehicle has pushed, accelerating air around the edges and rear-end of the large frontal vehicle and thereby creating an area of effectively "parted wind" behind it – this effect both causes a naturally lowered drag force against the rear following vehicle (due to the frontal slipstream air which is travelling forward at some positive speed relative to the pavement, which therefore creates lower relative speed against the windshield of the drafting driver who is travelling in the same direction) to reduce the required engine output power necessary to maintain constant speed and therefore improves fuel-efficiency. Our dynamical description of the effect likely also explains why some informal road experiments demonstrate in fact better results of the effect at 10 foot distance compared to extremely close distances such as 2 feet – since the vehicle is then so close to the frontal vehicle that there is less contact with the created forward-travelling air slipstream which is created by the friction with the *edges* of the large frontal vehicle, which may exceed the lateral expanse of the drafting driver's vehicle at such close distances (distances so close as to render this consideration a purely theoretical pondering). Some sources even state that drafting produces a small fuel-efficiency benefit for the frontal driver, due to increases in rearwards air

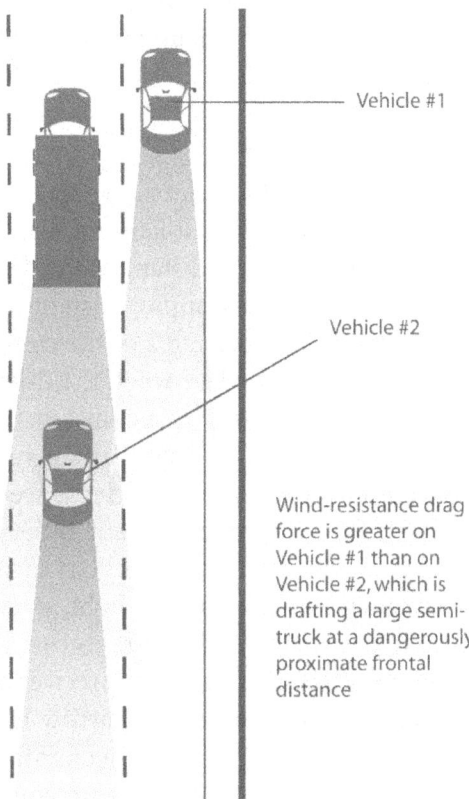

Figure 15 – Visualization of the "wind-shadow" sought by the drafting technique

pressure between the two vehicles, although this lacks sufficient justification either from scientific proof or experimental traffic research as would be necessary to consider it one of the primary benefits to drafting. Nevertheless, the concept is theoretically sound and incontrovertible in its energy-savings potential, as it is commonly known and employed in competitive NASCAR drag-racing and even high-speed cycling events. Our critical position towards drafting, therefore, unsurprisingly stems from its plethora of negative safety consequences which are almost guaranteed to outweigh the fuel-efficiency optimization from any meaningful manifestation of the tactic in an overwhelming majority of circumstances.

Critique of drafting

Travelling so closely to another vehicle, let alone such a vehicle of characteristically greater mass and size, violates the basic safety tenets of maintaining frontal following distance in order to afford both greater reaction time and larger stopping distance in the event that the frontal vehicle brakes or decelerates to the degree that a dangerous speed differential is created between the driver and the frontal vehicle, which is bound to result in a collision. The few who advocate drafting as a remotely acceptable or safe highway practice argue that the greater mass of the frontal vehicle, as well as the general comparative design of semi-trucks or any other type of large frontal vehicle necessary for the technique, prevent such vehicles from braking nearly as quickly as a following, light, maneuverable, four-wheel passenger vehicle could, and that therefore drafting drivers are able to regulate speed in a safe and precise manner behind a large frontal vehicle to maintain the narrow following distance. This argument is flawed on multiple accounts; we therefore propose unto its advocates the following contradictory objections:

1. While the raw dynamical fact that stopping distance at a given speed is greater for large semi-trucks than for light and maneuverable four-wheeled vehicles, stopping time is a

composite parameter of (at least) two primary constituent factors, physical stopping distance and driver-brake reaction time (termed "perception-reaction time" (PRT) and "maneuver-time" (MT) in the American Association of State Highway and Transportation Officials terminology), the latter of which is not controlled for in this present narrow-minded argument in support for drafting (i.e., there is some critical intervehicular proximity at which a collision will occur before the drafting driver even reacts to the braking or deceleration of the frontal vehicle, which represents the distance travelled by the vehicle during the reaction-time constituent of the total stopping time parameter);

2. The stopping distance for a drafting and purportedly "maneuverable" vehicle is vastly increased, and its "maneuver-time" (MT) vastly decreased, under these circumstances, perhaps even to a degree approaching (or, plausibly, even *exceeding*) that of the "heavy" and "slowly decelerative" frontal semi-truck (or whichever other frontal vehicle creates the drafting effect), since the road friction against the tires is massively decreased, since the downforce pressing the tires into the road is massively decreased, since wind resistance is smaller due to the vehicle's drafting (as vehicles are aerodynamically designed such that a component of the drag force is diverted down into the tires for improved maneuverability instead of into the longitudinal axis which opposes engine output force, and which furthermore explains why high performance sports vehicles are designed with a low aerodynamic profile);

3. All forms of vehicle maneuverability, including steering response (such as would likely be necessary to avoid collision by executing an evasive lane switch if the frontal vehicle were to rapidly decelerate), are severely compromised by the aforementioned decrease in aerodynamic downforce;

4. The very premise of this argument, that of precise and rapid regulation of speed by means of braking in order to maintain a precise distance behind the frontal vehicle, entirely defeats the purpose of drafting to begin with by wasting exorbitant amounts of frictional energy to the brakes of the vehicle – such rapid and wasteful usage of brakes which would not otherwise be necessary if regular and safe frontal following distance were appropriated in the first place; and

5. Even assuming perfect driver responsive reaction time of zero seconds, such rapid and immediate decelerations necessary to maintain an exact following distance to the frontal vehicle of such critically proximate dimensions would necessarily risk the driver's vehicle itself to become subject to rear-end collision, due to the rearwards driver who is invited to travel ever more closely to the speed-regulating large frontal (wind-blocking) vehicle and whose reaction time is not known to be anything other than average – that is, if it is argued against our objection #1 above that a superhuman driver has a reaction time of zero seconds and therefore the capability to exactly match his or her vehicle's speed with that of the large frontal vehicle, then the vehicle to the rear is invited to follow what is effectively the large frontal vehicle (from a speed-differential, collision-likelihood point of view) with less-than-recommendable following distance perceiving his or her frontal driver, by the vehicle's plain appearance, to be a regular four-wheeled vehicle and not a large semi-truck, even though the two are "tied" together in speed in this hypothetical retort to the first objection above.

And clearly even the last enumerated hypothetical is unrealistic, as driver reaction times to frontwards changes in speed are indeed greater than zero, and therefore the drafting driver would be found slamming on the vehicle's brakes to make likely a collision with the rearwards vehicle, even if collision with the frontal wind-blocking vehicle could be avoided, and in fact, quite possibly, a collision involving all three vehicles if the two following are sufficiently proximate. In such an event, the comparative fuel expense of having abandoned the dangerous drafting technique and having allowed proper, copious following distances would be quite minimal compared to the fuel expense of each vehicle's fuel tank violently and catastrophically being ruptured during the course of the aforesaid drafting-caused collision, spilling and perhaps combusting their whole fluid contents across a remarkable span of marred freeway pavement. It is clearly quite the fuel-efficiency optimization to avoid such happenings, which can be achieved by abandoning the drafting "optimization", or at least by adopting the wisdom to perform the technique with conservative and only moderately undershot following distance in proper understanding of the risks which short following distances are known to create. It is not such that maintaining proper following distance behind a frontal vehicle entirely negates any sort of drag reduction benefit inherent to the "convoy" or "platoon" setup of longitudinally successive isolane vehicles, which is only taken to an extreme in the aggressive drafting case; studying convoys of commercial vehicles, Gotz (1983) found that even with 40 meters of frontal following distance at 50 mph (which is not by any means close to the disturbingly narrow frontal margins which extreme manifestations of drafting establish), the drag force on a following vehicle can still be reduced by up to 30%[5]. This quantification should further call into question the necessity of dangerously close following distances even to reap a large portion of the drag reduction benefits which drafting has to offer.

The potential dangers of the drafting practice are not, however, limited to such circumstances of rear-end collision caused by rapid deceleration of the frontal vehicle and insufficient following distance for defensive, collision-avoiding braking. Concerns have even been expressed of engines overheating, the frontal air-intake

---

[5] Gotz, H., 1983. Bus Design Features and their Aerodynamic Effects. *International Journal of Vehicle Design, Impact Aerodynamics on Vehicle Design,* Volume SP-3, pp. 229-255.

grill of the drafting vehicle being cut-off from cooling headwind airflow in so far as following distance is shortened (this being, of course, a proportionally higher concern in hot weather). Significant safety hazards may accompany the drafting driver in the event that the large frontal vehicle (typically an eighteen-wheeled truck, in the canonical example of "fuel-efficient" drafting) loses a wheel-cap at high speeds, or even more commonly, ejects an airborne fragment of tire retreading that has delaminated from one of the truck's tires. Tire retreading is a pervasively common remanufacturing practice in the trucking industry in which tread replacements are installed over worn tires as opposed to replacing the entire worn tire, which achieves significant cost savings. The treads also have a common negative reputation for coming loose from trucks at highway speeds and for being typical pieces of "road rubber" industrial ejecta commonly found on shoulder regions of the highway, which pose safety hazards even resting there. While reputable research has contradicted the widespread negative attitude against retreaded tires, showing that they are of relatively comparable safety to that of new tires (Hammond, 2009)[6], this does not exculpate them (or any potentially hazardous tire debris, new or retreaded) in their likelihood to become an extreme hazard to drafting drivers if drafting becomes adopted on the large scale. An illogical argument sometimes purported in defense of drafting with regards to truck debris ejecta hazards such as retreads states that the relative velocity between any truck debris and a following, drafting vehicle is minimal and therefore not very dangerous, since the debris was formerly attached to the freeway-speed truck vehicle. However this does not hold true for delaminated tire retreads, since they are pressed by the gravitational force of the weight of the vehicle into the pavement, and therefore are frictionally linked to the velocity of the pavement, which is the freeway-travel-speed slower than the drafting vehicle. Therefore, should one of these loosened tire retreadings be vertically shot or pulled into the air, whether by the rotational force of the partially attached wheel while detaching, or

---

[6] Hammond, P. J., 2009. *Retreaded Tire Use and Safety: Synthesis*, s.l.: s.n.

by the turbulent air slipstream which the truck leaves behind when fully detached, then it may crash into windshield of the following driver's vehicle at however fast it is travelling, perhaps over 70mph, in what may come to be a tragic safety disaster. While the drafting act is certainly not responsible for the truck's ejection of loosened debris, the shortened following distance it creates nearly guarantees that there will be insufficient reaction time to evade the piece of debris by deceleration or by evasive lane switching. Special sensitivity must be had to this risk especially in hot weather, when the risk of retread delamination is much greater; performed field analyses of tire fragments and casings have found that excessive heat was involved in the ejection of 30% of the tire fragments examined (Svenson, 2009)[7].

Additional safety arguments against drafting can be made from very basic understandings concerning the risk of minimizing frontal following distance; if, for instance, the frontal truck driver switches lanes in an attempt to avoid a rapidly decelerative (or even stationary) area of traffic ahead in his or her lane, and if the following, drafting driver is unable to follow the truck in its quick lane switch due to an allovehicular obstruction behind the truck in its new lane, then the following driver will be left with very little reaction time to decelerate for the original frontal hazard which prompted the trucker's lane switch in the first place; this would not have been the case had the driver lengthened following distance to a sufficient degree, or had switched lanes and passed the large frontal vehicle altogether – neither of which involve the generally dangerous technique of drafting.

Non-drafting intervehicular effects

We have shown that drafting is a characteristically dangerous practice in which the appropriate balance of safety and fuel-efficiency is almost always bound to yield a certain compromise

---

[7] Svenson, A. L., 2009. *Commercial Medium Tire Debris Study*. Rosemont, IL, s.n.

following distance of sufficient length as to lower the amount of active "drafting" use to such subjectively low levels that the term "proper following distance" would do better do describe what is less significantly "minimal drafting". Still, the drafting fuel-efficiency phenomenon may still hold some beneficial effect at generally safe distances behind a large vehicle and provides the professional driver with a widened set of options in rare, emergency, fuel-critical circumstances. There are, however, other aerodynamic factors on the highway, often ignored, besides drafting which can wield an effect on drag force and therefore fuel-efficiency. Any vehicle travelling at highway speeds creates an air slipstream around it not limited to that of the rearwards region but also extending around the top, side, and even bottom surfaces of the vehicle. Therefore, travelling side-by-side with another vehicle or even passing at high velocities can create aerodynamic interference effects between the two vehicles which can generally approach the approximate aerodynamic form as if the two vehicles were one solid mass travelling through the air fluid at freeway speeds. These effects are therefore exponentially greater with both higher speed and lateral proximity. Travelling in areas of heightened air velocity surrounding a lateral allovehicle represents the opposite of the drafting technique's intended purpose, as such would increase the drag force by increasing air velocity as it pushes the vehicle, exerting a stronger opposing force on the engine. Drafting can therefore be taken as an inverse reminder of what the professional driver does *not* do: instead of sacrificing safety by closely travelling in the air-wake of a vehicle, the professional driver should *increase* safety by *avoiding* the *higher* air-velocity areas of the vehicle's slipstream, which typically peak on the lateral regions of the vehicle just before the front of the windshield, as Computational Fluid Dynamics (CFD) models of airflow around passenger vehicles demonstrate for common body designs (Tsubokura, et al., 2009)[8]. In this instance, fuel-efficiency optimization and safety optimization harmoniously agree on the

---

[8] Tsubokura, M. et al., 2009. Computational visualization of unsteady flow around vehicles using high performance computing. *Computers & Fluids*, 38(5), pp. 981-990.

importance of lateral safety margin distance in decreasing collision likelihood from allovehicular attempts at ignorant, dangerous lane switches and in decreasing the drag force by laterally removing the vehicle from the areas of quickened air flow around the sides of the vehicle. Such aerodynamic considerations provide an excellent overture for our following discussion on intervehicular dynamics, since they illustrate the finely dynamical and mutually influential relationships which every freeway vehicle's spatial motion imposes on every other surrounding vehicle.

CHAPTER 8

Intervehicular Dynamics

Having established the core principles of our tactical model for spatial maneuvering, through our discussions on lane, speed, and fuel-efficiency optimization, we will now analyze a selection of more specific topics and situations which are interconnected to the above topics as to make impossible their being forced into any of the previous chapters. The following discussion on intervehicular dynamics will therefore provide a space for these discussions which principally involve the professional driver's reality in a majority of non-rural freeway circumstances of navigating a fluid stream of vehicular traffic in which other vehicles can represent slowing obstructions to freeway-vacant ideal travel speed at best (such as in high-traffic situations), or lethal collisional objects at worst. These discussions should therefore be viewed in the overarching lens of collision avoidance, since vehicular accidents (especially on the freeway) do obviously run contrary to any conjurable safety or efficiency optimization. The at-times theoretical optimizations discussed in the previous chapters must therefore be put in the higher perspective of collision-avoidance, since a misappropriation of the former which increases the risk of the latter is certainly not optimal from the view of basic probability. The aforementioned drafting technique of fuel expenditure reduction is a classic example of such a misappropriation, unwisely overemphasizing a moot benefit for comparatively much greater risk of collision. All intervehicular dynamical topics should therefore remind of the quintessentially dangerous nature of high-speed, metallic, human-containing objects travelling together in close proximity, and of the professional driver's resulting responsibility to ensure safe intervehicular navigation through sound spatial awareness and tactical response measures.

Intervehicular aerodynamics

At the conclusion of our discussion on fuel-efficiency optimization, we elucidated the fine nature of air-flow around the lateral regions of a vehicle, its increased velocity in this position, and therefore the fuel-efficiency and safety optimization agreement in maintaining copious lateral safety margin distances. This statement could perhaps be extended to the basic intervehicular safety measure of avoiding travel in another highway-traveler's blind spot – if, for instance, the professional driver is travelling in the left lane with an anterolateral allovehicle in the lane to the right and of such longitudinal advancement as to be unable to see the driver in his or her mirrors. Depending on the type and aerodynamic nature of the vehicle, this blind spot zone may be well ahead of the air-velocity-reduced drafting region and in fact right in the turbulent slipstream wake of the anterolateral vehicle. Although Computational Fluid Dynamic (CFD) simulations typically tend to show that the highest increase in air velocity to the side of a travelling vehicle occurs at a more frontal region, approximately just behind the windshield, it is still suboptimal from a vehicular stability point of view to travel in the massively turbulent slipstream wake that is likely to occupy the blind-zone region – especially if created by large semi-trucks. This advocates the general safety recommendation of either speeding up or slowing down to escape such a region, and to travel ahead or behind of the anterolateral vehicle, outside of its blind spot, respectively. While this might not be possible in high traffic-density circumstances, such circumstances are likely to have lowered freeway travel speed to the degree at which such aerodynamic factors do not have as much influence, being exponentially tied to the linear velocity of the air flow in question. Tsubokura's aforementioned CFD simulation research of air-flow around a passenger vehicle clearly demonstrates the existence of door-mirror and body-side vortices which travel down the lateral edge of the vehicle's air-flow to create high turbulence in what is typically the blind-spot region of a vehicle, negatively affecting the stability of another vehicle travelling there. Azim and Gawad (2000) extended the mere solitary case of vehicular air flow to that of downscaled vehicle pairs travelling in a wind tunnel to characterize certain "side forces and yawing movements" exerted on vehicles (especially on lighter vehicles) by aerodynamic interference factors in two intervehicular situations: side-by-side travel, and the general passing (i.e., "overtaking") maneuver[1]. Side-by-side travel is unsurprisingly found to increase the velocity of air flow between the vehicles, increasing drag (due to an extra frictional surface layer's resistance against a flow of increased velocity – whereas the single vehicle case creates a lateral flow of lesser velocity and with only one frictional surface), decreasing interstitial air pressure between the two vehicles, and therefore creating a small attracting force between the two (clearly being at odds against lateral collision avoidance) insofar as lateral vehicular proximity and speed are maximized (as well as a potential imbalance in mass between the two vehicles, with a heavy truck being far less effected yet more effecting than a light hybrid four-wheeled vehicle, which is much more susceptible to the present effect). This increase in interstitial, lateral air velocity between the two vehicles should also harken back to the fuel-efficiency debate of window-open cooling vs. air conditioning system cooling, as actual velocity passing the window on this side of the vehicle and under these conditions (of tight lateral safety margins and high speed) would be greater than the overall velocity of the vehicle, and would proportionally advocate air conditioner usage at a lower speed, creating also a louder noise disturbance if the window is opened which may challenge the professional driver's auditory spatial awareness capability – which is probably of only any significant import in such exact tight, high-speed situations when signaling horn usage of another vehicle is likely. Azim and Gawad discovered similarly relevant aerodynamic interference effects in the high-speed passing process between the passing and being passed vehicles; in the case of a left-lane driver overtaking an anterolateral vehicle to the front and in the lane to the right, a rightwards "yawing" (or turning) force is observed to push the front of the

---

[1] Azim, A. F. A. & Gawad, A. F. A., 2000. A flow visualization study of the aerodynamic interference between passenger cars. *SAE Technical Paper Series*, Volume 2000-01-0355.

passing vehicle towards the passed vehicle and its back away from the passed vehicle once the passing vehicle's front achieves the longitudinal position of the passed vehicle's back, due to the effects of the positioning of the slipstream and side wake which the passed vehicle creates. This force decreases with the continued longitudinal advancement of the passing vehicle (as their more even longitudinal positions more closely approximate their aerodynamic treatment as a single mass, in which the laterally attractive force of the side-by-side case temporarily holds) until the force is reversed when the front of the passing vehicle exceeds the front of the being passed vehicle, in which the passing vehicle's front is yawed away from the passed vehicle and its rear towards the being passed vehicle. The professional driver is cognizant of these subtle aerodynamic forces, however minimal, in such situations and especially in conditions of tight lateral proximity and high travelling velocity, due to their entirely conceivable ability to challenge vehicular stability enough to risk lateral collision when allovehicular drivers are being carless to their interlane position, whether being distracted by manual device usage or being impaired by psychoactive substances.

As it concerns the intervehicular aerodynamics of two isolane vehicles, one frontal and following, we have already discussed the lion's share of relevant information in our analysis of the drafting fuel-efficiency optimization technique. We should repeat that the effect of lessened drag force exerted on the vehicle due to the rearwards wake of the frontal vehicle is not constrained to the very proximate distances which warranted our safety concerns in the prior section on drafting; this effect, to some meaningful extent, propagates back to distances even of normal following distance. The drag reduction effect can be further enhanced when travelling through narrow tunnels (Gotz, 1987)[2]. Dynamically speaking, circumstances of decreased frontal drag can affect the handling of the vehicle, depending largely on the specific aerodynamic profile and design of the vehicle in question. The professional driver is

---

[2] Gotz, H., 1987. "Aerodynamics of road Vehicles". In: W. Hucho, ed. *Commercial vehicles*. s.l.:Butterworths.

ideally familiar with the handling and "feel" of the vehicle's steering and acceleration at different speeds (and how air resistance and wind gust loads affect this handling), and can therefore account for the aerodynamic effects which decreased drag can have on handling. Brakeless deceleration, for instance, by easing the throttle can be expected to produce slower reductions in speed when the frontal vehicle's rear air slipstream wake is lowering drag, since the high-velocity momentum of the vehicle is less forcefully resisted (which follows quite simply from Newton's second law of motion, $F = mA$, since drag force F is decreased and vehicular mass m is constant, and therefore deceleration A must also decrease – deceleration being the signed negative of acceleration, as force F is negative in this case, and as the two negative signs on each side cancel).

Topographic factors

While some freeways are near-entirely flat for the whole of their expanse, others traverse topological aberrations which create certain intervehicular effects of which the professional driver must be aware, especially to the degree that surrounding traffic density is high. We first consider the visible onset of an approaching hill; as illuminated in our discussion on fuel-efficiency optimization, the increase in grade causes the necessity of increased engine output power to maintain constant speed. Therefore, the predicted likelihood of changes in speed of allovehicles warrants attention due to the safety relevance of altered longitudinal-axis following distance margins.

Following distance effects

Overall, a reduction in allovehicular speed can be expected at the initial portion of ascent, wherein grade has just increased and drivers are responding to the increase in grade by applying additional throttle to the engine. This temporary decrease in speed, which is not certain in every case (due to attentive drivers' premonitory acceleration into the zone of increased grade, which can keep speed relatively constant) but is a sound general pattern, must be noted for its effect of decreasing frontal following distance since the frontal allovehicle encounters the region of increased grade before the driver does, since the frontal vehicle achieves the forward position of the hill first. The professional driver should therefore predictively facilitate a wise increase in following distance before the ascent of a hill, if traffic density conditions warrant, in anticipation of the likely imminent deceleration of the frontal vehicle. This increase in frontal following distance, facilitated by means of light deceleration, is better done just before the onset of the hill rather than on its initial increase in slope, due to potential narrowing effects with the rearwards vehicle, if any. The professional driver's vehicle will also, just as the others, be moved to a slower speed due to the incline if not compensated by additional throttle, and will therefore narrow the rearwards longitudinal-axis following distance in the same manner as the frontal vehicle is expected to come closer by virtue of its deceleration on the onset of the hill. This natural reduction rearwards safety margin distance (under circumstances of decreased in isothrottle velocity), combined with the driver's intent *deceleration* to accommodate the frontal vehicle, would naturally narrow the rearwards following distance to a degree at which being rear-end collided would be of concern. Therefore, decelerating and lengthening frontal following distance just *before* the onset of the hill will give the driver not only safe distance from the frontal vehicle, but room in which to accelerate for the avoidance of the rearwards vehicle by lengthening rearwards following distance. Decelerating slightly before the hill is also likely to lengthen the whole intervehicular isolane space, since the rearwards driver will be made to decelerate by virtue his or her frontal driver's deceleration.

This small defensive tactic of slightly decelerating before a hill, predicting the deceleration of other vehicles, does not necessarily insist that all vehicles are maintaining constant throttle and will slow down upon achieving the onset of the hill; however, if every allovehicular driver happens to intently accelerate on the upwards phase, then the increased following distance the driver has created is certainly no harm. Use of cruise control, whether by the driver or by allovehicular drivers, can delay isotachic throttle-increase response to the increased grade to the point at which the driver's having created the additional safety space may be quite useful, as various cruise control software implementations adopt their own specific sensitivity and responsivity to load-induced changes in speed which will prompt automatic acceleration at some point on the hill. This responsivity, however, is likely to be less than that of manual driver speed regulation by the engine throttle, and accordingly is more likely to increase speed on the downwards phase than manual driver regulation (of using brakes). Whether or not allovehicular drivers brake for speed regulation on the accelerative downwards phase of a hill, a general increase in speed after the hill's crest (if any) can be expected on the way down for the same reasons a general pattern of acceleration is expected on the way up. The professional driver must therefore be aware of the generally unsafe speed differentials which can be created between two vehicles on the downward slope of a hill, if one is using speed-permissive cruise control (which naturally resists braking) and another using conservative, manual braking speed-regulation, insofar that the downwards grade is steep and extended.

Visibility obstruction

The other large component of topographical factors' relevance to the professional driver is their potential to obstruct the driver's spatial awareness scanning of the path-of-travel beyond some high point. This frontal space in which immediate recognition of a frontal hazard would prompt vehicular stopping is called the "stopping sight distance" and is limited by the crests of hills on the upwards section, increasingly insofar as the hill is steep. If a frontal hill is steep enough, the driver's upwards-tilted viewing angle will not encompass the invisible contents of the road beyond the present hill's crest, thereby creating a safety hazard of limited Assured Clear Distance Ahead (ACDA) in the severest case. Driver body height and vehicular design circumstances that place the driver's eye level above ground at shorter than average height increase the potential visibility limiting risks which vertical hill crests can impose on spatial awareness. Insofar as road steepness and lowered eye-level height create this situation, additional cause is given for preparatory deceleration before approaching a hill, since speed must be attenuated to ensure minimum stopping distance's ability to halt the vehicle before a potential hazard just beyond the crest of the hill which was invisible to the driver (and also to ensure compliance, therefore, with the basic speed rule). The intervehicular safety recommendations of ascending steep hills therefore concords with that of fuel-efficiency optimization in that speed should be lowered on the upwards phase relative to that of flat highway travel in the same location and circumstances. For these reasons, lane optimization comes into play at the predicted or visible onset of a hill, as it would temporarily increase the importance of being in a lane with permissive allovehicular safety margins due to the potential hazards which hills can create. Conventional highway design does not typically permit the existence of curved hills which are banked to the degree that slope on one lane is much different than that of slope on another lane, so therefore the topology-related risk analysis of each lane can practically be considered identical. In addition to the obvious heightened lane optimization desire to increase following distance, optimization of the curve-distance interlane disparity effect becomes increasingly more at odds against safety in cases of curved hills, since in fact the outer lane would typically afford better visibility circumstances of path-of-travel at a steep crest due its longer given visible distance per fixed unit of forward linear highway distance at the curve-crest. This effect, however, is not as important as that of safety margin distance, since occupying a lane with marginally better visibility around the curve-crest yet tightly spaced between other vehicles would certainly be more dangerous than that of being in a less traffic-dense inner lane. Since increasing following distance before a hill becomes a marginally greater concern which can be satisfied by lane-switching into a less traffic-dense lane, therefore the aforementioned recommendation of decelerating slightly before hills additionally may afford better opportunities for executing such a safe lane switch, giving the driver more longitudinal space and (therefore merging opportunities) in which to conduct one. Most hills on the highway are of slight enough grade as to render these considerations less impactful than may be evident, but in the sporadic occurrence of sufficiently steep topological freeway aberrations, accounting for such resulting intervehicular effects could mean the difference between safe travel and rear-end collision.

Road Curvature

Turning our attention from the intervehicular effects which proceed from a freeway's vertical components (termed its *profile* in highway construction terminology), we now examine that of its horizontal curvature (or *alignment*). Horizontal curves during the professional driver's freeway driving experience may be subdivided into two distinct categories: that of the naturally curvaceous entrance and exit ramps, and that of curves and bends of the actual freeway itself during interstate travel. From a safety hazard perspective, traffic research indicates the first of these to be the more hazardous and accident-prone.

Entrance and exit ramp hazards

Analysis of hazards on the entrance ramp is a relevant topic to the present discussion on intervehicular dynamics, since slowed or disabled vehicles in front of the freeway-entering driver will affect his or her merging abilities and may cause excessive deceleration as to challenge the driver's task of afterwards accelerating to highway speed in time for the merge. Curvature on entrance ramps is almost certain to be greater than that which can be expected on the freeway itself due to the lowered design speed; the hazard of road departure (potentially leading to fatal sliding off the highway into a lowered ditch beside a raised entrance ramp) or vehicle rollover on the entrance ramp becomes exponentially increased when speed on the curve is increased linearly. This hazard especially applies to vehicles whose center of gravity is far above the road surface, such as trucks. It has been estimated that over 20% of freeway truck accidents occur on entrance ramps, though the total length such interchanges constitutes less than 5% of total freeway mileage (Firestine, et al., 1989)[3]. High speed is to be blamed for the majority of highway entrance ramp curvature-related accidents; speed around curves increases the rotational G-force exponentially to some point at which tire friction is no longer able to keep the vehicle attached to the pavement. The professional driver is aware of the risks of high speed on entrance and exit ramps of pronounced curvature, and is also aware that the radius of freeway ramp curvature often becomes smaller as the ramp progresses. That is, the curvaceousness of a freeway ramp (especially that of exit ramps) may suddenly increase after an inexperienced driver has adjusted speed to the maximum safe threshold for the prior radius of curvature, in the assumption that such radius of curvature would remain. When his or her vehicle achieves the region of even more tightened curvature, then an unsafe slamming on the brakes will be necessary to reduce vehicle speed so that total loss of control does not enable the vehicle's momentum to carry it and the driver in a straight tangential departure path off the ramp and into whatever ditch, wall, guide-rail, or (in the case of multi-lane entrance ramps) perhaps even other vehicle exists there. Slippery road conditions, obviously, should increase even more the conservatism with which the professional driver regulates speed around curvy highway entrance and exit ramps.

Intrafreeway curvature

While ramp curvature concerns mostly general safety hazards and less intervehicular factors, curvature in the actual freeway can produce a host of decidedly intervehicular effects. The higher the radius of curvature on the freeway, and the higher a vehicle's travel speed, then the faster a driver must respond to subtle steering adjustments from hand-eye coordination feedback to keep the vehicle in the middle of the present lane. Since the professional driver is not distracted by manual device operation nor by any tasks

---

[3] Firestine, M., Toeg, P. & McGee, H. W., 1989. *Improving Truck Safety at Interchanges: Final Report to the Federal Highway Administration*, s.l.: s.n.

which would take his or her eyes off the frontal path-of-travel for any period of time as would cause dangerous drift in interlane position during the curve, therefore allovehicular attention should be prioritized towards that of lateral vehicles (if any) who are not guaranteed to maintain proper interlane position. While travelling beside a vehicle in a different lane is clearly undesirable and preferentially avoided, as we have stated before, it is at times a necessary reality of passing or of high traffic-density situations. Attention must be given to the lateral regions of the vehicle, in this case, during a curve to ensure that such lateral allovehicles do not stray out of their lane and into a lateral collision with the professional driver's vehicle[4]. Clearly, the side on which the tangential velocity of the allovehicle would bring it towards collision with the driver's vehicle should be prioritized, since for the purposes of interlane drift during a curve, the vehicle on the other side would be moved towards going *away* from the driver's vehicle. Predictive observation of driver impairment, fatigued driving, or distracted driving in such circumstances should proportionally increase spatial awareness attention to the curve-interior-side lateral allovehicle, to ensure that it does not drift dangerously close to the professional driver's vehicle, and to make corrective, defensive adjustments if it does. Clearly, the desirable nature of not travelling beside another vehicle in another lane is given special attention and relevance before the onset of a curve, and should prioritize lane-switching and/or passing which would establish safer circumstances in which the pertinent lateral region is clear of other vehicles. Driver foreknowledge of road curvature can therefore enable him or her to make such preparatory maneuvers knowing which side of the vehicle would be threatened by allovehicular interlane position drift during a curve (the right side for right bending curves, and the left side for left bending curves). Clearly, being on the interior left-most or right-most lane in such curves would prevent the risk of allovehicular lane drift collision, since there is then no more curve-interior lane in which such vehicles may travel. We happily point out

---

[4] See Chapter 12, accident situation #8

the exciting agreement (in this instance, at least) between this general curve-related safety factor and that of optimizing the curve-distance interlane disparity effect, which would advocate travel in the same curve-innermost lane for reducing the amount of required travel distance and enabling lower speed therefore to achieve equal linear forward position on the freeway.

In our discussion on lane optimization, we discussed the general efficiency benefits of the curve-distance interlane disparity effect but ignored the significant intervehicular effects it can impose on highway traffic flow around a bend. Given the gradual increase in travel distance needed to achieve equal forward position on the highway for each successive lane away from the interior of the curve, vehicles maintaining even position with each other will experience a disparity in speed (with the outer vehicles needing to go faster in order to keep up with their lateral counterparts) around a curve. Accordingly, isotachic vehicles at first laterally parallel to one another maintaining even speed will experience a decrease in their forward position, increasing outwards from the innermost lane (i.e., if four vehicles in four distinct lanes follow a curve at exactly 60mph, having been perfectly side-by-side before the curve, then the vehicles will end up staggered and longitudinally disjunct after the curve reverts to a regular straight highway section, with the outer lane vehicles being further behind, due to the increased distance they needed to travel around the curve). The specific manifestations of this bidirectional disparity effect depends on specific driver behavior. Since the left-most lane is typically occupied with faster and more aggressive drivers than that of the more right lanes, curves which bend to the right can be slightly more likely to provoke an isoposition response (and therefore, necessary speed acceleration) in the drivers of the left-most, outer lane than in left-bending curves, where the typically more conservative right-most lane drivers (the right-most lane now being the outer lane) are more disposed to an isotachic response in which forward position slightly decreases. In any event, the professional driver should expect that what may be a clear lateral region before a curve may come to be occupied by a vehicle whose forward position is either decreasing or increasing due an isotachic response to the curve-distance interlane disparity effect. The professional driver (especially if driving a long vehicle, such as an eighteen wheeled semi-truck) should therefore be aware of not only lateral but also all posterolateral and anterolateral vehicles before a curve, due to their possibility of coming into the vehicle's lateral region and colliding with the vehicle if being inattentive and drifting out of their lane, as discussed above. In this way, right-curving bends would prioritize predictive monitoring of the lane to the left's anterolateral vehicle (due to its likelihood to disadvance into the driver's left lateral region) and especially the lane to the right's posterolateral vehicle (due to not only its likelihood to advance into the driver's right lateral region but also its possibility to drift outside its lane and collide with the vehicle) and, inversely, left-curving bends would prioritize predictive monitoring of the lane to the right's anterolateral vehicle (due to its analogous likelihood to disadvance into the driver's right lateral region) and especially the lane to the left's posterolateral vehicle (due to its same analogous predictive likelihood as stated above). The professional driver should remark at the curve-distance interlane disparity effect as a unique opportunity to advance in relative forward-position without increasing speed (and therefore without increasing traffic-enforcement-stop risk), or at least while increasing it to a lesser and therefore less-risky degree than would be necessary on a straight section, while executing a maneuver such as passing. Passing during a curve is therefore most wise when the passing vehicle is on the inner-lane of the curve and the passed driver on the bordering outer lane, since the opposite configuration would impose a *challenge* instead of an *aid* to the passing driver's passing (needing to travel faster than normal rather than slower than normal to execute the pass), and would also put the being passed inner-lane vehicle in a position where careless lane-exiting drift could cause a collision with the passing vehicle. Lane optimization is therefore needed (or at least massively beneficial) before the curve if passing is intended, since curves of such nature make analogous passing maneuvers either safer and easier or more dangerous and risky, depending on whether or not the passing driver is on a more inner-curve or more outer-curve lane (relative to the passed vehicle's lane) respectively. The curve-distance interlane disparity effect can even cause unintentional passing between two vehicles whose positions are changed relative to each other due to isotachic handing of the curve, and intent acceleration by aggressive drivers (feeling a sense to "keep up" with a lateral, curve-interior vehicle whose forward position would be naturally aided by the curve).

The professional driver should be aware that the cross-slope (or *cant*) of the freeway is "superelevated" on the outer edge of the freeway surface in order to create a slight "banked" turn such that gravity can supply part of the centripetal force necessary to keep the vehicle in-lane around the curve. While straight sections of highway are typically cross-sloped on each side (leading to a peak along the road centerline which aids drainage) to a minimal enough degree as to be largely negligible to vehicular dynamics, sharper curves can prompt slopes of greater magnitude which are of note when slippery winter conditions causes travel speed to be much lower than the maximum design speed of the freeway (the speed which dictates heightened curve cross-slope), and therefore the direction of the gravitational force caused by the cross-slope may challenge traction a small bit in slippery and slow conditions. Combined with the obvious need for slow travel at curves for avoiding loss of traction and vehicular straying off the highway in a straight tangential path, this factor dictates that extra caution and safety margin distances be appropriated at curves in such slippery conditions. Truck rollover accidents are also to be predictively avoided, in slippery conditions or not, by ensuring that travel beside a truck on an outer-curve lane does not occur, especially if traffic conditions are likely to prompt the truck's necessary and rapid braking on the curve, which can lead to a lethal rollover accident. Even with cross-slope superelevation, truck rollovers at curves can and do occur in the freeway context. Traffic research confirms the potential dangers which large truck handling of curves can have on the truck's driver and the surrounding drivers; the Federal Motor Carrier Administration analyzed 239 truck rollover accidents in the

Large Truck Crash Causation Study, finding that "it is in handling curves, mostly on- and off-ramps, that excess speed becomes the biggest factor, accounting for 77 rollovers, two-thirds of all those that are speed-related ... five rollovers occurred when drivers failed to realize early enough that vehicles ahead had slowed and they were unable to stop in time. The primary cause was inattention, with one case due to insufficient following distance" (McKnight & Bahouth, 2009)[5]. The professional driver is aware of these hazards at curves in a freeway's horizontal alignment, whether driving a large truck him or herself or driving a passenger vehicle in proximity to one.

General Passing

Incentives and procedures

As it is known to novice highway drivers, due to the physical obstruction which a frontal isolane vehicle can have on longitudinal position, the "passing" or "overtaking" maneuver is executed when speed motivations (compared to the alternative speed of remaining behind the frontal vehicle) outweigh safety costs in changing lanes, accelerating past the obstructive vehicle, and reverting to the original lane. If lane optimization analysis does not evince a strong preference for the original lane for whatever reason, then the passing driver may not immediately or ever merge back into the original lane of travel in front of the obstructing vehicle, which would not formally constitute a whole canonical highway pass in that event (however the majority of the relevant characteristics of one, in particular the lateral overtaking phase, still hold). Passing therefore requires lane-switching and is therefore optimally avoided, due to the inherent risks to lane-switching (which vary greatly depending on circumstance). The professional driver is aware, however, of the situations in which safety and optimization benefits do indeed warrant a passing maneuver, with speed optimization being the most obvious of these. There is an ambiguous and

---

[5] McKnight, A. J. & Bahouth, G. T., 2009. Analysis of Large Truck Rollover Crashes. *Traffic Injury Prevention,* 10(5), pp. 421-426.

indeterminable line between "passing" and general lane optimization, with the former concerning smaller, tighter (and therefore more dangerous) movements, whereas a lane optimization maneuver may switch out of the present lane in which a frontal vehicle is seen a quarter of a mile away and into an entirely free lane, for the purposes of frontal safety margin optimization, seeing that the distant frontal vehicle is travelling more slowly than the driver and will at some point catch up longitudinally. At some later point, after the vehicle overtakes this once-frontal vehicle in the new lane, the driver may decide to switch back into the original lane far ahead of the vehicle. While these decisions and maneuvers, separated by perhaps minutes, certainly do not resemble that of a fast and proximate highway "passing", it is formally identical in its three distinct phase (lateral lane switch, longitudinal overtaking, and original lane return). Our discussion of passing is generally distinguished therefore by situations in which the freeway is not nearly as sparse as in the above example, and in which relatively allovehicular-proximate maneuvers will (unfortunately and sub-optimally) need to take place. Such close-range passing should therefore not be a common activity for the professional driver, being favored only in some circumstances. In addition to maintaining chosen freeway-vacant ideal travel speed, passing may also afford the benefit of avoiding lateral hazards by advancing forward position (if decreasing forward position is not possible). If, for instance, an uneducated frontal driver of a small passenger vehicle is travelling exactly beside the front of a large semi-truck in the neighboring lane and therefore forcing the following professional driver to travel in the truck's dangerous blind zone, and it being impossible for the professional driver to sufficiently decelerate due to the rearwards vehicle, then the professional driver will preferentially pass to the left, overtake the careless frontal driver, and return to the lane (if lane optimization still holds the original lane as optimal) having passed the driver and being safely out of the blind zone of the truck.

Passing on the right

Special attention should be given to the case of passing on the right, such as would be the case in the lateral inverse of the above example (which would be very uncommon, due to either left lane travel restrictions for semi-trucks or for the driver's likely slower travel speed being in a righter lane). Passing on the right is technically illegal in many jurisdictions under some circumstances, as it does violates the general traffic principle of faster traffic keeping left. In the freeway context, however, North American regulations typically provide for an exception to the right-side-passing prohibition when sufficient lane width and frontal space enable the maneuver's safe execution. The qualification "passing on the right" is of course as ambiguous as passing's definition in the first place, as we showed above, since any long-range maneuver of rightwards lane switching followed by restorative leftwards lane switching is formally identical to that of "passing on the right" if a vehicle in the leftwards adjacent lane happens to be longitudinally overtaken during the process. Regardless of legal technicalities, passing on the right is generally undesirable due to some drivers' being unused to being passed on the right and their slightly higher resulting likelihood to execute a rightwards (and potentially collisional) lane switch without checking their sides, whereas they may be more expecting of faster, passing traffic on the left and therefore more careful with leftwards lane switches[6]. Passing on the right is also more likely to involve risky safety margins due to the general highway tendency of right-lane traffic to travel more slowly than left-lane traffic. Generalities aside, passing on the right is sometimes a justifiable and optimal maneuver when and only when the incentives to passing significantly outweigh the disincentives, with ample spatial clearances on the right side being guaranteed and visually confirmed by the driver before attempting the pass. This is

---

[6] Tijerina, L., Garrott, W. R., Stoltzfus, D. & Parmer, E., 2005. Eye glance behavior of van and passenger car drivers during lane change decision phase. *Transportation Research Record: Journal of the Transportation Research Board*, 1937(1), pp. 37-43.

a common situation in left-most-lane travel, as we will see in a future section reviewing passing lane situations.

The existence of right-side passing illuminates the potential for a peculiar situation about which the professional driver is at all times cognizant when executing any lane change maneuver. On a multi-lane divided highway with three or more lanes, it is conceivable that two different vehicles may be attempting to merge into the same longitudinal position in the same lane at the same time, but from the two different, adjacent lanes on either side. Put more simply, two vehicles separated by one lane between them could be attempting to laterally switch into the same spot in the center lane, which would cause a lateral collision. This situation is much more of a concern in the passing context, marked by fast maneuver execution and proximate safety margin distance, rather than the more general lane optimization context in which there is time for thoroughly comprehensive spatial awareness scanning to ensure that such a situation does not occur. The passing driver must likewise ensure a similar thoroughness in his or her spatial understanding of the allovehicular positions in the road ahead of the being passed vehicle, and ensure that such lateral collisions do not occur. This occurrence becomes a particular concern in right-side passing since, in a three-lane example highway, a left-most lane anterolateral driver, merging into the center lane, would not expect a driver from the right-most lane to speed up and pass his or her own posterolateral driver, who is of sufficient rearwards longitudinal position in order to execute the lane switch, nor even be able to see such a right-passing driver who may be obstructed visually by the being-passed center-lane

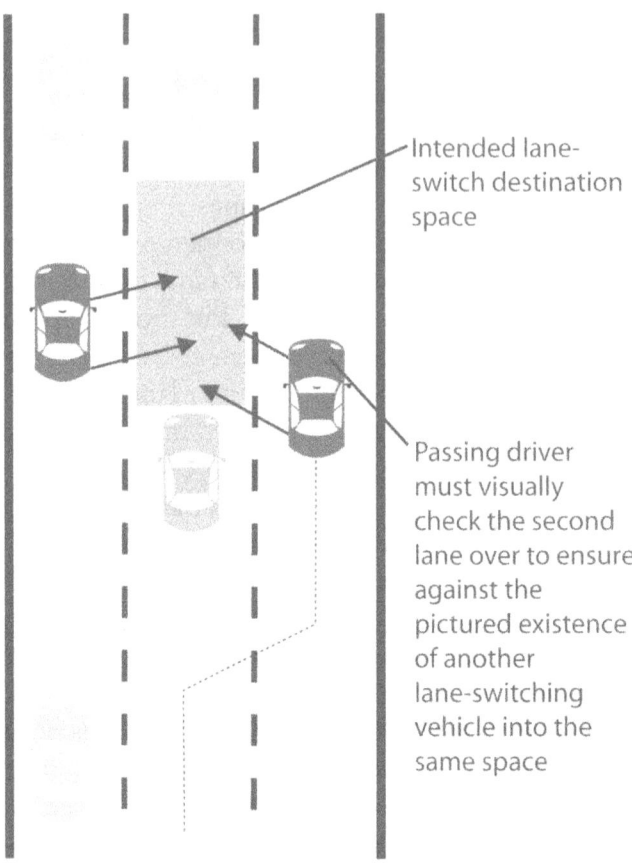

Figure 16 – The rare yet concerning situation of two vehicles simultaneously merging into the same lane-space from opposite adjacent lanes

vehicle, and therefore the left-lane driver may begin to execute the lane switch, thinking that spatial margins have been confirmed to be clear of allovehicles, and proceed to collide with the passing vehicle on the right who is returning to the center lane after executing his or her right-side pass. The question of which isolane-entering vehicle has right of way is of little concern, since the professional driver will be aware of and respond to the behaviors of the other-lane switching driver in order to avoid a lateral collision. Some jurisdictions have wonderfully clear legal definitions of the right of way in such rare circumstances however, such as found in the Texas Transportation Code:

> "On a roadway divided into three or more lanes and providing for one-way movement of traffic, an operator entering a lane of traffic from a lane to the right shall yield the right-of-way to a vehicle entering the same lane of traffic from a lane to the left."[7]

This precedent of North American highway convention strangely gives the right of way to vehicles on the *left*, who would be merging right, further necessitating the careful attention of any right-side passing driver. This would agree with our statement at the conclusion of our discussion on highway entrance merging of weave lanes, that the freeway-exiting (and therefore, left-side) vehicles have right-of-way over the freeway-entering (and therefore, right-side) vehicles in such lane. Though not every jurisdiction's legal corpus of traffic regulations provides as clear of a statement on the matter as that of the Texas Transportation Code (or even acknowledgement of the situation whatsoever), we repeat that this is of little significance to the professional driver, who at all times performs comprehensive spatial awareness checks to avoid such a collision, especially during the undesirable practice of passing on the right.

Speed responses to being passed

The professional driver's understanding of highway passing is not limited to the active hemisphere of initiating and executing the pass, but also entails the passive hemisphere of tactics and responses to *being* passed by other freeway vehicles. The two general collision-risk decreasing responses are (1) increasing lateral safety buffer distance, if possible to do without compromising that of the other side, by slightly adjusting interlane position, and (2) slightly decelerating in order to increase the relative speed between the passing and being

---

[7] *Texas Transportation Code Section 545.061.* s.l.:s.n.

passed vehicles, which will contribute to the maneuver's being finished more quickly (since the relative overtaking distance is constant), which minimizes the time in which the two vehicles must sub-optimally travel side-by-side to each other. In this narrow hypothetical, we assume that the driver is to remain in the present lane to begin with, either due to the non-existence of an evasive lane to the other side or for some other reason, since in practice the professional driver may very well have moved over to another lane to prevent the rearwards driver from needing to pass in the first place (a common passing-lane situation we will analyze in a future section). Speed response to being passed is always preferentially decelerative from a safety-only point of view, however some drivers are tempted to accelerate while being passed in order to require the passing driver to go even faster in order to complete the pass. This manipulative tactic capitalizes on the passing driver's human psychological tendency and desire to "finish what has been started", being perhaps half-way through the passing maneuver when the passed driver's acceleration begins, in order to decrease legal risk of speeding for the passed driver, since he or she must still be necessarily travelling more slowly than the passing vehicle in order for the pass to be accomplished, and also taken in conjunction with the assumption that any present traffic enforcement officer is constrained to pulling over only one vehicle and would therefore naturally target the faster, passing vehicle. While isotachic speed maintenance or *slight* acceleration during rare high-urgency situations may be justified, we unsurprisingly discourage the aggressive driving behavior of accelerating while being passed for the following reasons: (1) the underlying assumption that a traffic enforcement officer must or even is largely more likely to pull over only the fastest vehicle is flawed, since may speeders who are pulled over are not the fastest momentary speeders on the freeway, but are merely the most convenient or inauspiciously positioned vehicles who were seen first, and since such perceptive and comparative radar-scanning ability between near-equally speeding vehicles of relative speed differential of only a few miles per hour is likely an impossible or extremely difficult task to begin with; (2) it is highly likely to instigate a road-rage situation with the passing driver who may perceive that his or her attempt to longitudinally exceed the vehicle has been confrontationally "challenged"; (3) it is likely to begin with that overshooting the tactic by accelerating too much will cause the driver to abort the passing maneuver, decelerate in his or her adjacent lane, and remerge behind the vehicle into the original lane, which poses further collision risks to all surrounding vehicles (and which is still likely to instigate road rage); and (4) the arrival-time optimization benefits of momentarily increased speed, lasting only for the few seconds of the passing maneuver's duration, and speed necessarily needing to be restored to normal thereafter lest legal risk be increased, are absolutely insignificant, completely negligible, and not at all worth the associated risks in anything but the highest-urgency speed-necessary circumstances. Furthermore, accelerating while being passed obviously lengthens the duration of the maneuver, increasing the risky lateral exposure time of being in such undesirably close proximity to the passing vehicle. The professional driver will therefore almost always hold speed constant or even slightly decelerate if being passed. If the professional driver him or herself is driving the passing vehicle, and the being passed vehicle exhibits the aforementioned aggressive accelerating behavior, then the professional driver remains keenly and objectively aware of the risks and consequences inherent to increasing speed compared to that of aborting the pass by decelerating and, if necessary, returning to the original lane – not being influenced by the psychological tendency in unprofessional drivers to feel a need to complete that pass which they have started, even if it becomes suboptimal and associated with greater safety risks than benefits which the maneuver would warrant. In such a case that the being passed driver accelerates while the professional driver is passing him or her, then this is to be taken as a sign of aggressive driving and therefore a good indication that this vehicle may more wisely not be made a rearwards vehicle (such would do the successful continuation and completion of the pass), who may intently decrease rearwards following distance by "tailgating" the professional driver. This would serve not only as an incentive to abort the passing maneuver, but in fact also to represent a lane optimization dissuasion towards being in the same lane either behind or in front of this allovehicle; the professional driver may then decide to abort the pass by travelling at a new appropriate speed in the new lane which had been being temporarily used for passing, or to pass another vehicle in said lane for longitudinal overtaking of the aggressive vehicle (or, of course, decelerating) – in order to get out of the way of the aggressive driver's behavior which was evidenced by his or her acceleration while being passed.

Large allovehicle aerodynamic optimization and safety passing

Inherent to our statements above on passing is the general safety motivation of not travelling beside another vehicle, and therefore the heightened spatial attention which must accompany any passing maneuver. We should highlight a particular emphasis on this concern when travelling beside large trucks. The common highway driving mantras "never drive in a truck's blind-zone" (also called its "no-zone"), or even "never travel beside a truck", are entirely justified. In addition to the allovehicular blind-spot visibility limitations brought about by travelling in such a region, one risks wind and/or curvature related truck rollover hazards, truck retreading ejecta debris hazards, increased aerodynamic drag and turbulence, decreased lateral safety margin distance, and decreased lane-optimization opportunities for both vehicles. The lateral region of trucks in the adjacent lane should therefore be "passed" by the professional driver (although this is not the full conventional definition of a traditional highway pass, since it may lack the initial and final lane-change phases, it is still a "pass" in the geometric sense). The region besides the truck should be passed with greater than regular speed, in order to decrease the time spent along the fixed longitudinal distance lateral to the truck in which there are heightened safety risks as we stated above. If lane switching opportunities afford, it would be optimal to maintain the freeway-vacant idea travel speed by switching into a free lane two lanes over from the truck's longitudinal position, in which the truck-related lateral risks are precipitously lowered. It may often be necessary, however, to overtake large semi-trucks in the lane adjacent to them, and in which the general acceleration incentive must be regulated with (1) assured sufficient frontal following distance extending through the dangerous lateral zone of the truck, (2) anterolateral attention to the lane adjacent to the present lane (i.e. in the direction away from the truck), if any, to ensure that there are no allovehicular inwards merging attempts into the path-of-travel (which would be an extremely questionable lane-change maneuver on their part to begin with, since they would be merging into the inherently dangerous truck-lateral zone), and (3) at times a momentary decelerative increase in frontal following distance before entering the truck's lateral/immediately-anterolateral zone in order to ensure sufficient distance for the acceleration necessary to pass the truck with greater speed and thereby minimize time-exposure to the risks of travelling next to the truck. It is important, however, not to wait too long after assuring sufficient passing distance next to the truck to initiate passing acceleration, since leaving the truck's lateral region open and clear could induce the truck to execute a dangerous lane switch as the passing driver enters its blind zone – which is especially concerning if the truck is being passed on the right (therefore dangerously lane-switching to the left), which is very much preferentially avoided.

Passing lane situations

We should give special attention to the intervehicular effects and situations commonly encountered on wide multi-lane divided highways during vehicular passing and travel involving the passing lane (the left-most lane of the freeway, which is typically occupied by the highest travel-speed vehicles) and the lane to the right of it, the first of which is distinguished by a total lack of leftwards lateral escape opportunities (with the exception of rare left exists), guaranteeing that any travelling vehicles in it (1) must at some point lane-switch to the right, (2) can be expected to attract the most aggressive and/or speeding drivers on the freeway, and (3) that if passed, they must be passed on the right as there is no alternative.

Passing lane situation #1: slower adjacent-lane travel

Let us first consider travelling not in the left-most lane but in the adjacent lane to the right of it, and the case of a faster vehicle approaching from behind in the passing lane (i.e., a posterolateral vehicle) as is very likely to occur given the speed tendencies of the vehicles of both lanes. The existence of a heavily faster flow of traffic passing on the left, in this case, would create a large speed differential between the vehicle and those surrounding it and would therefore incentivize acceleration to decrease or eliminate the speed differential for the following reasons:

1. The passing lane vehicles' travelling much more quickly will cause them to keep passing the driver's vehicle on the left, which narrows lateral safety clearances and risks lateral collision if one of them should lane-switch out into the right without looking;

2. Due to the left-lane vehicles' greater speed than that of the adjacent lane's slower hypothetical professional driver, the professional driver must expend more frequent visual scanning spatial awareness resources on these vehicles since their relative position to the vehicle is changing so rapidly (compared to their relatively static intervehicular position if the driver were travelling at the same speed);

3. Any faster vehicles in the left-lane which encounter a frontal hazard have shorter stopping distance than the slower-travelling adjacent lane driver and therefore may require (or just reflexively react by, in a split second) rapid rightwards lane-switching into the adjacent lane, which could risk a lateral collision with the adjacent lane driver; and

4. Any aggressive driver in the left lane passing another frontal left lane driver on the right may have naturally constricted longitudinal passing distance margins in the adjacent lane

due to the adjacent lane's frontal driver travelling at such a lower speed, which can risk collision between the passing vehicle and either the being passed vehicle, the adjacent-lane slow vehicle, or both (since the distance the passer would see on his or her right may at first seem sufficient for passing, being limited by the slow adjacent-lane frontal vehicle, but this space is in fact rapidly diminishing due to the speed differential between the two vehicles and may be insufficient for a safe pass by the time the passing driver longitudinally overtakes the being passed vehicle in the adjacent lane).

Especially with regards to this last fourth point, the professional driver travelling in the lane adjacent to the left-most passing lane is always keenly scanning the allovehicular dynamics of that which is going on behind him or her, and will make safety optimizing speed adjustments if necessary such as accelerating if possible (in this case) if an aggressive posterolateral passer needs more space to conduct a maneuver which is already in full execution (or to dissuade its occurrence, if the maturity of its execution is sufficiently nascent, by decelerating – however this would require more care and is generally less attractive that the permitting, accelerative option, since the latter allows the aggressive, passing posterolateral vehicle to proceed away from the driver once the pass is completed, whereas the former decelerative response would both retain this aggressive driver's vehicle in the rearward zone and may prompt road-rage-characteristic feelings in them, having been shut out of consummating his or her momentary aspirations to pass the other vehicle).

Immediate speed response options

Another common speed optimization occurrence in the present situation of slower adjacent-lane travelling to that of faster passing-lane vehicles concerns the same phenomenon which we discussed in our general comments on passing above of speed response options while being passed. While we had demonstrated the excessive rarity with which a professional driver should ever aggressively accelerate while being passed in the conventional, isolane, and traditional sense, this speed response option is certainly more safely viable when the "passing" vehicle arrives from and continues away in another (in this case, the left-most passing) lane. That is, since such faster left-lane drivers are not concerned with the travel of the vehicles to their right, nor are in a psychological state of attempting to "overtake" the once-frontal vehicle when laterally passing on the left (as opposed to the traditional "highway pass" which originates from an isolane slower frontal vehicle), then therefore the response of accelerating while being "passed" (in this sense) on the left is far less likely to instigate a road-rage situation or to risk collision in tight lane-return switches that do not occur in this case. That is, if the professional driver is in the lane adjacent to the left-most lane and is travelling more slowly than a faster vehicle to his or her left which is longitudinally overtaking the vehicle, and if legal risk analysis had played a large enough component in the professional driver's decision to travel at this slower speed to begin with, then slight acceleration for the momentary instance of being passed may be optimal in high-urgency circumstances. We still repeat some of the inherent dangers to this response which we elucidated for the traditional case of passing in which the passing driver begins and ends in the same lane as the being passed driver: that time-exposure to dangerous lateral proximity is largely increased, and that arrival-time optimization only marginally increased.

<u>Allovehicular-driver psychological optimization of passing-lane-entrance directional signal activation</u>

In this circumstance of travelling to the right of faster, approaching, and passing left-passing-lane traffic, if the driver seeks to lane switch to the left, safe use of precise directional signal timing can aid the process of clearing passing vehicles in order to execute the lane switch more safely and quickly. If, for instance, a posterolateral vehicle directly on the driver's 7 o'clock is obstructing the execution of a lane switch, and if its future speed pattern of acceleration or deceleration relative to the merging vehicle's longitudinal position is unknown (or if it seems slower than would be ideal for getting this vehicle out of the way so that the lane switch can be done confidently), than intentionally timing the activation of the directional signal as to make the passing-lane driver more nervous of a lateral collision will cause him or her, if the signal is noticed (which is likely), to decide either to accelerate faster or decelerate in order to get out of the way of the lane switch. In practice, this should and will most often prompt the passing vehicle's acceleration, leaving safe following distance in which to finish the lane-switch maneuver. Comparing this precisely timed activation of the left directional signal with that of earlier activation, the latter would not have prompted an immediate sense of nervousness in the passing driver since he or she would have been safely behind the longitudinal position of the vehicle if, in their perspective, it decided to proceed with the lane switch, causing them to decelerate and make space. But since this allovehicle's travel speed had formerly been (in the hypothetical case we describe) greater than that of the slower adjacent lane professional driver's determined freeway-vacant ideal travel speed to begin with, eliciting an accelerative response in the passing allovehicle is desirable since (1) they will not have to slam on the brakes as to cause a dangerous reduction in rearwards following distance behind them and (2) since their pattern of faster travel compared to the present driver indicates that they would preferably serve as a frontal rather than rearwards vehicle relative to the professional driver once he or she has merged into the passing lane, since the other vehicle's generally greater speed would reduce following distance while being a rearwards vehicle but would increase following distance being a frontal vehicle. Therefore, precise timing of the leftwards turn-signal lane-switch assertiveness declaration, relative to the faster left-lane-driver's longitudinal position to the vehicle, is likely to create a useful and safety-augmenting sense of alarm in this driver who will be more likely to accelerate out of the way of the merging vehicle than if directional signal activation had been done earlier (as explained above) or later (since they would likely not even see the directional signal once they have entered the lateral region of the vehicle, and even if they did see it, they would be less concerned that the merging driver would be careless enough to merge into a visibly present lateral vehicle, whereas occupying the posterolateral region should and does often create fears of blind-spot visibility limitation). Although this tactic is most applicable to this particular passing lane situation (travelling in the adjacent lane with faster traffic in the passing lane), it is applicable to any lane switching situation in which there is an approaching faster posterolateral vehicle in the sought lane.

Passing lane situation #2: faster adjacent-lane travel

In the less common case that the professional driver is travelling *faster* in the adjacent lane than that of the traffic to his or her left in the left-most passing lane, then the same speed-differential dangers are seen in a somewhat inverse fashion. In this case, the professional driver should be influenced to decrease speed, since whatever circumstances of decreased traffic-density which afford the higher speed in this adjacent lane, compared to the likely high traffic-density circumstance which are correlated with the lower speed in the passing lane, would likely effect a very favorably seeming prospect of lane-switching into the right, faster lane for the slower allovehicles in the passing lane – and therefore, the professional driver must be vigilant against rear-end collision with a frontal vehicle which may rapidly and carelessly lane-switch into the faster lane without checking for approaching posterolateral vehicles or even activating their directional signals. While this interlane traffic speed setup is only likely to occur during relatively slow overall flow of heavy traffic, backed up left exists can create this very effect to a concerning degree, should any slowed or stalled vehicles decide to leave the traffic, merge back into the fast-moving freeway, and find an alternate route. This dangerous interlane speed differential situation of course more commonly exists with backed-up right exists, but is exacerbated in the rare left exit case due to the tendency and highway convention of faster traffic to travel in a more leftwards lane.

Passing lane situation #3: faster passing-lane travel

Let us now examine some archetypal passing lane situations with the professional driver travelling in the left-most lane, the passing lane, and his or her response options to isolane allovehicular flow of higher or lower speed. Firstly we should remind that travel in the passing lane is illegal in many states, however it is common informal practice in many areas for the fastest vehicles to travel in this lane (some of which, such as Massachusetts, even formally prohibit the practice, unknown to the majority of left-lane participants in the common practice) which therefore suite it towards accompanying a higher determined freeway-vacant ideal travel speed. We will therefore start with the case of encountering a slower frontal vehicle in this lane compared to the driver's speed; clearly the driver must either decelerate to maintain basic safe frontal following distance or initiate a pass on the right by switching into the adjacent lane. The latter would only be removed from the realm of aggressive driving if the slow frontal vehicle were travelling precipitously slower than the driver, or to an unreasonable degree below the flow of traffic. The professional driver must analyze the subjective factors which influence the risks inherent to the rightwards pass by thoroughly examining the nearest vehicles in the adjacent lane, and must understand that their likely slower speed will require a large and safe open distance in which to conduct the rightwards pass. Depending on the frontal vehicle's slowness relative to the allovehicular flow in front of it, the professional driver may not be guaranteed a space in which to merge back into the passing lane after overtaking the slow vehicle if indeed the vehicle was obstructing the view of another vehicle in front of it that was causing the first frontal vehicle to travel slowly. The professional driver must therefore ensure sufficient open frontal distance in the adjacent lane if a rightwards pass is to be attempted, which should render the maneuver mostly safe from that point onwards, since there is no risk of lateral collision with a co-lane-switching driver into the same lane from the other side (a potential we discussed above) since there is no farther lane on that side. If a slower vehicle is seen approaching in the passing lane, and if the adjacent lane is clear, and if it does seem by the degree of the speed differential that rightwards passing will be optimal for the professional driver, then it is preferable to switch into the adjacent lane in preparation of overtaking the frontal vehicle sooner rather than later, (1) since the dangerous reduction of frontal following distance between the driver and the slow vehicle, as it is approached, is avoided by switching out of the lane earlier and therefore being in a much safer position if the slow driver were for some reason to slam on his or her brakes, (2) since delaying the initiation of this rightwards-pass initial lane switch would involve some prior deceleration in order to maintain safe frontal following distance, which may waste energy to the brakes and which more importantly could elicit a rearwards driver (especially if they are aggressive) to initiate a rightwards pass around the professional driver him or herself, being the slowed vehicle in the perspective of the rearwards vehicle's driver, which would constrictively box the professional driver in behind the slow vehicle, being unable or at least delayed in the ability to pass given the other, rearwards vehicle's usage of the adjacent lane for the same purpose, and (3) since the professional driver will have earlier and more distant forwards path-of-travel spatial comprehension of the adjacent lane, which may limit the rightwards pass from being safely accomplished, which would accordingly prompt the professional driver either to switch back into the passing lane and decelerate to safely follow the vehicle or continue travel in the adjacent lane until circumstances safely permit overtaking the original slow vehicle. Especially to the degree that an early lane switch into the adjacent lane is made in the attempt to overtake a slow passing-lane vehicle, the professional driver must give heightened attention to the directional signals, interlane position, and overall spatial behavior of the slow, being passed, anterolateral vehicle up front and to the left since its sudden merging into the adjacent lane (being, perhaps, made nervous by the faster approaching vehicles behind it and not caring to shoulder-check the rightwards blind spot, occupied by the professional driver who was about to pass on the right) could risk a posterolateral collision into the professional driver (or, returning to the professional driver's perspective, an anterolateral collision with the slow passing-lane driver) as it switches into the lane directly in front of the about-to-pass professional driver who was naturally travelling more quickly than the slow vehicle given his or her having been about to overtake it. The inherent potential dangers to passing should prompt serious consideration of the need to pass a slower left-most lane vehicle in the first place, since simple deceleration to safely travel behind it is not likely to constitute a massive impact on destination arrival time. If the frontal "slow" vehicle is already going, for instance, 5mph over the post speed limit, it is severely doubtful that the professional driver would rightly attempt to pass it, as the required speed for such a maneuver (let alone the choice of freeway-vacant ideal travel speed indicated by the arbitration of the insufficiency of the frontal speed) is quite likely to be sub-optimally too fast.

Passing lane situation #4: slower passing-lane travel

The final common passing lane situation we will analyze places the professional driver in the left-most passing lane yet while travelling more *slowly* than the isolane allovehicular traffic as opposed to more quickly as in the former situation. Our general attitude towards this well-known phenomenon is that travelling significantly slower than the isolane flow of traffic creates safety hazards; research has confirmed that such speed differentials are dangerous on the highway, regardless of the posted speed limit. It seems subversive to suggest that safety may be improved in some cases by exceeding the speed limit, however in such left-lane high-speed travel circumstances, both the freeway-vacant ideal travel speed and raw safety optimizing speed would likely agree on a figure somewhere around or perhaps up to 5mph over the speed limit in many cases. In our discussion on speed optimization, we examined the exponentially increasing safety hazards and efficiency losses which limit ideal speed at some point above (or even in some circumstances, below) the speed limit. Regardless of the posted speed limit obedience, the raw intervehicular dynamics of being an aggravatingly slow driver in the fast passing lane must be considered. Though a circumstance in which the travel speeds of the other vehicles in the passing lane are so excessively and dangerously high is conjurable, most speed differential situations commonly observed in the left lane are such that the slow, aggravating driver could, with ease and virtually no speed-related increase in legal risk, temporarily increase speed until a lateral escape opportunity enables lane-switching into the adjacent lane or even into the next one over, in which the slow driver could comfortably return to their preferred freeway-vacant ideal speed without aggravating rearwards drivers. Driving more slowly than the flow of traffic in the passing lane creates the following intervehicular hazards: (1) decreased rearwards following distance by both the linear mathematics of the relative speed and position between the slow and rear vehicles, and also by the likely anger of the rearward vehicle's driver and its effect to promote tailgating (intentional close following by the rearwards vehicle), (2) the same effect for those following the rearwards vehicle, (3) a massive incentive for all following vehicles to pass on the right, which creates multiple collision opportunities between not only those passing but also those already travelling in the adjacent lane, and (4) a general (and well-assured) instigation of allovehicular driver anger and road-rage situations, which is likely to lead to other aggressive driving hazards. Being that perhaps the largest dissuading factor towards travel at a higher speed (at some point) is legal risk to begin with, and given the utter statistical minimization of this factor while travelling at or below the speed of the flow of traffic of multiple allovehicles, then it is quite hard to conjure a justified situation in which the professional driver would create such a situation him or herself in the passing lane. That is not to say that the professional driver should join what is sometimes aggressive speeding behavior often undertaken by the inhabitants of the left-most lane (which is often an illegal travelling position to begin with), but instead to suggest that if the professional driver is indeed to travel at that much slower of a comparative speed, then he or she has absolutely no place in the left-most lane to begin with, which is for faster vehicles (at best – and is formally for passing only in most locations), when clearly lane optimization would yield a different choice of lane given the speed of traffic therein and its effect on the necessity of maintaining safe following distance both behind and in front of the vehicle. Assuming that lane optimization analysis does yield a selection of the left-most lane as the optimal choice, and assuming more sparse traffic circumstances, than it can be concluded that a sound response towards seeing an approaching faster isolane rearwards vehicle in the center mirror while travelling in this lane would be to predictively switch into the adjacent lane, let the faster vehicle pass, and then switch back into the passing lane if conditions still warrant. Persistent slower-than-traffic travel, however, in the left-most lane, when creating a large obstruction to the flow of traffic, is not responsible nor professional driving behavior for the reasons of the created safety hazards explained above, regardless of any superficial justifications claiming legal obedience to the posted speed limit or what not. In such situations, the basic speed rule should be referenced, which has priority over posted speed limits, and which only prohibits travel above speeds which are "reasonable and prudent" with full regard to the present situation, including allovehicular traffic. An argument could be made even from a legal perspective, therefore, that travelling slightly over the speed limit in order to prevent dangerous road-rage, congestion, and rightwards passing situations is not even illegal to begin with.

Two-lane freeway considerations

Some full-speed interstate highways, such as long stretches of Vermont's Interstate 91, afford the professional driver with only a binary choice between a left and a right lane. Lane designation compliance may wield a disproportionally larger influence over lane choice if indeed the law prohibits travel on half of the highway unless passing is being attempted. Perhaps in this circumstance and likely even more with travel freedom in both lanes, lane optimization may be nearly simplified into the selection of greater following distance. That is, a common phenomenon will occur in sparse traffic especially on these roads wherein the lane switch of an anterolateral vehicle into the frontal zone (perhaps, for instance, in preparation for exiting the freeway) should prompt the professional driver to conduct an immediate resulting lane switch into the original lane of the frontal driver, for the restoration of frontal following distance. This "lane swapping" phenomenon of proper lane optimization is also used by the professional driver on traditional wider highways of more than two lanes in highly traffic-sparse conditions when the anterolateral vehicle's lane switch simply limits following distance and a responsive switch into the other lane restores that distance to its original (or at least, a greater) length. Travel on two-lane freeways should emphasize the critical importance of safe following distance margins, since rapid deceleration and/or collision avoidance lane switches are necessarily limited to that of one escape lane, whereas travel in the middle lane of a wide and sparse highway would afford more ample evasive opportunities.

High urgency situations

A driver of urgent purpose is naturally disposed to accept increased safety risks for the benefit of arrival-time optimization, however we have indicated the absolutely exponential increase necessary of the former to yield only linear increases in the latter. The behavior of such a driver will unavoidably involve narrowing safety margins between other vehicles from both a theoretical and dynamical point of view; theoretically, vehicular traffic flow behaves as a fluid and exhibits analogous qualities to speed, pressure, and density – an individual particle's travelling through the fluid flow at a higher rate of velocity (akin to a speeder weaving through traffic) requires force to counter the molecular collisions which would resemble vehicular collisions on the highway. This dynamically represents itself in passing situations; being free to accelerate through frontal following distance, the speeding driver must overtake the frontal vehicle, which is limiting forward position, by passing the vehicle on either side. Increased traffic density, of course, yields greater difficulty in performing this task, since sufficient longitudinal space between the being passed vehicle and the frontal vehicle in the temporary lane will be hard to find. The professional driver is aware by means of spatial awareness of when his or her vehicle is bordering such an attempt to "squeeze" through traffic by making tight passes by an aggressive, speeding driver; one is either driving the being passed vehicle, which should decelerate to allow the speeder to merge back into the lane, or driving the frontal limiting vehicle in the temporary passing lane, which would be noticed during spatial awareness checks in the side and center mirrors, and should therefore generally accelerate to allow the aggressive driver's merge into the adjacent lane and continue through the flow of traffic. The professional driver, of course, should not allow the passing maneuver (and should intently discourage it by acceleration and deceleration, respectively, in the above cases) if an analysis of speed patterns of the neighboring vehicles indicates that the aggressive driver's pass simply will not be possible – perhaps due to an impending overall slowing in the flow of traffic (causing smaller following distance gaps) or due to a change in the comparative interlane speed between the two present lanes unfavorable to the passing aggressive driver. In these cases, it is best to shut down and dissuade the aggressive maneuver in order to avoid the likely collision which will occur in proximity to the professional driver. However in the prior cases, it is best to allow the aggressive driver to pass and get out of the professional driver's immediate space so that any future accidents which the aggressive driver causes do not involve the professional driver. The professional driver him or herself in a high urgency circumstance will be able to appropriately balance the aggressiveness of tactics with a firm understanding of the increased risks and decreased benefits which additional speed and aggression bring beyond some point – also knowing the legal risk of such actions, which if severe enough can enable traffic enforcement officers to conduct a full seizure, which would be massively detrimental to arrival-time optimization on the scale of hours or even days. From solely an arrival-time optimization point of view, moderate speeding (such as 10mph to 15mph over the speed limit) is almost always preferable to that of egregious speeding (for instance, over 30mph over the speed limit), since the former is at least non-seizureable and likely to constitute time costs (of being pulled over) on the order of twenty minutes instead of twenty hours. Even in a high urgency circumstance, the professional driver's extensive understanding of the risks inherent to speeding and aggressive driving would very unlikely warrant a freeway-vacant ideal travel speed of over 10mph over the speed limit.

High-congestion traffic conditions

Drivers travelling in high-density traffic conditions are more statistically prone to vehicular collision due to the tighter spatial safety margins separating vehicles and the high speed differential situations created by recurring stop-and-start, "crawling" traffic patterns at such low speeds. Unsurprisingly, lengthened frontal following distance is the primary mechanism by which the professional driver decreases the risk of such collisions, since any rapid deceleration of the frontal vehicle, caused by, for instance, its driver's momentary inattention to the road and near collision with his or her own frontal vehicle, is far less likely to create a dangerous deceleration situation for the present driver due the slower minimum necessary deceleration speed made possible by the lengthened frontal space. This decreases the chances of not only rear-end colliding but also of being rear-end collided, due to the very same less-rapid deceleration. As we discussed in chapter five, the professional driver must be attentive towards anterolateral vehicles who may merge into the frontal region if it is of sufficient length, which would then prompt an according reduction in speed for the restoration of proper following distance. High traffic conditions on the highway can also create seeming discrepancies in travel speed between different lanes of traffic, which can frustrate drivers stuck in a slow or stalled lane seeing others move at a higher velocity, which may even further cause aggressive shortenings on following distance than would the general frustration of slow traffic to begin with. Even more dangerously, this can create an urge for impatient drivers to switch over into a momentarily faster lane, risking collisions from nearly every direction in the tightly compacted congress of vehicles. The professional driver puts such differences in interlane speed into perspective in such circumstances, realizing that they are usually of such a stochastic nature as to be entirely coincidental and that there is equal probability of either the present lane speeding up soon or the once-desirable other lane slowing down, which can further aggressive driving behavior if expensive and careful lane switches were just conducted to get into that lane. This follows from the natural fluid nature of highway traffic, since any such comparatively more-sparse, "low-pressure" areas of traffic will attract an influx of vehicles from "high-pressure", high traffic-density regions which themselves will become more free from the exodus of drivers out of that area. In some predictable and narrow circumstances (such as an approaching and very locally popular exit, necessitating the right-wards lane-switching of many vehicles), the different regions of high-traffic flow speed may indeed be representative of a more permanent and improvement-likely status which would provide greater attraction to the professional driver of executing a lane switch to move into the faster region. In such circumstances, if the lane switch can be executed safely enough, this may very well constitute both a safety and arrival-time optimization since there will be less travel time spent in the slow bumper-to-bumper, start-stop crawl of traffic in the slow lane, in which the chances of a light rear-end collision (colloquially, a "fender-bender") are statistically very high. In any case, however, the professional driver in heavy traffic circumstances is aware of the heightened dangers to lane-switching, especially into faster adjacent lanes in which a high-speed vehicle may be approaching from behind[8], and will therefore ensure comprehensive, 360-degree spatial awareness understanding before executing any maneuver which could otherwise result in a collision.

A natural criticism of our inherently safety-prioritizing tactical model for the professional driver's actions in high-congestion traffic circumstances (and on the freeway in general) is that both local and systemic arrival-time is decreased by conservative behaviors such as

---

[8] See Chapter 12, accident situation #6

increasing following distance and permitting allovehicular merges in the frontal zone. There is a positively enormous body of research and literature on the theory of traffic flow, which entirely exceeds the scope of this book on tactics and which we will therefore not even begin to dissect, lest we include a whole second book in one. We will dismiss, however, the traffic-flow theories that encourage the theoretical "optimality" of aggressive behavior since their method of analysis, even if accurate in the first place, focuses solely on maximizing highway flow-rate and optimizing arrival-time – whereas there are other constituent factors to the driver's high-level strategy than solely arrival-time optimization. That is, both fuel-efficiency and (especially) safety are compromised in the dictates of many theoretical traffic flow models of optimum driving behavior for maximum throughput; we repeat our general advocacy of maintaining large following distances and non-combative interactions with allovehicular drivers due to the largely underestimated safety costs of adopting an alternative freeway-driving tactical model, as the present model is developed to discover an ideal balance between safety, speed, fuel-efficiency, and all of the other smaller risks and factors we have formerly analyzed.

CHAPTER 9

Other Defensive Tactics

Vehicular proximity response

The professional driver's best tactic in critically decelerative, high collision-risk circumstances is to have avoided them in the first place by sound application of the defensive safety measures already discussed; however, we should analyze the various vehicular proximity response options among which the driver must choose if indeed a presently urgent reality should come to necessitate their usage, for whatever reason.

Longitudinal proximity

The first of these concerns frontal versus rearwards collision prediction in high speed differential situations. Simply put, if the frontal vehicle slams on its brakes and if the professional driver must brake with excessive force and decelerative magnitude in order to avoid rear-end colliding the frontal vehicle (due to some rare circumstance which prevents the establishment of copious frontal following distance in the first place), then collision risk turns from rear-end colliding to that of being rear-end collided by the rearwards vehicle, who may not have the acute reaction time necessary to brake fast enough to avoid collision, and whose potential dangerous tailgating was the reason for which the professional driver had temporarily limited rearwards following distance in the first place. Since the professional driver is aware of surrounding vehicles from proper spatial awareness technique, this situation (in which the professional driver could choose between frontal and rearwards collision) is plausible. In it, we emphasize the universal responsibility (which applies also to other drivers) of needing to decelerate for the frontal vehicle; drivers who are rear-end collided from behind are never considered guilty in a traffic litigation context when their deceleration was prompted by the sound and proper response of decelerating due to their frontal vehicle's deceleration. In low-speed traffic circumstances when true risk of injury from such accidents is mostly low and therefore outweighed likely by accident liability considerations (the same low-speed, high-traffic circumstances in which the vast majority of such collisions on the highway occur), it is nearly impossible to justify any response other than sufficient deceleration to avoid collision with the frontal vehicle – while completely ignoring the rearwards vehicle and failing to care whether or not it collides into the present vehicle due to the execution of the proper frontal-collision-avoiding response, due to the professional driver's spatial knowledge that the speed differentials involved in such high-traffic, "fender-bender" collisions are relatively low, having seen the rear driver in the center mirror, and having arbitrated that its speed renders absolutely inconsequential safety hazards in its gently colliding with the rear of the vehicle compared to that of the legal and insurance burdens which would entail rear-end colliding the frontal vehicle. With regards to situations of higher driver or passenger collision sensitivity, lessened concern for accident culpability, and (exponentially so) higher speed, this analysis must increasingly exhibit the opposite behavior of disregarding the legal aspect and prioritizing solely safety (with the former only rarely differing from that of the latter, since such high-speed deceleration-critical circumstances are likely to involve the necessary collision of both vehicles, and so the prospect of avoiding a frontal rear-end collision becomes increasingly unlikely). Clearly the professional driver has already attempted to exit this example whole intervehicular isolane space of such small margins and tried to lengthen it by decelerating and pushing back the rearwards vehicle – regardless, if in a critical circumstance the professional driver is caught in a deceleration-critical high-speed circumstance of tight longitudinal following distance margins both in the frontal and rearwards regions, and evasive lane switching being impossible, and it being arbitrated that an impending collision with both vehicles is unavoidable, then he or she must in a split second decelerate with a decidedly optimized balance between frontal and rearwards collisions so that some of the forces cancel out, instead of colliding full-force with the frontal vehicle, and then being nearly full-force collided again by the rearwards vehicle. The professional driver's having the time and spatial awareness to perfect this balance would be an incredibly rare (and at worst, solely theoretical) situation – however, insofar as spatial awareness affords immediate knowledge of the distances and speeds of each vehicle, the professional driver will minimize collisional force between the two vehicles by braking immediately to slow the force of the frontal collision, knowing however that a resulting rearwards collision is highly likely in high-speed, low-rear-following-distance circumstances.

Lateral proximity

Though not as potentially dramatic as that of longitudinal collisions, lateral challenges to safety margin space must be constantly monitored for the evasion of a side collision. Whenever the professional driver's speed exceeds that of an anterolateral vehicle in an adjacent lane, a large priority of spatial attention should be given to its directional signals and interlane position to ensure that its driver does not attempt a lane switch while being longitudinally passed, which would create a lateral collision. Interlane position monitoring must complement that of turn signal monitoring since a distracted or inebriated driver may not intend to drift out of lane while being longitudinally passed (especially if they are on the inner bend of a curve, as we examined before). Once this errant allovehicular driver or even the other surrounding drivers notice the impending collision, nervous and over-corrective jerks to the steering wheel can easily create a collision elsewhere with another vehicle. Irrational braking may also accompany such panicked moments of a drifting lateral driver, who may then collide with its rearward vehicle. Furthermore, the professional driver (in the longitudinally opposite case) must monitor any posterolateral vehicles in an adjacent lane if they are going faster and therefore bound to longitudinally pass at some future time. This is, however, nowhere near as great of a concern as the first case of watching about-to-be-passed anterolateral drivers, since the passing posterolateral drivers are much more likely to see that which is in front of them than the being-passed anterolateral drivers are to see that which is behind them. And naturally, in any event of preferentially avoided travel alongside an adjacent-lane allovehicle in the lateral zone, large spatial awareness scanning prioritizations should be made towards the side of the opposite adjacent lane, if any, in order to secure an evasive escape path if the lateral driver comes too close, or even in which to immediately lane-switch to remove the lateral vehicle from proximity.

Collision response procedure

As in any case, if a collision does occur, the professional driver (nor the common driver with even a modicum of common sense) never exits the vehicle on the freeway even in traffic-halted or entirely stopped circumstances; deaths have been documented from vehicle-person collisions after drivers have exited their vehicle post-vehicle-vehicle collision. Proper accident response procedure always calls for the activation of hazard lights and induces the involved vehicles to pull over to the right where safe in the breakdown lane, away from the flow of traffic, and only then to exit the vehicle. The advent of cell phones has rendered freeway call boxes mostly obsolete and found with decreasing frequency along interstates; this further decreases the immediate need to exit the vehicle in many circumstances when phone communication to emergency management is already at hand, even having pulled over in the breakdown lane, at least until traffic enforcement support arrives and is able to procure greater safety by inducing larger space between the travelling vehicles and the disabled, breakdown-lane vehicles, whether by temporary lane closure in severe cases or the by the mere presence of traffic enforcement vehicles and their lights.

Driver impairment and road rage

While we have discussed driver behavior profiling to a cursory degree in our discussion on freeway entrance merging, these indications derived largely from visual sight of the driver's body which is difficult or impossible in many (especially nighttime) circumstances. The professional driver must therefore be able to identify and react to dangerous allovehicular drivers by analyzing their vehicle's maneuvering patterns from a safe distance, which is founded upon proper and attentive spatial awareness technique. Drivers who are impaired due to intoxication or fatigue must be identified and spatially evaded by the professional driver in order to predictively avoid collisions which are likely to occur in their immediate region. The professional driver constantly monitors signs of such impairment, including but not limited to:

- Highly variable interlane position, issuing corrections thereunto at regular intervals to correct for the allovehicle's errant drifting
- Deactivated headlights at night
- Erratic acceleration and deceleration patterns
- Travelling significantly below the speed limit compared to other drivers, perhaps in an attempt to avoid traffic enforcement stops
- Utter ignorance of lane-marker designations, travelling over them and failing to use directional signals which switching between lanes

While single instances of any of the above are more likely to indicate the temporary distraction of an un-impaired yet unexperienced driver (allowing such distractions from, for instance, electronic device usage, to impact their freeway driving in a noticeable fashion), a conjunctive synthesis of any of the above in the pattern of recurring behavior serves as an excellent logical indicator that such behavior will indeed continue, risking collision with any surrounding drivers. Upon longitudinally overtaking (or, less likely, being overtaken) by such a vehicle, the professional driver will adjust speed and lane position in order to evasively maximize intervehicular distance to the impaired driver's vehicle during the passing phase. The possibility that such impaired drivers may be travelling more quickly than the driver reinforces the importance of continuous, 360-degree spatial awareness scanning information, as rearwards identification of such a driver either in the center or wing mirror will be necessary for their pre-emptive identification.

The phenomenon of road rage encapsulates another field of dangerous allovehicular behaviors about which a sizeable corpus of research has been written. Though in no way constrained to the freeway context, the existence of aggressive driving behavior on the highway caused by driver frustration is foreign only to novice freeway drivers. A 1995 study in the UK surveyed 526 drivers, 90% of whom had experienced a road-rage situation in the past year (Joint, 1995)[1]; an attempt to quantify the formal manifestation of such incidents resulted in the following response rates:

- Aggressive tailgating (62%)
- Headlight flashing (59%)
- Obscene gestures (48%)
- Deliberately obstructing other vehicles (21%)
- Verbal abuse (16%)

The two primary forms of road rage therefore demonstrate the phenomenon's particular relevance to the freeway context and also substantiate our former statements on discouraging slower-than-traffic left-lane travel, which is nearly guaranteed to instigate aggressive tailgating at the very least. This study's findings concerning the perceived aggressiveness of headlight flashing, at least in some situations, is positively shocking and quite illuminating, since headlight signaling can be a normal and appropriate form of driver signaling (for instance, passing notification) which augments safety in some circumstances, as we will discuss in a later section. The professional driver should therefore be aware that some drivers may perceive being headlight-flashed as a confusing, aggressive, and/or bothersome behavior, which should therefore limit its usage to situations in which its prompting of spatial awareness knowledge in the recipient driver

---

[1] Joint, M., 1995. Road rage.

outweighs this factor in its safety benefit. A Canadian review of newspaper reports from 1998-2000 confirms many of the road-rage associated behaviors of Joint's study and additionally posits an 8.5% female perpetration rate dwarfed by a whopping 96.6% male perpetration rate (Smart & Mann, 2002)[2], a fact which can aid the professional driver's subjective analytical perception of the existence and likelihood of aggressive road-rage behavior (or likely future behavior) in a visually identified allovehicular driver. Such observed behaviors should induce the same evasive maneuvers as the identification of impaired drivers would merit, with the only difference that intentional challenges to safe distance margins (or even collision) supplants that of the impaired driver's unintentional elicitation of the same dangers.

Stationary object anticipation and avoidance

We have formerly discussed predictive avoidance and identification of road-surface hazards in the lane optimization context, but have not yet analyzed proper response and evasion procedures in the full intervehicular context of our whole tactical model for spatial maneuvering. The two primary tactical considerations upon spotting a frontal road hazard are identifying (1) the evasive escape vector(s), relative to the present vector of vehicle motion, which will yield a safe avoidance of the obstacle, and (2) the potential intervehicular and/or structural hazards which such a change to vehicle speed and heading could create. Considering the balance of options created by these two factors, the professional driver must choose the most optimal response that minimizes chance of collision or which minimizes collision severity, in the case that collision avoidance is impossible. In a freeway-vacant environment, the second factor concerns only fixed structures such a side-rails, concrete divider structures, or posted signage, for instance, and would quite favorably afford the professional driver much space through which

---

[2] Smart, R. G. & Mann, R. E., 2002. Deaths and injuries from road rage: cases in Canadian newspapers. *Canadian Medical Association Journal,* 167(7), pp. 761-762.

to conduct an evasive maneuver without intricate consideration of the collateral risks of secondary vehicular collision (due to avoiding collision with the first hazard) since there are no other vehicles on the road. This clearly does not capture the majority of circumstances, and therefore the professional driver's response options will most likely be limited by the rear vehicle and the vehicles travelling in any adjacent lane(s) which could prevent lateral, lane-switch-induced escape of the hazard. If the hazard is directly frontal, and lateral escape is not possible, then the evasive vector should point exactly 180-degrees opposite to the direction of travel (i.e., away from the hazard), which would evince a strong deceleration and admittedly risky collision with the rearwards vehicle if following distance is small. Due to this, the professional driver must make an approximate subjective assessment of the mass and height of the frontal hazard; if it is short enough to afford security that the windshield of the vehicle will not be impacted, and if it is massless enough as to lower collision risk enough (such as may be the case with a blown-over traffic barrel while driving an SUV at 68mph), then the apparent non-lethality of the impending collision must be weighed against the potentially worse consequences of full rearwards deceleration under tight following distance circumstances (the caused frontal accelerative force of which may even occasion the additional collision with the frontal hazard at a speed not even much less than that of the original travel speed) when responsive deceleration is taken to the absolute maximum of the vehicle's physical ability. For this reason, the proper tactical response to such a situation of limited lateral escape opportunities while approaching a proximate and sudden frontal hazard must consider the relative mass and velocity of the driver's vehicle and the rearward vehicle; in one extreme, if the professional driver is operating a light Prius in front of a positively massive eighteen-wheeled semi-truck, which is unable to decelerate with any remotely comparative suddenness (and which would be a foolish lane position to occupy without establishing copious rearwards following distance to begin with, for these same reasons), then the potential danger of sudden braking in front of the truck is quite likely to outweigh that of collision with the frontal hazard, especially insofar as it is light, since rapid deceleration of a light vehicle just in front of a truck is not unlikely to yield lethal consequences. In such a case, if the frontal hazard is light enough, the professional driver may even accelerate into the object to lengthen rearwards following distance in preparation for the inevitable deceleration which collision with the frontal object is bound to yield, in an attempt to decrease the likelihood of being collided by the massive and forceful rear truck. In the opposite case that the professional driver is operating a heavy vehicle in front of a light vehicle, both the consequences of colliding with the frontal hazard and being collided by the rearward vehicle are largely minimized, which should prompt a conservative deceleration in order to reduce impact velocity. It is fortunate that the more-difficult lateral escape opportunities of such larger and heavier vehicles is balanced by the comparatively lesser danger in which they may collide with a frontal hazard compared to a lighter and more agile vehicle.

The professional driver's spatial awareness scanning affords visibility not only to the frontal but also anterolateral regions, especially when anterolateral vehicles are present. The professional driver must predictively anticipate the lateral evasion of an anterolateral driver into his or her own frontal region, which may also be dangerously accompanied by a rapid deceleration on the evading vehicle's part due to their being utterly overwhelmed by avoiding the hazardous object as to be ignorant of any rearwards (and originally posterolateral) vehicle in the lane into which they have just evasively switched. The professional driver should preferably either pass ahead or increase longitudinal space relative to such present anterolateral drivers, especially if there is judged to be a high probability that they may encounter a hazard on and protruding from the shoulder, or even any frontal hazard, which could prompt their immediate and careless lateral evasion into the frontal region. This holds especially true when travelling in the second-to-left-most lane due to the commonness of left-shoulder debris (such as detached tire retreadings) and perhaps also due to line-of-sight visibility obstruction to such hazards from the existence of frontal vehicles.

Interlane position in high traffic density

Spacious lateral safety margins, as we have shown before, are absolutely essential to collision avoidance on the freeway due to the plurality of situations in which other vehicles may come dangerously close to the sides of the vehicle, by which collision may easily occur if interlane position if offset enough from the center of the lane. A potential benefit, however, of adjusted interlane position is increased frontal path-of-travel visibility that would otherwise be obstructed by the frontal vehicle (to the extent that the profile of the frontal vehicle is narrow enough). The professional driver will seek to maintain sufficient frontal following distance as to render such information (of that which extends beyond the frontal driver) not entirely necessary – however it may be marginally beneficial in high traffic circumstances, when the immediate braking of the vehicle in front of the frontal vehicle and delayed response of the frontal vehicle would create a rapidly decelerative situation for the observing driver, who could more smoothly apply the deceleration with visual forewarning of the second-in-front vehicle's stoppage if it is visible due to adjusted interlane position. While this hypothetical is technically plausible, it is still unlikely that the benefits of such interlane position adjustment would outweigh the potential safety costs inherent to lane drift. Even in slow high-traffic circumstances, offset lane position to a sufficient degree could prompt an adjacent lane driver's attempt to merge into the space which appears to be empty from behind, but is in fact filled with a lane-offset driver. This could easily cause a collision if the mis-assuming driver initiates the lane switch and then must either continue into the space or abort and return to the original lane. The professional driver should in all standard circumstances remain attentive to lane borders and maintain properly centered interlane position.

Part IV

Vehicular Control and Interface Tactics

CHAPTER 10

Vehicle Control

Having concluded and fully specified our precise tactical model for spatial maneuvering on the freeway, we must now examine the local and internal vehicular control tactics which will enable the professional driver to put such maneuvers into effect during the course of freeway travel. Although this encompasses any manual or foot operation of a vehicle interface component, the two primary constituents are unsurprisingly grouped into that of speed control and steering control.

Speed control

The professional driver's options concerning speed control are characteristically divided between that of manual accelerator/brake pedal operation and that of using the vehicle's isotachic cruising feature, called "cruise control" (or "autocruise" or even "tempomat"), which is both standard to nearly every modern vehicle and which is also a positively massive asset to the professional driver which we have not had the opportunity yet to explore (due to its irrelevance to the former sections). In reality, it is not accurate to portray such absolute division between the two classes of speed control methods since the professional driver will often blend a hybrid integration of both speed control tactics as situational factors accord. Let us examine the advantages, disadvantages, and proper utilizing of both.

Cruise control vs. manual speed control

In general, we are quite fond of cruise control and supportive of its place in the professional driver's repertoire of highway driving vehicle control tactics. Proper usage of cruise control can (1) increase the effectiveness of maintaining the determined freeway-vacant ideal travel speed in traffic sparse circumstances, thereby decreasing higher legal risks incumbent to irregular speed peaks which may be caused by traditional acceleration/deceleration control (which would only tend to approximate the chosen speed by slightly-over and slightly-under alternating intervals, insofar as the driver is not skilled with precise speed maintenance with the accelerator pedal), (2) remove the arrival-time costs associated with lull periods in such variable speeds (if the average of such speed vacillations happens to be lower than the target, approximated freeway-vacant ideal travel speed), (3) simplify the driving task by removing the need to precisely regulate accelerator depression pressure to keep speed even by delegating this task to the control software of the vehicle (as such cruise control speed regulation is done digitally in a vast majority of modern vehicles), and (4) increase fuel-efficiency on flat, traffic-sparse, long-distance trips by decreasing brake usage frequency (even though we did review the circumstances in which cruise control is not fuel-efficiency optimal in our discussion on fuel-efficiency optimization). Cruise control is therefore most suited to situations of low predicted speed differential, whereas an increased likelihood of needing to adjust speed (such as in any moderate-to-high traffic density circumstance) would call for the speed responsivity of increased immediacy which the accelerator and brake pedals offer. The common criticism of cruise control that immediate responsive changes to speed are made more difficult, therefore, is almost wholly invalidated due to the driver ability to activate brakes or depress the accelerator pedal, taking cruise control out of effect immediately. The aforementioned objection is only valid to the extent that prolonged cruise control usage and the resulting (and only seeming) lack of foot-pedal interface necessity may tempt the driver into positioning his or her feet in a more relaxing position from which additional time would need to be taken to responsively depress the brake or accelerator pedal in a time-critical situation compared to that of the already engaged foot positions which would accompany a cruise-control-eschewing driver. Another concern which has prompted the criticism of cruise control has pointed out that over-fatigued drivers are more likely to fall asleep at the wheel and continue straight off the highway or into a frontal vehicle in a perhaps-lethal collision, due to the lack of a decelerative stimulus which would accompany the falling asleep (and therefore, ankle muscle relaxation) of an over-fatigued driver, which would either issue a corrective "wake-up" response or would at least result in the safer deceleration of the vehicle. While both of these concerns are valid from a global conspectus of the cruise control feature, the professional driver is able to overcome such safety concerns by (1) only using cruise control in situations not calling for rapid speed changes, (2) always maintaining "ready" foot position to depress the brake (or even accelerator) if a sudden situation so dictates, and (3) by remaining bright and alert during the driving process, never driving under such dangerous circumstances of fatigue. Cruise control usage is also obviously unwise in slippery road conditions, due to the heightened possibility of skidding.

Tactical model for cruise control usage

The professional driver is aware of the functional inputs to a vehicle's cruise control system, traditionally including an On/Off switch, a "SET/ACCEL" button, a "RES" button, a "CRUISE" button, and switches on the brake pedal (and clutch pedal, in the case of an automatic transmission vehicle). The functions of each are as follows:

- The On/Off switch (either taking the form of two separate buttons adjusting a cruise control activation status indicator or of a single depression-switch button) which simply activates the cruise control functions and awaits further user input (i.e., the whole system's solely being switched "On" does not by itself activate any cruise control features, yet only enables their future activation by further user input)

- The "SET/ACCEL" button, which sets the current speed and begins speed maintenance, and which then (after setting a speed) functions as an accelerative incrementor button for the set speed (usually by 1mph per button press)

- The brake pedal switch (and clutch pedal switch, if applicable) which deactivates the current cruise control set speed and returns acceleration control to the throttle position of the accelerator pedal (and which will prompt cruising to a stop if speed is not restored by the accelerator or the following control)

- The "RES" button, which restores the most recent set speed once it has been deactivated by the brake pedal, the clutch pedal, or the following control (if applicable)

- Sometimes a separate "CANCEL" button which achieves the effect of stepping on the brakes and deactivating cruise control without necessitating brake pedal usage

- The "CRUISE" button, which usually will perform the same function above (of unsetting the cruise control speed) when held down, and of decrementing the set speed when tapped

Although this general outline of cruise control user inputs applies to many traditional systems, the professional driver is specifically knowledgeable of the system he or she is operating which may contain slight variations from the above. The most common of these would be the omission of the "CRUISE" button, inclusion of a "CANCEL" button, and the "SET" and "RES" buttons acting as the incremental and decremental (or the converse) speed buttons during an actively set cruise control speed. In such user interfaces, the "SET" and "RES" button increments (potentially co-labeled "+" and "-", or the converse) during an actively set speed may adjust speed by a larger interval when held down for an extended period (such as 5mph, as in the case of the Chrysler 2012 Town and Country implementation of the cruise control interface) as opposed to tapped – however we remind that cruise control is usually unsuited for large changes in speed (due to the time-extended nature in which the control system applies them), especially if they are to be appropriated in a time-sensitive nature, in which a reversion to traditional accelerator and brake pedal usage is appropriate. Further variations on the traditional cruise control design can link the "SET" and "CRUISE" buttons, requiring an opposite "RES" and "ACCEL" button, inverting the order in which each button's speed-unset function is related to its speed-set function. Some vehicles' driver interface designs even remove the necessity of pressing buttons and place the totality of such cruise control manual functions on a stick.

Cruise control systems require that the driver first bring the vehicle up to speed with the accelerator pedal before a set speed is kept in place, and as such the professional driver will activate cruise control only after highway entrance merging. Most cruise control systems do not allow the driver to set a speed below some minimum threshold, typically around 20mph or 25mph, which presents no obstruction to the freeway driver since travel speed of such slowness could only be caused in circumstances of high traffic density and/or challenging road surface or visibility conditions which themselves would already prevent wise cruise control usage. Once (and if) a circumstance of relatively constant predicted future speed of the vehicle arrives, the cruise control feature should be turned on and the "set" function activated to lock in the current speed (causing the automatic speed maintenance to begin only after both of these steps are executed, as merely turning on the cruise control feature does not automatically set the speed in most vehicles). It is redundant to declare cruise control usage inappropriate when there are moderately proximate vehicles surrounding the vehicle, since this would naturally provoke the anticipation of needing to change speed (as a defensive intervehicular maneuver or as a simple following distance maintenance response to a frontal vehicle's adjustment in speed) which characterizes the proper place and time for manual brake and accelerator pedal usage for speed regulation.

Once a speed is set and being actively maintained by the vehicle, the professional driver can make small adjustments by using the incrementing and decrementing controls which typically add or subtract 1mph to the set speed. This is quite useful for facilitating the type of minute, long-range changes that may come about to influence the freeway-vacant ideal travel speed in sparse, long-distance travel. If and when circumstances require more immediate and precise adjustment to speed as would warrant the use of braking and accelerator pedals instead of cruise control, then the desired acceleration should be carried out by pressing the accelerator or the desired deceleration carried out by pressing the brake in an exactly normal fashion as would be constantly necessary for the driver of a cruise-control-lacking vehicle. There are some circumstances and special considerations which occasion the interaction between cruise control and normal speed control and which slightly complicate the above oversimplified model for integrating the two, as follows:

- If cruise control is on and an active speed is set, accelerating the vehicle by throttling the acceleration pedal does not necessarily disengage cruise control such as activation of the brake pedal universally does. In fact, it does not in most vehicles. The driver must know the specific behavior of his or her own vehicle in this regard (if there is, for instance, a speed or time cutoff beyond which the cruise setting will in fact be deactivated) and until then must always be aware that the vehicle may begin to decelerate back to the set speed once the accelerator pedal is no longer being pressed, or to decelerate to a stop if indeed the cruise control setting has been deactivated.

- Deceleration can be accomplished more quickly by disengaging the speed setting (generally accomplished by pressing the "CANCEL" button or holding the "CRUISE" button) than by decrementing the speed by the 1mph increment many times. Some vehicles' cruise control speed increment and decrement button interfaces are designed not to be responsive to over a certain amount of clicks in a short time – for instance decreasing the speed by 15mph with fifteen consecutive rapid, split-second, vibrational clicks in some vehicles will not be registered as a full 15mph decrease to speed. Simply deactivating the cruise setting in deceleration-anticipated circumstances, or in circumstance of needing to significantly decelerate over a long stretch of time, allows the vehicle to slowly cruise to a lower velocity in a fuel-efficient manner (analogous to the "gliding" phase of the pulse-and-glide fuel-efficiency optimization technique). If more rapid deceleration is needed, then regular braking should be used.

- Deceleration by any means of cruise control (that is, by any method which does not involve depressing the brake pedal) does not activate the rearwards brake lights of the vehicle as does braking, which can be extremely important for the visual awareness of a rearwards driver especially if they are careless and travelling too closely behind. In situations of limited rearwards following distance, decelerating by means of equal braking, though perhaps less fuel-efficient, affords the important safety benefit of flashing and activating the bright-red, alerting brake lights for the rearward vehicle's observation, whereas cruise control reliance for decelerative purposes never activates brake lights.

- The cruise control system is regulated by a PID (proportional, integral, and differential) algorithm which adjusts throttle position according to a synthetic sum of (1) linear (proportional) error in speed (i.e., the difference between travel speed and set speed due to change in external forces impacting engine load), (2) the magnitude of the time--integrated distance error (i.e., the current vehicle position subtracted from the hypothetical vehicle position were speed properly controlled for the error period), and (3) the instantaneous accelerative tendency of current speed (acceleration being the derivative of speed). The practical result of this control system design to the professional driver is that the cruise control system will experience some time-delay upon encountering a cause of speed error, such as approaching and ascending a hill, before issuing a corrective change in engine throttle to restore speed to the set point. Manual accelerator usage is therefore guaranteed to enable more even and regular speed control when engine load increases in this way, such as ascending a hill or even sudden wind gust loads in windy environments.

- This also means that a cruise-control-enabled vehicle will almost always overspeed on the downwards slope of a hill; since the set speed is already configured at the freeway-vacant ideal travel speed, this behavior could dangerously and riskily increase speed beyond the desired level and cause a speed-related traffic enforcement stop. The professional driver, therefore, should either employ manual speed control at hills, or, if sufficient rearwards longitudinal safety distance exists, decrease the cruise control speed before the crest of the hill in order to compensate for the over-acceleration on the way down. Most vehicles will *not* apply the brakes automatically in order to slow the vehicle down to the set speed, and therefore manual braking is quite likely to be necessary on any precipitously downwards section of freeway, insofar as a fuel-efficiency-optimizing and according decrease in speed is not previously undertaken on the uphill phase. Regardless, we have already mentioned the fuel-inefficient performance of cruise control in hilly terrain and now demonstrate a safety cost of its potential to overspeed the vehicle in such conditions.

Knowledge of these considerations while using cruise control, taken in conjunction with a proper understanding of when cruise control is to be seamlessly overtaken by manual pedal-based control methods, allows the professional driver to incorporate the feature into his or her vehicle control tactics without sacrificing safety. Our control loop model would suggest that the removal of the constant necessary attention to throttle position for precise isotachic cruising with the accelerator pedal would in fact, by itself, constitute a safety improvement since information processing and coordination resources are freed for spatial awareness scanning and processing. The professional driver therefore uses cruise control in the type of appropriate traffic-sparse, speed-constant situations which we described above.

Braking

Many situations on the freeway will not permit the preferable avoidance of braking by well-timed predictive coasting (facilitated either by digitally decrementing the cruise control setting or removing pressure from the throttle pedal) nor by the prior extension of following distances; especially in rapidly decelerative collision avoidance and evasion circumstances, the professional driver must understand the braking techniques and capabilities of the vehicle which he or she operates on the freeway. An understanding of braking capabilities is best elicited by taking the extreme example of full-force depression of the brake pedal to stop the vehicle as quickly as possible.

Braking distance

The distance traveled with the brakes fully activated before the vehicle comes to a stop is known as the braking distance, and is therefore shorter than the total stopping distance which also includes the distance traveled during the initial perception-time phase. As is taught in most introductory driving courses, braking distance is not linearly related to speed, but rather increases exponentially with every linear increase to speed. In the freeway context, this constitutes an increasingly whopping safety risk incumbent to higher speeds when traffic circumstances may at any sudden moment dictate the need of forceful braking. Braking distance is increased in regions of downhill grade (and accordingly decreased on an uphill grade), though this effect is minimal compared to that of speed's influence in stopping distance, since gravitational potential energy (represented by $GPE = mgh$) is an entirely linear relation, whereas the vehicle's kinetic energy ($KE = \frac{1}{2}mv^2$) contains a second-degree, exponential relationship to velocity. Braking must do work equal in magnitude to the forward-moving kinetic energy of the vehicle in order to bring it to a stop; work equals force times distance, and in this case the force is the frictional force between the tires and the road surface, which is represented by $F = \mu mg$, where g is the gravitational constant, m is the mass of the vehicle, and μ is the coefficient of static friction (i.e., how slippery or sticky the frictional tire grip is); putting together the relation, it is seen that total braking work is given by $W_b = F \cdot d = \mu mg \cdot d$; therefore, since the braking work W_b must match that of the velocity-given kinetic energy of the vehicle, a decrease in the coefficient of static friction (i.e., as with wet, icy, snowy, or otherwise slippery roads) must accordingly increase d – the braking distance – in order to fully stop the vehicle. The professional driver is therefore always aware of the increased braking distance in slippery road conditions and seeks to decrease speed accordingly, which decreases kinetic energy and therefore the amount of work which braking must accomplish, allowing it to be accomplished in a shorter distance. While variations in braking distance do accord to different vehicle types and masses, it is a common error to assume that a lighter vehicle can be stopped so much more quickly as to justify excessive speed in the appearance of an "agile" capacity to stop suddenly if necessary, unlike a heavier vehicle. This should never be assumed since although mass is a component to the frictional force stopping the vehicle, increasing the downforce and therefore the friction, it is also a factor in the kinetic energy equation and so the mass factor would cancel out on both sides, arranging the two equations in a $KE = W_b$ equality; in other words, although heightened mass does increase downforce and therefore tire traction, it also increases the kinetic energy of the vehicle which must be stopped by braking. Therefore, extreme care to speed should be taken in slippery conditions even in a light and seemingly "agile" vehicle.

Downforce

We should examine the tire friction force relationship, $F = \mu mg$, which is more accurately written $F = \mu F_d$, wherein the coefficient of friction is multiplied by F_d – the *downforce* being pressed into the tires, which only under normal circumstances is equal to mg, the weight of the vehicle. In practical reality, there are many other factors which influence the downforce being pressed into the tires above and beyond the weight of the vehicle which itself is not evenly distributed among the tires during turns. The largest of these in the freeway context is the *aerodynamic downforce* which is caused by the air resistance drag force being diverted into the tires by means of the vehicle's precisely designed aerodynamic profile. Imagining the basic slanted design of windshields (slanted planarly upwards from the road surface), it is easy to imagine how the air passing the vehicle pushes into the tires and increases traction. Unlike heightened vehicle mass itself, which does indeed increase traction but also increases the amount of work the frictional traction force must do to stop the vehicle, since it is heavier and therefore bearing greater kinetic energy, increased air resistance only increases the traction capacity of the tires. Driving with a tailwind, therefore, lengthens braking distance. The professional driver should also identify the aerodynamic downforce as an additional factor contributing to the dangerousness of the drafting technique, since not only is frontal following distance shortened, but also braking distance in fact *lengthened* due to the lower air drag force and therefore aerodynamic downforce which would press the vehicle's tires into the ground for better stopping traction. However, in the drafting technique, the frontal vehicle obstructs a large part of said air resistance and allows the following vehicle's tires to gently glide on the surface of the road with decreased stopping capacity – a potentially lethal situation if the frontal vehicle rapidly decelerates.

Tire slip

Since the braking force is carried out through the friction force between the tires and the road surface, a brief understanding of tire dynamics is necessary for the professional driver to understand the differences in braking technologies and techniques. The term "slip" refers to the relative increase in tire-turn distance per unit distance that the vehicle travels; that is, if the circumferential tire-turn distance exactly matches that of vehicular distance traveled on the pavement, then there is no slip as the tire has maintained full traction with the road. The peak traction force of tires, however, occurs when there is a small bit of slip – an amount which varies according to tire design, weight transfer, and road surface characteristics. Applying the concept to manual braking, there is some optimal pressure applied to the brakes which elicits the maximum potential traction force against the tires to stop the vehicle. If the tires are wholly stuck to the ground as they turn, there is no slip and better traction could be gained by more forceful braking. If the driver brakes so hard that the wheels lock up and the vehicle goes into a skid, then there is clearly far too much slip (there is absolutely no wheel turning per unit distance traveled, in the extreme example of applying brakes full force as to cause wheel lock-up) and the driver could obtain better traction by easing up slightly on the brakes. The optimal skid amount varies but is, predictably, a generally low percentage figure, which is usually between 10% and 20% for road vehicles and which can even be as low as 4% in racing tires. The ideal slip amount is marginally higher with wet pavement than with dry pavement, however wet road conditions decrease overall surface traction to the point that driving technique and choice of speed should severely minimize the likelihood of needing to conduct a full-force stoppage of the vehicle. Regardless, in almost all situations, the maximum-force brake pedal depression pressure possible by the driver's lower body muscles is not the ideal braking force, since this will likely cause total wheel lock-up and resulting skidding which has lower traction than decreased brake pressure at the optimal slip amount. Becoming familiar with the optimal slip amount requires a familiar and experienced knowledge of the particular vehicle's "feel" and handling. Braking just at the point of slippage is called "threshold braking" or "limit braking" in racing contexts and is rooted in the general comparative superiority of the coefficient of static friction (tire gripping the road) than that of kinetic friction (tire locked up and skidding on the pavement).

Brake fade

Ideal braking is, unsurprisingly, slightly more complicated than constant application of the right pressure which achieves the ideal tire slip amount. Even in light braking circumstances (which are far more common than rapidly decelerative, stopping-immediate situations), constant and extended application of light braking pressure does a great deal of wear to most brake systems and can cause them to overheat, whereas braking with more severe, short intervals is generally better for the internal braking components (this of course requiring spacious rearwards following distance to avoid being rear-end collided). Brake fade is caused when any type of friction-based braking system (such a drum brakes or disc brakes) overheats due to excessive and/or high-speed usage which decreases stopping distance. Furthermore, drum brakes are susceptible to a phenomenon when logged with water (for instance, as a result of driving through a deep puddle) in which braking friction is temporarily reduced or eliminated due to a film of water's lubricating an activated brake shoe which pushes out against the brake drum; a somewhat antiquated driver's education teaching therefore recommends the light and continuous application of brakes after driving through a puddle in order to dry them out and restore their efficacy. While this is technically valid in the limited context to which it applies, it is mostly antiquated and irrelevant to the professional freeway driver since (1) disc brakes have overwhelmingly supplanted drum brakes in the last thirty years in the American market, being even more common in Europe, which do not exhibit this effect (that is, not to any comparable degree), (2) even small applications of continued braking force on the freeway are much more likely to cause a dangerous reduction in speed which may challenge proximity to the rearwards vehicle than that of the secondary and local road contexts to which the brake-drying aphorism is intended, and (3) puddles do not occur on modern, well-maintained freeways with proper draining and would only be found in circumstances of heavy rain and potential hydroplaning at which speeds should already be slow. Some vehicles have drum brakes for the rearwards tires and disc brakes for the front tires, in which the drying technique may still bear some relevance, yet this is still limited by the frontal tires' greater contribution to stopping force (in almost every case) than that of the rear tires due to weight transfer.

Cadence braking and ABS

In an emergency stop or accident evasion situation, it is possible that the professional driver may need both to brake and steer concomitantly, even though the physical dynamics of the former naturally constrains the execution of the latter. Cadence braking is a technique in which the brakes are pumped in a pulse-like fashion to afford better steering during rapid deceleration (allowing greater frictional rotation freedom for the tires to turn in the relaxed stages of the braking pulses) and also capitalizing on the increased coefficient of static versus kinetic friction between the tires and the ground by means of its reduction of wheel-locked skidding. Cadence braking therefore has merits even in the context of straight-line emergency stops when steering is not necessary, especially if there is variable friction across different tires either through variations of brake fade or (more likely, and perhaps more severely) different surface road conditions, such as a patch of ice or a hydroplaning pool of water on the left two tires with dry pavement contact on the right two tires. In such circumstances, cadence braking would allow the professional driver to issue corrective steering maneuvers during the relaxed phase of the braking pulses to overcome the potentially dangerous difference in traction between the two sides, whereas continuous braking pressure would likely cause the vehicle to veer to the side of increased traction, which could easily cause a lateral collision. Most modern vehicles are equipped with digital ABS (Anti-lock Brake System) which executes this process in faster intervals than a human driver could approximate, mostly rendering the cadence braking technique only relevant to those older vehicles which do not have ABS. The professional driver is therefore aware of the braking technologies built into his or her vehicle and is cognizant of the presence of ABS. Anti-lock Braking Systems have been confirmed to shorten braking distance and decrease vehicular collusions; a 1999 NHTSA report confirmed that "for most stopping maneuvers on most surfaces, ABS-assisted full pedal brake application stops were shorter than those made with the ABS disabled", except for that of loose gravel surfaces in which an average 27 percent *increase* in stopping distance was found (Forkenbrock, et al., 1999)[1]. Fortunately, loose gravel is not a road-surface construction characteristic encountered by the professional freeway driver travelling on any highways which are within the limits of our knowledge, at least.

Foot position and left-foot braking

A sufficient discussion on braking would not be complete without a cursory exploration of foot interface methods. The traditional method of alternating the right foot's upper sole position between the accelerator and neighboring brake pedal, with slight lateral position adjustment to heel-floor contact or even with keeping it fixed, is used by most drivers and taught near-universally. Left-foot braking is an unconventional method which assigns the left foot to the brake (and clutch, if any) and the right foot to the accelerator, with the apparent benefit that switching from accelerator to brake pedal can be done with faster speed. We substantiate our advocacy

---

[1] Forkenbrock, G. J., Flick, M. & Garrott, W. R., 1999. NHTSA light vehicle antilock brake system research program task 4: a test track study of light vehicle ABS performance over a broad range of surfaces and maneuvers. *US Department of Transportation, National Highway Traffic Safety Administration,* January.Volume DOT HS 808-875.

for the traditional foot position on account of the following reasons:

1. The foot-depression switch from accelerator to brake can be executed with near-immediate speed to an accustomed, professional driver, calling into question the true braking-speed optimization benefit which left-foot braking offers

2. The left-foot configuration may cause dangerous confusion at times, easily creating a collision (for instance, if a driver is used to a manual transmission vehicle and is switching to an automatic, he or she may inadvertently brake when intending to operate the clutch pedal)

3. The vehicle's speed is more immediately responsive to the brake pedal than to the accelerator pedal, which increases the potential intervehicular safety consequences of accidental depression which may occur if indeed the left foot is resting on the pedal

4. The activation of brake lights does not typically require much pressure from the applying foot, and therefore the resting of the left foot on the brake could result in erroneous brake light signals to the rearwards following vehicle (notwithstanding potential brake wear and overheating consequences)

5. The standard passenger vehicle is ergonomically designed to support the traditional foot position, which therefore often requires an awkward and uncomfortable extension of the left foot into the right region for brake pressure application, causing uneven seating position, steering errors, and leg soreness.

Steering control

Although steering control's proportional relevance to that of speed control is far greater in the broader driving context and smaller in the freeway context, it is still essential that the professional freeway driver should have precise and immediate control over the heading of the vehicle. While steering comes into play on the freeway normally under the limited categories of entrance ramp steering lane-switching/merging, of general lane-switching, and of maintaining proper interlane position around bends or slight curves, more aggressive forms of steering may be necessary in defensive maneuvers such as evasive lane switches. Automobile handling refers to the physical dynamics of vehicle, particularly along the lateral axis, while executing any sort of change in heading necessary in everything from an urgent evasive maneuver to a simple lane switch. Although a full discussion of automobile handling is beyond the scope of this book and is sizable enough to easily occupy a whole other one, the professional driver must be aware of some factors which may indeed be influential on the freeway – especially if high-speed evasive lane switches need to be made in defensive circumstances. In such circumstances, especially if slippery road conditions are at hand, the professional driver must avoid maneuvers of such severity as would risk skidding, any loss of traction by one tire of the vehicle, or in an extreme case, even rollovers.

Handling and dynamics

The most simple control principle which can be applied to avoid these risks is avoiding sudden "jerk" or rapid motions with the steering wheel (especially if the driver is concurrently braking, which is highly likely in such rare defensive circumstances) since this may increase the steered tires' slip angle and therefore cornering force beyond that which the static friction between the tires and road can sustain, causing them to skid. Moreover, such a skid is not guaranteed (nor even likely) to occur with each wheel skidding in the same direction and with the same magnitude, or even skidding to begin with, causing a lateral deformation to the vehicle's path-of-travel which may cause it to collide with other vehicles. This is a particular likelihood when over-corrective steering/braking maneuvers are undertaken on slippery surfaces; "fishtailing" refers to this occurrence with the rear wheels and can be exacerbated in rear-wheel drive vehicles. Regardless of the drive type of the vehicle, which is known to the professional freeway driver in order account for its resulting dynamical ramifications, uneven losses of traction may occasion the four-wheel road traction system in a multitude of ways. This is traditionally explained by the phenomenon of weight transfer (or "load transfer", though they are not technically synonymous in all contexts), wherein vehicular momentum and structural mass combine to exert varied magnitudes of weight vertically pushing down on each tire, causing variable tire traction and therefore pronounced steering effects. Weight transfer's effects on steering come primarily from transverse imbalances between the right and left wheels, whereas longitudinal weight transfer (the transfer of weight to the rear during acceleration and to the front during braking) is typically only relevant to steering if it is concomitantly undertaken with acceleration or braking; i.e., if (assuming front-wheel-only steering, which is most common) a vehicle has front-wheel drive, steering traction will be increased during braking, due to the frontwards weight transfer, and decreased during acceleration, due to the rearwards weight transfer. In rear-wheel drive vehicles, although the same weight transfer increase or decrease is applied to the front steering wheels, there is less total weight above the steering wheels due to the lack of engine components bearing down over the axle, and so rapid steering ability will be generally inferior to that of front-wheel drive vehicles. Changes to the center of gravity of the vehicle can affect weight transfer on both the transverse or longitudinal axes of the vehicle's suspension system; having the left side of the vehicle occupied by obese passengers and the other side left empty would proportionally increase traction on the left side and would cause a naturally leftwards shift in the vehicle's path-of-travel if not corrected by steering. Longitudinally, heavy intravehicular weight imbalances can influence both steering and braking due to weight transfer effects; as we stated before, braking transfers weight to the front of the vehicle and accelerating to the rear, but the respective tire-traction effects of this can be either negated or enhanced depending on whether intravehicular weight (such as is caused by passengers) is positioned more heavily in the front or back, attracting the vehicle's center of gravity to a different point. Inclining and declining slopes in road profile also create analogous weight transfer effects.

Steering hazards

This weight transfer phenomenon is related to the "torque steering" effect, which contributes to the importance of firm hand grip on the steering wheel while accelerating. Especially in older vehicles unmediated by digital power assisted steering systems, the internal engine torque can have an erroneous "tugging" effect on the steering components which will cause the vehicle to drift out of the intended path-of-travel if the professional driver does not issue corrective adjustments. While certainly the professional driver has no cause ever to remove hand grip from the steering wheels, it is even more dangerous to accelerate without steering wheel control due to this effect. Novice freeway drivers may remark at the straightness of a certain stretch of highway and their vehicle's straight interlane alignment, therefore thinking it acceptable to remove hand grip from the steering wheel momentarily in order to perform some other manual task; especially if combined with acceleration during the inattentive window of time, this error could easily turn into a lateral collision when significant interlane position drift motions the vehicle into the side of a lateral vehicle. As we stated in our discussion on intervehicular dynamics, the professional driver encountering a bend in the road fears this same dangerous behavior in other drivers and makes defensive scanning checks to the ends of avoiding it; however the driver him or herself must ensure the maintenance of their own vehicle's interlane position, taking care therefore to avoid errors in steering. Steering errors are classified broadly into oversteer and understeer respectively; understeer (not steering enough or steering too late) will bring the vehicle dangerously out of the lane away from the center of a curve and perhaps even off the freeway surface if traction is insufficient either due to regular skidding or slippery road surface conditions – both avoidable by lowered initial pre-curve speed. Oversteer (steering too much or too early) will of course, in an opposite fashion, deflect the vehicle's path-of-travel too far into the center of curvature. While severe understeering which approaches the frictional limit of the vehicle's tires will take the vehicle in a stable, wide-radius curve (in itself dangerous due to allovehicular collision or road-runoff possibility), severe oversteer situations are dynamically unstable and far more likely to put the vehicle into an uncontrollable spinout. Some (mostly older) vehicles are susceptible to a form of oversteer called lift-off oversteer, in which the accelerator pedal is let up around a curve, transferring the weight load off the rear tires and onto the front tires, decreasing rear tire traction and perhaps even causing a spin in the turn's direction. This may be of particular relevance on highway exit and entrance ramps, wherein there is extended steering accompanied by the type of accelerative/decelerative weight transfers which can cause this effect. While Electronic Stability Control (ESC) systems in recent times have largely decreased the likelihood of such risks by their capacity to monitor changing tire traction conditions and issue according reductions or increases in engine power to different tires, the professional driver is still aware of basic vehicular dynamics in order to avoid the types of hazards which can result from overactive steering.

Rollovers are the most severe form of steering-related safety threats which the professional driver has a dual responsibility in both avoiding in his or her own vehicle and also in detecting and evading in other vehicles. Cornering any curve naturally creates "body roll" by disrupting even weight transfer by shifting weight to the outer-curvature tires, thereby giving them more frictional contact with the road. The lateral G-forces which facilitate rollovers increase not linearly with but rather exponentially, as the centripetal force F is defined as the product of acceleration and mass: $F = ma = m\dfrac{v^2}{r}$ in conventional Newtonian rotational dynamics, acceleration being

Chapter 10: Vehicle Control

310

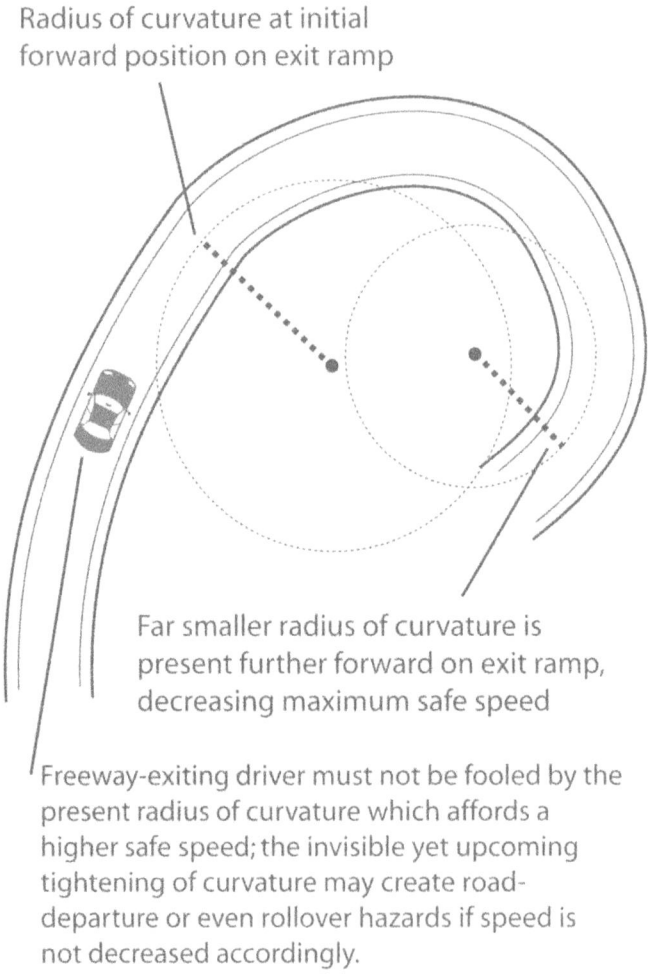

Radius of curvature at initial forward position on exit ramp

Far smaller radius of curvature is present further forward on exit ramp, decreasing maximum safe speed

Freeway-exiting driver must not be fooled by the present radius of curvature which affords a higher safe speed; the invisible yet upcoming tightening of curvature may create road-departure or even rollover hazards if speed is not decreased accordingly.

Figure 17 – Shortening radius of curvature on a highway exit ramp

related to the square of velocity. It is therefore crucial to avoid large excess of the posted advisory speed limit on highway exit ramps since the G-force is exponentially affected by linear increases in speed, and as the turning radius r often decreases in many exit ramp designs (for example, an exit ramp curving 270 degrees under an overpass containing the exited freeway). It is clear that care against over-accelerating on entrance ramps is also essential for rollover avoidance, yet rollover hazard is likely to be greater on exit ramps due to the near-freeway speeds at which they are typically entered. Rollover danger is furthermore increased in vehicles which have a high center-of-gravity (such as trucks and SUVs), whereas the professional freeway driver of a low-profile sports car would be mostly concerned with allovehicular rollover identification and avoidance on actual freeway curves – especially if wind direction and magnitude are such that they aid the body roll tilt of the large surface area of, for instance, a tall semi-truck around a high-speed freeway bend.

Grip and hand position

The driver's grip on the steering wheel largely determines the speed, firmness, and precision with which he or she will be able to issue corrective steering gestures either to keep the vehicle within lane, to adjust for proper road curvature, to execute lane switches, or to execute evasive maneuvers if an accident is imminent. Firm steering wheel grip also allows for resistive, tactile feedback from the tires and internal steering system, which can help facilitate a better "feel" for the vehicle's handling – an extraordinarily rare example of non-auditory, non-visual sensory information useful to what is indeed spatial awareness information (in the strange and highly literal sense that such awareness concerns the precise geometries and forces of the tires and internal vehicle components rather than large-scale exovehicular factors which typically command the meaning of the term "spatial awareness"). Other than firmness, equal (that is, symmetrically mirrored) radial position between the left and right hands is the only substantial recommendation. Assuming that firmness and evenness describe a manual grip configuration, as it concerns specific radial hand position on the steering wheel, there is not a very strong necessity to support one specific positioning over another, especially as there is high variability between vehicles which may suit one or another better to a certain driver's preferences (such as the non-existence of power assisted steering in old vehicles, or a varied steering ratio – which is defined as the ratio between steering wheel angle and tire steering angle; that is, some vehicles' steered tires are more responsive to steering wheel input than others). The traditional recommendation is to keep hands at the 10 o'clock and 2 o'clock position, however many modern vehicle safety experts now favor a lower positioning, such as even 9 o'clock and 3 o'clock, since the higher positioning has caused hand and arm injuries during steering-wheel airbag deployment if a collision does occur. While we concede the veracity of that risk, the point of view of the professional driver is almost always that an accident can be avoided through proper tactics, and therefore the arguably more-precise control of the 10 o'clock and 2 o'clock position must be considered for each driver's personal judgment of preference. In contrast to these hand-over-hand steering grip methods, the hand-to-hand configuration affords marginally less strong and less full control over the wheel but can improve comfort for long freeway trips, in which hands are positioned lower with the left hand generally between 7 o'clock and 8 o'clock and the right hand generally between 4 o'clock and 5 o'clock. The steering wheel is then "fed" or "pushed" by one hand and "received" or "pulled" by the other. The hand-to-hand method is naturally more suited to long-duration, low traffic-density circumstances whereas the hand-over-hand method is preferable in moderate-to-high traffic density when the likelihood of requiring a sudden evasive maneuver is higher. Any steering wheel interface method, however, can be mastered and therefore the choice of configuration is not as important as experience and attentiveness to the road. In the freeway context, travel at such high speeds requires very minimal adjustment to steering wheel angle for the vast majority of situations, such as lane switching – especially since there is a double-integral relationship between steering angle and position (i.e., increasing angular offset to the steering wheel not only varies heading but varies the *rate* of change in heading, and heading itself is the rate of change in lateral position), which is responsible for the very short time which such high-speed, slight steering maneuvers as lane switching take to achieve their goal of lateral position displacement.

Control loop effects of operating devices

Vehicle control is inherently dependent on its share of attention given by the professional driver, cyclically executing the sensory-input-responsive "control loop" process which we theoretically described in Chapter 2, and therefore must share finite psychological resources with other constituents of the total freeway-driving mental demand. It is not unsurprising nor likely unknown to the reader that research indicates the substantial vehicle control losses brought about by conflicted sensory processing and physical control time resources spent on a device-human system rather than on the spatial awareness-vehicle control system. The corpus of academic literature written on the topic, broadly categorized under the header of "distracted driving", is absolutely enormous and fittingly so, considering the potentially lethal consequences of sacrificing spatial awareness and vehicle control attention for driving-unrelated tasks. Research has attributed nearly 40% of all accidents to "inattention or perceptual errors" (Hendricks, et al., 1999)[2], which significantly questions how much less significant this figure would be if limited solely to the freeway environment, wherein such accidents have higher potential lethality due to the possibility of far greater speed differentials than could be easily achieved on a local or secondary road. Mostly due to increased cell-phone use in developed societies, increasing rates of fatalities from distracted driving have been strongly correlated with statistical indications of distracting-device usage (such as number of cellphone subscriptions or text-message volume) since 2005 – which continue to increase (Wilson & Stimpson, 2010)[3]. The focused professional driver is therefore situated in a freeway of passive danger; lethal rear-end collisions can occur if rapid traffic-related deceleration

---

[2] Hendricks, D. L., Fell, J. C. & Freedman, M., 1999. The relative frequency of unsafe driving acts in serious traffic crashes. *National Highway Traffic Safety Administration, U.S. Department of Transportation.*
[3] Wilson, F. A. & Stimpson, J. P., 2010. Trends in fatalities from distracted driving in the United States, 1999 to 2008. *American Journal of Public Health*, 100(11), pp. 2213-2219.

occurs in front of a device-distracted driver, therefore validating many of our past discussions concerning lane and speed optimization advocating the maintenance of spacious rearwards as well as frontal following distance. However the driving impairment effects of operating external devices unrelated to the vehicle system extends beyond that of simple delay of visual scanning activities for spatial awareness; Strayer et al. (2003) studied the effects of *hands-free* phone conversations on drivers in a driving simulator, concluding that even the cognitive engagement of holding a conversation "[impairs] implicit perceptual memory", causing even greater alarm for activities such as composing emails or SMS messages while driving, since these tasks both distract immediate visual memory of acquired spatial awareness and obstruct further visual scanning by requiring eyesight removal from the appropriate spatial awareness regions[4]. The professional driver, aside from obviously being wholly focused to the task of safe and optimal driving, is also skilled in visual identification of allovehicular drivers who may be distracted by the visible operation of a device, prompting preferentially evasive maneuvers away from such a potentially dangerous vehicle.

Driver communication

High-beams

The most common and obvious form of external communication between drivers is the directional signal or "turn signal", the use of which we have already reviewed according to circumstance. The professional driver is also keenly able to use and interpret the high-beam headlights of his or her vehicle for appropriate tactical purpose. On usage, high-beams are often used to alert a frontal vehicle that a passing attempt is underway, which is only likely to prompt beneficial change, causing its driver either to slow down and allow the pass to occur more quickly or to speed up and clarify the

---

[4] Strayer, D. L., Drews, F. A. & Johnston, W. A., 2003. Cell phone-induced failures of visual attention during simulated driving. *Journal of Experimental Psychology: Applied*, 9(1), p. 23.

immediate impossibility of the pass. In high-traffic circumstances, flashing the high-beams can signal an unsure anterolateral merge-attempting driver into the frontal lane space that his or her attempt has been acknowledged and that tolerant space will be made so that the lane switch can be finished. In traffic-sparse nighttime circumstances, their steady activation aids frontal spatial awareness for the identification of obstructive road hazards such as wildlife, however care must be taken to ensure that there is no frontal driver within range of the high-beams, as such lights are strongly reflected by most mirrors and can aggravate frontal drivers as well as impairing their own spatial awareness capacity. In general, flashing high-beams can be interpreted as an aggressive gesture in the absence of an obvious context such as signaling the permission (colloquially, the "go-ahead") for a frontal merge-attempting vehicle. Travelling slowly in the left lane at night is quite likely to aggravate rearwards drivers, as we have analyzed in our discussion on intervehicular dynamics, and to attract high-beam flashing signals from behind as a declared pressure to move faster or as an indication of a rightwards passing attempt. On interpreting high-beam flashes from the rearward vehicle, it is critical that the professional driver does not misinterpret sinusoidal body roll about the transverse axis of the rearwards vehicle caused by travel over a bump or other road disturbance as high-beam flashing (that is, oscillating load transfer on the frontal tires of the rearward vehicle, modulating in a spring-like fashion by the vehicle's suspension system, waving the regular lights up and down above and below a critical reflection point in the driver's center mirror which may cause the appearance of flashing high-beams). Such road surface aberrations which may cause this behavior are plentiful on highways that are not excellently maintained, especially in the left-most lane and in areas of road work, therefore requiring visual identification in the center mirror of a genuine high-beam flash rather than the false-positive "light-bouncing" behavior before an interpretative identification of the high-beam flash is made. Foreknowledge of any such road aberrations which would cause such suspension turbulence in the isolane rearwards vehicle, by virtue of having crossed them first (being in front of the rearwards vehicle), may predictively aid in the identification of false yet seeming rearward-vehicle high-beam activation.

Brake lights

Brake lights are an obvious third light source which aids driver communication in a very simple and mundane fashion, being tied to the brake pedal and necessarily to the function thereof. The only known alternate use of the brake lights is that of pulsing three or four extremely rapid, staccato taps on the brake pedal to symbolically evince a "thank-you" message to the rearwards driver, perhaps in response to a graciously permissive deceleration for lane entrance. While this practice carries the psychological tendency to reduce road-rage situations, it still necessitates the unnecessary and inefficient activation of the brake pedal to some small degree. Its tactical significance is limited as much by its disutility as by its extraordinary rarity.

Part V

Additional Considerations

CHAPTER 11

Driving Environment

Low-lighting and night conditions

Special conditions apply to spatial awareness at night or under circumstances of otherwise limited lighting. While allovehicles generally become easier to notice due to strong lighting contrasts between vehicle lights and the darkness surrounding them, this might not necessarily hold true for that of lateral allovehicles which may more easily fade into the dark veil of the vehicle's blind spot than in the day, when peripheral vision may be more able to catch unlit parts of such a vehicle's exterior. Proper frontal region scanning mediates this effect since the headlights of such an approaching posterolateral vehicle would be projected ahead along the vehicle's path-of-travel (although outward bending curvature and passing the crest of a hill could limit this effect by removing the vehicle's frontal path-of-travel from the colliding with the projected light beam of an approaching posterolateral vehicle, and so reliance on frontal scanning alone is not sufficient at night just as it is not during the day). The professional driver therefore increases his or her visual sensitivity to allovehicular light sources at night by minimizing the amount of interior l0ight up unto the degree that dynamic information sources, such as speed or navigation data, are not compromised. The same form of distracted driving discussed in the previous section of electronic LCD-screen device operation may furthermore decrease visual light-sensitivity to allovehicular lights, further increasing the potential hazards of such behavior at night (though clearly also a behavior foreign to the professional driver). While medium-range allovehicular spatial awareness may be aided at night due to the strong lighting contrasts created by brakelights/headlights with the surrounding dark void, long-distance forward path-of-travel scanning may be severely limited due to insufficient reach of projected headlight illumination. The primary focus of collisional object identification and avoidance generally shifts, therefore, from vehicular to non-vehicular targets in night conditions, since dangerous non-vehicular road obstruction errata such a dead animals or ejected truck tire retreadings are typically not outfitted with brightly illuminated, red rear safety lights as are all vehicles by design and by regulation. While we have discussed the occasional place for high-beam headlight activation on the freeway, we should emphasize its wise usage in scanning for and evading such non-vehicular road hazards (1) at night or in otherwise low-light conditions (2) with no frontal drivers or drivers in the other side of the highway whom would receive the projection of the high-beams, (3) especially while travelling in either the left-most or right-most lane, due to the highest statistical probability of such errata to be along the two respective shoulders, and (4) especially while following the outer rim of curvature, due to the decreased visual perception time afforded by the angular offset of the path-of-travel to the tangential beam of the headlights and due to the rotational G-forces which act opposite to the direction of an evasive maneuver which would avoid such errata at a curve of this shape, leading perhaps to a spin-out or even a rollover if the speed, curve radius, and evasive maneuver dynamics are sufficient. As it concerns speed optimization, some jurisdictions impose special night-time speed limits lower than that of the regular daytime speed limit which would accordingly adjust the freeway-vacant ideal travel speed by whichever degree of balance legal risk and spatial awareness limitations merit in a given case.

Atmospheric and solar effects

Hydrometeors

Precipitation of every hydrometeoric form has an effect on road surface traction, calling for appropriate reductions in speed (due to the consequently increased stopping distance) and for increases in safety margin distances accordingly. Pavement surface traction categories may be divided into four categories, (1) that of wet though drained and non-freezing pavement, (2) that of undrained pools of water, (3) that which lies on a spectrum of wintry slippery hydrometeoric substances from snow accumulation to ice, sleet, and slush, and (4) that of hard ice accretion. The first two and last two in this list are classified by non-freezing and freezing categories of road conditions respectively, the identification of which is the first step in the professional driver's analysis of road surface conditions.

Identifying warm-wet and frozen-wet road surfaces

Generally speaking, if external air temperature (which is very commonly indicated by a vehicle sensor) is above the 32 degree Fahrenheit freezing point, it is unlikely that hazards #3 or #4 will be present on the freeway. Road surface materials have a higher specific heat capacity than has air, which basically means that they are more resistant to changes in temperature (such is why coastal climates are more moderate than inland climates, due to ocean water's similarly high specific heat capacity). Therefore the only circumstance in which the road pavement temperature could be below freezing when the air temperature is above freezing is if the air temperature had previously been below freezing, either to a large degree, for a long time, or both, and had more recently shot up dramatically in temperature (such as may occur after sunrise in some climates, due to the addition of solar radiative heating), prompting the roads to warm yet more slowly than the air temperature. If these effects are pronounced and well-timed enough, it is conceivable that the pavement surface temperature could be below 32 degrees Fahrenheit while the air is above 32 degrees Fahrenheit, discouraging the dangerous assumption that any present road wetness would be non-freezing and increasing speed accordingly (as, clearly, hazards #3 and #4 in the list above are far more dangerous and friction-limiting than is #1 – simple wet, warm pavement). Friction is essentially heat energy, which will endeavor to warm the surface of the freeway and convert any frozen, wintry substances into that of simple warm wetness with sufficient passing traffic, if temperatures are below freezing but close to the phase-change point. Therefore, if it is necessary to travel in wintry road conditions to begin with, the professional driver will favor lanes with increased traffic insofar as road conditions are slippery and insofar as road pavement temperature proximity to 32 degrees Fahrenheit is such that the passing tires have warmed the surface water and pavement enough to yield an improvement in traction. Erroneously altering interlane position in these conditions could lead to terrible losses in traction, since only the two longitudinal patches of intralane road surface which have been traversed by the passing vehicles experience pronounced frictional heating and melting, potentially forming a sharp boundary with more slippery surfaces laterally away from these narrow strips of allovehicular tire-road contact. Under such circumstances, tractive preference for higher-traffic lanes must of course be balanced against following distance optimization, in which freer lanes are preferable. Especially under circumstances of heavy though very cold (and therefore dry) snow, motorists as a whole may be tempted to vastly exceed the recommended speed which solely the decreases in visibility would permit, since road traction in cold, dusty, dry snow (i.e., the type that thinly wafts and waves in the air across the road surface instead of heavily sticking to the road) is admittedly far greater than that of slush, ice, or wet snow, causing the professional driver to respond by choosing either a freer lane or a skilled balance between traffic speed and speed which complies with the basic speed rule.

Visibility limitation

The consideration of varied precipitation types lends to a discussion on the other large field of precipitation's effects, visibility limitation. Even if the tractive losses resulting from precipitation could be eliminated, the existence of hydrometeors within the suprafreeway air layer limits visibility by both direct and indirect effects, necessitating a reduction in speed according to the given reduction in ACDA (Assured Clear Distance Ahead). While only heavy rain can accomplish this to a meaningful degree in non-freezing atmospheric conditions, such visibility limitation is much more easily created by snow, especially dry and cold snow, due to its optical and physical properties. Rain indirectly creates visibility problems in the large spray clouds that are created behind all vehicles travelling at highway speed on a wet asphalt surface, particularly by large semi-trucks. Not only are such effective jet streams of water visibility-limiting, they likely also challenge fuel-efficiency by creating additional drag on the receiving rearwards vehicle. Dry, blowing snow is subject to similar aerodynamic "stirring" into visibility-obstructive clouds in a wintry freeway environment. Therefore, especially in the case of heavy rain, the regular impetus of lane optimization and speed control to the purpose of lengthening frontal following distance is increased due to the added visibility hazards. Foggy conditions may impose an even greater challenge to forward visibility across the entire freeway surface and therefore do not provide for visibility-optimizing evasive maneuvers (such as switching out of a lane in which the frontal vehicle is causing a large spray cloud of rearwards water in wet though non-foggy conditions), prompting therefore an overall reduction to the freeway-vacant ideal travel speed.

Hard ice accretion

Returning to the list of hazardous conditions above, hazard #4 (hard ice accretion) carries the potential perhaps more than any other to cause lethal spinouts and total loss of vehicle control. Since areas of icing on the highway may be entirely uneven, it is possible for some tires to have tractive contact with the pavement while the tires on the other side exist on a slippery patch of hard ice when the driver is decelerating; as follows from our brief discussion on tire dynamics and steering control, the vehicle is likely to veer far off course due to the disparate friction between either side of the vehicle, creating a high likelihood that it will uncontrollably fly off the highway or into an adjacent lane allovehicle. While visual spatial awareness scanning of the path-of-travel may sometimes be able to identify such patches of ice, it is far more tactically wise to identify conditions in which such icing could be remotely possible to begin with, and then to travel at a reduced speed accordingly. In such conditions, it is also likely preferable to travel in the center of the road (that is, practically speaking, in the closest lane thereto) due to the drainage effects of the road canting which increase the likelihood of such patches in the side lanes. This is preferable especially in cases of elevated highways above a large drop-off, due to the greater lateral distance to the edge of the highway; highways with rapid and steep drop-offs beyond the shoulder can indeed evince the safety preferentiality of risking collision with allovehicles in the highway (by travelling in the center lane) than of risking slide-off and lethal rollover into a ditch beside the highway (by travelling in the according left-most or right-most lane). In any event, reducing speed in circumstances of potential hard-ice patches is fully essential and far more preventative of an accident than any of these comparatively minor lane optimizations, due the exponential increase of kinetic energy and therefore stopping distance brought on by merely linear increases in speed.

Hydroplaning

Hazard #2 from our list above remains the last unaddressed item, that of static pools of water in irregular topological aberrations on the freeway. While such puddles do not form on perfectly maintained, ideal freeway surfaces (since they are flatly sloped down from the central canting, causing rain water to drain as runoff from the sides of the road surface), aged freeways, freeways exposed to large temperature extremes, and/or freeways lacking constant maintenance are more than capable of sustaining surface damage as to create areas in which such pools of water can form in heavy rain conditions. When a vehicle's tire encounters a pool of water of sufficient depth and at high enough speed, the phenomenon of hydroplaning (or "aquaplaning") occurs, in which the tires loose massive amounts of road surface friction as they travel over a thin "film" of suspending water. In this way, patches of static water on the freeway surface can be nearly as hazardous as that of frozen ice due to their similar qualities of massive frictional limitation and of sporadic spatial nature as may affect one side of vehicle tires but not another, potentially causing dangerous road departures and spin-outs. Unlike loss of control due to hard ice hazards, however, the possibility for the hydroplaning phenomenon to occur can be near-completely eliminated simply by reducing speed, allowing the tires to hydrodynamically "split" the water off into either side and allow the inner rubber to contact the pavement. While the pavement in this case is still wet and tractively limiting to some extent compared to that of dry pavement, it is a far improvement over the severe tractive limitation of hydroplaning. An additional distinguishing factor from that of hard ice hazards is the solid and decelerative nature of pools of water; while a slipping tire would merely travel *over* a patch of hard-frozen ice, it must travel (to some degree) *through* a deep puddle of water, creating a decelerative force on the tires which may further propagate tractive imbalances between different sides of tires which can lead to loss of vehicle control. The theoretically ideal travel position in extreme heavy rain circumstances is therefore directly over the center of the road, with each side of the middle cant slope evenly distributed across the track of the vehicle, (1) due to the most minimal likelihood of water pools to form there, since the road slope shape is designed to let water roll down away from this region, (2) since topological aberrations on the freeway surface which allow puddles to form are least likely in this interior region and most likely on the sides of the freeway, and (3) perhaps since the opposite camber angles between the tire patch and road slope would exert a small, corrective camber thrust force if any lateral departure to this position were in progress, whereas driving wholly on one side of the road slope exerts an imperceptibly small lateral force away from the center of the road. We say this position is "theoretically" ideal due to the reality of lane markings and other vehicles on the freeway, with which collision is very likely if a driver were to travel consistently out of lane. Practically, therefore, we recommend travelling in whichever middle lane closest to the centerline of the freeway in conditions of extreme heavy rain as would produce the risk of hydroplaning. If the professional driver is unable to avoid hydroplaning by means of these lane optimization techniques and by that of overall speed reduction, and begins to hydroplane on a patch of water, then deceleration must be sought but not rapidly – and preferably not using the brake pedal, as this will compound the vehicular instability already brought about by the tires' lack of traction. The driver must sense which tires are hydroplaning, deduce the resulting change to the vehicle's path-of-travel vector, and then make an appropriate response depending on all of these circumstances and that of specific surrounding hazards – which are of course situations of too numerous possible configurations to enumerate here. Other than careful deceleration, a specific and precise understanding of the particular driven vehicle's vehicle control dynamics must dictate appropriate response to hydroplaning – which is ideally avoided in the first place by lowering travel speed.

Wind

We have devoted an examination to wind's effects on the freeway in our past discussions on lane and speed optimization. The only relevant further understanding to the professional driver concerns how wind factors may change during the course of freeway travel. As we have seen, the wind vector has a large influence on fuel-efficiency, rollover hazards (especially at curves), and intervehicular dynamics. Wind contemporaneous to heavy rain precipitation could either extend, attenuate, or divert the visibility-restricting water spray clouds which form at the tail end of high-speed freeway vehicles, depending on intensity and vector direction. Gusty conditions, that is, conditions of great instantaneous differential in wind speed, can have a large effect on vehicle handling and dynamics, requiring corrective steering to maintain proper interlane position – especially in the case of horizontal crosswinds and to the extent that the vehicle has a high aerodynamic profile. The professional driver should have foreknowledge not only of general wind conditions throughout a trip's spatial extent, but also – if meaningful wind speeds will be present – of the situation and layout of the freeway stretches to be traveled, as this can vastly alter wind conditions in a localized environment. For instance, if a freeway runs straightly through a flat yet densely wooded environment, then a wind parallel to the freeway is likely to exert a much stronger force than would a wind of equal magnitude perpendicular to the highway, since in the latter case, the surrounding canopy cover of the forest would prevent much if any wind to sweep down to the freeway level. In this way, changes in road and wind direction can have large dynamical effects on freeway traffic. In mountainous environments, in which higher wind speeds are more likely to begin with, relative curvature around topological protrusions could constitute the difference between a total lack of wind (due to the hill or mountain's windward prevention of wind over the freeway), a Venturi-accelerated wind speed (due to wind passing tightly around the sides of a steep topological protrusion, perhaps additionally funneled through a valley structure), or moderate windward-side wind. Returning briefly to the drafting fuel-efficiency optimization, the existence of a cross-wind can both largely eliminate the drag-decrease benefit for the following driver and reposition it into the vehicle of an adjacent lane driver, since a crosswind would laterally shift the "wind-shadow" region away from directly behind the vehicle. Therefore in the existence of a cross-wind, the drafting driver massively increases collision risk without even decreasing air resistance to much of an extent at all. Longitudinally parallel headwinds and tailwinds create perhaps even greater aerodynamic fuel-efficiency ramifications; a 25mph sustained headwind would massively decrease fuel-efficiency to a vehicle travelling 70mph, fighting against a drag force of equivalent 95mph wind. Conversely, such a vehicle could travel at the massively reduced drag force experienced at 45mph if such a 25mph wind were a perfect tailwind. Wind force also has a clear effect on stopping distance, increasing it whenever it resembles a tailwind (i.e., coming from behind) and decreasing it when it resembles a headwind (i.e., coming from the front).

Extreme heat and cold

Standard passenger vehicles with internal gasoline combustion engines are quite capable of tolerating a wide spectrum of outdoor temperature conditions, and therefore extreme temperatures create relatively limited considerations for drivers of such vehicles. In extreme cold, frozen door locks and insufficient ignition battery voltage considerations are at times valid, however their relevance far precedes the time at which the context of our current discussions – the freeway– is achieved on a given driving trip. The only substantive freeway consideration inherent to subzero temperatures (other than obvious exovehicular ice hazards, if water is present) is that of tire behavior. In general, tire pressure can be expected to decrease, rolling resistance to increase, and rate of air loss to increase – necessitating increased attention to tire pressure. In extreme heat, engine overheating and fuel-inefficient AC usage are the two primary considerations (likewise eschewing non-freeway-related dangers, such as excessive greenhouse-effect-heated indoor air temperature). For alternate automobile types such as electric vehicles, the considerations inherent to extreme temperature freeway travel are not as straightforward. The battery performance of electric vehicles can be precipitously impacted by extreme temperatures; A 2014 AAA Automotive Research Center study compared 20 degree Fahrenheit and 95 degree Fahrenheit travel (temperatures far from "extreme") to that of 75 degree Fahrenheit travel in an average Electric Vehicle (EV) battery, finding a 57% and 34% decrease in rage respectively. Drivers of electric vehicles must be aware therefore of the more-frequent recharging requirements of long-range freeway travel in extreme temperature conditions.

Glare and albedo

Strong light within the driver's field of view can negatively impact spatial awareness capability. While solar radiation is the chief cause of problematic glare, nighttime headlight glare (a common problem on two-lane bidirectional highways) is not foreign to the freeway context since various mirror configurations can reflect the light emitted by a closely following rearward vehicle's strong headlights into the eyes of the driver. Though the required geometric alignment is relatively uncommon, mirrors can also reflect direct sun-beam irradiation around sunrise and sunset if the involved angles match up, or around times more close to noon insofar as down-sloping road gradient provides proper angling. Unlike the solar case, rearwards vehicle nighttime glare can be fairly easily avoided with lane switching away from the rearwards driver. Frontal solar glare is far more difficult to overcome, especially when frozen external surfaces (as ice or fresh snow) reflect and irradiate even more of the light into the driver's vision (referred to as the "albedo"). If the professional driver is unable to adjust internal vehicle glare prevention equipment to satisfactory results, tactical choices on the highway must be changed to reflect the decreased perception-time ability at hand to identify a frontal hazard in the path-of-travel. In this way, the glare would limit the Assured Clear Distance Ahead (ACDA) to whatever maximum forward visual extent possible under the glare conditions, mandating a reduction in speed.

Pre-drive automobile optimizations

Other than routine vehicular safety and maintenance checks taught to novice drivers, maintaining proper tire pressure likely stands as the most significant pre-drive automobile optimization possible. While high-pressure tire inflation is known for its fuel-efficiency augmenting effects, it unsurprisingly bears a negative impact on handling ability, since a smaller rubber contact patch grips the road surface. Excessively low tire pressure significantly increases traction, yet is however dangerous due to tire overheating concerns (which may lead to tread delamination in extreme cases) and of course is quite fuel-inefficient. The professional driver should therefore regularly ensure that his or her vehicle's tires are inflated to the manufacturer's recommended pressure – which is typically lower than the maximum value engraved onto the tire itself. External aerodynamic profile adjustments constitute a far more wise pre-drive fuel-efficiency optimization than that of overinflating tires; storing cargo on the top of the vehicle – in the dead center of the high-velocity slipstream passing the roof at highway speeds – can massively decrease highway fuel economy, whereas storing such cargo on the rear-end of the vehicle would vastly improve efficiency. The small consequent safety cost is, of course, slightly increased vehicle length which therefore makes tight merging situations slightly less maneuverable.

Physiological considerations

Expert driving on the freeway is a task as physically demanding as it is mentally demanding, requiring constant responsive attention to at least two senses and constant, coordinated muscle movements. Age is a significant physiological metric correlated with crash risk; a 2008 NHTSA report indicated the two approximate "shoulder" age groups, 16 to 20 and 80 to 84, as the highest accident-involved groups, with fatalities per 100,000 population both around 30 in 1998 (National Highway Traffic Safety Administration and others, 2008)[1]. Whereas lack of driving skill is more causal in the younger age group, elderly declines in physiological factors as "vision", "cognitive functioning", and "physical" abilities are at least partly responsible for the heightened risks for this group (Owsley, 2004)[2]. The aged professional freeway driver should therefore take extra care to physiological conditioning for expert highway driving. This includes range-of-motion stretches and exercises, particularly involving the neck and shoulder muscles for critical spatial awareness scanning/head-checking ability, and cardiovascular conditioning for overall mobility and muscle function. Ideally, we recommend to the professional freeway driver the study of a martial art for its concomitant inclusion of both of these, as well as the type of defensive high-speed decision making psychological adaptations which are critical to evasive situations on the freeway.

---

[1] National Highway Traffic Safety Administration and others, 2008. Traffic safety facts: Older population, 2008. Volume DOT HS 811-161.
[2] Owsley, C., 2004. Driver Capabilities in Transportation in an Aging Society: A Decade of Experience. Technical Papers and Reports from a Conference: Bethesda, MD; Nov. 7–9, 1999.. *Transportation Research Board.*

Psychological considerations

Other than the aforementioned adaptations to high-speed decision making in stressful evasive circumstances, which can also be neurologically achieved with high-intensity cardiovascular exercise or a repeated form of cold-exposure conditioning such as cold showers, combating against fatigue represents the other large field of beneficial psychological adaptations which aids the professional driver's critical task – insofar as he or she must take long-duration trips on the freeway. We should immediately qualify the controversial words "combating against fatigue", as we do not mean to contradict the common and sensible safety advice that a driver should not persist against fatigue on the highway during a "combat against fatigue" involving lane drift, repeatedly nodding down and restoring vision, erratic speed, etc. The professional driver, though supremely capable over regular drivers, is keenly aware of his or her own human physiological limits and will always cease the driving task when capability to perform it at full attentiveness does not exist. However, the trained, experienced, and expert professional driver is more than capable of continuous freeway driving for 24 straight, conscious hours – at least – with only intermitted rest stops. This endurance must ultimately be built in the same way that cardiovascular endurance or muscle strength would be built – with progressively overloading running duration and resistance-training intensity respectively – and analogously, with repeated practice at long-distance freeway driving trips. Food can induce noticeable influences on attentiveness in the long-duration context; while most un-adapted individuals experienced decreased alertness in the prolonged absence of food, intermitting fasting on the scale of 18-24 hours actually increases alertness in many adapted individuals – whereas large and heavy meals prompt full and tired feelings, increasing digestive stress and likely diverting metabolic energy away from the mental and physical task of professional freeway driving. The professional driver should therefore, at most, eat sparingly during the course of a trip to remain alert, consuming water to stay hydrated or even a thermogenic substance (such as coffee or a caffeine and green tea extract substance) to aid in fatigue prevention. The "highway hypnosis" phenomenon is relevant along distant and perfectly straight stretches of freeway, in which the driver may have no memory of the driving the length of road in question as the conscious mind dissociatively focuses on another thing in this state, diverting the complex information-processing task of highway driving to subconscious processes – an example of automaticity. In the research context, this phenomenon is referred to as "driving without awareness" (DWA) and is regarded as very dangerous, especially for professional drivers undertaking long trips (Briest, et al., 2006)[3]. If the professional driver is situated in external air temperatures uncomfortably cold to the skin, and if the danger of fatigue outweighs the fuel-efficiency cost of opening windows at freeway speeds (which is quite likely), then the wonderful technique of lowering the windows to invite the uncomfortable cold air quite amazingly minimizes the likelihood of continued fatigue and shocks necessary alertness back into the driver – as opposed to the positively somnolent effects of comfortable heating system usage, which is foreign to the professional driver other than to maintain basic operable interior air temperature in the presence of freezing exterior air conditions.

---

[3] Briest, S., Karrer, K. & Schleicher, R., 2006. Driving without awareness: Examination of the phenomenon. *ision in Vehicles XI. Amsterdam: Elsevier Science Publishers BV*.

CHAPTER 12

Canonical Freeway Accident Situations and Avoidance Methods

Tying together the unified dictates of our established tactical model for freeway spatial maneuvering with the secondary considerations which we have now reviewed in full, we will now examine a few recurring, high-probability accident situations on the freeway to understand their causes and proper avoidance tactics.

1. Frontal collision due to rapid, unnoticed deceleration of frontal vehicle

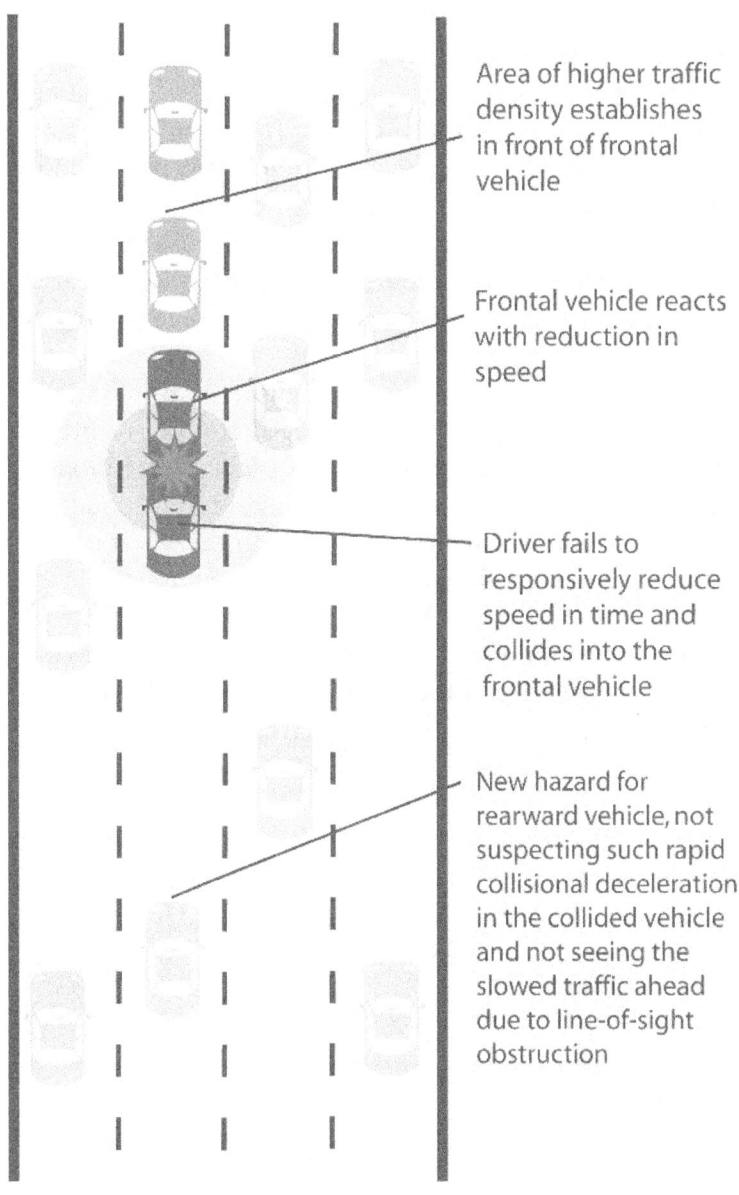

This collision, along with its analogous rear-end collision variety (when the perspective of the colliding vehicle is changed to that of the collided vehicle), is likely the most common freeway accident. It thankfully occurs most frequently in low-speed, high-traffic conditions which result in non-lethal "fender-bender" collisions; however, it can be thoroughly fatal at higher speeds. It is caused by two conjunctive direct and indirect effects: (1) extended driver ignorance of the frontal vehicle, delaying perception of its sudden deceleration beyond that which affords possible corrective deceleration to the frontal vehicle's speed before colliding with it, and (2) the driver's having travelled with minimal following distance in the first place. Thusly, from the perspective of the colliding vehicle, this accident is avoided by premonitory lengthening of frontal following distance and constant attention to the frontal vehicle, as it occupies the path-of-travel and therefore is a primary spatial awareness scanning priority. Misappropriated attention to hand-held devices in stop-and-start, "crawling" traffic conditions is very frequently responsible for this collision. In the worst case, if it is apparent that corrective deceleration will either not be able to prevent frontal collision or will cause a rearward collision, then the braking should be continued as lateral checks for an evasive lane switch dictate whether or not the hazard can be entirely avoided by a defensive, rapid lane switch into a more frontally spacious lane through which safe deceleration may be possible.

2. **Posterolateral collision due to tight passing attempt and accelerating posterolateral vehicle**

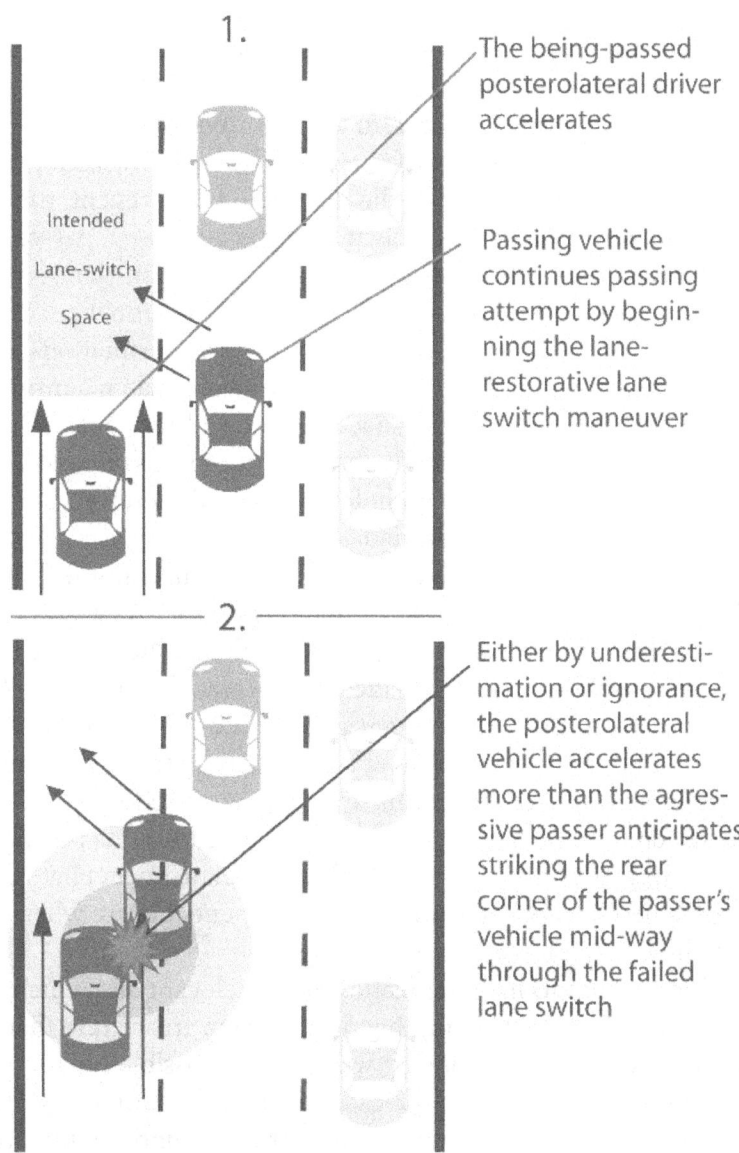

While the pictured diagram presents this accident situation in the context of an aggressive passing attempt, the momentary nature of the described situation may be taken under whatever historically preceding events should lead to the configuration – as long as the distinguishing factor of the dangerous-lane-switch volition remains (i.e., this setup would often occur from a decided passing attempt originating from behind the being-passed vehicle, however the aggressive passer could have been in the pictured lane to begin with when the longitudinal position of the two relevant allovehicles came to form the situation depicted in the diagram). In any event, this accident situation, from the perspective of the aggressive passer, concerns the high likelihood of collision inherent to any lane switch attempt of tight safety margins. In the diagram, a diagonal constriction is pictured between the posterolateral destination-lane vehicle and the frontal isolane vehicle. Such a lane switch simply must not be executed unless the space between all relevant allovehicles is sufficient – which it clearly is not in this situation. This accident situation can be completely avoided therefore by neglecting to pursue an aggressive maneuver which is clearly not safe. This conclusion could be extended to an infinite amount of spatial configurations and collision situations on the freeway – however, what distinguishes the solution for this particular situation from others of such simple avoidance of aggressive behavior is the pictured driver's distinct psychological tendency to want to "finish" the maneuver, due to this maneuver's tendency (1) to have seemed safe moments before, and (2) to have already attracted the "effort" or "investment" in the aggressive driver to come into this position, creating an irrational impulse to complete the maneuver. That is, if the vehicles had been sufficiently spaced moments before when the lane switch was first intended and declared, only for their acceleration vectors to have repositioned the relevant allovehicles as to narrow space between them, then it may seem frustrating that the maneuver must be aborted since it was entirely possible only moments before. Secondly, in the case that this situation originates from a full-on traditional passing attempt from behind the pictured posterolateral vehicle, then the aggressive driver has already expended the effort of switching lanes and overtaking the original vehicle in hope of passing it in front. The professional driver, being immune to these irrational psychological effects, understands the relevant application of the "sunk-cost fallacy" in this situation, will accordingly decrease speed or switch lanes to restore safe distance margins, and then will conduct a comprehensive spatial analysis anew and proceed with a safe choice. From the perspective of the being-passed posterolateral vehicle, one must be aware of such aggressive passing behaviors and the impulses which may motivate an unsafe passing attempt in the situation, so that safe adjustment of the passing space or altogether lane-switch evasion may be undertaken.

Chapter 12: Canonical Freeway Accident Situations

340

3. Anterolateral collision due to tight passing attempt and decelerating anterolateral vehicle

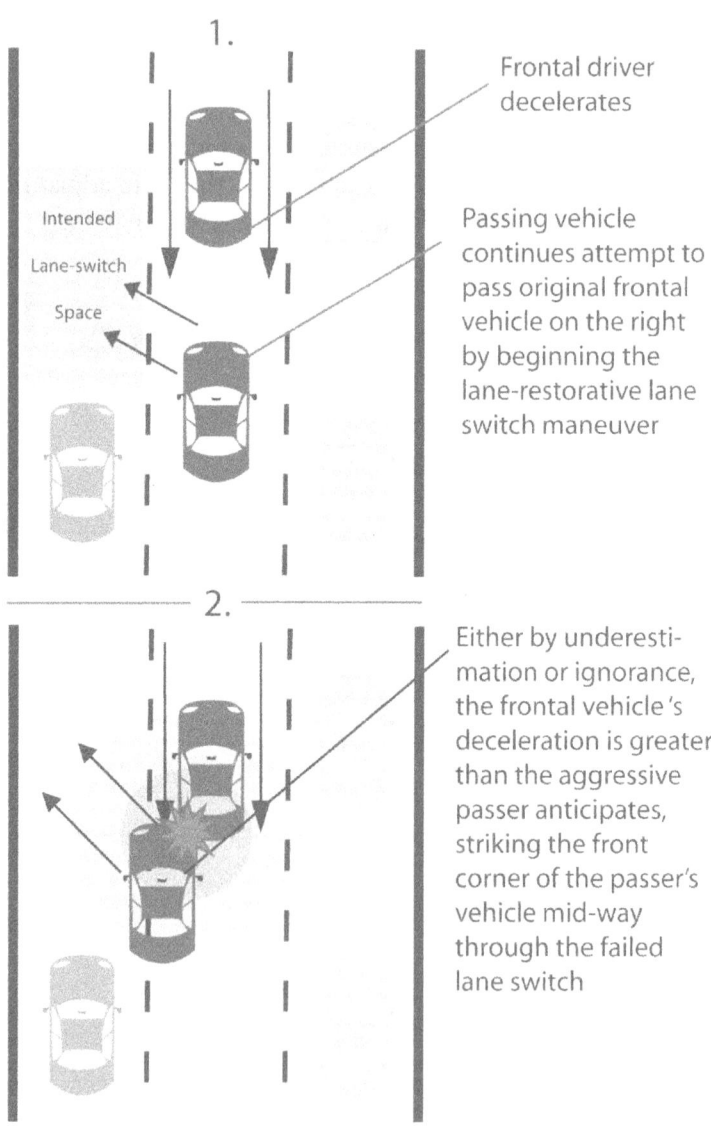

This accident situation is conceptually identical to the former, however the resulting collision of attempting to pass through the excessively narrow gap occurs with the frontal (or by the time of the collision, anterolateral) vehicle instead of with the posterolateral vehicle. It is therefore avoided in the same way. If this collision occurs first during the unsafe maneuver pictured in the diagram, then it is more than possible that a secondary collision will ensue (mimicking the former accident situation) with the posterolateral vehicle, due to the likely deceleration which will accompany such an accident as pictured. The professional driver therefore takes great care to disinvolve him or herself in such aggressive passing situations.

4. Lateral collision with vehicle in blind spot during lane switch

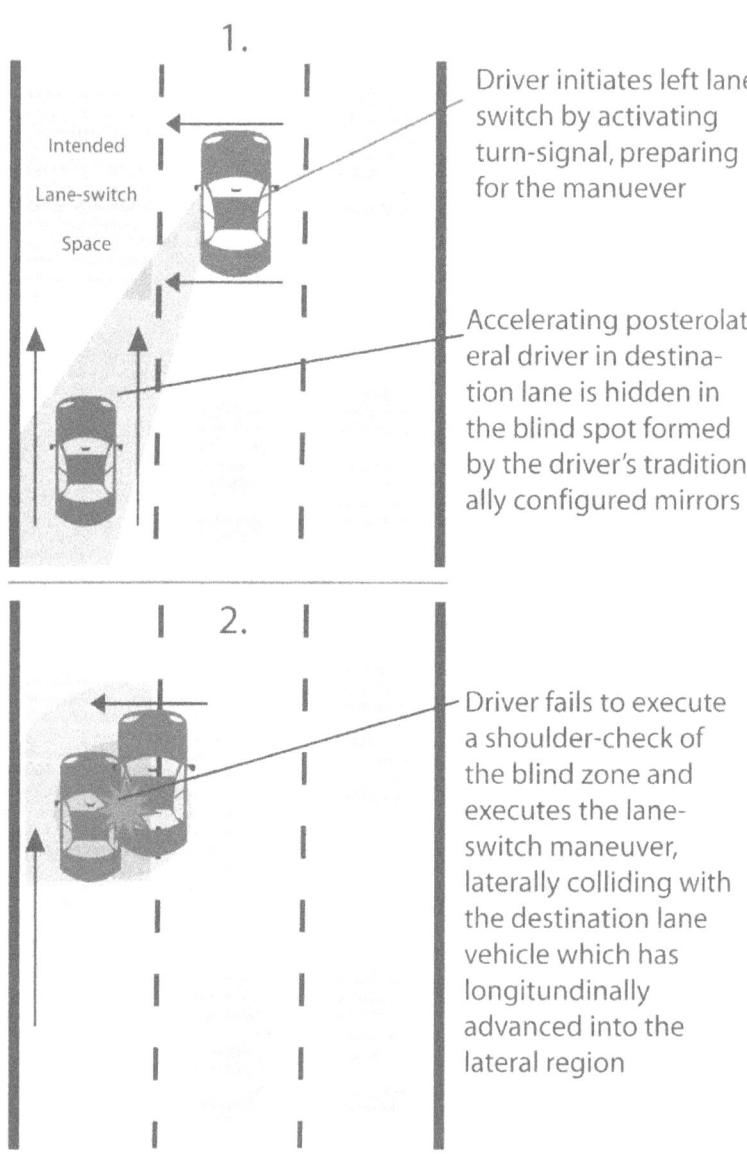

1. Driver initiates left lane switch by activating turn-signal, preparing for the manuever

   Accelerating posterolateral driver in destination lane is hidden in the blind spot formed by the driver's traditionally configured mirrors

2. Driver fails to execute a shoulder-check of the blind zone and executes the lane-switch maneuver, laterally colliding with the destination lane vehicle which has longitundinally advanced into the lateral region

This accident situation lies at the heart of arguments concerning proper mirror alignment, as it is the canonical blind-spot-related hazard leading to a lateral collision. Because of the blind region created by the traditional mirror configuration, which is approximately shown in the diagram above, the lane-switching driver in this case should be executing at least one proper and completed shoulder check of the blind region through the side windows of the vehicle in order to ensure the nonexistence of a posterolateral vehicle there. This would prevent the accident in the present situation, since the driver would then abort the lane switch seeing that another destination-lane vehicle exists in far too worrying proximity to the vehicle than would enable safe lane switching. If this crucial lateral spatial awareness step is omitted, and the lane switch therefore executed, the happening of an accident is reduced to the mere probability of the destination-lane vehicle's acceleration vector; if it is longitudinally stationary or longitudinally decelerating (relative to the merging vehicle), then a collision may be avoided by luck, however if it is accelerating (as it is in this case), the vehicle will collide with the destination-lane lateral vehicle which had formerly been invisible in the wing mirror view. Sole reliance on mirrors and frontal line-of-sight spatial awareness scanning is therefore quite likely to cause collision during lane switches; the professional driver must always execute proper head-checks to examine the lateral and posterolateral regions for a comprehensive, 360-degree spatial awareness that will ensure the safety of the lane switch maneuver.

5. Lateral collision from another vehicle switching lanes

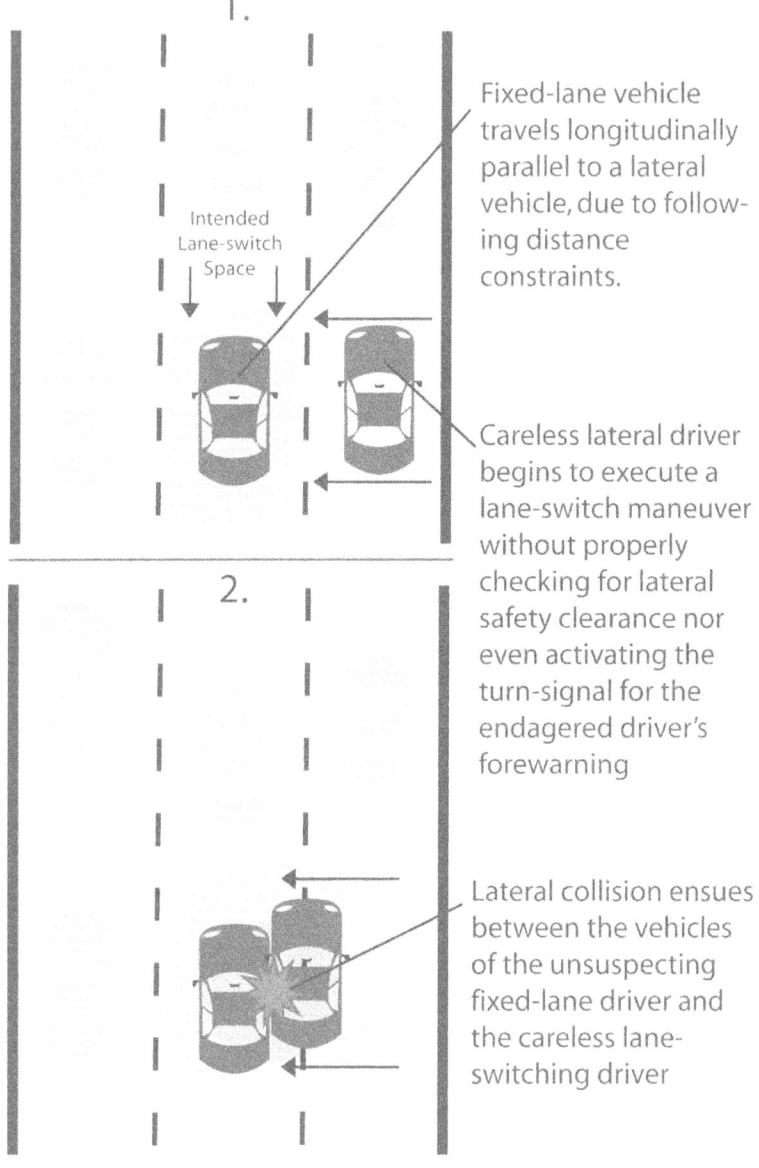

1. Fixed-lane vehicle travels longitudinally parallel to a lateral vehicle, due to following distance constraints.

Careless lateral driver begins to execute a lane-switch maneuver without properly checking for lateral safety clearance nor even activating the turn-signal for the endagered driver's forewarning

2. Lateral collision ensues between the vehicles of the unsuspecting fixed-lane driver and the careless lane-switching driver

This accident situation is formally identical to that of the former, with perspective shifted to that of the collided driver as opposed to the colliding driver. Avoiding lateral collisions from inattentive, inexperienced, aggressive, fatigued, inebriated, or otherwise impaired drivers is a task far more suited and notable for the professional driver than is the former situation's accident-avoidance technique of proper shoulder-checking before lane switching – which is an absolutely universal, essential, and novice skill necessary for every driver. Defensively speaking, the professional driver preferentially avoids travel in the lateral regions of an adjacent-lane vehicle in order to avoid the geometric possibility of this collision in the first place (as we alluded in our discussion on lateral safety margin distances), which can be accomplished by lane optimization, or even by adjusting interstitial, isolane position within the whole intervehicular isolane space so that all adjacent-lane allovehicles occupy either the posterolateral or anterolateral zones, leaving the directly lateral zones clear. Our discussion on intervehicular aerodynamics mentioned the general aerodynamic optimality of such distance from lateral vehicles as well. Aside from preventative measures as these, if the professional driver must travel beside a lateral-zone adjacent-lane allovehicle (which may commonly be the case, especially under moderate to high traffic-density conditions), then constant spatial awareness checks – intently prioritized on the relevant lateral region when occupied by an allovehicle – will afford warning of any insane allovehicular lane-switch attempt as depicted in the diagram. Increased spatial attention should also accompany the other side's lateral region, in the case that a lateral, adjacent-lane allovehicle is detected, for the premonitory appropriation of an evasion opportunity if one becomes necessary. Clearly, responsive acceleration or deceleration will be necessary to evade the combatively dangerous and positively insane allovehicular maneuver, balancing the forward position of the lateral vehicle with frontal and rearwards isolane following distance margins. (In this interesting way, extra longitudinal safety margin space aids even lateral hazards due to its affording more longitudinal escape options in a case as this.) Clearly, evasive lane switching away from the lateral driver would be preferred, however this is assumed not to be immediately possible at the given longitudinal spot within the whole intervehicular isolane space due to the existence of a constricting lateral vehicle on the other side (or the lack of another lane there to begin with, if travelling on the right-most of left-most lane), since the professional driver would likely have already executed such a lane switch to predictively increase lateral safety margin distance. Either way, evasive maneuvers in the case of such an insane and/or spatially unaware lateral driver will likely involve both immediate longitudinal escape, and then evasive lane switching where possible.

6. **Rearwards or lateral collision by lane-switching out of stalled high-traffic lane into high-speed neighboring lane**

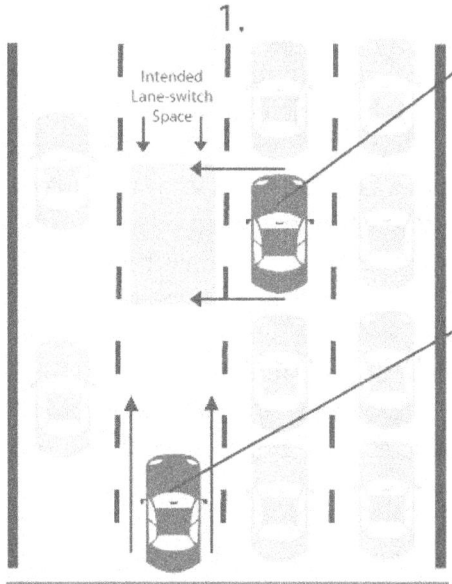

Driver in high traffic-density lane initiates lane switch attempt into adjacent low traffic-density lane for speed optimization

By means of improper spatial awareness procedure, whether by failing to check the blind zone or the posterolateral region altogether, a high-speed, approaching posterolateral vehicle in the destination lane is unseen by the lane-switching driver

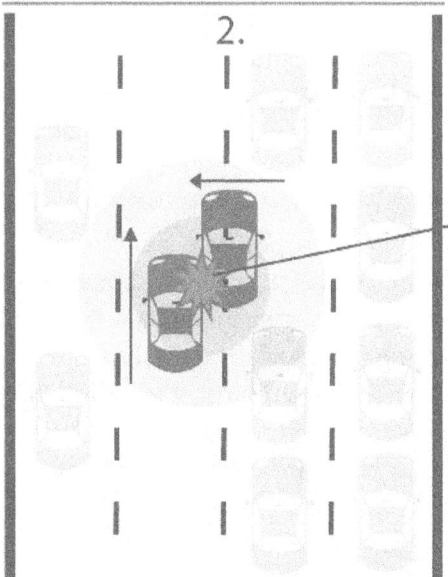

The high-speed destination-lane driver is unable to decelerate in time and collides into the posterolateral region of the careless lane-switching driver's vehicle

High traffic-density circumstances often lead to natural and fluid differentials in speed between lanes which are usually (but not always) smoothed out in variability as the distance narrows to the traffic flow constriction, such as multiple lane closures due to an accident or road work. The existence of a seemingly extreme disparity between sitting in stalled traffic and watching travelling traffic in an adjacent lane can exacerbate driver frustration beyond that which is already inherent to high-traffic conditions, as indeed some circumstances different to that of the example traffic obstructions listed above (such as a clogged exit ramp) can create veritable and persisting differentials in traffic speed between lanes. Drivers in such circumstances are therefore often tempted to merge out of the high-traffic lane and into the adjacent high-speed, low-traffic lane – which is on its face a sensible manifestation of arrival-time optimization and, more generally, the fluid nature of traffic flow in general. However, the extreme interlane speed gradients these situations can create are able to sustain a lethal collision as pictured in the diagram if neither rearwards, posterolateral, nor lateral regions are carefully examined with thoroughness before executing such a lane switch into the high-speed adjacent lane. In the case of a clogged exit ramp lane, a stationary and frustrated driver beside an adjacent lane of totally absent (visible, frontal) traffic could quickly merge over when indeed a 60mph-travelling posterolateral destination-lane driver was hiding in the unchecked blind spot, causing a lethal ~50mph speed differential rear-end collision. Clearly, this is avoided by extensive blind-zone and rear-zone spatial awareness pre-lane-switch, proper lane-switch signaling, and fast execution of the lane switch once cleared for safety. In such extreme interlane traffic speed differential circumstances, it is highly likely that another rearwards isolane vehicle's driver will make the same decision to merge into the fast adjacent lane; it is therefore preferable to wait for such a rearwards driver to do this, watching in the relevant side mirror, since their rearwards presence guarantees safety against a fast rearwards vehicle collision (since if one occurs, it will be with that other hastily merging vehicle and will absorb the impact energy, shielding the vehicles downstream of traffic). That is not to say that the existence of a fellow rearwards slow-lane-escaping vehicle guarantees entire safety and lack of need to execute comprehensive spatial awareness checks, since lateral attention is still necessary to ensure that a vehicle from the second lane over does not merge into the same space simultaneously, leading to a lateral collision. However, the existence of a rearwards vehicle executing the same slow-lane-escape lane switch at the same time is preferable from a safety perspective due to its shielding any potential fast rearwards vehicle. If no such "shielding" rearwards vehicle exists, being the lone-wolf (and perhaps impatient) slow-lane-escaping driver necessitates full and comprehensive rearwards spatial awareness, as well as of every other direction, to ensure that this highly lethal accident situation is avoided.

350

7. Rear-end collision due to overactive deceleration

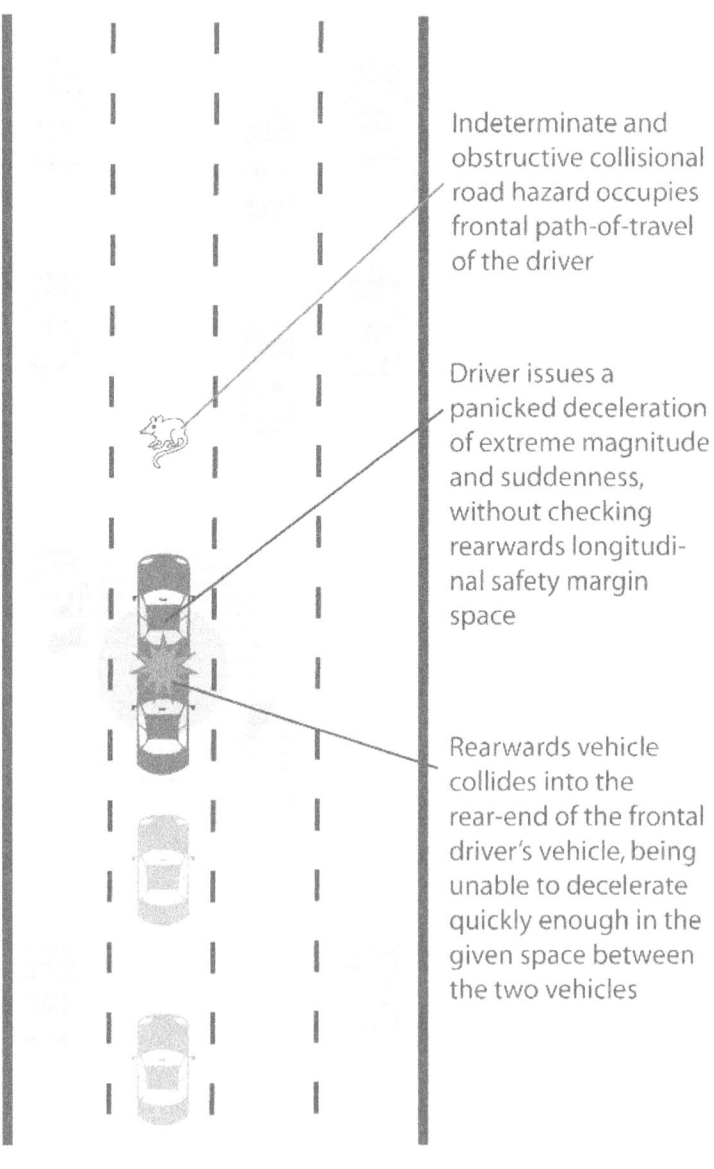

Indeterminate and obstructive collisional road hazard occupies frontal path-of-travel of the driver

Driver issues a panicked deceleration of extreme magnitude and suddenness, without checking rearwards longitudinal safety margin space

Rearwards vehicle collides into the rear-end of the frontal driver's vehicle, being unable to decelerate quickly enough in the given space between the two vehicles

Any freeway situation involving the presence of a rearward vehicle includes some certain risk-level of a rear-end collision insofar as braking or other deceleration is performed to a high degree, limiting the amount of time the rearwards driver has to react. In a plurality of genuine hazard-avoidance circumstances, as we have stated before, the primary focus on braking for avoidance of the frontal hazard should outweigh that of worrying over the chance of being rear-ended. Even from an exactly even force comparison of frontal to rear-end collisions, especially in long vehicles, the driver is longitudinally closer to the point of impact in the frontal case and perhaps less sheltered than that of iso-force collision from the rear vehicle (notwithstanding the potential mass-dampening effects of heavy engine components that are usually in the front), which perhaps lends an even further emphasis on frontal collision avoidance over that of rearwards collision. However, the professional driver may indeed encounter circumstances in which the preferential avoidance of a small frontal hazard must be balanced against the collisional consequences of slamming on the brakes in front of an aggressive tailgating vehicle. The pictured diagram demonstrates such a circumstance, though concededly in a perhaps exaggerated manner, in which the true risk of frontal collision may just be ignorable compared to that of impact collision of the rearwards, tailgating driver. As a preventative measure, the professional driver uses speed adjustments and lane optimization to increase rearwards following distance to begin with, which would massively decrease the risk of such a rearwards collision in a rapid-deceleration circumstance due to the increased reaction distance given to the rearwards driver. The importance and necessity of constant rearwards spatial awareness checks are therefore validated by this theoretical accident situation, since foreknowledge of the rearwards vehicle proximity will enable the professional driver to balance braking immediateness as to minimize collision dangers between both the frontal hazard and rearward vehicle.

Chapter 12: Canonical Freeway Accident Situations

352

8. Lateral collision due to drifting interlane position

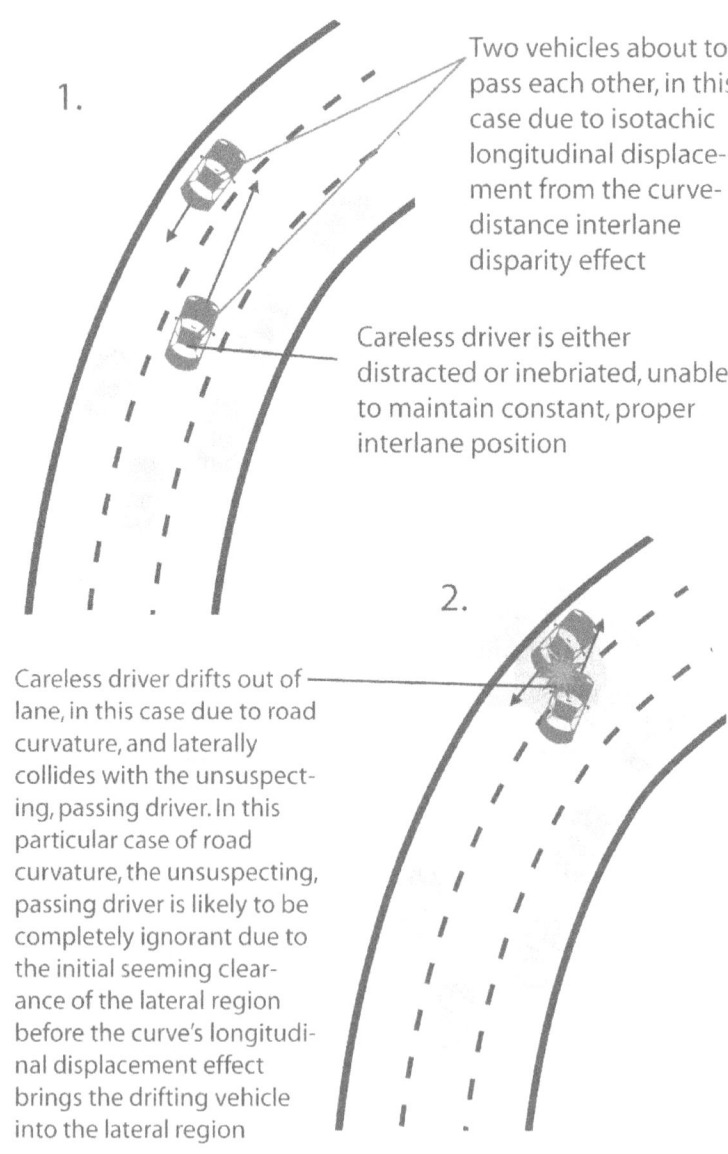

1. Two vehicles about to pass each other, in this case due to isotachic longitudinal displacement from the curve-distance interlane disparity effect

Careless driver is either distracted or inebriated, unable to maintain constant, proper interlane position

2. Careless driver drifts out of lane, in this case due to road curvature, and laterally collides with the unsuspecting, passing driver. In this particular case of road curvature, the unsuspecting, passing driver is likely to be completely ignorant due to the initial seeming clearance of the lateral region before the curve's longitudinal displacement effect brings the drifting vehicle into the lateral region

Though drifting interlane position can occur in any circumstance of road geometry, including that of a straight, flat section of road, a curve is indicated in the pictured diagram due to the heightened likelihood of lane departure over this road alignment. Failing to maintain centered interlane position risks not only collision with lateral allovehicles on the highway, but also collision with stationary obstructive objects on the freeway edge (as a rail-guards) or even rollover from a downhill highway fly-off if the edge of the highway sits above a large ditch. The driver must always maintain frontal spatial awareness scanning of the path-of-travel in order to issue corrective steering adjustments which maintain proper interlane position. This accident situation is therefore entirely avoided by constant spatial attention to lane bending and maintenance of interlane position – a task which is positively destroyed by removing visual attention from the road. Assuming otherwise unimpaired driver psychological conditions, distracted-driving is therefore the chief cause of this accident. Glaring for only moments at a handheld electronic device, especially around such a curve, can create lane departure drift easily of great enough magnitude to cause a lateral collision. The professional driver therefore remains fully focused on the driving task at hand of forward path-of-travel scanning and the resulting corrective adjustments to steering for centered interlane position.

9. Posterolateral collision in tight merging maneuver

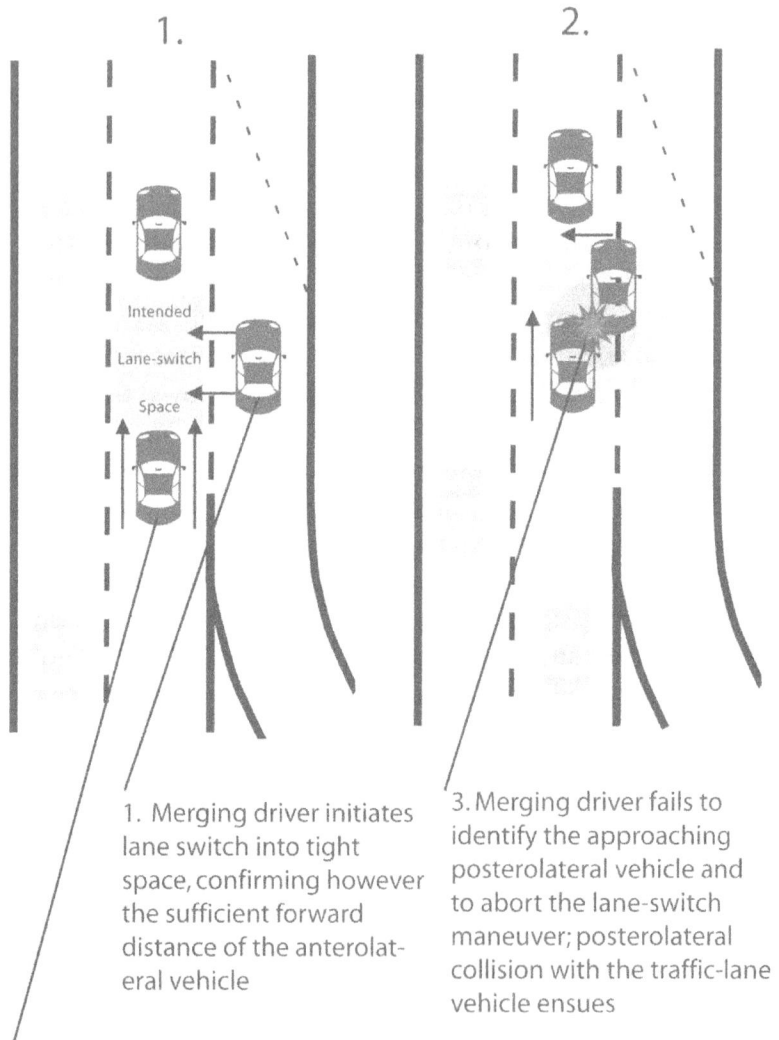

1. Merging driver initiates lane switch into tight space, confirming however the sufficient forward distance of the anterolateral vehicle

2. Merging driver however ignores the posterolateral vehicle, which is accelerating either due to ignorance or aggressive non-compliance with the merging attempt

3. Merging driver fails to identify the approaching posterolateral vehicle and to abort the lane-switch maneuver; posterolateral collision with the traffic-lane vehicle ensues

This collision situation of highway entrance merging is yet another unsurprising example of failed spatial awareness procedure. Whether the posterolateral, traffic-lane vehicle is hidden in the blind spot and the merging driver failed to shoulder-check the region, or if traffic-lane spatial awareness behind the frontal limits of peripheral vision were ignored altogether, this collision is still the fault of the merging driver since the traffic-lane vehicles have right-of-way. In most cases, an ignorant merger as pictured may be shielded from collision by the astute intelligence of the posterolateral traffic-lane driver, observing that the aggressive merge maneuver is underway and making appropriate deceleration to welcome the "cutting-off" vehicle. Dependence on such allovehicular driver awareness is however, clearly, insufficient for the professional driver, since ignorant and/or aggressive traffic-lane drivers, such as the one pictured, may assertively accelerate in order to close off the merging attempt, which is the precise situation pictured in the diagram. Though comprehensive lateral traffic-lane spatial awareness during the merging process solves the pictured risk of posterolateral merge collision, the pictured driver may still be left with a challenging highway-entrance merge upon aborting the first dangerous merge attempt if conditions are high-traffic and high-speed, especially if there are frontal merging vehicles decelerating to find an entrance gap as well. Therefore, we recapitulate our emphatic dictate from Chapter 4 of premeditatedly lengthening frontal following distance on the entrance and acceleration ramp, *before* the merging zone, to afford the merging driver far more spatial opportunities in such challenging merging conditions. Such preparatory lengthening of frontal following distance is likely to provide a merge opportunity gap of sufficient longitudinal space as to make unlikely to begin with such a dangerously tight merging maneuver as pictured in the diagram. In summary, proper highway entrance merging tactics microcosmically resemble a condensed and exaggerated version general freeway driving tactics, in that generous frontal following distance and comprehensive, 360-degree spatial awareness are key. Early declaration of the lane-switch attempt into the traffic-lane by means of directional signal activation is also essential to proper merging procedure, since it increases the possibility that the potentially collisional vehicle's driver will notice and graciously accede to the lane switch by deceleration – whereas his or her ignorance of the merging driver would guarantee that no such intentional and beneficial speed response will be undertaken.

10. Frontal collision during merging maneuver due to extended blind spot spatial awareness check and resulting ignorance of frontal vehicle deceleration

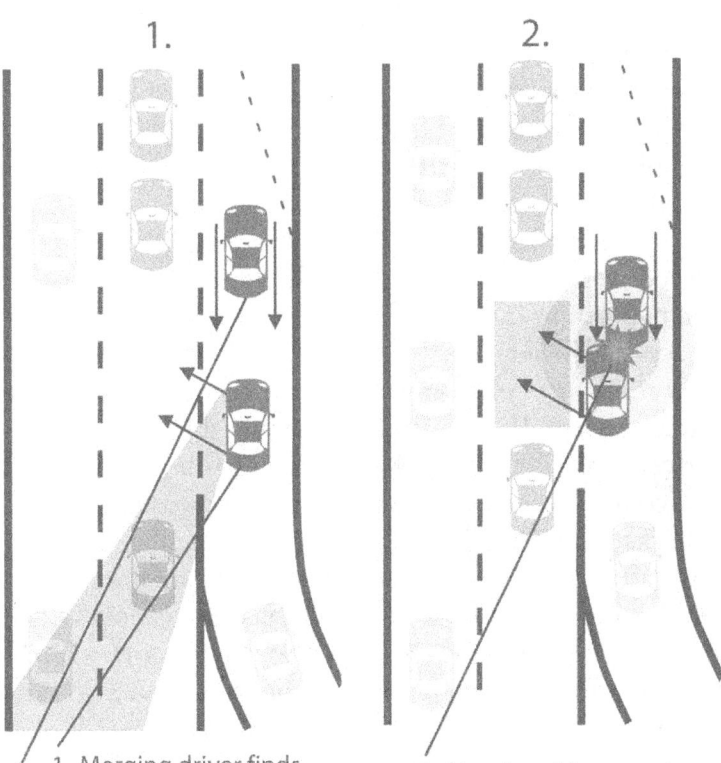

1. Merging driver finds appropriate merging gap and shoulder-checks blind spot to ensure sufficient distance and speed of the posterolateral traffic-lane vehicle

2. Frontal merging vehicle decelerates in merging lane due to lateral constrictions in the traffic lane, dangerously narrowing interstitial safety margin distance between the two merging vehicles

3. Merging driver, overly preoccupied with the posterolateral traffic-lane vehicle and overextending the shoulder-check duration, is ignorant of the frontal decelerating vehicle and proceeds by lane-switching into the anterolateral merging gap, colliding into the frontal merging vehicle

Extreme preoccupation with avoiding the prior accident situation (by means of longer-than-necessary posterolateral and lateral spatial awareness scanning) is likely to cause the presently described collision, since spatial awareness information is entirely robbed from the frontal zone. Thusly, any rapid deceleration of the frontal vehicle is likely to prompt a frontal collision due to the driver's fixation on such traffic-lane zones, which is quite possibly just as dangerous (or even more) than that of any lateral collisions which a misbalanced over-obsession with spatial awareness information on this region is hoped to prevent. Furthermore, such rapid and unnoticeable frontal merging vehicle deceleration is not unlikely if that vehicle's driver him or herself is rapidly adjusting relative longitudinal position to the traffic-lane vehicles in order to find a merging space (and is likely not looking in their rear mirror to ensure that a rearwards collision, from their perspective, does not occur by such actions). In the pictured diagram, the merging vehicle's driver is preoccupied with scanning the blind spot which does indeed contain a posterolateral vehicle in this instance; shoulder-checks must not be prolonged longer than the initial Boolean indication of whether or not an allovehicular hazard occupies the blind zone. Once line-of-sight visual contact has been made with the region, the driver must return his or her eyesight to the frontal region for path-of-travel scanning (as indicated in our discussion on proper head-checking procedure in Chapter 3). Novice drivers, needing to merge either way into the traffic-lane, may be hung-up over concern regarding the noticed posterolateral vehicle and may dangerously linger shoulder-rotated eye contact with it during the maneuver, to ensure that it does not speed up and that the lane-switch maneuver does not induce a posterolateral collision. This novice misappropriation of collision fear ignores the frontal and even perhaps anterolateral regions which could turn rapidly decelerative in a split-second. The professional driver must therefore prioritatively balance all relevant regions of spatial awareness and alternate view between them with speed and precision. When this is rehearsed and combined with practiced, fast head-checks, the comparative increase in posterolateral-vehicle spatial information gained by staring at it, head-tilted, for four solid seconds over that of two expert, quick shoulder checks spaced four seconds apart is extremely small – whereas the comparative decrease in frontal spatial awareness from the two fast visual departures (the professional driver) to the utter dearth of visual scanning (the preoccupied novice driver) is absolutely massive, for changes in posterolateral vehicular speed after the initial head-check take at least a second or two to manifest in a visible and meaningful way to begin with, further decreasing the sensible utility of extending a shoulder-check beyond its intended, quick, and proper duration. While the avoidance method we have given for this accident situation revolves on sound prioritization of spatial awareness scanning, a far simpler and recommended preventative measure would be the skillful (and unsurprising) extension of frontal following distance before the merging ramp to massively decrease risk of a frontal collision due to rapid frontal vehicle deceleration, affording greater perception-reaction distance to such an event.

Chapter 12: Canonical Freeway Accident Situations

360

11. Collision due to lack of road friction for corrective deceleration and/or steering

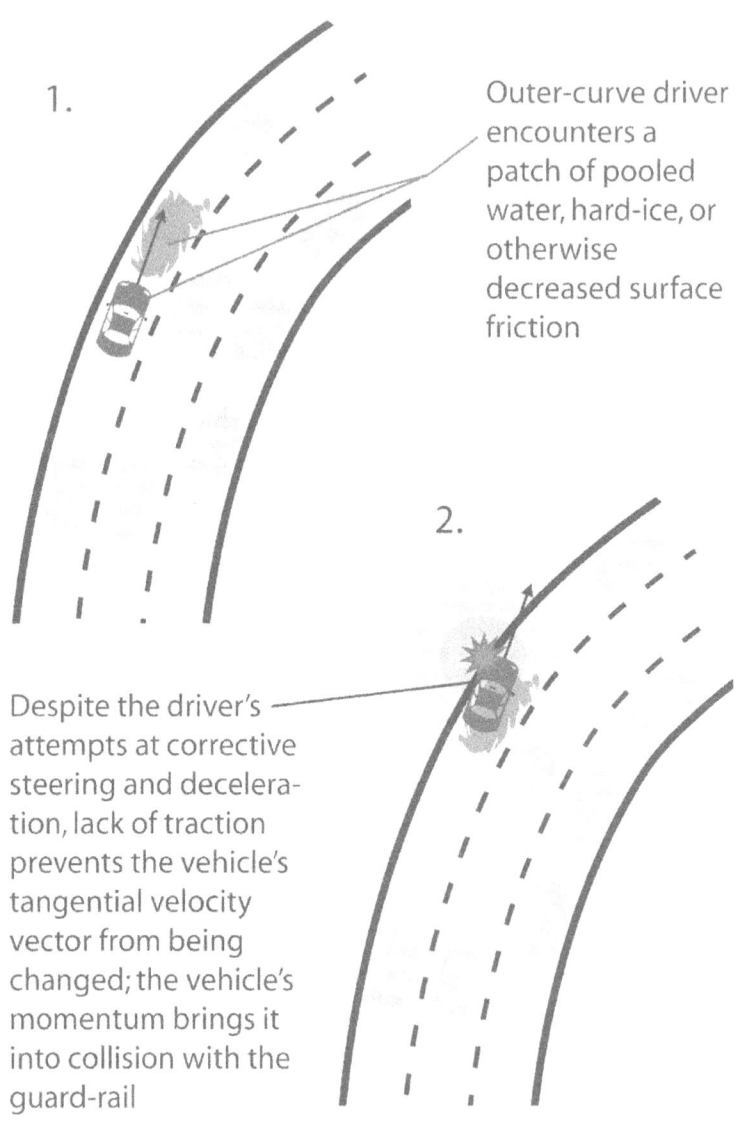

1. Outer-curve driver encounters a patch of pooled water, hard-ice, or otherwise decreased surface friction

2. Despite the driver's attempts at corrective steering and deceleration, lack of traction prevents the vehicle's tangential velocity vector from being changed; the vehicle's momentum brings it into collision with the guard-rail

As we examined in our respective discussions on vehicle control and precipitation effects on the freeway surface, losses of tire traction in circumstances of hydroplaning, hard-ice, slippery snow, wet pavement, or excessive speed around curves on dry pavement can throw the vehicle entirely out of driver control, leading to a host of possible collisions with allovehicles or, as pictured, with fixed structures. The best accident avoidance measures for these situations are therefore primarily preventative rather than responsive; while decreasing speed and increasing following distance both significantly lower the probability of a collision of this type, it is astute spatial awareness scanning which unsurprisingly equips the driver with a first line of defense against such hazards, since their intent *identification* is necessary first to justify the arrival-time costs of decreased speed. Some of these circumstances are trivially easy to identify, such as heavy precipitation, wet pavement around or below 32 degree Fahrenheit air temperature, or visibility limitations from fog or tire-spray precipitation clouds. However, the professional driver must never abandon all-important path-of-travel spatial awareness scanning to identify anomalous and unpredictable hazards as oil spillage slicks, lone patches of black ice, or even faulty hydrological infrastructure which could cause a pool of hydroplaning-viable water in dry, sunny circumstances. Hazards of these types require both premonitory deceleration (and lane-switch evasion, preferably) and prior identification not from general situational awareness but from precise, careful, and constant spatial awareness scanning of the vehicle's frontal path-of-travel – perhaps the single most critical task of anyone operating a motor vehicle in any context whatsoever.

Part VI

Conclusion

Conclusion

Freeway driving is a task as critical and relevant to modern industrial society as it is nuanced, detailed, and at times daunting. Carefully decided and masterfully rehearsed tactics carry the potential to improve the overall social utility of freeway travel by means of eliciting safety and optimization improvements. In summary, the largest fields of optimization we have discussed have been that of safety, arrival-time, legal risk, and fuel-efficiency – and in that descending order, as all objective interpretations of our tactical model would unanimously indicate. We have however prefaced this tactical model for freeway spatial maneuvering with a brief discussion on high-level driver strategy which informs specific choice of tactics, and which therefore could conform to an individual's different ordering of the above optimization priorities. While our position of advocating the supremacy of safety is firmly rooted, other individual persuasions may place fuel-efficiency or arrival-time optimization at a strategically higher level in the ranking of potentially intercompeting tactical optimizations which our specific discussions on freeway traffic dynamics illuminate. The important topic of fuel-efficiency in particular is tied to environmental concerns, and therefore a careful study of vehicular emissions remains a relevant topic unexplored by this book which may hold great relevance to one whose highway driving strategy emphasizes environmentally responsible driving.

On the whole, advanced highway driving resembles in itself a finely intricate martial art, combining its constituent aspects of elegant kinetics, potentially violent collisions, sage and high-speed decision-making, muscle-memory-programmed hand-eye-coordinated neurological adaptations, and a deeply psychological interplay between attacker and defender – or, analogously, the external freeway environment and the professional driver. Defensively speaking, there is nearly complete harmony among the foremost recurring recommendations of our tactical model for freeway spatial maneuvering that continuous circumspective spatial awareness checks and attention to large safety margin distances around the vehicle are the most basic and essential prerequisites both to facilitating economically attractive driving optimizations and to ensuring basic highway safety for all users of the freeway system.

Freeway driving's comparatively nascent history recalls only perhaps half-a-century of age and experience, at least in a way which resembles its modern and large-scale form of high-capacity four-lane expressways which constitute a positively critical infrastructure for the transportation of goods, people, and services between spatially distant centers of population. Therefore, although all forms of machine-aided transportation seem to become obsolete at some point, it is quite likely that freeway driving will maintain its pressing relevance to developed society for many decades to come – promising the extended, continued utility of this book's discussions for the visible future. We duly note, in fact, that the relevance and importance of driving altogether, along with the crucial study of safe driving practices, will quite increase only in short time.

Part VII

Appendices

US Listing of Location-Specific Considerations by State

As it concerns the elements of our tactical model for highway spatial maneuvering that involve the preferential avoidance of legal risks, primarily in the form of traffic-enforcement stops which we have shown to be suboptimal in every light from arrival-time optimization to fuel-efficiency, the professional driver must be aware of the specific traffic regulations which pertain to the course of his or her travel along the relevant stretches of freeway. Given our primary focus on the U.S. Eisenhower Interstate System, we attempt to summarize the salient points of such considerations in each of the systems's fifty crossed states — by far, regulations on the left-most passing lane are the most (if not the only ones) relevant of these to the advanced highway driver. Data are as of 2010 or more recent.

Alabama

Although Alabama regulations permit left-lane travel on roads that are "divided into three marked lanes" (i.e., freeways), vehicles "proceeding at less than the normal speed of traffic at the time and place and under the conditions then existing shall be driven in the right-hand lane" if not passing[1]. Therefore, left-lane travel is recommended only if the freeway-vacant ideal travel speed is determined to be equal to or greater than the "normal" speed of traffic flow.

Alaska

Specifically excepting emergency vehicles, Alaska's left-most lane traffic regulation requires keeping right if "proceeding at less than

---

[1] Code of Alabama, Section 32-5A-80

the maximum authorized speed of traffic"[2] and not passing, making it one of the few states to do so. Referencing the speed limit instead of the "normal speed of traffic" (as does the Uniform Vehicle Code), though questionable from a regulatory point-of-view, affords the professional driver with greater lane occupation opportunities if his or her determined freeway-vacant ideal travel speed lies at or just over the speed limit, which would typically be too slow to satisfy the Uniform Vehicle Code requirement of traffic-characteristic speed in the presence of allovehicles[3]. We have already detailed, however, the reasons for which the professional driver avoids creating large isolane speed differentials, even if this behavior is legally protected by odd regulations as Alaska's. The law seemingly forbids sub-speed-limit left-lane travel in blizzard and/or downpour circumstances, in which slow speed and large following distances (as are brought about by full traffic dispersion across all lanes) are clearly necessary for safety. It is quite likely that the professional driver's rational speed assessment in such circumstance would defy the regulation, decelerate in the left lane if there to begin with, and only lane-switch out if safety margin distances would be augmented by a compliant lane position.

Arizona

Arizona's left-lane travel regulation is nearly identical to that of the first enumerated, which is shared by a majority of states. We will

---

[2] Alaska Administrative Code, Title 13, 2.050

[3] Uniform Vehicle Code, Article III, 11-301 (b): "Upon all roadways any vehicle proceeding at less than the normal speed of traffic at the time and place and under the conditions then existing shall be driven in the right-hand lane then available for traffic, or as close as practicable to the right-hand curb or edge of the roadway, except when overtaking and passing another vehicle proceeding in the same direction or when preparing for a left turn at an intersection or into a private road, alley, or driveway. The intent of this subsection is to facilitate the overtaking of slowly moving vehicles by faster moving vehicles."

refer to this regulation from now on as the "speed of traffic-flow" requirement (synonymous to the Uniform Vehicle Code's "normal speed of traffic" qualification); unless if passing, vehicles "proceeding at less than the normal speed of traffic"[4] must keep right.

Arkansas

Though mostly identical to the former "speed of traffic-flow" requirement, Arkansas's regulation employs unique wording in its left-lane travel prohibition; travelling "continuously in the left lane of a multilane roadway whenever it impedes the flow of other traffic"[5] is forbidden, carrying the two liberating qualifications permitting *brief* as opposed to *continuous* left-lane usage in such conditions and forbidding only rearwards traffic *impediment* perhaps as opposed to only *slightly* lower speed. It is still questionable why a professional driver's motives would take advantage of these qualifications to reduce speed from that of the flow of traffic, especially being that the non-legal-risk factors of the freeway-vacant ideal travel speed typically advocate higher speed limited by traffic regulation factors, rather than the converse.

California

The California regulations not only impose the typical "speed of traffic-flow" requirement, but even wonderfully clarify that speed-limit obedience in such circumstances is insufficient justification for slower travel in the left lane.[6] This is most likely to be relevant to

---

[4] Arizona Revised Statutes, 28-721

[5] 2010 Arkansas Code, 27-51-301

[6] California Vehicle Code 21650 (a): "notwithstanding the prima facie speed limits, any vehicle proceeding upon a highway at a speed less than the normal speed of traffic moving in the same direction at such time shall be driven in the right-hand lane..."

the professional driver's perspective in providing some additional justification for executing a rightwards pass when located behind such a vehicle. California traffic regulations also seemingly permit temporary usage of the breakdown lane just before an exit in high-traffic circumstances to achieve the start of the exit ramp lane.[7]

Colorado

The Colorado traffic regulations are somewhat unusual in their having a dedicated passing-lane regulation instead of relying on general "keep right" principles; while following the "speed of traffic-flow" requirement on roads below 65mph speed limit, left lane travel on highways with a 65mph or greater speed limit is characteristically forbidden unless passing or unless it is unsafe to merge into the adjacent, "nonpassing" lane.[8]

Connecticut

In addition to the common "speed of traffic-flow" requirement, highways must generally be "divided into three or more marked lanes for traffic" in order to sanction any non-passing left lane freeway travel[9] or rightwards passing (a feature common to many states' traffic regulations). Connecticut's traffic regulations also explicitly prohibit any non-trivial manifestations of the drafting

---

[7] California Vehicle Code 21650 (f)

[8] Colorado Revised Statutes 42-4-1013

[9] 2011 Connecticut General Statutes, Chapter 248, 14-230

technique[10] and recently require the removal of ice and snow from vehicular surfaces[11].

Delaware

Delaware traffic code simply follows the "speed of traffic-flow" requirement, permitting left-lane travel on highways of three lanes or more provided that the vehicle is not "proceeding at less than the normal speed of traffic".[12]

Florida

Floridian traffic regulations mimic the common "speed of traffic-flow" requirement, with the added restriction that a left-lane driver must yield by switching to the right lane "if the driver knows or reasonably should know that he or she is being overtaken in that lane from the rear by a motor vehicle traveling at a higher rate of speed."[13]

Georgia

Similar to that of the prior, Georgia's traffic regulations defer to the Uniform Vehicle Code's general "speed of traffic-flow" requirement[14] and now include (as of July 2014) the same particular yielding requirement when knowledge of a rearwards passing-

---

[10] 2011 Connecticut General Statutes, Chapter 248, 14-240

[11] 2011 Connecticut General Statutes, Chapter 248, 14-252 (a)

[12] Delaware Code, Section 4114

[13] 2014 Florida Statutes, 316.081

[14] Georgia Code, 40-60-40

volitional vehicle is had[15]; they also include a clarified prohibition on "impeding" traffic flow, similar to the piece of Arizona regulation already discussed.

Hawaii

Hawaiian traffic regulations simply defer to the general "speed of traffic-flow" requirement.[16]

Idaho

Idaho traffic regulations simply defer to the general "speed of traffic-flow" requirement.[17]

Illinois

As of January 2004, a very efficient traffic regulation has belonged to the Illinois statutes which particularly singles out "Interstate highways [and] fully controlled access" highways and prohibits left-lane travel on them, which does not apply:

> "(1) when no other vehicle is directly behind the vehicle in the left lane;
>
> (2) when traffic conditions and congestion make it impractical to drive in the right lane;
>
> (3) when snow and other inclement weather conditions make it necessary to drive in the left lane;

---

[15] Georgia Code, 40-6-184

[16] Hawaii Revised Statutes, §291C-41

[17] Idaho Statutes, 49-630

(4) when obstructions or hazards exist in the right lane;

(5) when a vehicle changes lanes to comply with Sections 11-907 and 11-908 of this Code;

(6) when, because of highway design, a vehicle must be driven in the left lane when preparing to exit;

(7) on toll highways when necessary to use I-Pass, and on toll and other highways when driving in the left lane is required to comply with an official traffic control device; or

(8) to law enforcement vehicles, ambulances, and other emergency vehicles engaged in official duties and vehicles engaged in highway maintenance and construction operations."[18]

The Illinois left-lane travel regulation is therefore a flexible mandate near-impossibly at odds with the professional driver's proper execution of lane optimization given only the first two exceptions, which describe a vast majority of circumstances in which left-lane travel should be properly sought to begin with.

Indiana

Indiana traffic regulations simply defer to the general "speed of traffic-flow" requirement.[19]

---

[18] 625 ILCS, 5/11-701

[19] Indiana Code, 9-21-8-2

Iowa

Iowa traffic regulations simply defer to the general "speed of traffic-flow" requirement.[20]

Kansas

As of recently, Kansas traffic regulations explicitly prohibit left-lane non-passing travel.[21] The list of exceptions does not share the accommodating liberality of the Illinois statute and is constrained to the common and trivial exceptions concerning temporary lane closure and traffic diversion, standard passing, etc.

Kentucky

Kentucky traffic regulations prohibit left-lane travel on limited access highways of four lanes or more and of at least 65mph speed limit, except "in overtaking a slower vehicle, yielding to traffic coming onto such a highway, or when traffic conditions exist which would prohibit safe use of the right or center lanes".[22]

Louisiana

Louisiana traffic regulations prohibit left-lane travel on multi-lane highways "except when directed otherwise, preparing for a left turn at an intersection or private road or driveway, overtaking or passing another vehicle proceeding in the same direction, or when right-

---

[20] Iowa Code, 321.297

[21] Kansas Statutes, 8-1522

[22] Kentucky Revised Statutes, 189.340

hand lanes are congested"[23] and also repeat a prohibition on impeding isolane rearwards traffic in the left lane.

Maine

In general, on limited-access highways of 65mph or greater speed limits, non-passing travel in the left-most lane is prohibited; in the excepted case of passing, the qualification that one "must return to the right-hand lane at the earliest opportunity" after the pass's completion is added[24].

Maryland

The Maryland traffic regulations include a "special rule for slow-moving traffic" which affords seeming protection for dangerous-situation-causing slower passing-lane vehicles, only requiring rightwards travel for vehicles "going 10 miles an hour or more below the applicable maximum speed limit or, if any existing conditions reasonably require a speed below that of the applicable maximum, at less than the normal speed of traffic under these conditions".[25] The professional driver should have heightened frontal awareness in this region if travelling at normal speeds in the left-most lane in order to safely respond in the case that any ignorant drivers may feel justified by the spirit of this regulation to create dangerous isolane intervehicular travel speed differentials, the onset of which may occur at travel far faster than a whole 10 miles per hour below the speed limit as is legally protected by this puzzling regulation.

---

[23] Louisiana Revised Statutes 32:71

[24] Maine Revised Statutes, 29A-2052

[25] 2010 Maryland Code, 21-301 (b)

Massachusetts

The Massachusetts General Laws (MGL) and their constituent traffic regulations are written in a quaintly laconic and antiquated fashion as fits their general prohibition on left-lane travel "upon all ways" (with no specific regard to the freeway context) in the absence of passing or "or when preparing for a left turn", the latter of which is clearly irrelevant to the freeway context.[26] The Massachusettensian regulations also include a memorable prohibition against increasing speed while being passed.[27]

Michigan

In stark contrast with the refreshing clarity of the MGL regulations above, Michigan's traffic regulations on lane designation in this regard are discomfortingly vague and circumlocutive. We seize the opportunity to reproduce the relevant parts of the seemingly incoherent section:

> "(2) Upon a roadway having 2 or more lanes for travel in 1 direction, the driver of a vehicle shall drive the vehicle in the extreme right-hand lane available for travel except as otherwise provided in this section. However, the driver of a vehicle may drive the vehicle in any lane lawfully available to traffic moving in the same direction of travel when the lanes are occupied by vehicles moving in substantially continuous lanes of traffic and in any left-hand lane lawfully available to traffic moving in the same direction of travel for a reasonable distance before making a left turn.

---

[26] Massachusetts General Laws, Part I, Title XIV, Chapter 89, Section 4B

[27] Massachusetts General Laws, Part I, Title XIV, Chapter 89, Section 2

(3) This section shall not be construed to prohibit a vehicle traveling in the appropriate direction from traveling in any lane of a freeway having 3 or more lanes for travel in the same direction."[28]

After explicitly requiring right-most-lane travel (along with extending the promising, expectation-creating qualification "except as otherwise provided in this section", which is unfortunately an expectation bound to end in disappointment as one continues reading the indecisive statute) on freeways in the first sentence of paragraph (2), the proceeding sentence provides an exception permitting travel in any of the mysterious "lawfully available" lanes, which is itself qualified by the even more ambiguous "continuous lanes of traffic" modifier. Since the latter seems to refer to high traffic density, a concept which other traffic regulation corpuses have no difficulty in articulating with clear choice of language, but is still insufficient to the end of defining "lawfully available", it is therefore an easily defensible position that a form of *circulus in probando* fallacy is evident in this statute's utterly circular logic, being the exact body responsible for defining "lawfully available", and doing so with none other than circular, unqualified reference to itself. Paragraph (3) further solidifies the interpretational difficulty of this deficiently-written regulation, indicating that there are indeed lawful circumstances in which a freeway (of over three lanes, with travel in the same direction) driver may travel in the left-most lane. There is, however, absolutely no clear language describing the permitting circumstances which allow for paragraph (3) exceptions in light of the first sentence of paragraph (2); while every other traffic-regulation statutory body in the United States of America is deftly able to enumerate such circumstances with simple and clear terms (such as, "if the vehicle is overtaking another", "if the vehicle is an emergency vehicle or law enforcement officer", or even more simply, "if the vehicle is moving at the normal speed of traffic"),

---

[28] MCL 257.634

Section 634 of the Michigan Vehicle Code achieves no more than the loosely related description of "vehicles moving in substantially continuous lanes" – a term so spatially and conceptually vague, carrying so many conjurable meanings, that it is to be wondered if Michigan State Troopers' informal having interpreted the law in the general light of "left lane for passing only or high traffic conditions" comes from a place of instinctive good sense next to a legal text of infinite interpretational possibilities rather than from an actual, clear exegesis of the statute's plain meaning.[29] We now proceed from our likely over-extended critique of the Michigan regulation and posit a supplementary exhortation to Michigan legislatures to replace the risibly convoluted statue, borrowing perhaps from the helpful example of all the other forty nine United States' comparatively laudable regulations in this regard.

Minnesota

Minnesota traffic regulations simply defer to the general "speed of traffic-flow" requirement.[30]

Mississippi

Mississippi traffic regulations simply defer to the general "speed of traffic-flow" requirement.[31]

---

[29] Administrative office memoranda at the Michigan Department of Transportation have indicated this same quaintly simplistic interpretation of MCL 257.634, which seems to be therefore solid *de facto* understanding; this does not however excuse the statute's basic linguistic deficiencies and general ambiguity.

[30] 2014 Minnesota Statutes, 169.18

[31] 2013 Mississippi Code, 63-3-603 (d)

Missouri

Missouri traffic regulations simply defer to the general "speed of traffic-flow" requirement.[32]

Montana

Montana traffic regulations simply defer to the general "speed of traffic-flow" requirement.[33]

Nebraska

Nebraska traffic regulations simply defer to the general "speed of traffic-flow" requirement.[34]

Nevada

Nevada's set of traffic regulations eschews the standardized Uniform Vehicle Code language to communicate nearly the same concept; if a vehicle travels at a "speed so slow as to impede the forward movement of traffic proceeding immediately behind the driver", a triple-conditional instructive process is required, which most relevantly to the freeway context is "to use alternate routes whenever possible".[35] Fascinatingly, in this narrow excerpt, there is no specific relation to the left-most lane in specific.

---

[32] Missouri Revised Statutes 304.015.1

[33] Montana Code Annotated, 61-8-321(2)

[34] 2014 Nebraska Revised Statutes, 60-6,131(2)

[35] Nevada Revised Statutes 484B.627

New Hampshire

New Hampshire traffic regulations simply defer to the general "speed of traffic-flow" requirement.[36]

New Jersey

New Jersey is one of the few states which explicitly forbids general left-lane travel, mandating that "a vehicle shall normally be driven in the lane nearest the right-hand edge or curb of the roadway when that lane is available for travel, except when overtaking another vehicle or in preparation for a left turn".[37] There is also a technical requirement to declare a passing maneuver by sounding the horn or using an "other warning device" while "not within a business or residence district".[38]

New Mexico

New Mexico traffic regulations simply defer to the general "speed of traffic-flow" requirement.[39]

---

[36] New Hampshire Revised Statutes Annotated (RSA), Section 265:16 (II)

[37] 2013 New Jersey Revised Statutes, 39:4-88

[38] 2013 New Jersey Revised Statutes, 39:4-85

[39] 2013 New Mexico Statutes, 66-7-308

New York

New York traffic regulations simply defer to the general "speed of traffic-flow" requirement.[40]

North Carolina

North Carolina's "keep-right" traffic regulation references the requirement of a vehicle to be "proceeding at less than the legal maximum speed limit"[41] for the prohibition of left-lane travel; the professional driver should therefore assumed heightened awareness of dangerous slower frontal vehicles in the passing lane, which are afforded regulatory protection in North Carolina provided that they only match or exceed the speed limit.

North Dakota

North Dakota traffic regulations simply defer to the general "speed of traffic-flow" requirement.[42]

Ohio

Ohio is one of the few states which (seemingly) references speed limit travel speed or greater as justification for left-lane travel, however not without the unique and somewhat confusing, conjunctive qualification that references normal traffic flow speed; the regulation bans left-lane travel for vehicles "proceeding at less than the prevailing and lawful speed of traffic at the time and place

---

[40] New York Code, 1120 (b)

[41] North Carolina General Statutes, 20-146

[42] North Dakota Century Code, 39-10-08

and under the conditions".[43] Clearly, the second qualification of "lawful" would almost always constrain that of the first "prevailing" qualification; therefore the referenced cutoff speed is to be interpreted as the lowest of these two, by their conjunctive and co-necessary relation, rendering the interesting language in this Ohio statute effectively synonymous with regular reference to the speed limit as is found in the few examples formerly discussed. The only theoretical, semantic difference brought about by the special wording herein would concern the improbable (under normal conditions) case that the flow of traffic were *below* the speed limit, in which case a left-lane driver would be permitted to travel thereon at that sub-speed-limit speed, unlike under the standard examples of such regulations which reference only the speed limit. This formal difference can, for all intents and purposes, be practically ignored.

Oklahoma

In addition to deferring generally to the "speed of traffic-flow" requirement[44], Oklahoma traffic regulations include an additional supplementary clarification that any "vehicle proceeding at less than the maximum posted speed, except when reduced speed is necessary for safe operation, shall not impede the normal flow of traffic by driving in the left lane"[45] in highways divided into four or more lanes.

---

[43] Ohio Revised Code, 4511.25 (b)

[44] Oklahoma Statutes, 47-11-301

[45] Oklahoma Statutes, 47-11-309

Oregon

Oregon traffic regulations simply defer to the general "speed of traffic-flow" requirement.[46]

Pennsylvania

Pennsylvania traffic regulations essentially defer to the general "speed of traffic-flow" requirement[47], however include a supplementary freeway-specific regulation requiring right-lane travel when a vehicle is not using the left lane for the commonly enumerated purposes (passing, left exits, etc.) *nor* is "traveling at a speed greater than the traffic flow"[48]. Pennsylvanian traffic code therefore explicitly permits left-lane freeway travel as long as speed exceeds that of the traffic flow. An interesting peculiarity to the language of Pennsylvania's two concurrent regulatory statutes on "keeping right" is that left-lane travel at exactly the speed of traffic flow is illegal (all speed zones other than that of above the speed limit having been explicitly forbidden for non-passing left-lane travel), whereas the general "speed of traffic-flow" requirement in most states, borrowing from the Uniform Vehicle Code, is worded as to prohibit non-passing traffic only which is *slower* that the traffic flow. Though as semantically unrealistic and impossibly over-particular as the notion of exact "equal speed" between any two vehicles in a flow of traffic to begin with, this oversight in the Pennsylvanian code seems technically to require compounding increases of speed in the left lane *ad infinitum*, since travelling at the kept speed of traffic flow in this lane is forbidden; we therefore proceed by acknowledging the practical identity of Pennsylvania's

---

[46] Oregon Revised Statutes, 811.315

[47] Pennsylvania Consolidated Statutes 75-3301(b)

[48] Pennsylvania Consolidated Statutes 75-3313(d)

left-lane usage regulation to that of the general "speed of traffic-flow" requirement of many other states and leave a brief exhortation to Pennsylvanian legislatures to replace "greater than" with "greater than or equal to" in Pennsylvania Consolidated Statutes 75-3313 (d) paragraph 1.

Rhode Island

Rhode Island traffic regulations simply defer to the general "speed of traffic-flow" requirement.[49]

South Carolina

South Carolina traffic regulations simply defer to the general "speed of traffic-flow" requirement.[50]

South Dakota

South Dakota traffic regulations omit both the general requirement pertaining to the normal speed of traffic and any specific requirements pertaining to travel under fixed freeway speed, having only a "keep-right" rule for "slow moving vehicles".[51] The South Dakota Department of Public Safety has informally clarified that "left lanes on divided highways are not restricted to passing maneuvers".[52]

---

[49] 2012 Rhode Island General Laws, 31-15-2

[50] South Carolina Code, 56-5-1810

[51] South Dakota Codified Laws, 32-26-1

[52] South Dakota Department of Public Safety website, "FAQs"

Tennessee

Tennessee traffic regulations simply defer to the general "speed of traffic-flow" requirement.[53]

Texas

Texas traffic regulations simply defer to the general "speed of traffic-flow" requirement[54], however "left lane for passing only" signs on particular sections are both widespread and legally authorized[55].

Utah

Utah traffic regulations both refer to the general "speed of traffic-flow" requirement[56] and include a supplementary requirement that left-lane travelling vehicles, upon the approach of a faster rearwards vehicle, must "yield to the overtaking vehicle by moving safely to a lane to the right" and "may not impede the movement or free flow of traffic in the left general purpose lane"[57]. The appellation of the left lane as a "general purpose lane" is an Utahan idiosyncrasy as unique as it is illuminating of the generally liberal and sensible regulation which redundantly clarifies the general primary requirement with the aforementioned secondary freeway-specific regulation.

---

[53] 2010 Tennessee Code, 55-8-115

[54] Texas Transportation Code, 545.051

[55] Texas Transportation Code, 544.011

[56] Utah Code, 41-6A-701

[57] Utah Code, 41-6A-704

Vermont

Vermont traffic regulations simply defer to the general "speed of traffic-flow" requirement.[58]

Virginia

Virginia traffic regulations both refer to the general "speed of traffic-flow" requirement[59] and include an explicit yielding requirement for slower left-lane vehicles to any faster approaching, rearwards traffic, upon "audible or light signal"[60], by switching into the right adjacent lane.

Washington

Washington traffic regulations permit non-passing left-lane freeway travel "when traveling at a speed greater than the traffic flow" and clearly prohibit driving "continuously in the left lane of a multilane roadway when it impedes the flow of other traffic".[61]

West Virginia

West Virginia traffic regulations simply defer to the general "speed of traffic-flow" requirement.[62]

---

[58] Vermont Statutes Annotated 23-1031

[59] Code of Virginia, 46.2-804

[60] Code of Virginia, 46.2-842.1

[61] Revised Code of Washington, 46.61.100

[62] West Virginia Code, 17C-7-1

Wisconsin

Wisconsin traffic regulations simply defer to the general "speed of traffic-flow" requirement.[63]

Wyoming

Wyoming traffic regulations simply defer to the general "speed of traffic-flow" requirement.[64]

---

[63] Wisconsin Statutes, 346.05

[64] Wyoming Statutes, 31-5-201

Eisenhower Interstate System Signage and Conventions

The professional driver travelling on America's Eisenhower Interstate System may be occasionally aided in a tactically significant way by a working knowledge of the conventions and signage formats which pertain to the entire system – especially in quick navigational decision-making on unfamiliar interstate trips.

Primary interstates are numbered with one or two digits and are classified as either east-west or north-south in the axis of their general motion; they are given an even number in the former case and an odd number in the latter. The numbering generally increases as geographic location of the highway is more easterly for even-numbered interstates and more northerly for odd-numbered interstates. Decided and researched pre-trip navigation knowledge must confirm the proper travel direction in a given interstate trip, since defaulting to geographic spatial awareness by comparing a known destination to either the "east/west" or "north/south" direction designation could lead to navigation failure and travel in the reverse direction, since all interstates are not mapped to perfectly horizontal or vertical lines of arc but involve natural heading variation which can in some places make a given direction designation seem questionable or perhaps, in fact, entirely backwards.

Auxiliary interstates are denoted by three digit numbers and frequently take the shape of circular belts which surround major population centers (there is a great deal in redundancy between these numbers across the system due to their plurality). The last two digits are taken from the parent interstate from which the auxiliary route originates; an even first digit indicates that the auxiliary route returns to the parent interstate, and odd first digits signify that the route terminates (in which case it is classified a spur highway).

Stopping Distance at Various Speeds

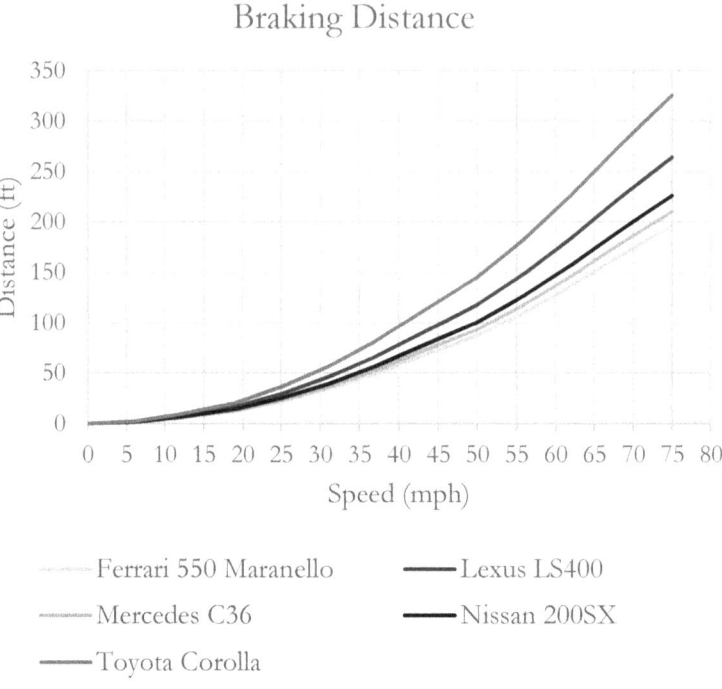

Source: © Wood, E. Australian Senior Mathematics Journal

Comparative visual reference should be had to the speed regions on this graph which span the range of observed freeway speed. Assuming a speed limit of 65mph and a 10mph departure therefrom, the braking distance variation between that of 55mph and 75mph is absolutely massive (mean 111.63ft, std. dev 20.34ft, n=5), which confutes the seeming unimportance which our precise analysis of fine speed margins on the freeway may indicate at first glance. Total stopping distance is of course a sum of the pictured braking distance and reaction time distance, the latter of which also increases with speed (although linearly).

Table of Figures

Figure 1 – Formal differences between the path-of-travel and the line-of-sight, illustrated by their divergence at a curve. 41

Figure 2 - Common vehicle body styles and corresponding pillar identifiers. Reproduced from public domain materials. 60

Figure 3 - Mirror visibility zones and blind spot coverages of the traditional alignment method 65

Figure 4 - Modern "Wide" or "SAE" mirror configuration method, showing the creation of two additional (yet smaller) blind spots 66

Figure 5 – Exovehicular spatial zones to which we heavily refer throughout this book 77

Figure 6 – An approximate graphical shading of a simplified, idealized highway entrance ramp demonstrates the relative demarcations between the three zones. 79

Figure 7 – A shaded graphical demonstration of turn-signal activation on the entrance ramp; the professional driver never delays such merge-intention declaration until a final maneuver is underway 111

Figure 8 – A weave lane, which further necessitates comprehensive lateral spatial awareness attention during merging, since intrafreeway vehicles may be merging into the same merging lane for highway exiting 119

Figure 9 – Two different lane-switch lateral position profiles, the first of which demonstrates slower lateral speed 124

Figure 10 – A geometric visualization of the curve-distance interlane disparity effect 130

Figure 11 – Potential negation of the curve-distance interlane disparity effect from two symmetrically opposite curves 134

Figure 12 – The whole intervehicular isolane space, longitudinally divided into its two constituent frontal and rearwards following distances 143

Figure 13 – The professional driver responds to changing frontal following distance spaces by executing optimal lane switches which increase safety margins for collision avoidance. 156

Figure 14 – HOV lane designation 173

Figure 15 – Visualization of the "wind-shadow" sought by the drafting technique 229

Figure 16 – The rare yet concerning situation of two vehicles simultaneously merging into the same lane-space from opposite adjacent lanes 256

Figure 17 – Shortening radius of curvature on a highway exit ramp 310

Glossary

"The driver"/"The professional driver"

The instructive, first-person frame-of-reference driver which is used as the subject of our discussions. We describe sound maneuvering tactics on the freeway by referring to this idealistic, perfect, conceptual driver and contrast him or her with that of the other drivers on the highway in order to maintain clarity in long descriptions of accident setups, intervehicular situations, etc.

ACDA

The Assured Clear Distance Ahead – essentially the linear extent of the path-of-travel from the vehicle to the farthest point which is guaranteed to be safe of hazards. See Chapter 6, "Determination of the Freeway-vacant ideal travel speed", "Assured Clear Distance Ahead (ACDA)" subsection.

Adjacent lane (in general)

A lane next to and bordering the given lane of reference. Interior lanes have two adjacent lanes, and the right-most and left-most lanes have only one adjacent lane. In two-lane freeways, there never more than one adjacent lane since the breakdown lane is not considered a normal lane of travel (under standard circumstances).

"Adjacent lane" (Chapter 8, Passing lane situations)

Our discussion on passing lane situations refers to the adjacent lane next to the passing lane, which is almost always the left-most lane of the freeway, making the adjacent lane the one to the right of the left-most passing lane in this context. This is more dynamically relevant to freeways of three lanes or greater, in which there is much choice in whether or not to travel on the left side or not. Two-lane freeways characteristically have one passing lane and one "adjacent lane" from the reference point of the former.

Allovehicular

Pertaining to an allovehicle – an *other* vehicle on the freeway distinguished from the professional driver's first-person frame-of-reference vehicle.

Anterolateral

Pertaining to the anterolateral zone (forward and to either side). See Figure 5 in Chapter 4, "Allovehicular terminology and spatial zones".

Basic speed rule

The overarching legal requirement of drivers to operate vehicles at not a greater speed than that which is "prudent and reasonable" given the totality of present variable circumstances. See Chapter 6, "Determination of the Freeway-vacant ideal travel speed", "Basic speed rule" subsection.

Control loop

> Our simplistic traffic-psychology mental processing model in which drivers repeat a continuous, responsive process of observing external factors from sensory information, processing such information, and responding with vehicle control to execute a certain tactic. Attention to visual and auditory sensory inputs therefore requires the professional driver to abstain from distracting behaviors while driving. See Chapter 2, "'Control loop' mental processing model".

Curve-distance interlane disparity effect

> The effect which longitudinally displaces isotachic vehicles distributed across different lanes around a curve in the freeway's alignment, deriving from the larger linear travel distance required on the outer-lane edges of the curve. See Chapter 5, "Geometric economy: the curve-distance interlane disparity effect".

Directional signal

> The manual exterior vehicular illumination signal, also called a "turn-signal", "directional", or "blinker", which alerts other drivers of impending and/or desired lateral motions of the vehicle, and which is divided into right and left sides.

Exovehicular

Pertaining to all factors outside the vehicle (i.e., not interior).

Freeway-vacant ideal travel speed

The theoretically optimum travel speed at which the professional driver should travel given all variable circumstances other than present traffic conditions on the freeway; the latter may naturally restrict travel at this decided, optimum speed in some circumstances, however choice of driver tactics would reveal a preference to match or at least approximate it where possible. See Chapter 6, "Determination of the Freeway-vacant ideal travel speed".

Frontal vehicle

The isolane vehicle, if any, in the front of the vehicle being referenced. See Figure 5 in Chapter 4, "Allovehicular terminology and spatial zones".

Head-check/shoulder-check

The critical spatial awareness tactic in which the driver momentarily angles his or her head to obtain visual spatial awareness information about the lateral and posterolateral exovehicular regions by means of vision through the rear side windows of the vehicle. The recommended traditional mirror configuration may not afford full view of such regions, necessitating head-check procedure. See Chapter 3,

"Visual information source #3: Usage of the rear-lateral windows of the vehicle", "Head-check procedure" subsection.

HOV lane

A "high occupancy vehicle" lane formally reserved for vehicles of plural passengership

Interlane position

The spatial term used to describe lateral position on the freeway, which should almost always be maintained over the exact centerline of the present lane of travel.

Intrafreeway

Pertaining to all factors within the actual freeway surface, as opposed to (for instance) exit and entrance ramps.

Isolane

Pertaining to all factors within the same lane as is being referenced.

Isotachic

Pertaining to the same speed: to the maintenance of equal speed or to the parity of speed between two or more vehicles.

Lane position

>The choice of travel lane in a multi-lane divided highway.

Lateral

>Spatial term pertaining to the sideways right-and-left axis.

Line-of-sight

>The direct line of vision which extends out from the driver's eyes and onto the target surfaces, which may be limited by vehicular factors (such as body pillars and head restraints, creating blind spots) or by exovehicular factors (such as the crest of a hill).

Longitudinal axis

>Spatial term pertaining to the forwards-backwards, fore-aft, longitudinal axis parallel to the direction of freeway travel.

Merging gap/entrance gap

>The space into which a merging vehicle intends to lane-switch, which may be enclosed by frontal and rearwards destination lane vehicles, in which their interstitial space must be sufficient for safe merging.

Merging lane

> The lane fed from a highway entrance ramp from which a vehicle entering the highway usually must merge, due to its forwards termination at some point.

Merging lane risk coefficient

> A conceptual value which indicates the degree to which traffic conditions are hazardous for merging, which is equal to the degree to which traffic is concurrently fast and dense (two inversely proportional factors), or equivalently to the product of traffic speed and density.

Passing lane

> A lane designated for passing or potentially even reserved for passing only, which is so commonly the left-most lane of the freeway that the term may be taken as a direct synonym for the left-most lane (and is prevalently used in this context throughout our discussions).

Path-of-travel

> The forwards surface area about to be occupied by the vehicle, given its momentary travel direction and speed.

Posterolateral

> Pertaining to the posterolateral zone (rearwards and to either side). See Figure 5 in Chapter 4, "Allovehicular terminology and spatial zones".

Rearwards vehicle

> The isolane vehicle, if any, in the rear of the vehicle being referenced. See Figure 5 in Chapter 4, "Allovehicular terminology and spatial zones".

SAE mirror alignment method

> The widespread modern alternative mirror alignment method which increases the angular displacement of the side mirrors' field of view from the longitudinal axis of the vehicle (i.e., widening their view). The SAE method removes view of the regions directly along the side of the vehicle and behind, creating a dangerous posterolateral blind spot which is mostly responsible for our supporting the traditional mirror alignment method. See Chapter 3, "Visual information source #3: Usage of the rear-lateral windows of the vehicle", "Traditional vs. wide mirror alignment" subsection.

Safety/following distance buffer/margin

> Safety margins/buffers in general refer to the exovehicular spaces which separate the vehicle from the surrounding allovehicles on the freeway and are critical for safety and optimization. The "following distance" variety of such safety margins refers to

their longitudinal frontal and rearwards constituents. See Chapter 5, "Longitudinal-axis safety margin and following distance optimization"

Spatial awareness

Knowledge of physical exovehicular factors. See Chapter 3.

Suprafreeway

Pertaining to the spatial volume immediately above the freeway surface area.

Tactical vs. strategic

The theme introduced in Chapter 2 which describes the interplay between a driver's high-level strategy (i.e., overall reasons and outlook for using the freeway in his or her personal model of utility maximization) and the according low-level, specific spatial maneuvering tactics (the subject of our discussions) which serve whichever goals are strategically valuable for a given driver (whether arrival-time optimization, safety optimization, avoidance of legal risks, improvements to fuel-efficiency for economic or environmentally sensitive purposes, etc.).

Traditional mirror alignment method

The method of aligning the side mirrors so that their inner edge, when viewed from the driving head position of the driver, runs directly parallel along the side of the vehicle, affording view of the direct lateral and posterolateral zones. This creates a blind spot in a known and constant region which can and must be checked with quick head-check maneuvers. See Chapter 3, "Visual information source #3: Usage of the rear-lateral windows of the vehicle", "Traditional vs. wide mirror alignment" subsection.

Traffic lane (Chapter 4)

We distinguish the "traffic lane" from the "merging lane" in Chapter 4 to reference the initial intrafreeway destination lane of the merging driver into which he or she must initially lane-switch before occupying any other lane in the freeway. This is usually the right lane, but may be the left lane in the case of left-side entrance ramps.

Transverse

An adjectival synonym of *lateral*.

Weave lane

The special type of merging lane which terminates by going into an exit ramp, therefore concurrently serving as both an exit lane and entrance-merging lane.

Whole intervehicular isolane space

Our spatial term which refers to the entire longitudinal space between the frontal and rearwards vehicle, which the professional driver seeks to maximize in order to obtain safe following distances in both of its constituent rear and frontal zones. The professional driver should usually prioritize frontal following distance over rearwards distance, whose vehicle is therefore not typically in the exact longitudinal center of the whole intervehicular isolane space. See Figure 12 in Chapter 5, "Longitudinal-axis safety margin and following distance optimization".

Bibliography

Aljanahi, A. A. M., A. H. Rhodes and Andrew V. Metcalfe. "Speed, speed limits and road traffic accidents under free flow conditions." *Accident Analysis & Prevention* 31.1 (1999): 161-168.

Azim, Ahmed F. Abdel and Ahmed F. Abdel Gawad. "A flow visualization study of the aerodynamic interference between passenger cars." *SAE Technical Paper Series* 2000-01-0355 (2000).

Baruya, A. and D. J. Finch. "Investigation of traffic speeds and accidents on urban roads." *Proceedings of Seminar J Held at the 22nd PTRC European Transport Forum, University of Warwick, England, September 12-16, 1994.* London: PTRC Education and Research Services, Ltd., 1994.

Bhise, Vivek D, et al. "Driver head movements in left outside mirror viewing." *SAE Technical Paper Series* 810761 (1981).

Briest, Susanne, Katja Karrer and R. Schleicher. "Driving without awareness: Examination of the phenomenon." *ision in Vehicles XI. Amsterdam: Elsevier Science Publishers BV* (2006).

Burg, Albert. "Lateral visual field as related to age and sex." *Journal of Applied Psychology* 52.1 (1968): 10-15.

—. "Vision test scores and driving record: Additional findings." (1968).

Charissis, V. and M. Naef. "Evaluation of prototype automotive head-up display interface: testing driver's focusing ability through a VR simulation." *Intelligent Vehicles Symposium, 2007 IEEE* (2007).

Davis, Gary A and Joel Swenson. "Identification and Simulation of a Common Freeway Accident Mechanism: Collective Responsibility in Freeway Rear-end Collisions." (2006).

Farrington, R. and J. Rugh. "Impact of Vehicle Air Conditioning on Fuel economy, Tailpipe Emissions, and Electric Vehicle Range." *NREL Report* No. CP-540-28960 (2000).

Firestine, M., P. Toeg and H. W. McGee. "Improving Truck Safety at Interchanges: Final Report to the Federal Highway Administration." U.S. Department of Transportation, 1989.

Forester, Thomas H, Robert F McNown and Larry D Singell. "A cost-benefit analysis of the 55 mph speed limit." *Southern Economic Journal* (1986): 631-641.

Forkenbrock, Garrick J., Mark Flick and W. R. Garrott. "NHTSA light vehicle antilock brake system research program task 4: a test track study of light vehicle ABS performance over a broad range of surfaces and maneuvers." *US Department of Transportation, National Highway Traffic Safety Administration* DOT HS 808-875 (1999).

Garber, N. J. and R. Gadiraju. "Factors influencing speed variance and its influence on accidents." *Transportation Research Record* 1213 (1990): 64–71.

Gotz, H. ""Aerodynamics of road Vehicles"." *Commercial vehicles*. Ed. Wolf-Heinrich Hucho. Butterworths, 1987.

—. "Bus Design Features and their Aerodynamic Effects." *International Journal of Vehicle Design, Impact Aerodynamics on Vehicle Design* SP-3 (1983): 229-255.

Hammond, Paula J. "Retreaded Tire Use and Safety: Synthesis." Transportation Synthesis Report. Washington State Department of Transportation, 2009.

Hendricks, D. L., J. C. Fell and M. Freedman. "The relative frequency of unsafe driving acts in serious traffic crashes." *National Highway Traffic Safety Administration, U.S. Department of Transportation* (1999).

Hill, William, et al. "Affect [sic] of Windows Down on Vehicle Fuel Economy as compared to AC load." *SAE Automotive Alternate Refrigerant Systems Symposium*. 2004.

Huff, Shean, Brian West and John Thomas. "Effects of Air Conditioner Use on Real-World Fuel Economy." *SAE Technical Paper Series* 2013-01-0551 (2013).

Joint, Matthew. "Road rage." (1995).

Kiefer, Raymond J and Jonathan M Hankey. "Lane change behavior with a side blind zone alert system." *Accident Analysis & Prevention* 40.2 (2008): 683-690.

Letirand, Frédéric and Patricia Delhomme. "Speed behaviour as a choice between observing and exceeding the speed limit." *Transportation Research Part F: Traffic Psychology and Behaviour* 8.9 (2005): 481-492.

Liu, Cejun and Chou-Lin Chen. "An analysis of speeding-related crashes: Definitions and the effects of road environments." *US Department of Transportation, National Highway Traffic Safety Administration* DOT HS 811-090 (2009).

Macuga, Kristen L, et al. "Changing lanes: inertial cues and explicit path information facilitate steering performance when visual feedback is removed." *Experimental brain research* 178.2 (2006): 141-150.

Mannering, Fred. "An empirical analysis of driver perceptions of the relationship between speed limits and safety." *Transportation Research Part F: Traffic Psychology and Behaviour* 12.2 (2009): 99-106.

Marottoli, Richard A and Emily D Richardson. "Confidence in, and Self-rating of, Driving Ability among Older Drivers." *Accident Analysis and Prevention* 30.3 (1998): 331-336.

McKnight, A. James and George T. Bahouth. "Analysis of Large Truck Rollover Crashes." *Traffic Injury Prevention* 10.5 (2009): 421-426.

National Highway Traffic Safety Administration and others. "Traffic safety facts: Older population, 2008." DOT HS 811-161 (2008).

National Highway Traffic Safety Administration. "Study of diver performance/acceptance using aspheric mirrors in light." *US Department of Transportation, National Highway Traffic Safety Administration* DOT HS 810-959, 33 (2008).

Office of Highway Policy Information. "Table VM-1." *Highway Statistics Series* (2011).

Olson, Paul L. and Christopher B. Winkler. "Measurement of crash avoidance characteristics of vehicles in use. Final report." (1985).

Owsley, C. "Driver Capabilities in Transportation in an Aging Society: A Decade of Experience. Technical Papers and Reports from a Conference: Bethesda, MD; Nov. 7–9, 1999. ." *Transportation Research Board* (2004).

Parry, M.H. *Aggression on the Road.* London: Tavistock, 1968.

Platzer, George. "The geometry of automotive rearview mirrors-why blind zones exist and strategies to overcome them." *SAE Technical Paper Series* 950601 (1995).

Sen, Basav, John D. Smith and Wassim G. Najm. *Analysis of lane change crashes, DOT HS 809-571.* U.S. Department of Transportation Research and Special Programs Administration. Washington, D.C.: National Highway Traffic Safety Administration, U.S. Department of Transportation, 2003.

Sivak, Michael, Brandon Schoettle and Matthew P. Reed. "Influence of visibility out of the vehicle cabin on lane-change crashes." *Accident Analysis & Prevention* 38.5 (2006): 969-972.

Sivak, Michael, et al. "Body-pillar vision obstructions and lane-change crashes." *Journal of safety research* 38.5 (2007): 557-561.

Smart, Reginald G. and Robert E. Mann. "Deaths and injuries from road rage: cases in Canadian newspapers." *Canadian Medical Association Journal* 167.7 (2002): 761-762.

Stewart, R. M. and T. W. Selby. "The relationship between oil viscosity and engine performance - a literature search." *SAE Technical Paper Series* 770372 (1977).

Strayer, David L., Frank A. Drews and William A. Johnston. "Cell phone-induced failures of visual attention during simulated driving." *Journal of Experimental Psychology: Applied* 9.1 (2003): 23.

Svenson, Alrik L. "Commercial Medium Tire Debris Study." *SAE Commercial Vehicle Engineering Congress.* Rosemont, IL, 2009.

"Texas Transportation Code Section 545.061." n.d.

Tijerina, Louis, et al. "Eye glance behavior of van and passenger car drivers during lane change decision phase." *Transportation Research Record: Journal of the Transportation Research Board* 1937.1 (2005): 37-43.

Tranter, Paul Joseph. "Speed Kills: The Complex Links Between Transport, Lack of Time and Urban Health." *Journal of Urban Health* 82.2 (2010): 155-166.

Tsubokura, Makoto, et al. "Computational visualization of unsteady flow around vehicles using high performance computing." *Computers & Fluids* 38.5 (2009): 981-990.

Wang, Jing-Shiarn and Ronald R. Knipling. "Lane change/merge crashes: problem size assessment and statistical description." *US Department of Transportation, National Highway Traffic Safety Administration* DOT HS 808-075 (1994).

Wilson, Fernando A. and Jim P. Stimpson. "Trends in fatalities from distracted driving in the United States, 1999 to 2008." *American Journal of Public Health* 100.11 (2010): 2213-2219.

Yowell, Robert O. "The evolution and devolution of speed limit law and the effect on fatality rates." *Review of Policy Research* 22.4 (2005): 501-518.

Zeeger, Charles V and Carolyn Williams. "Calculation of Accident Rates by Roadway Class for HSIS States." *University of North Carolina Highway Safety Research Center* (1994).

www.ingramcontent.com/pod-product-compliance
Lightning Source LLC
Chambersburg PA
CBHW071311150426
43191CB00007B/581